Governing Truth

Governing Truth

NGOs and the Politics of Transitional Justice

KELEBOGILE ZVOBGO

OXFORD
UNIVERSITY PRESS

Oxford University Press is a department of the University of Oxford.
It furthers the University's objective of excellence in research, scholarship,
and education by publishing worldwide. Oxford is a registered trade mark of
Oxford University Press in the UK and in certain other countries.

Published in the United States of America by Oxford University Press
198 Madison Avenue, New York, NY 10016, United States of America.

Library of Congress Cataloging-in-Publication Data
Names: Zvobgo, Kelebogile author
Title: Governing truth : NGOs and the politics of transitional justice /
Kelebogile Zvobgo.
Description: New York : Oxford University Press, [2026] |
Includes bibliographical references and index.
Identifiers: LCCN 2025027780 (print) | LCCN 2025027781 (ebook) |
ISBN 9780197815670 paperback | ISBN 9780197815663 hardback |
ISBN 9780197815687 epub | ISBN 9780197815700
Subjects: LCSH: Human rights. | Transitional justice. |
Transnational advocacy networks.
Classification: LCC JZ5584.T56 Z86 2026 (print) | LCC JZ5584.T56 (ebook)
LC record available at https://lccn.loc.gov/2025027780
LC ebook record available at https://lccn.loc.gov/2025027781

DOI: 10.1093/oso/9780197815663.001.0001

Paperback printed by Marquis Book Printing, Canada

The manufacturer's authorized representative in the EU for product safety is
Oxford University Press España S.A. of Parque Empresarial San Fernando de Henares,
Avenida de Castilla, 2 – 28830 Madrid (www.oup.es/en or product.safety@oup.com).
OUP España S.A. also acts as importer into Spain of products made by the manufacturer.

For Ruvimbo, with great love and affection.

Contents

List of Figures

List of Tables

Preface

This is not the book I intended to write.

I entered graduate school with a deep interest in perpetrators' involvement in transitional justice (TJ). I had studied truth commissions in college and written an undergraduate thesis on institutional design features of commissions that influence perpetrator participation. An article-length version of the thesis became my writing sample for graduate school applications and, later, my first peer-reviewed publication. A proposal to expand the project helped me secure a three-year graduate research fellowship from the National Science Foundation. I was off to a running start.

But while taking courses my first two years in graduate school, I struggled to come up with my next big idea, one that was "big enough for a book" and that would allow me to apply the mixed-method approach that I believed rigorous social science requires. Data on perpetrators' involvement in TJ is scant and hard to compare across cases. I could continue doing work in this vein in "side projects," I thought, but I needed a different set of questions for the dissertation and future book. Seeking inspiration, I became a voracious reader of the quantitative TJ literature while studying for my comprehensive exams in the summer of 2017. And inspiration came.

I was struck by the TJ field's largely mixed results on the question of "impact." Some studies found that TJ tools like truth commissions, trials, and amnesties support democracy, peace, the rule of law, and respect for human rights. Other studies, to my surprise, found the exact opposite, suggesting that commissions and other TJ mechanisms can undermine these outcomes. Still other studies fell somewhere in the middle, suggesting a limited impact for TJ measures under narrow conditions. Quantitative research on commissions' positive effects intrigued me. While I, of course, wanted to find that commissions support these macro outcomes (I did not enter graduate school to study failed or failing institutions), I wondered what exactly about commissions could do so. I landed on an idea.

A distinguishing characteristic of truth commissions is the recommendations they make to policymakers—about prosecutions, memorialization projects, reparations programs, and legal and personnel reforms, among others. I thought that maybe, and just maybe, if a government implemented, for example, electoral reforms, a country would be more likely to transition to and maintain democracy. Maybe, if a government made reparations to survivors and rehabilitated perpetrators, the country would be more likely to hold on to a hard-won peace. Maybe, if a government conducted trials, the country would be more likely to uphold human rights and the rule of law. Maybe. So, to establish causal links between commissions and the macro outcomes about which comparative politics and international relations scholars are so deeply concerned, I needed to understand the implementation of commission recommendations. To what extent does the implementation of recommendations influence human rights, democracy, peace, and the rule of law? That is the question I set out to answer. That is the question some hoped I *would* answer, that some thought I *should* answer. But it is not the question I *could* answer, at least not right away.

Inspired by new quantitative data projects seeking to measure the microfoundations of TJ projects and ascertain their impacts, I had decided in the autumn of 2017 to build my own quantitative dataset—coding for the first time the global landscape of truth commission recommendations and implementation—and match my data with existing data on political regimes, human rights performance, peace and conflict, and the rule of law. This was going to be a straightforward project. Or so I thought. Over a period of months, conversations with my advisors made me realize that this would not be the case.

After hearing my ideas, they said something along the lines of, "Okay, but truth commissions don't all recommend the same things, do they?" Probably not. I figured commission recommendations likely varied across countries and world regions due to historical factors, including different experiences of violence and different development trajectories. So I would have to explain, or at least account for, variation in types of commission recommendations in my empirical models before explaining implementation and impacts. Fine. My advisors pressed, "And commissions aren't all created equally, are they?" No, commissions are not created equally. I knew as much, based on my prior research on commission design. So I would have to explain variation in commission design before explaining variation in recommendations, implementation, and impacts. I started getting nervous, and my advisors pressed further: "And not every country that could have a commission does, right?" Also no, not every country that that could have a commission has one. So I would have to explain variation in commission adoption, before explaining variation in design, before explaining variation in recommendations, implementation, and impacts. My straightforward project turned out to be anything but. (Over the years, I have learned to greet with skepticism projects that seem "straightforward" because they rarely are.) I could not do all of this in a single project and with less than three years to complete it.

Through this iterative process and dialogue with my advisors, I pulled the timeline of my investigation from the post-commission stage to the pre-commission stage. By examining earlier stages of commissions, and providing scholars guidance about issues of sample selection in post-commission TJ, my project would set the stage for future research assessing commissions' long-term impacts around the globe.

As I strove, then, to explain why truth commissions are adopted in some countries but not in others, why some commissions are designed for success while others are not, and why only some commission recommendations are implemented while many others are not, nongovernmental organizations (NGOs) kept cropping up. I discovered that the story I had to tell about commission adoption, design, and implementation of recommendations, and for which I would build not a single dataset but multiple datasets, was a story about civil society, about burden sharing between and among groups domestically and internationally. This story was also not just about commissions but about TJ processes more generally. Commissions were just a case of a larger phenomenon: TJ governance by transnational civil society actors.

This project shifted my perspective on what factors shape important outcomes: actors (notably, civil society) *through and with* TJ institutions and programs (for example, truth commissions), not TJ institutions or programs by themselves. This project also transformed my scholarly identity. I realized I could not be a TJ scholar without also being an NGO politics scholar. I had to be both to do right by the questions that preoccupied my thoughts, to do right by the stories that stirred my heart and elevated my political consciousness, to do right by the victims, survivors, relatives, and human rights advocates whose ordinary and extraordinary lives have changed mine forever.

With great joy, some trepidation, a good deal of urgency, and deep gratitude and humility, I share with you my first book, *Governing Truth: NGOs and the Politics of Transitional Justice*—a labor of grief, love, and hope, and the product of a truly global village.

Acknowledgments

Governing Truth was born in the autumn of 2017, shortly after I passed my qualifying exams at the University of Southern California (USC). I had been anxious about finding an idea big enough for a book. Inspired by a quantitative TJ panel at the American Political Science Association (APSA) annual meeting, including Laia Balcells, Cyanne Loyle, and Monika Nalepa, and by a series of conversations with my advisors, I homed in on that idea. I would explain the reason transitional justice is the way it is around the globe: transnational civil society. To do this, I would use truth commissions as my point of departure and leverage new comprehensive and granular quantitative data that I would build.

I could not have asked for a better advisor and mentor than Wayne Sandholtz. He asks tough questions, keeps view of the big picture, and is exceedingly generous with his time, feedback, and encouragement. During my time at USC, Wayne gave me invaluable professional guidance and personal support. Though I stumbled at times and my self-confidence wavered, he always let me know that he believed in me and in my work. Ben Graham's training and mentorship were pivotal for me. He taught me how to build a codebook, train a research team, collect data, manage a high-volume project pipeline, and build a compelling research and teaching profile. He provided resources that few could dream of at my career stage, including funding for research assistants, and was always ready to talk whenever I popped my head into his office. Abby Wood's comments helped me clarify the project's core concepts, tighten the empirics, and tousle with alternative explanations. She was my advocate for various professional opportunities, shared resources to support my productivity, and reminded me to prioritize my health and well-being. Few people have made me think more critically and work harder than Bryn Rosenfeld has. She inspires excellence as a scholar, mentor, and colleague. She was the last missing piece in my committee, and I am so glad she joined. Wayne, Ben, Abby, and Bryn, I owe you a great debt.

I likely would not have pursued a political science PhD were it not for my advisors and professors at Pomona College, especially Heather Williams, Pierre Englebert, and Heidi Haddad. Heather shepherded me through my early years at the college and introduced me to Priscilla Hayner's *Unspeakable Truths*—a catalytic event in my formation as a student of TJ. Pierre taught my senior thesis seminar and encouraged me to build the data I needed to answer the questions that mattered to me. So many of my data projects owe to his guidance at this earliest stage of my career. Heidi was in her first semester as an assistant professor when she agreed to be my thesis advisor. Only when I became an assistant professor myself did I fully understand what a gift her time and mentorship were that year. She also set me on the path to publishing my thesis as a peer-reviewed article. More than a decade has passed since I graduated from college, and you three have remained a part of my life. I am so thankful.

William & Mary (W&M), where I started as a pre-doctoral fellow and am now a tenured associate professor, provided an ideal setting for completing this book. I am grateful to Mike Tierney, Sue Peterson, Paul Manna, and colleagues at the Global Research Institute (GRI) and in the Government Department for this incredible launching pad for my career. Veridiana supported me in countless ways throughout my PhD. Alexa, Becky, Claire C., Claire G., Francesca, Guillermo, James, Jessica, Kiela, Peay, Rachel, Suparna, and Matt provided tremendous support from near and far as I transitioned to life in Virginia. They helped keep me sane during the COVID-19 pandemic and the national struggle over race, and they provided spiritual, emotional, and practical support when I lost my father and, later, my childhood best friend. Nick was always so proud of me and my accomplishments, even as he was fuzzy on the details of my life in academia. He was my person, and I miss him dearly. Mark and Terri gave me the gift of home away from home. William showed me great love, grace, and support as I completed this project.

Chapter drafts were presented at the Institute for Qualitative and Multi-Method Research, the International Studies Association (ISA), UC-Santa Barbara, USC, and W&M. I received helpful feedback from my discussants at these venues: Alison Brysk, Julia Morse, and Oskar Timo Thoms, among other workshop and conference participants. This project also benefited from conversations with Onur Bakiner, Miriam Barnum, Genevieve Bates, Austin Carson, Brett Carter, Shauna Gillooly, Jim Goldgeier, Cyanne Loyle, Amanda Murdie, Kyle Reed, Daniel Solomon, and Eric Wiebelhaus-Brahm. Jonathan Markowitz's natural skepticism kept me on my toes, his fantastic research design course gave me important tools for my work, and his advice and example challenged me to "always be submitting" my work for publication and never (again) sit on a rejected manuscript for almost a year.

Laia Balcells, Geoff Dancy, and Monika Nalepa provided invaluable advice at multiple stages of the project and generously served as discussants at my manuscript review workshop at W&M in the autumn of 2021. In addition to providing feedback on this and other research projects, they have generously promoted my work among TJ scholars. I am very grateful to you. I also wish to thank my W&M colleagues, Sharan Grewal, Steve Hanson, S.P. Harish, Paula Pickering, Phil Roessler, and Maurits van der Veen, who also participated in my manuscript review workshop, along with Francesca Parente at Christopher Newport University, whose friendship and collaboration I deeply cherish.

The *Varieties of Truth Commissions* datasets analyzed in this book would not have been possible without seventeen brilliant undergraduate research assistants, who gathered and coded data, accompanied me on field research trips, and commented on and helped copyedit chapter drafts. At USC, there was Shir Attias, Loleï Brenot, Nastaran Far, Chandra Ingram, Daniel Liu, Anthony Momo, Bridget Mulrooney, Hailey Robertson, Jack Schwartz, and Amanda Scott, and, at W&M, there was Alexandra Bryne, Gabrielle DeBelen, Nitya Labh, Nathan Liu, Zoha Siddiqui, Johanna Weech, and Bilen Zerie. Together with Alexandra and Bilen, Samantha Jennings, JT Kaufmann, Zola Sayers-Fay, and Leo Sereni provided valuable editorial support as I revised the manuscript.

For their research participation, I am grateful to current and former leaders and staff members at the International Center for Transitional Justice (ICTJ), Marianne Akumu, Ruben Carranza, María Carolina Carter, Rim El Gantri, Salwa El Gantri, Didier Gbery, Sibley Hawkins, Priscilla Hayner, Alec Knight, Virginie Ladisch, María Cielo Linares, Kelen Meregali, Jesse Mugero, Agatha Ndonga, Mateo Porciuncula, María Margarita Rivera, Anna Myriam Roccatello, Mohamed Suma, and Howard Varney; from Argentina's Comisión Provincial por la Memoria, Ernesto Alonso, Roberto Cipriano García, Diego Diaz, Rodrigo Pomares, Sandra Raggio, Samanta Salvatori, and Yamila Zavala Rodríguez; Philip Luther from Amnesty International; Param-Preet Singh from Human Rights Watch; Cristián Correa from Chile's Comisión Nacional Sobre Prisón Politica y Tortura, Chile's Comisión de Derechos Humanos, and the ICTJ; Zoe Dugal from Kenya's Truth, Justice, and Reconciliation Commission and Sierra Leone's Truth and Reconciliation Commission; Karine Duhamel from Canada's National Inquiry into Missing and Murdered Indigenous Women and Girls; Eduardo González from Peru's Comisión de la Verdad y Reconciliación and the ICTJ; Emilio Crenzel from the Universidad de Buenos Aires; Carlos Beristain from Guatemala's Recovery of Historical Memory (REMHI) Project and the Inter-American Commission on Human Rights Interdisciplinary Group of Independent Experts for the Ayotzinapa Case; Margarette Macaulay from the Inter-American Commission and Court of Human Rights; and an anonymous interviewee.

In Guatemala, I wish to thank Dora Mirón from the Asociación Civil Verdad y Vida, Rafael Herrarte and Erwin Melgar from the Centro de Análisis Forense y Ciencias Aplicadas (CAFCA), Fabiola García from the Centro para la Acción Legal en Derechos Humanos (CALDH), Carlos René Fernández Pérez from the Centro Internacional para Investigaciones en Derechos Humanos (CIIDH), Rosalina Tuyuc Velásquez from the Coordinadora Nacional de Viudas de Guatemala (CONAVIGUA), José Felipe Sarti Castañeda and

Elizabeth Pedraza from the Equipo de Estudios Comunitarios y Acción Psicosocial (ECAP), Erica Henderson from the Fundación de Antropología Forense de Guatemala (FAFG), Manuel Farfán from the Asociación de Familiares de Detenidos y Desaparecidos de Guatemala (FAMDEGUA), Hilda Pineda from the Fiscalía de Derechos Humanos, Andy Javalois from the Fundación Myrna Mack (FMM), Maya Juracán from Fundación Paiz, Mario Polanco and Carlos Juárez from the Grupo de Apoyo Mutuo (GAM), César García from the Instituto Internacional de Aprendizaje para la Reconciliación Social (IIARS), Julio Solórzano Foppa from the Memorial para la Concordia, Juana Tipaz from the Movimiento Nacional de Victimas, Patricia Ogaldes and Carolina Rendón from the Oficina de Derechos Humanos del Arzobispado de Guatemala (ODHAG), María García Ortíz from the UNDP Programa de Acompañamiento a la Justicia de Transición (PAJUST), Alejandro Reyes from the Procuraduría de los Derechos Humanos, and Emir de Jésus Mejía y Mejía from the Secretaría de la Paz. I am grateful, too, to my interpreter, Crystal.

In South Africa, I wish to thank Thandeka Kathi and Sithuthukile Mkhize from the Centre for Applied Legal Studies (CALS), Hugo van der Merwe from the Centre for the Study of Violence and Reconciliation (CSVR), Katarzyna Zdunczyk from the Foundation for Human Rights (FHR), Shirley Gunn from the Human Rights Media Centre (HRMC) and South African Coalition for Transitional Justice (SACTJ), Betzi Pierce from the National Institute for Crime Prevention and the Reintegration of Offenders (NICRO), and Marguerite Holtzhausen from the Trauma Centre for Survivors of Violence and Torture.

For participating in my research on Timor-Leste, I wish to thank Patrick Burgess from Asia Justice and Rights (AJAR) and, previously, the Comissão de Acolhimento, Verdade e Reconciliação (CAVR), UN Transitional Administration for East Timor (UNTAET), UN Mission of Support to East Timor (UNMISET), and ICTJ; Galuh Wandita from AJAR and, previously, the Asosiasaun Chega! Ba Ita (ACbit), Forum Komunikasaun Ba Feto Timor Loro Sa'e (FOKUPERS), and ICTJ; Hugo Fernandes from the Centro Nacional Chega! Instituto Publiku (CNC! I.P) and, previously, the CAVR and Timorese–Indonesian Commission of Truth and Friendship (CTF); Pat Walsh from the CNC! I.P and, previously, the CAVR and Post-CAVR Technical Secretariat; John Miller from the East Timor and Indonesia Action Network (ETAN); Nélson Belo from the Fundasaun Mahein and, previously, the Judicial System Monitoring Programme (JSMP); Casimiro dos Santos and Jose Pereira from JSMP; Charles Scheiner from La'o Hamutuk, the International Federation for East Timor (IFET), and, previously, ETAN; Adriana Sri Adhiati and Mark X from TAPOL; and, again, Cristián Correa and Eduardo González.

At Oxford University Press, I would like to thank Angela Chnapko for her interest in my manuscript, belief in me as an author, and guidance through the publication process. I would also like to thank Rachel Blaifeder at Cambridge University Press for considering the manuscript. While a book can only be published at one press, this book is what it is because of both sets of anonymous readers' serious engagement with the text and their constructive feedback. Tom Bedford carefully copyedited the book, Barry O'Keefe designed the beautiful cover art, and Andrea Smith shepherded the work through production. Thank you all so much.

My parents, who met at afternoon tea in the Senior Common Room at the University of Zimbabwe many moons ago, are the reason I am here. My baba, Chengetai, now late, imparted to me a strong work ethic and a deep hunger to conduct academic research—to read more, write more, and share more. When I experienced difficulties in my PhD training, I found comfort in knowing that he also traversed this path more than forty years earlier in Edinburgh, Scotland. "If he could do it then," I would think to myself, "I can do it now." I so wish he could have seen me complete my PhD and publish this book. But I know that he sees me, loves me, and is proud of me. My mama, Kebokile, with whom I share a name, has been my rock, guide, and inspiration—in every season of life. My first teacher, she taught me to love learning. As I grew up, she gave me the fortitude and determination to persist, whatever the obstacles I encountered. Her love, humor, encouragement, occasional stern word, and prayers keep me going. I dedicate this work to my sister Ruvimbo Heather, who left us just three weeks before I started graduate school but who has been with me every step of the way. Love you, always.

Governing Truth is based on my PhD dissertation, which won the APSA Award for Best Dissertation in Human Rights and the ISA Lynne Rienner Publishers Award for Best Dissertation in Human Rights in 2022. An earlier version of Chapter 6 won the ISA Lawrence S. Finkelstein Prize in International Organization in 2021. The project was made possible by fellowships from USC (Provost Fellowship in the Social Sciences) and W&M (GRI Pre-doctoral Fellowship for Academic Diversity). In addition, this material is based on work supported by the National Science Foundation Graduate Research Fellowship Program under Grant No. DGE-1418060. Any opinions, findings, and conclusions or recommendations expressed in this material are mine and do not necessarily reflect the views of any organization.

This book is derived in part from an article published in *International Studies Quarterly* (2020) copyright Oxford University Press, available online at doi.org/10.1093/isq/sqaa044. The data underlying this book are available online at dataverse.harvard.edu/dataverse/zvobgo.

All for God's glory.

Abbreviations

ACbit	Asosiasaun Chega! Ba Ita/Chega! For Us Association
AJAR	Asia Justice and Rights
CAFCA	Centro de Análisis Forense y Ciencias Aplicadas/Center for Forensic Analysis and Applied Sciences
CALDH	Centro para la Acción Legal en Derechos Humanos/Center for Legal Action in Human Rights
CALS	Centre for Applied Legal Studies
CAVR	Comissão de Acolhimento, Verdade e Reconciliação/Commission for Reception, Truth and Reconciliation
CEH	Comisión para el Esclarecimiento Histórico/Historical Clarification Commission
CIIDH	Centro Internacional para Investigaciones en Derechos Humanos/International Center for Human Rights Research
CNC! I.P	Centro Nacional Chega! Instituto Publiku/Chega! National Center Public Institute
CONAVIGUA	Coordinadora Nacional de Viudas de Guatemala/National Coordinator of Guatemalan Widows
CSVR	Centre for the Study of Violence and Reconciliation
ECAP	Equipo de Estudios Comunitarios y Acción Psicosocial/Community Studies and Psychosocial Action Team
ETAN	East Timor and Indonesia Action Network
FAFG	Fundación de Antropología Forense de Guatemala/Forensic Anthropology Foundation of Guatemala
FAMDEGUA	Asociación de Familiares de Detenidos y Desaparecidos de Guatemala/Association of Relatives of the Detained and Disappeared of Guatemala
FHR	Foundation for Human Rights
FMM	Fundación Myrna Mack/Myrna Mack Foundation
FOKUPERS	Forum Komunikasaun Ba Feto Timor Loro Sa'e/East Timorese Women's Communication Forum
GAM	Grupo de Apoyo Mutuo/Mutual Support Group
HRMC	Human Rights Media Centre
HRO	Human Rights Organization
HRW	Human Rights Watch
IACmHR	Inter-American Commission on Human Rights
IACtHR	Inter-American Court of Human Rights
ICTJ	International Center for Transitional Justice

IFET	International Federation for East Timor
IIARS	Instituto Internacional de Aprendizaje para la Reconciliación Social/International Institute of Learning for Social Reconciliation
IJR	Institute for Justice and Reconciliation
INGO	International Nongovernmental Organization
IO	International Organization
JSMP	Judicial System Monitoring Programme
KSG	Khulumani Support Group
NGO	Nongovernmental Organization
NICRO	National Institute for Crime Prevention and the Reintegration of Offenders
ODHAG	Oficina de Derechos Humanos del Arzobispado de Guatemala/Human Rights Office of the Archbishop of Guatemala
OHCHR	Office of the United Nations High Commissioner for Human Rights
PAJUST	Programa de Acompañamiento a la Justicia de Transición/Transitional Justice Accompaniment Programme
REMHI	Proyecto Interdiocesano Recuperación de la Memoria Histórica/Interdiocesan Recovery of Historical Memory Project
SACTJ	South African Coalition for Transitional Justice
SAHA	South African History Archive Trust
TAN	Transnational Advocacy Network
TRC	Truth and Reconciliation Commission
UN	United Nations
UNDP	United Nations Development Programme
UNMISET	United Nations Mission of Support to East Timor
UNTAET	United Nations Transitional Administration for East Timor

About the Companion Website

www.oup.com/us/governingtruth

Oxford has created a website to accompany *Governing Truth: NGOs and the Politics of Transitional Justice.* Material that cannot be made available in a book, namely supplementary statistical tables and figures, as well as additional information on the study's quantitative and qualitative data, is provided here. The reader is encouraged to consult this resource in conjunction with the chapters. Material available online is indicated in the text with Oxford's symbol ⯈.

1
Introduction

In 1997, Indonesian human rights activist Galuh Wandita cofounded the East Timorese Women's Communication Forum (FOKUPERS) to resist Indonesia's occupation of Timor-Leste. The nongovernmental organization (NGO) called for an end to the violence, counseled women survivors of conflict-related violence, facilitated visits for international monitors, mobilized support for an independence referendum, and advised the United Nations transitional administration on gender policy. FOKUPERS also lobbied for and helped implement a variety of transitional justice (TJ) initiatives, including the Commission for Reception, Truth and Reconciliation (CAVR), established in 2001.[1]

Wandita helped draft the truth commission's mandate and appoint commissioners. She also served as the commission's deputy director. Today, she directs Asia Justice and Rights (AJAR), an international nongovernmental organization (INGO) in Southeast Asia that, among other activities, advocates before, assists, and substitutes for the Timorese government in implementing the CAVR's policy recommendations.[2] At the helm with Wandita is Patrick Burgess, a former deputy to the late Brazilian diplomat Sérgio Vieira de Mello—the UN transitional administrator in Timor-Leste, from 1999 to 2002, and the UN high commissioner for human rights until 2003, when he was killed in Iraq just days after the UN assistance mission opened in Baghdad. Burgess, an Australian attorney, served as the human rights director for the UN's two missions to Timor-Leste and as the CAVR's principal legal counsel.[3]

Cristián Correa collaborated with Burgess, Wandita, and other CAVR leaders, with support from domestic civil society representatives, to craft the commission's recommendations. An international TJ expert from Chile, Correa began his career as a student member of the nonviolent resistance movement during the Augusto Pinochet dictatorship. He was later the legal secretary for the National Commission on Political Imprisonment and Torture, from 2003

[1] Amnesty International 1998, 1999; FOKUPERS 1999; Hunt 2016; Niner 2016; UNCHR 2001; UNSG 1999; Wandita et al. 2006.

[2] Author interview with Galuh Wandita. See online Appendix D for interview questions and information on participants (i.e., name, organization, mode of participation—survey, interview, and/or focus group—and location and dates).

[3] Author interview with Patrick Burgess.

Governing Truth. Kelebogile Zvobgo, Oxford University Press. © Oxford University Press (2026).
DOI: 10.1093/oso/9780197815663.003.0001

to 2005, and went on to help implement Chile's national reparations program and serve as a human rights advisor to President Michelle Bachelet, from 2006 to 2007.[4] He later became a senior expert at the International Center for Transitional Justice (ICTJ), the preeminent TJ INGO, cofounded by Priscilla Hayner in 2001, as the South African Truth and Reconciliation Commission (TRC) concluded and debates around the Timorese CAVR began. The same year, Hayner published *Unspeakable Truths*, the first book to comprehensively study truth commissions globally. When I interviewed her, she was part of the UN Standby Team of Senior Mediation Advisers.[5]

Eduardo González was a member of Hayner's early team of ICTJ senior associates, moving to the organization's New York headquarters after two leadership positions in the Truth and Reconciliation Commission in his native Peru, from 2002 to 2003. In addition to Correa, González met Burgess and Wandita at the ICTJ, where the two worked for half a decade between their time at the CAVR and AJAR. González also met there Ruben Carranza, a former high-level defense official in the Philippines government, and Howard Varney, a human rights defender and attorney from South Africa, both turned TJ advisors and consultants. Carranza, González, and Varney have worked on an impressive eighteen commissions around the world, eight of them together.[6] Among other contributions, González and Varney wrote the ICTJ's guides on designing commissions.[7]

Burgess, Carranza, Correa, González, Hayner, Varney, and Wandita are seven of the nearly eighty individuals I engaged in my research for this book. They are part of what I term the "global transitional justice network," a collective of domestic and international civil society actors that I argue governs the constellation of norms, practices, and institutions collectively known as "transitional justice." Like global governors in other political realms, members of the TJ network are "authorities who exercise power across borders for purposes of affecting policy. [They] thus create issues, set agendas, establish and implement rules or programs, and evaluate and/or adjudicate outcomes."[8] Rowen takes this further, calling actors mobilizing for TJ, including the mass public, a "movement."[9]

4 Author interview with Cristián Correa.
5 Author interview with Priscilla Hayner.
6 Author interviews with Eduardo González and author survey of current and former ICTJ leadership and staff.
7 González 2013; González and Varney 2013.
8 Avant et al. 2010, 2. See Henry and Sundstrom (2021) for more on civil society actors, especially NGOs, and how and why they decide to "go global" and to what effect. Gready (2010, 5) queries whether TJ is "now led by an epistemic community (an international, knowledge-based, elite professional and donor network) rather than locally rooted victim-survivor or social movements." This book shows domestic and international civil society actors *work together* in the global TJ network, playing different roles at different stages, to achieve shared goals.
9 Rowen 2017.

Members of this transnational network influence governments to adopt TJ institutions and programs, design them to succeed, and follow up on them with additional measures. They accomplish this through their advocacy, technical expertise, and operational assistance to governments. In some cases, they even substitute for governments. TJ network members derive their power and authority from, and do their work on behalf of, their constituents, the parties most interested in truth, justice, reparation, and nonrepetition: survivors of political violence, victims' families, and their communities.[10] The thesis and through line of this book is this: Whatever we get, as much or as little as we get, is because of civil society.[11]

With this argument, I depart from mainstream international relations scholarship, which has traditionally elided non-state actors in global governance.[12] I join a movement of scholars dislocating and decentering states as the primary, if not exclusive, governors in world politics, and centering civil society, particularly in the human rights and TJ space.[13] Importantly, I formalize the idea of a "global TJ network," parsing what specific members of the network do at specific stages of the TJ life cycle. I argue and demonstrate that, together, they are TJ governors: Domestic and international civil society actors help explain similar outcomes—TJ adoption, strong design, and implementation and follow-up—across dissimilar contexts and countries around the globe.[14]

To demonstrate my argument, I analyze an ambitious set of quantitative and qualitative data, including from the *Varieties of Truth Commissions* and focus groups and interviews that I conducted with government officials, former commission officials, representatives of international organizations (IOs), and domestic and international NGO advocates from thirteen countries: Argentina, Canada, Chile, Costa Rica, Guatemala, Indonesia, Kenya, Peru, Sierra Leone, South Africa, Timor-Leste, the United Kingdom, and the United States.

[10] Some prefer the term "victim" or "victim-survivor" to "survivor" for individuals who have not been killed. Throughout this book, I will generally use "survivor" to refer to the living and "victim" to refer to the deceased.

[11] Lessa's analysis of "justice seekers" in the Southern Cone deeply resonates with my analysis of the "global TJ network" across world regions. Lessa "draws attention to proactive and strategic attempts by justice seekers to generate networks to support transitional justice processes. These individuals actively promote accountability, and their efforts at the national and international levels create the conditions necessary for justice to be achieved" (2022, 8). The importance of this last point cannot be overstated: Transnational civil society actors *create the conditions for justice*, even if governments do not respond by providing justice or do not provide justice to the fullest extent possible.

[12] For this criticism, see Alter (2014), Avant et al. (2010), Barnett and Finnemore (2004), Bush (2015), Danner and Voeten (2010), Henry and Sundstrom (2021), Lessa (2022), Murdie (2014), and Stroup and Wong (2017).

[13] Arthur and Yakinthou 2018; Bakiner 2014; Brysk 1993, 2013; Burt 2007; Collins 2010; Correa et al. 2020; Crenzel 2012; Della Porta and Tarrow 2005; González-Ocantos 2020; Hayner 2011; Hertel 2006; Keck and Sikkink 1998; Kim 2014; Lessa 2022; Medie 2020; Michel 2018; Price 2003; Risse et al. 2013; Roht-Arriaza 2001; Rowen 2017; Sikkink 2011.

[14] Zvobgo 2020. Per Henry and Sundstrom (2021, 3), NGOs "shap[e] how the world is governed."

My survey of ICTJ leaders and staff also covers members of the organization in the field, including in Colombia, Côte d'Ivoire, the Gambia, Tunisia, and Uganda.

Transitional Justice: A Field of Practice and Scholarship

TJ began as accountability for a small number of leaders in international criminal tribunals in Nuremberg, Germany, and Tokyo, Japan, but quickly expanded to regional and domestic courts and later grew to encompass nonretributive truth-seeking processes.[15] As the twenty-first century approached, human rights courts and treaty bodies helped refine and strengthen the concept of TJ, promulgating new rights for victims of human rights violations, specifically the rights to truth, justice, reparation, and to a guarantee of nonrepetition.[16] These "pillars of transitional justice," it was believed, would help combat impunity, heal social wounds, secure peace, and advance human rights.

With the turn of the century, optimism about TJ and its possible effects on violence-affected societies soared, as truth commissions, human rights trials, and other measures spread globally.[17] Activists asserted that truth seeking would bring victims healing and restore broken social orders.[18] The late Nobel laureate and South African TRC chairperson, Archbishop Desmond Tutu, underscored time and again that "there is no healing without truth."[19] Similarly, legal practitioners and analysts argued that trials would help secure peace because criminal justice "dampens motives for revenge" and "breaks the cycle of violence by stamping out impunity."[20] Academics likewise urged that institutional reforms would "[remove] an important cause of future war and wartime abuses."[21] For their part, leaders like Kofi Annan, the late former UN secretary general, encouraged that reparations would help "turn the page" on the past.[22]

While TJ as a normative and policy framework held—and continues to hold—great promise for violence-affected societies, TJ as a practice has been fraught with controversy. Take, for instance, judicial measures. At the international level, criminal tribunals are hotly contested. They are criticized for being illegitimate, biased, and ineffective.[23] Concurrently, there is widespread impunity at the

[15] Minow 1998; Teitel 2003; Tepperman 2002.
[16] UNCHR 1997.
[17] Gready 2010; Sikkink 2011; Tepperman 2002.
[18] Kiss 2000, 72; Scharf 1996, 400.
[19] Quoted in Kiss 2000, 72.
[20] Scharf 1996, 400.
[21] Mendeloff 2004, 361. Scholars and practitioners operationalize guarantees of nonrepetition as institutional reforms.
[22] Annan 2007.
[23] This started with the Nuremberg and Tokyo trials and continues today with the International Criminal Court (ICC). Regarding the former, see, among many others, Bass (2002) and

domestic level. Perpetrators of gross violations of human rights routinely evade judicial and nonjudicial proceedings. And, when they are confronted, they deny responsibility.[24] TJ processes also do not necessarily produce positive results. Some research indicates TJ mechanisms do not improve support for the rule of law.[25] Other research goes further to say they can have a negative effect on respect for human rights and the durability of peace.[26] Yet other work concludes that they have no effect.[27]

The debate over whether TJ works invites scholars to address a more fundamental, interrelated set of questions. First, who governs TJ, at what level of politics, and whose interests do they represent? Second, how do TJ governors realize their goals, and what challenges and challengers do they face? Third, to what extent are TJ governors successful, and why? Without answers to these questions, demonstrated through systematic evidence from around the globe, scholars and practitioners are not well equipped to comprehend variation in TJ emergence, characteristics, and, very importantly, effects.

This book begins to answer these questions, arguing that transnational civil society actors representing the interests of survivors and victims' families govern TJ. Domestic and international civil society groups collaborate strategically, working above, below, with, and without the state to realize their goals—TJ adoption, strong design, and delivery and follow-up—amid non- and anti-TJ interests in myriad political contexts. As this book will show, civil society actors have made monumental strides toward achieving truth, justice, reparations, and reforms for affected communities. But they, and the states they engage, have a distance still to go. Yet, as previously stated, whatever we get, as much or as little as we get, is because of civil society.

Key Concepts

I examine TJ through the lens of truth commissions, with civil society actors, NGOs in particular, as central protagonists. These groups have coalesced into a transnational advocacy network (TAN) that encompasses groups that "name

Smith (2012). Regarding the latter, see, among others, Chaudoin (2023), Cronin-Furman (2013), Escribà-Folch and Wright (2015), Helfer and Showalter (2017), Hillebrecht (2021), Zvobgo (2019*b*), and Zvobgo and Chaudoin (2025).

[24] See, for example, Hirst and Varney (2005) on Timor-Leste, and Jackson (2005) on Sierra Leone.

[25] Stromseth et al. 2006.

[26] Snyder and Vinjamuri 2003/2004. Perpetrators and those aligned ideologically with them can also create and exploit backlash against TJ policies. See, among others, work by Villamil and Balcells (2021).

[27] Sikkink and Walling 2007; Wiebelhaus-Brahm 2010. Some research does show a positive effect in select cases. Consider, for example, Appel (2018), Dancy and Thoms (2022), Kim and Sikkink (2010), Lie et al. (2007), Nalepa (2022), Nalepa and Powell (2016), Olsen, Payne, and Reiter (2010), and Prorok (2017).

and shame" governments, offer technical expertise and operational assistance, and fund TJ initiatives. The theoretical model advanced in this book and the empirical evidence presented center on the first two groups.

My concept of advocacy is transnational rather than transcalar.[28] The primary level of TJ politics and policy is national and so too, therefore, is the focus of advocacy.[29] The primary target of advocacy is the state, which is led by a new or restored government and its successors.[30] Under international law and the normative regime of TJ, the state is the actor primarily responsible for delivering TJ for past abuses, whether or not the current government perpetrated the abuses in question.[31]

Advocacy involves "outside strategies," such as shaming and protest, and "inside strategies," such as lobbying and technical assistance. NGOs' strategies depend both on the stage of the TJ life cycle in which they are operating and their relative strengths. As I will elaborate, domestic members of the network are sometimes better positioned to lead while international members follow. In a similar fashion, international members are sometimes better positioned to lead while domestic members follow.

Structure (the TJ life cycle and comparative advantages) and agency (to lead or to follow) interact, leading domestic and international NGOs to burden share, with the goal of realizing TJ adoption, strong design, and delivery and follow-up.[32] This strategic cooperation is the outcome of a long learning process: Every national TJ process is new, and its successes and failures both build on and contribute to this cumulative knowledge.[33]

[28] According to Pallas and Bloodgood (2022, 6), "[The] strategies and actions [of transcalar advocates] concern issues, or have impacts, that extend beyond their geographic locale and across levels of politics."

[29] TJ advocacy in one national context is not necessarily intended to affect advocacy or policy in another national context. Thus, it is more likely to be transnational than transcalar. One exception might be advocacy for accountability for international crimes. In this case, the level of advocacy could be national, regional, and/or international.

[30] To continue with the exceptional case of legal accountability for atrocity crimes, other advocacy targets could include IOs like the ICC and other states, based on passive personality or universal jurisdiction.

[31] The state is not the only actor that delivers TJ, but it bears the duty to do so. This duty can sometimes apply to multiple states, not just one, for a particular set of abuses. To continue with the example of legal accountability for atrocity crimes, third-party states, whether through passive personality or universal jurisdiction, are also duty bound to deliver accountability for perpetrators and justice for victims. To be sure, actors not implicated in abuses, like NGOs, sometimes deliver or help deliver TJ (e.g., through memorialization projects), but they are not bound to do so as are states. Rather, they take on this work, usually when states have declined to do so themselves.

[32] Taking these points together, my thinking differs from Pallas and Bloodgood, who see modern advocacy as "a series of sequential, strategic choices by advocacy initiators: to choose the scale or level at which to conduct advocacy; to choose a specific target or targets; to choose a strategy, such as inside or outside lobbying, with which to engage those targets; and to select (or eschew) partners to assist in this effort" (2022, 191).

[33] Author interviews with Priscilla Hayner and Eduardo González.

Truth Commissions

Truth commissions are temporary, government-sponsored bodies that investigate political violence, usually in the "recent past," or within living memory of affected populations. Commissions determine systems and patterns of abuse over time, using a wide array of evidence, including statements from survivors, victims' relatives, perpetrators, and other witnesses.[34] Quasi-judicial in nature, commissions aim to advance truth and justice through comprehensive, authoritative accounts of the past.[35]

Some scholars give commissions short shrift, counterposing them against trials and characterizing them as "second-best alternatives."[36] Others go further, arguing that commissions distract and detract from justice, and can even undermine the rule of law.[37] Yet commissions often presage—and, indeed, provide the normative and evidentiary basis for—trials, reparations programs, memorial projects, and state reforms. Because they typically precede and uniquely complement these other TJ measures, commissions are critical institutions in transitional politics. Commissions generally culminate in a report with recommendations designed to redress past harms and safeguard against future harms.[38]

Commissions have been established in diverse political contexts—new democracies, post-conflict states, consolidated democracies, and even autocracies—as the norm of redress for political violence has been developed and institutionalized around the globe.[39] However, commissions are likely to be most consequential during political transitions,[40] when broader processes of peacebuilding and/or democratization are under way; hence, this book's primary interest in transitional commissions (i.e., those inaugurated within ten years of the end of internal armed conflict, government killings of civilians, or autocracy).

Commissions are deeply political and contentious: They are the site of the contest about whether or not to seek the truth. They are also often the first—and sometimes only—step toward acknowledgment, remedy, and reform.

[34] Hayner 2011, 11–12.

[35] Tepperman 2002. Quasi-judicial bodies operate in other arenas, including climate (e.g., the Aarhus Compliance Committee), development finance (e.g., the World Bank's Inspection Panel), and treaty regimes (e.g., the Committee on Economic, Social and Cultural Rights). See Reiners (2022), Schoner (2023, 2024), and Zvobgo and Graham (2020).

[36] See, for example, Call (2004, 103–104). See also Kiss (2000).

[37] Collins 2010, 9–10; Osiel 2000, 134–137. These scholars are not alone. International Criminal Tribunal for the Former Yugoslavia prosecutor Carla del Ponte moved against a commission in Bosnia, concerned that it would impede her cases.

[38] Bakiner 2015, 106; González-Ocantos 2020, 28; Hayner 2011, 93–97, 167–171.

[39] Loyle and Binningsbø 2018; Posthumus and Zvobgo 2021; Skaar and Wiebelhaus-Brahm 2013; Winston 2021.

[40] Ben-Josef Hirsch et al. 2012; Minow 1998.

Commissions are imperfect. But, per Tepperman, "[their] imperfections stem from the imperfect situations out of which they arise."[41]

Civil Society and NGOs

Civil society encompasses "all associations and networks between the family and the state in which membership and activities are 'voluntary'—formally registered NGOs of many different kinds, labor unions, political parties, churches and other religious groups, professional and business associations, community and self-help groups, social movements and independent media."[42] Though I use the terms "civil society" and "NGOs" interchangeably, my theory, data, and analyses center on NGOs—the most formal and institutionalized civil society groups.

NGOs are legally registered, voluntary, not-for-profit groups that employ a professional staff to pursue a variety of political, economic, and social projects, including promoting human rights, democracy, development, and education.[43] They operate at multiple levels: locally, nationally, and/or internationally. Domestic NGOs work in one country, and the bulk of their work is in that country, though they may engage in transnational activities.[44] INGOs, by contrast, operate in multiple countries.[45] To meet their missions, NGOs seek political and financial support from private individuals, governments, and IOs, among others. Their strategies range between cooperating with, challenging, and circumventing states.[46]

NGOs are key players in domestic and international politics, as they sometimes fulfill the role and responsibilities of states.[47] As a consequence, IOs have created space for NGOs, in rule development, negotiation, promotion, oversight, and enforcement.[48] Relative to more loose groups of citizens and less institutionalized social movements, NGOs can more easily define and pursue a unified message and agenda. This makes it easier for governments and IOs to engage, collaborate, and negotiate with NGOs, on the one hand, and harder for governments and IOs to dismiss them, on the other hand.

NGOs are not saints, to be sure, and we do not always know what their political interests are.[49] They can influence domestic and international politics in

[41] Tepperman 2002, 145.
[42] Edwards 2009, 20.
[43] Bush 2015; Hendrix and Wong 2014; Herrold 2020; Murdie and Davis 2012.
[44] Henry and Sundstrom 2021, 18.
[45] Murdie and Davis 2012.
[46] Henry and Sundstrom 2021; Stroup and Murdie 2012. See also Stroup and Wong (2017), who, focusing on INGOs, talk about groups collaborating with, competing with, and condemning their targets.
[47] Chaudhry Forthcoming.
[48] Alter 2014; Haddad 2018; Henry and Sundstrom 2021; Medie 2020. IOs also regularly support civil society advocacy.
[49] Wong 2014, 5.

ways that are not always beneficial. In a transitional setting, for example, they could intentionally or unintentionally drive a TJ process in a direction that does not support peace and justice.[50] They could also fail to represent their constituents in the process.[51] Indeed, the separation between NGOs borne out of mutual support groups (e.g., groups of widows or relatives of the disappeared) and NGOs created by professional human rights defenders has created some agency problems, opening up the possibility of representation failure and fragmentation.[52]

Still, in general, I assume—and this book shows—that NGOs working on TJ issues are principled, morally driven actors. In many instances, this is because NGOs working on TJ issues have survivors of violence and victims' relatives as founders, board members, leaders, staff, and supporters. So there is a degree of built-in, internal accountability and responsiveness to communities.[53] Burden sharing reflects the practical need to collaborate, incentivizing coordination, and creates another "check" on mission drift.

Transnational Advocacy Networks

TANs are comprised of domestic and international civil society groups that bind together to further their political goals.[54] Their partnerships are based on the exchange of ideas, knowledge, and resources. Conferences, trainings and workshops, and collaborative research projects facilitate this exchange, and, through it, TAN members develop strategies for realizing their shared goals—for example, pairing domestic protest with international shaming to lead governments to adopt TJ institutions and programs. Of course, TAN relationships and activities rely on voluntary cooperation, and members at both the domestic and international levels face time, personnel, and other resource constraints. This means that advocacy effort and advocacy success may not always be correlated.

[50] Subotić (2009, 2015) finds that domestic political actors can inconsistently and problematically interpret and implement international TJ norms. Emerging research also shows how conservative activists seek to reinterpret, or outright challenge, international human rights norms and standards (Ayoub and Stoeckl 2024; Vilán Forthcoming).

[51] See Yoshioka (2014) for a typology of representational roles that advocacy organizations can play. They can be delegates, trustees, and/or educators, serving members, constituents, and/or the public. There can be, but there is not always, perfect overlap. See also Kagan (2024). Madlingozi (2010) calls for dismantling international TJ experts' trusteeship role, arguing that it reproduces colonial relations. There can indeed be a "dilemma of representation," where, per Henry and Sundstrom (2021, 26), "[t]he more an NGO emphasizes the global aspects of its advocacy, the more its claim to represent domestic audiences may erode."

[52] Madlingozi 2010; Rudling 2019. In the 1980s and 1990s, NGOs in the TJ space were essentially the same. But as TJ has become a more technical process, many new NGOs—such as the ICTJ—have been created by professionals who advocate on behalf of violence-affected populations.

[53] Wells and Anasti describe such groups as also being able to draw on their "'grassroots' identity to achieve legitimacy" (2020, 1134). This "descriptive representation" may enhance "substantive representation," per LeRoux (2009).

[54] Keck and Sikkink 1998. On civil society–IO partnerships, see Medie (2020).

Domestic and international NGOs collaborate across multiple fields related to human rights, including democracy and good governance, economic development, environmental protection, law and courts, physical integrity rights, and TJ, among others. We could think of groups working in each of these areas as composing different TANs, and thus we could say that there are multiple human rights TANs. However, I see networks in human rights as branches of a single tree because many core issues are closely connected.

For example, groups working on TJ may collaborate with groups working to improve respect for physical integrity rights, as both sets of groups seek to redress past physical integrity rights violations and prevent future violations from occurring. To give another example, groups working on TJ may collaborate with groups working in law and courts and on environmental issues, as they all have a stake in governments and IOs mitigating environmental harms and meting out justice for environmental crimes whose impacts are often felt most acutely by historically oppressed communities such as Indigenous peoples.

The focus of this book is NGOs within the global TJ network. Many members of the network have a remit that goes well beyond TJ, so I do not refer to them using the narrow term "TJ NGOs." In keeping with the literature, I will sometimes use the term "HROs," signifying human rights NGOs, when discussing advocacy groups (rather than operational groups) working primarily at an international level (rather than at a domestic level).

The Global Transitional Justice Network

The global TJ network's central goal is redress for past abuses and prevention of future abuses—hence, the network's interest in truth commissions, trials, reparations, and reforms, among other TJ modalities.

International members. Amnesty International (hereafter, Amnesty), Human Rights Watch (HRW), and the ICTJ are central international members of the TJ network. Together, they have standardized, certified, funded, and campaigned for certain TJ ideas and practices.[55] Some are involved in other branches of the human rights TAN. For example, Amnesty and HRW principally work on physical integrity rights. Thus, they are involved in both the TJ branch and the branch working to improve respect for physical integrity rights. In contrast, other members (e.g., the ICTJ) work exclusively on TJ issues—a quasi-epistemic community within the TAN.[56] In general, groups working on TJ have a broader set of concerns beyond physical integrity rights, including economic, social, and cultural issues related to past (and sometimes recurrent and ongoing) violence and injustice. Some international members of the TJ branch mostly engage in advocacy (e.g., via shaming and litigation), whereas others principally offer

[55] Ancelovici and Jenson 2013; Clark 2010; Rowen 2017.
[56] Haas 1992.

technical expertise and operational assistance to governments. Amnesty and HRW are examples of the former, while the ICTJ is an example of the latter. Other members, still, are mostly funders (e.g., the Aspen Institute, Ford Foundation, and Open Society Foundations).

Domestic members. A range of domestic civil society groups have proven helpful, if not pivotal, for the development, operation, and monitoring of truth commissions since their first uses in the 1970s and 1980s—NGOs, churches, economic associations, lawyers' guilds, and so on. With respect to commission adoption, NGOs like the Mutual Support Group (GAM) in Guatemala—a women-led organization that engaged in nonviolent protests during and after the internal armed conflict—have gained national and international attention and support, as they have lobbied their governments for commissions.[57] In terms of commission operation, collectives like Khulumani Support Group (KSG) in South Africa, founded by survivors of apartheid-era human rights violations, have supported witnesses testifying before commissions.[58] And, regarding post-commission activities, organizations like the Direct Action Centre for Peace and Memory—founded by former fighters in South Africa's freedom struggle—have worked to mitigate against future violence by raising awareness of issues of social inequality and injustice through commemorative actions.[59]

Certainly, the TJ network's contours are always changing.[60] NGOs have expanded their mission field over the past five decades, from local justice to international peacebuilding and democracy promotion—the outcome of a learning process.[61] International advocacy organizations like Amnesty have in some cases offered technical assistance (e.g., by sharing best practices for effective commissions), while domestic groups have provided advice and trainings to their counterparts in other countries. This transnational community has learned over time to share the burden of helping to realize TJ.

Who Leads? Who Follows?

Throughout this book, readers will be introduced to different members of the TJ network. Groups burden share, with different groups playing different roles at different stages of the TJ life cycle. Domestic NGOs play a leading role in institutional adoption, initiating demands for truth and justice, with INGOs in a supporting role. International groups then play a leading role in design, drawing on their professional expertise and prior experience designing TJ mechanisms,

[57] Ross 2006.
[58] Duke 1998.
[59] Grunebaum 2017.
[60] Rowen 2017.
[61] Subotić 2012.

with domestic groups in a supporting role. Last, domestic NGOs once again take the baton at the implementation and follow-up stage, lobbying governments to act on the results of the preceding process, with support from international groups.[62]

My work complements Bakiner's but departs from it in some important respects.[63] Truth commissions are the central actors in his book, whereas civil society groups are the central actors in mine. Where he emphasizes commissions' help to civil society, I emphasize civil society's help to commissions. Groups carry commissions' work forward, as Bakiner observes, but they do so because, as the actors that helped initiate commissions, they are invested in commissions' long-term impact. I do not go so far as to say commissions *induce* civil society into monitoring government human rights policy, as Bakiner does. This is already part of their work. Commissions have independent relevance, to be sure, but they are limited because they are temporary. To generate long-lasting impacts, commissions require the intermediation of other actors. This is actually something one of Bakiner's cases, Peru, shows us.[64] Ongoing civil society mobilization saved the commission's legacy long after it concluded.[65]

The civil society groups at the heart of this book chronologically precede and succeed truth commissions and shape them in important ways. Because they are created by states, but operate separately from and independently of states, commissions have power, authority, capabilities, and resources that civil society lacks. This makes commissions helpful partners.

Among broader civil society movements, NGOs want governments to create commissions that conduct investigations that result in comprehensive, authoritative accounts of past violence. NGOs cannot do this on their own. NGOs also want governments to design commissions well so that commissions can meet their missions. In addition, NGOs want commissions to make policy recommendations based on their investigations—recommendations to remedy past harms and safeguard against future harms. While NGOs can prescribe policies to governments, policy prescriptions from NGOs do not necessarily carry the same weight as policy prescriptions from commissions because NGO activities are not backed by states, whereas commission activities are backed by states, at least to some degree. Last, NGOs want commissions to extend beyond their operations, and so NGOs advocate for implementation of commission recommendations. NGOs help and are helped by commissions.

[62] Mutual deference (Avant et al. 2010; Stroup and Wong 2017) is essential in the TJ network.

[63] Bakiner 2015.

[64] See Bakiner's (2014) article.

[65] We see the opposite in El Salvador, where the commission's impact has been muted because of a weak civil society, Carlos Beristain, an investigator for the Inter-American Commission on Human Rights, said to me in an interview.

Transitional Justice: A Theoretical and Empirical Puzzle

What explains similar outcomes—TJ adoption, strong design, and implementation and follow-up—across dissimilar contexts and countries around the globe? This section summarizes existing scholarship, outlines my theory and empirical strategy, and presents my project's core contributions.

The State of Scholarship

Prior scholarship tends to depict TJ as a set of *government-led* policies and institutions.[66] From this, we could infer that TJ outcomes are primarily, if not exclusively, shaped by governments.[67] Yet we observe similarities in the adoption, design, and implementation and monitoring of TJ processes across countries with dissimilar governments, politics, and histories. Importantly, TJ is first and foremost for survivors and victims' families; they are the most interested parties and have the most to gain from the process, not governments. What's more, before TJ was a framework for addressing abuses during authoritarian regimes and armed conflicts on a national level, it was a set of individual rights and individual remedies, recognized and provided by courts and quasi-judicial bodies.[68] Besides, in post-violence settings, establishing a truth or accountability process is not always among governments' priorities, and, in some instances, leaders see such measures as threats to regime stability.[69] This is not to say that non- or anti-accountability interests necessarily prevail.[70] Rather, these competing interests suggest that it is unlikely that governments alone determine TJ. In other words, governments might not be TJ governors, and they might not represent the interests of survivors and victims' families.

Previous research also casts TJ as a set of *domestic* policies and institutions encompassing trials, truth commissions, reparations, and reforms.[71] From

[66] Benomar 1993; Grodsky 2010; Sutter 1995.

[67] Among others, Price (2003) challenges such a state-centric approach to understanding world politics.

[68] See, for example, *Bleier v. Uruguay* (UN Human Rights Committee 1981), *Velázquez Rodríguez v. Honduras* (Inter-American Court of Human Rights 1988), and *McCann v. United Kingdom* (European Court of Human Rights 1995). For an in-depth treatment of the topic, see Ariav (2012), among others.

[69] Cronin-Furman 2022. See also Collins (2010, 8–9) and Kochanski (2021, 130–131). Following armed conflict, governments may prioritize peace over justice. Similarly, in the aftermath of atrocities, leaders may wish to deflect responsibility. Likewise, former authoritarian elites may trade new democratic elites stability for impunity.

[70] See, for instance, Michel on trials: States can fail to investigate and prosecute crimes "but victims' relatives and civil society still somehow find a way to prevent the case from falling into impunity and oblivion" (2018, 3).

[71] Bates et al. 2020; Loyle and Binningsbø 2018; Olsen, Payne, and Reiter 2010; Powers and Proctor 2016.

this, we could surmise that, beyond taking on similar institutional forms and even names, TJ processes in different parts of the world are otherwise unrelated to each other.[72] Yet, as discussed, TJ has deep international roots and has been refined, institutionalized, and normalized by an international community of experts and NGOs representing the interests of survivors, victims' families, and the broader affected population.[73] So, TJ is more than a domestic process.

Affected communities' interests in and governments' potential interests against truth and justice, coupled with the global development and local implementation of TJ, prompt me to study the actors who navigate the space between them and who leverage global and local resources to realize truth and justice: civil society.[74] Some scholarship refers to domestic civil society actors as *local implementers* and *service providers* in TJ contexts and recognizes international civil society actors as *technical experts* and *advisors*. But little work takes seriously the idea that they may be *policy entrepreneurs*[75] who develop, champion, and export policy ideas around the world.[76]

Moreover, no work, to my knowledge, argues that transnational civil society actors are *TJ governors*. (Recall that global governors, per Avant et al., "are authorities who exercise power across borders for purposes of affecting policy. [They] thus create issues, set agendas, establish and implement rules or programs, and evaluate and/or adjudicate outcomes."[77]) Despite their historical influence on domestic and international politics—including advocating for TJ around the world, drafting TJ mechanisms' rules and procedures, and participating in and sometimes leading TJ implementation—civil society actors are generally not seen as governing in this public policy realm or in others.[78]

[72] For example, we have seen "truth and reconciliation," "historical clarification," "truth, justice, and peace," and "truth and dignity" commissions, among others.

[73] Ancelovici and Jenson 2013; Rowen 2017; Subotić 2011; VanAntwerpen 2009. Madlingozi (2010, 225) offers the challenge that in "representing" victims, international experts "'produce' *the* victim" and reproduce colonial relations. This is a topic for which I cannot give a full treatment in these pages. This book is less about the normative aspects of transnational activism and more about the empirical reality of its existence, operation, and effects.

[74] Backer 2003. For work on civil society mediation in global governance institutions, see Henry and Sundstrom (2021).

[75] Policy entrepreneurs can operate "in or out of government, in elected or appointed positions, in interest groups or research organizations. But their defining characteristic, much as in the case of the business entrepreneur, is their willingness to invest their resources—time, energy, reputation, and sometimes money—in the hope of a future return" (Kingdon 1984, 122). They are "agents of change" (Brouwer 2015) who "try to influence a given public policy in order to open up new horizons of opportunities" (Arieli and Cohen 2013, 238).

[76] Ancelovici and Jenson (2013), Rowen (2017), and Subotić (2012) are exceptions.

[77] Avant et al. 2010, 2.

[78] Author interviews with practitioners, including Priscilla Hayner, Sandra Raggio, director of the Provincial Commission for Memory in Argentina, and Mario Polanco, director of GAM in Guatemala.

Additionally, little work addresses how domestic and international civil society actors collaborate to realize their shared goals across TJ contexts.[79]

The paucity of scholarship on the myriad ways transnational civil society actors are operative in TJ globally reflects Subotić's observation that "much of the role of civil society NGOs is uncritically accepted."[80] Essentially, the extant literature recognizes that civil society actors can be important for TJ, and scholars have identified some of the ways they are influential. However, scholars have not theorized and systematically analyzed how, why, and to what extent civil society is influential—not just in terms of TJ adoption but also in terms of design and implementation and follow-up.

Beyond scholarship's limited understanding of TJ governance and inadequate attention to one highly plausible set of governors, transnational civil society actors, there is a dearth of detailed data on TJ mechanisms, their origins, inputs, outputs, and outcomes—the exact types of data needed to compare global experiences and evaluate the nature of, reasons for, and degree of civil society's influence.[81]

Resolving the Puzzle: NGOs as Global Governors in Transitional Justice

This book advances the field's theoretical and empirical understanding of TJ by focusing on civil society groups to explain TJ in countries with a history of widespread political violence. As they advocate before, advise, assist, and substitute for governments, TJ network members exercise their comparative advantages in information, experience, material resources, and political power. They alternate leadership and support roles among themselves at the TJ adoption, design, and implementation and follow-up stages. By so doing, they maximize scarce resources and increase their chances of success.[82] My project thus produces a new model of TANs: *the burden sharing model.*

[79] There are noteworthy exceptions, including González-Ocantos (2020) and Lessa (2022).

[80] Subotić 2012, 112. For an exception, see Rowen (2017), who shows how transnational actors have helped translate TJ into domestic political action in Bosnia and Herzegovina, Colombia, and the United States. See also Merry (2006) on NGOs translating global human rights norms and Medie (2020) on women's justice norms.

[81] I use "outcomes" to capture "successes" and "failures." Outcomes can be "mediate" or "final." To illustrate, acknowledgment is a positive mediate outcome, while reconciliation and peace are positive final outcomes (De Greiff 2012). Mediate outcomes can support final outcomes. For instance, acknowledgment can support reconciliation and peace. As for "outputs," I use the term throughout the book primarily to refer to truth commission reports.

[82] Fyall and McGuire (2015) challenge the dichotomization of groups as advocates *or* service providers; as choosing insider *or* outsider strategies; and as working in one arena *or* another. Networks and coalitions like the ones I describe in this book can overcome these dichotomies—by working together and sharing the burden of realizing TJ.

The empirical predictions of the burden sharing model are as follows: (1) Governments are more likely to adopt TJ mechanisms in countries where domestic groups are stronger, international groups concentrate their shaming efforts, and domestic and international groups are more formally connected; (2) governments are more likely to design strong mechanisms when they are advised by international experts; and (3) governments are more likely to follow up with specific remedies that domestic groups propose based on the results of the country's previous mechanisms.

There can be some variation in domestic NGO activity across stages of the TJ life cycle. Some groups, like GAM, are active at all stages, from advocating for a TJ process like a truth commission to monitoring its operation, results, and follow-up measures. Others get involved later, like KSG during the South African TRC. Generally, once groups like KSG are involved in TJ issues, they stay involved. Among INGOs, however, there is more variation in activity.

Readers will see advocacy groups like Amnesty working with domestic partners during the period of repression and violence to shame states into accountability, expert groups like the ICTJ assisting with mechanism design, and monitoring groups like Impunity Watch working to oversee governments' post-commission activities. Naturally, then, Amnesty's shaming is an explanatory variable in Chapter 3 (on institutional adoption), the ICTJ's involvement in a country is an explanatory factor in Chapter 4 (on institutional design), and Impunity Watch is one organization in a coalition of INGOs that I capture to explain implementation of further TJ measures in the single-country chapters (Chapters 6 to 8).

To be clear, the TJ network's success is not inevitable or guaranteed. And there is variation in practice; domestic and international groups do not always agree on goals or methods, and do not always collaborate as described. Rather, their success depends on whether or not they do.[83]

Case Selection and Evidence for the Theory

I take truth commissions as my point of departure and show that governments create commissions, afford them strong investigative powers, and implement their recommendations (which include trials, memorials, and reparations) largely because of the advocacy of transnational NGOs. NGOs do not wait for or rely solely on governments to enact these further measures, to be sure. They work with and separately from the state to realize further TJ when governments are

[83] Arthur and Yakinthou's (2018) volume also illustrates the problem of "missed connections" between civil society groups, donors, and governments.

unable or unwilling to do so. Consequently, NGOs do not simply assist with TJ, as prior research suggests; rather, they help govern it, at every step. Given this, TJ in general and commissions in particular are a transnational, civil society-led institution.

I present evidence from statistical analyses of a series of novel datasets, the *Varieties of Truth Commissions*, that I built over a three-year period with the assistance of seventeen research assistants at two universities. The datasets jointly capture (1) the universe of commissions, (2) their mandates and investigative powers, (3) their recommendations, and (4) levels of implementation across recommendations. My data are unusual, both for their comprehensive coverage of commissions and their granularity. They offer significant descriptive value, illuminating important variation at multiple stages of TJ—institutional adoption, design, and delivery and follow-up—and the factors behind this variation. They help us better understand the advocacy and power of civil society, the decisions of governments, and the promise and limits of TJ and its global spread.

I also present case studies and probe causal pathways using evidence from my fieldwork, including interviews and focus groups with government officials, former commission officials, IO representatives, and domestic and international NGO experts and advocates in more than a dozen countries. Thus, I engage key stakeholders at all levels in global TJ.

Contributions to Scholarship and Practice

At a time when impunity for political violence threatens the global human rights regime, scholars must draw greater attention to the actors who prompt, architect, and help carry out TJ processes, the strategies they employ, the challenges and challengers they face, and their successes and failures. Likewise, given that many governments around the world continue to restrict civic space and crack down on civil society actors via physical repression and administrative controls, it is vital that scholarship elucidates how and where advocates are nevertheless successful, with a view to supporting and sustaining their efforts.[84]

This book's distinctive contribution is providing a complete theory, with testable hypotheses, of TJ adoption, design, and delivery and follow-up globally, with truth commissions as its entry point. The book positions NGOs as governors in global TJ, and addresses not only their advocacy but also their role in designing, implementing, and monitoring TJ processes. The book explains and provides evidence for how transnational civil society groups work together to influence government TJ policy at multiple stages: They burden share.

[84] Chaudhry 2022, Forthcoming.

The theory helps explain similar outcomes across dissimilar contexts. Moreover, the statistical analyses encompass a range of regime and conflict types, and the case studies cover countries with different experiences of violence in different parts of the world.

Building on this, my work contributes to broader debates in comparative politics and international relations about the extent to which civil society helps advance important micro outcomes like strong institutional design and critical macro outcomes like governments' respect for human rights. I find that civil society actors are essential to "the before, during, and after" of TJ. One implication is that external actors, whether academics, activists, attorneys, or donor governments, should view with a critical eye processes that sideline civil society at any and all of the key stages that I identify.

The findings also add to a growing quantitative TJ research program that builds on pioneering single-case and small-*N* comparative studies about the impact of TJ mechanisms. Leveraging comprehensive datasets and employing a mixed-method approach, this body of research seeks to systematically evaluate TJ's impact on post-violence societies.[85] My research shows that low political will among decision makers, corruption, government turnover, and fluctuating economic resources are key barriers to positive TJ impacts. A robust TJ process—like a truth commission that is designed well, conducts a serious investigation, publishes a comprehensive and accurate report on past violence, and proposes a range of relevant remedies—may nonetheless have a limited impact where governments are unwilling or unable to act on the results of the process (e.g., commissions' findings and policy proposals).[86]

Moreover, my project is noteworthy for its evaluation of commission recommendations, which have been largely neglected in scholarship, limiting our understanding of TJ legacies in violence-affected societies.[87] Studying what commissions recommend gives us a global view and understanding of social and political problems in the aftermath of violence—problems that commissions seek to address. And studying what recommendations are implemented and are not implemented—and why—illuminates opportunities for and barriers to commission impact.

Finally, my work invites scholars, practitioners, and policymakers to deliberate whether it is reasonable to expect TJ institutions and programs to support

[85] Ang and Nalepa 2019; Appel 2018; Balcells et al. 2022; Dancy 2018; Dancy and Thoms 2022.

[86] This is consistent with Cronin-Furman's (2022) conclusion that TJ processes are hampered when individuals responsible for—or complicit in—atrocities hold power.

[87] Byrne et al. (2024) and Skaar et al.'s *Beyond Words* project are rare exceptions. But Byrne et al. (2024) limit their study to recommendations pertaining to memorialization, while the *Beyond Words* researchers limit their investigation to select Latin American countries (Martín et al. 2022; Skaar et al. 2022*a*, 2022*b*, 2025; Wiebelhaus-Brahm et al. 2023).

democracy, human rights, peace, and the rule of law, particularly in countries where governments are not committed to acting on the results of a TJ process.[88] This problem may have less to do with TJ itself and more to do with politics, specifically what actors in a particular context want, what they promise or are promised, and what they think is possible.

Plan of the Book

To summarize the discussion so far, this book investigates how TJ is governed and realized. I ask why some national governments but not others adopt TJ institutions and programs, design them to succeed, and act on their results. I argue that members of the global TJ network guide governments in TJ adoption, institutional design, and delivery and follow-up. They do this by burden sharing: Domestic groups take the lead when they are better positioned to do so, with international groups in a supporting role. Inversely, international groups take the lead when they are better equipped to do so, with domestic groups in a supporting role. Through burden sharing, domestic and international activists and experts maximize scarce resources and improve the likelihood of their joint success.

I focus on truth commissions and document TJ network members' shifting roles across three stages: commission adoption, design, and implementation of recommendations. Given their contributions to each stage, I argue that civil society actors are not simply local advocates and service providers, as much prior research indicates. Rather, they govern commissions and, more generally, global TJ norms, practices, and institutions.

Chapter 2

In Chapter 2, I present my theory of TJ as a transnational, civil society-led institution, and I situate my argument in existing scholarly debates. I consider how prior research has positioned civil society actors in domestic and international politics and characterized their roles and importance for TJ in general and for commissions in particular. I then elaborate on the means by which civil society groups influence the presence, nature, and consequences of commissions. I focus on how domestic and international civil society groups create, share, and transmit information—both among themselves and to and beyond their government targets—to realize truth and justice. Last, I lay out my empirical strategy.

[88] Gready (2010, 7), for instance, wonders if TJ has taken on more than has been shown it can achieve.

Chapter 3

Chapter 3 investigates transnational advocacy and truth commission adoption. I analyze whether governments are more likely to establish commissions in countries where domestic groups are stronger, international groups concentrate their shaming efforts, and domestic and international groups are formally connected.

I evaluate my expectations using a comprehensive dataset covering the universe of transitions from internal armed conflict, government killings of civilians, and autocracy from 1970 to 2018. I also leverage my interviews with INGO leaders, interviews with Guatemalan NGO leaders, and a focus group with Argentinian human rights defenders.

This research design is well suited to test the implications of the burden sharing model for TJ adoption because it exploits cross-national data to establish global patterns and draws on eyewitness accounts of individuals on both sides of domestic–international civil society partnerships (i.e., the central protagonists of my transnational politics story of TJ). Supportive evidence from the quantitative and qualitative analyses should make us confident of the burden sharing model's value.

I find a strong association between domestic civil society strength and commission adoption and between concentrated international HRO shaming and commission adoption. These results hold, even when controlling for a range of domestic and international political and institutional factors, including pre-transition levels of human rights abuse, judicial independence, and aid dependence. I also find some evidence for formal ties between network members enhancing prospects for a commission.

The interviews and focus group corroborate the idea that international HRO advocacy strengthens domestic advocacy; however, all participants maintain that domestic advocacy is the determining factor.[89] Thus, I find support for the first part of the burden sharing model: Domestic groups are in the leading role at the TJ adoption stage and help explain similar outcomes across dissimilar contexts.

Chapter 4

Chapter 4 studies technical expertise and truth commission institutional design. I interrogate whether governments advised by international experts, notably the ICTJ, are more likely to endow commissions with strong investigative powers, specifically the power to investigate a range of abuses, trace antecedents of abuses, subpoena testimony, and preserve evidence.

[89] Readers who are skeptical of INGOs' impact should take heart: INGO representatives themselves emphasized domestic NGOs' importance above their own.

To evaluate these expectations, I draw on my new data, which code operational and jurisdictional powers stipulated in commissions' legal mandates. I document the presence (absence) of international experts prior to and during a country's commission. I supplement the cross-national data with my interviews with current and former ICTJ leadership, as well as a focus group with current leadership and staff.

This is an appropriate research design to evaluate the implications of the burden sharing model for TJ design because it makes use of cross-commission data to demonstrate global trends in design and capitalizes on first-hand accounts of the individuals who have been—and are—in the rooms where decisions are made. It is on their experience, expertise, and advocacy for strong TJ institutions and programs around the world that my theory in this chapter rests.

I find a strong relationship between international experts' advice and strong commission designs, including such features as the power to trace antecedents and to preserve evidence. I find this to be the case across transitional and non-transitional truth commissions while also controlling for commissions' subject matter (armed conflict or authoritarian rule) and regional and global precedents (i.e., diffusion). However, I do not find experts' advice has a similarly strong effect on commissions' power to consider a range of abuses or to compel testimony.

These findings are based on an analysis of individual powers, not combined powers. Additional statistical tests show a robust relationship between international expert involvement and overall stronger commission designs. A strong domestic civil society is strongly associated with just one commission power: the power to compel testimony.

Consistent with the second part of the burden sharing model, I find that international experts, those with the professional experience and technical know-how, are typically in the leading role at the TJ design stage and help explain similar outcomes across dissimilar contexts.

Chapter 5

Chapter 5 argues that NGOs use truth commissions' outputs, specifically their policy recommendations, to influence governments' post-commission policy agenda. Using a variety of political strategies, domestic groups, with international support, lean on governments to produce additional TJ measures (e.g., prosecutions, reparations, reforms, memorials, and others) based on a commission's results. And where governments are unwilling or unable to do so, civil society groups attempt to substitute for the state.

To ground the argument and situate in broader perspective the three cases that I study in depth in Chapters 6 to 8, I use *Varieties of Truth Commissions* data to define the universe of recommendations for which NGOs could advocate. I present, for the first time, the global landscape of recommendations and explore how they relate to different political contexts.

Commissions in different contexts have made remarkably similar recommendations. They have proposed measures for truth like education, measures for justice like trials, measures for reparation, both material and symbolic, and measures for reform, including of security services. Across time and space, commissions have tended to emphasize institutional reforms above all other measures. This isomorphism evinces again the transnational nature of commissions (owing to transnational actor involvement) and disentangles conventional diffusion explanations for this isomorphism.

After this discussion, I lay out the theory and hypotheses that I evaluate in the subsequent trio of chapters focused on Guatemala, South Africa, and Timor-Leste, and I present the research design. In brief, I argue that domestic NGOs, supported by their international partners, strategically lobby for recommendations. In turn, governments are more likely to implement recommendations backed by NGOs.

Chapters 6, 7, and 8

Part One of Chapters 6 to 8 explores how NGOs define the terms of what additional TJ measures should follow a truth commission (i.e., how they set the agenda), with a focus on advocacy for commission recommendations. Here, I leverage my third dataset, which contains information on NGOs working in different issue areas in Guatemala, South Africa, and Timor-Leste, and the recommendations they have lobbied policymakers to implement. I also trace NGO advocacy through case studies that present organizations framing problems and solutions, navigating prohibitive political conditions, and mobilizing their resources and networks. I also track international civil society actors' assistance to their domestic partners.

Guatemala, South Africa, and Timor-Leste are ideal for evaluating the arguments presented because their post-violence governments have contended with both domestic and international attention and pressure to deliver truth and justice for past violence. If NGOs ever leverage commissions' outputs to pursue additional TJ measures, we should see them doing so here, where they engaged in essential advocacy during periods of violence in their respective countries and, later, the transitions. If we see NGOs using the outputs of TJ processes in these three countries, we may see them doing the same in other countries. However, if we do not detect this work in these emblematic contexts, it is not likely that we will observe it elsewhere. In addition to the quantitative data, the analysis draws on my fieldwork interviews with members of victims and human rights groups, government officials, and IO representatives.

I find that instead of focusing solely on recommendations related to their previous work and expertise, as some prior research would lead us to expect, NGOs, at commissions' prompting, largely diversified their issue portfolios, spurring knowledge and resource sharing within the domestic human rights community and tightening links between and among NGOs. Throughout, INGOs and even IOs provided operational and political support. Thus, I find support for the third part of the burden sharing model: Domestic groups are in the leading role in the first half of the implementation and follow-up stage.

Part Two of Chapters 6 to 8 discerns the extent to which NGOs prevail on governments to implement truth commission recommendations. I also evaluate whether and to what degree domestic groups, with the material and political support of international partners, substitute for governments that are unwilling or unable to deliver on recommendations. Here, I present the capstone of the *Varieties of Truth Commissions*, which codes implementation across nearly 650 policy prescriptions from the Guatemalan, South African, and Timorese commissions. I rely on quantitative data on implementation—which track whether a given proposal was initiated, the level of implementation that was reached, and the presence and breadth of NGO coalitions in different areas—and qualitative data from my fieldwork.

Since Guatemala, South Africa, and Timor-Leste vary in terms of the types of political violence they experienced—internal armed conflict, race-based authoritarian government, and foreign occupation and conflict, respectively—I can rule out potentially competing explanations for policy adoption at the post-commission stage, like similar violence and post-violence development trajectories. In addition, since the cases vary by region—Central America, Southern Africa, and Southeast Asia, respectively—I can also rule out conventional diffusion explanations for policy adoption. Moreover, I can hold constant across the cases the unique window of opportunity that political transitions represent for policy adoption.

While quantitative analyses do not show a statistically significant relationship between NGO advocacy and government initiation of recommendations in Guatemala, they do show a statistically significant relationship between NGO advocacy and the level of implementation reached. By contrast, in South Africa and Timor-Leste, the quantitative data indicate NGOs influencing initial policy uptake but not policy completion. Strikingly, across all three cases, I find that, where governments have not provided additional remedies, NGOs have intervened, assisting governments in those areas where there is a modest commitment to a positive outcome and substituting for governments where there is not such a commitment.[90]

Consistent with the burden sharing model, domestic advocates have remained in the leading role in this second half of the implementation and follow-up stage. INGOs and IOs have lent financial, logistical, and political support, but this has not been a panacea for such challenges as low political will, corruption, government turnover, and fluctuating economic resources.

These are important findings: Many hold up Guatemala, South Africa, and Timor-Leste as paragons of TJ, yet civil society continues to struggle for TJ. Despite the ongoing dialogue between scholars and practitioners, scholarly research has lagged behind the pace of practical knowledge.[91] With a wider temporal lens and data from an array of sources, we see how states have limited, and sometimes obstructed, TJ, even in these emblematic cases.

Chapter 9

Chapter 9 re-presents the arguments in broader perspective and discusses the implications of the findings for the TJ, human rights advocacy, and global governance literatures. This book empirically demonstrates how transnational civil society actors propel truth commissions and, more broadly, TJ norms, practices, and institutions. They shame, lobby, advise, partner with, and substitute for states. They are not just local advocates or service and technical assistance providers. They are governors.

[90] NGOs can help states build up their "TJ capabilities," per González-Ocantos (2020). See also Salamon and Toepler (2015) in the broader literature on nonprofits.

[91] Hayner 2001, 2011.

2
Burden Sharing: How NGOs Govern Transitional Justice

In this book, I argue that TJ is a transnational institution led by domestic and international civil society actors who have coalesced into a global network. This argument innovates on extant accounts of TJ as a domestic process driven by states and builds on a growing body of work that examines TJ advocacy networks. While social scientists have examined related networks in the global movement to improve respect for physical integrity rights, few have extended their insights to TJ, which succeeds periods of widespread abuse. Importantly, research has not hypothesized and scrutinized the discrete activities that TJ network members undertake at different stages to transform their preferences into policy.

Consistent with research on other human rights networks, I do not assume that international members of the TJ network are stronger, more savvy, or more influential than domestic members of the network.[1] The difference between them lies in their comparative advantages at different stages of the TJ life cycle. As such, domestic and international groups alternate leading and support roles. Relatedly, in my model, partnership and collaboration are not predicated on domestic groups needing international groups' support per se, as in the traditional "boomerang" model of advocacy.[2] Both sets of groups need each other in different ways.[3]

Transitional Justice: A Story of Domestic or International Politics?

Comparative politics scholarship and international relations scholarship pose a twin set of questions relevant for understanding TJ origins, contours, and consequences: To what extent do countries' domestic politics shape outcomes in the international system, and to what degree does the international system influence

[1] Pallas and Bloodgood 2022.
[2] Keck and Sikkink 1998.
[3] Zvobgo 2020.

Governing Truth. Kelebogile Zvobgo, Oxford University Press. © Oxford University Press (2026).
DOI: 10.1093/oso/9780197815663.003.0002

domestic politics? Prior research shows that domestic political factors—such as a country's regime type, legal tradition and institutions, and civil society—influence commitment to and compliance with human rights treaty regimes.[4] Meanwhile, research on international law, norms, and institutions elucidates how states create but are ultimately constrained by these regimes, due in part to the actions of compliance partners and compliance constituencies such as NGOs.[5] Still other research tracks the interaction between domestic and international political factors and the effect of this interaction on outcomes. Of note, established models of transnational advocacy such as the boomerang illustrate how domestic and international NGOs converge on repressive governments to change their behavior.[6]

Much of the existing TJ literature provides a domestic politics story. Consider, for instance, research on truth commissions. Some researchers consider commissions to be the fruit of local advocacy and elite sympathies.[7] Yet others view commissions as the product of a power struggle between elites and the masses, or simply among elites.[8] Even so, other researchers find themselves in between, describing commissions as the cause and consequence of autocratic breakdown and democratization.[9]

Certainly, commissions have emerged from domestic elite bargains. For example, in South Africa, the now-famous TRC was a key element of the transition from apartheid to democracy. However, international actors—including civil society actors who had fought for and helped implement commissions in Latin America—also influenced the content and outcomes of the negotiations.[10]

Some research offers an international politics story. In the critical literature especially, scholars describe commissions—and TJ more generally—as a foreign imposition in many instances.[11] For example, in Sierra Leone, the TRC was a term of the peace accords that brought protracted internal armed conflict to an end. But external actors' involvement in the accords' construction generated skepticism, even criticism, from locals.[12] Meanwhile, scholarship on the "justice cascade" or "revolution in accountability" suggests that the expansion of human rights norms like TJ and related initiatives are positive and all but inevitable.[13]

[4] Sandholtz 2017; Simmons 2009.

[5] Alter 2014; Barnett and Finnemore 2004; Keohane 1984; Koremenos 2016; Lebovic and Voeten 2006; Sandholtz 2000.

[6] Keck and Sikkink 1998.

[7] Kim 2012*a*, 2014.

[8] Grodsky 2010.

[9] Arenhövel 2008.

[10] Roht-Arriaza 2001; Hayner 2011. In addition, the international anti-apartheid movement, involving political and economic sanctions, helped bring the apartheid government to the negotiating table with the African National Congress.

[11] Gready 2010; Nagy 2008.

[12] Jackson 2005.

[13] Lutz and Sikkink 2001; Sikkink 2011; Sriram 2003; Teitel 2003.

Taken on their own, domestic and international politics stories are limited in their ability to explain TJ. Domestic politics stories neglect international actors and institutions that can influence domestic actors' preferences and capabilities.[14] In turn, international politics stories dismiss domestic actors' agency—to advance or undermine truth and justice.[15] Moreover, both sets of stories rely on evidence from cases that are not especially representative of global TJ processes. Strikingly, many existing accounts do not seriously query TJ institutional design. Neither do they systematically examine "post-transitional justice" outcomes like the implementation (or nonimplementation) of truth commission recommendations.[16]

I propose instead a transnational politics story—one that helps explain not only TJ adoption but also TJ design and post-TJ outcomes. This story centers domestic and international civil society actors who are part of a global network of activists and practitioners. This book thus advances scholarship on truth commissions, TJ, transnational advocacy, and global governance.[17]

Civil Society: Local Partners or Global Governors?

Another core question in the study of comparative politics, and to a growing extent research in international relations, is how and to what degree civil society actors shape political outcomes.[18] Much scholarship on political transitions considers civil society groups to be crucial players. Whether agitating under repressive authoritarian governments or traversing conflict zones, at great risk these organizations offer an affecting critique of the architects and agents of political violence. In the context of autocratic rule, this criticism "inevitably spills

[14] Henry and Sundstrom 2021.

[15] Per Lessa (2022, 8), "[T]he frequent pitting of the national vs. international spheres... and of civil society against the state... leave[s] numerous hidden nuances unaccounted for... [J]ustice seekers operate both domestically and internationally... within civil society and state institutions." Civil society groups, per Henry and Sundstrom (2021, 6), "act as 'mediators' between global and domestic political arenas... promoting global solutions at home."

[16] Collins 2010. There are exceptions, on which I build. First, using a global, mixed-method analysis, I scale up Bakiner's (2015) qualitative case comparisons of civil society activism in post-commission Chile and Peru. I likewise scale up Kim's (2014) research on South Korea, and Rowen's (2017) examination of Bosnia, Colombia, and the United States. In terms of commission recommendations, I cast a wider net than Skaar et al. (2022*a*, 2022*b*, 2025), who examine a selection of Latin American cases, and Byrne et al. (2024), who concentrate on memorialization projects.

[17] Bakiner (2015) is one of my project's inspirations. Drawing on Chile and Peru, he shows how civil society mobilization helps explain commission impact, even if delayed by governments. Bakiner gives more weight to commissions for shaping post-TJ outcomes, whereas I give more weight to civil society. Still, our work is generally complementary. The bigger difference is that I stretch the timeline to examine both pre- and post-commission advocacy.

[18] Alter 2014; Avant et al. 2010; Barnett and Finnemore 2004; Bush 2015; Danner and Voeten 2010; Henry and Sundstrom 2021; Keck and Sikkink 1998; Lessa 2022; Medie 2020; Michel 2018; Sikkink 2011; Stroup and Wong 2017; Vilán Forthcoming.

over to include political and social rights."[19] Likewise, in the midst of inter- and intra-state conflicts, civil society actors campaign for peace, provide essential services, and offer counseling and rehabilitation.[20] Moreover, as countries move from autocracy to democracy, and from conflict to peace, domestic and international NGOs representing survivors and victims' families possess great moral authority and a wealth of experience and knowledge that, together, position them to provide and help implement a framework for confronting the past—that is, TJ.[21] However, civil society actors are not typically viewed as governors in this policy realm.[22]

Civil society actors are generally characterized as local advocates and service providers in TJ processes. In the context of truth commissions, civil society actors represent and support survivors and victims' families and assist in localizing truth seeking and truth telling within a variety of social, cultural, and political contexts. They are local representatives, statement takers, trauma counselors, program evaluators, and community liaisons.[23] For many scholars, this is the extent of their contributions; civil society actors are not seen as policy entrepreneurs.[24] As in other public policy domains, much of the existing research on TJ attributes transnational policy transfer to states and IOs.[25] But the spread of TJ processes around the world as a response to political violence cannot be solely attributed to states. Individuals and groups, from above and below, are driving policy in this and other realms.[26]

Civil society actors have played essential roles in developing and implementing TJ globally through their savvy use of information, contacts, expertise, and resources. However, prior scholarship has not systematically investigated the TJ network's activities and members' roles at different stages. How exactly does the network operate, and what are the keys to its success? For guidance, I turn to the literature on NGOs and TANs in adjacent policy domains.

NGOs in Comparative Politics and International Relations

NGOs are conventionally viewed as providers of various political benefits, both to governments and publics. In terms of political benefits, NGOs mediate between the state and the public, channeling citizens' interests in an organized

[19] O'Donnell and Schmitter 2013, 60.
[20] Gizelis 2011.
[21] Sikkink 2011.
[22] Ancelovici and Jenson 2013.
[23] Backer 2003.
[24] Ancelovici and Jenson 2013.
[25] Fletcher and Weinstein with Rowen 2009.
[26] Finnemore 1996*b*; Rowen 2017; Sikkink 2011.

manner.[27] In addition, NGOs train citizens to articulate their grievances using the language of human rights, which calls for different remedies for different harms.[28]

NGOs also provide economic resources and offer essential services that governments may not otherwise be able to afford, particularly in developing contexts. And in many places around the world, NGOs are central channels of foreign funds, partly because of donor governments' belief that official aid is more likely to reach its intended targets when NGOs are involved. NGOs are also key targets of private philanthropy, receiving and transferring billions of US dollars each year.[29] NGOs not only receive and transfer resources, they can also close doors to resources, notably when they criticize governments for violating human rights.[30]

NGOs' most noteworthy contribution is perhaps the research and advocacy they undertake, particularly in the human rights field. Similar to IO secretariats, NGOs enjoy as a result of their work different types of authority in domestic and international politics.[31] To start, NGOs document and transmit local information on abuses, often in place of foreign governments and IOs. They thus enjoy a type of delegated authority.[32]

In addition, by pleading the cause of individuals and communities who have suffered and are suffering political violence, NGOs enjoy great moral or principled authority.[33] They also reduce monitoring costs for third parties, decrease the costs of applying pressure on target governments to modify their behavior, and increase the salience of necessary change.[34]

Moreover, NGOs supply vital technical assistance. For example, they compile briefs, offer legal aid to survivors and victims' families, and deliver expert testimony in domestic and international human rights trials.[35] They sometimes even work as auxiliary or third-party prosecutors.[36] What's more, they "field build"—that is, educate citizens on how to articulate their messages, cultivate support, and implement powerful tactics such as nonviolent protest.[37] In this way, NGOs enjoy expert authority.

[27] Chaudhry Forthcoming; Henry and Sundstrom 2021.
[28] Simmons 2009.
[29] Dietrich 2013.
[30] Dietrich and Murdie 2017.
[31] Barnett and Finnemore 2004; Stroup and Wong 2017. Authority is "mak[ing] rules or set[ting] standards that other relevant actors in world politics adopt," per Green (2013, 35).
[32] Raustiala 1997.
[33] Murdie 2014; Reimann 2006; Stroup and Wong 2017.
[34] Bob 2002; Meernik et al. 2012.
[35] Shelton 1994.
[36] Martínez 2017; Michel 2018.
[37] Chaudhry Forthcoming.

Based on the delegated, moral, and expert authority that NGOs earn by providing the aforementioned benefits, they can direct governments and publics toward public policies that meet the needs, desires, and interests of those who have suffered political violence.[38] Building on Avant and coauthors' concept of authority as deference,[39] Stroup and Wong highlight how NGOs "work without force . . . [and] speak with conviction and information" to draw support.[40]

But how exactly do NGOs at the domestic and international levels—among broader civil society movements—relate to each other? How do they plan, operate, and accomplish their policy goals? Dominant models of transnational advocacy and advocacy networks, discussed below, have helped us understand how domestic–international partnerships produce outcomes like improvements in governments' respect for their people's physical integrity rights. However, these models do not help us understand how different members of these networks complement each other in the multistage process that is TJ adoption, design, and delivery and follow-up.

Existing Models of Domestic–International NGO Partnerships in Human Rights

Scholars tend to think about transnational advocacy in two main ways that are germane to TJ. The first theoretical model is *strategic complementarity*, where international HROs more frequently target countries where domestic groups are stronger. The logic of strategic complementarity undergirds expectations about the boomerang and when and where it will matter for outcomes.[41] In brief, international civil society actors are interested in concentrating pressure from above and below, because that is where they have the highest expectation of success.[42] A second model is *strategic substitution*, where international HROs more frequently target governments where domestic groups are weaker.[43] Essentially, they focus their attention on the countries where they are most needed and attempt to mind the gap, making up for domestic groups' limited power.

Missing from these models is a framework for understanding how domestic and international groups work together in TJ and how groups leverage each other's relative strengths and compensate for each other's relative weaknesses.

[38] States are not NGOs' only targets. Stroup and Wong (2017) draw attention to corporations and other NGOs as other key audiences. Henry and Sundstrom (2021) also highlight NGOs' role as mediators between corporations and communities.

[39] Avant et al. 2010.

[40] Stroup and Wong 2017, 26.

[41] Keck and Sikkink 1998.

[42] For more, see Brysk (1993). Also, see Bob (2005) on INGO partner selection.

[43] See, for example, Murdie and Urpelainen (2015).

Civil society organizations in the TJ realm engage in critical advocacy and provide essential technical and operational assistance before, during, and after the establishment of TJ mechanisms. Yet we lack a comprehensive theory and corresponding hypotheses that address activism at each of these stages, and we lack a systematic, cross-national assessment of their efforts.

Existing Evidence of Domestic–International NGO Partnerships in Transitional Justice

Scholars, practitioners, and scholar-practitioners have long argued the essential role that civil society groups play in TJ processes, though the state is usually the starting point and civil society is treated as the residual category for what the state does not do or cannot do.[44] Scholars, practitioners, and scholar-practitioners have also shown the importance of domestic and international cooperation for TJ success[45] and recognized how the synergies produced by domestic–international NGO cooperation facilitate TJ.[46] But scholarship lacks an overarching theory and systematic evidence to show that this happens across political contexts and world regions. Moreover, scholarship rarely addresses all stages of the TJ life cycle: adoption, design, and delivery and follow-up. Regarding truth commissions, many scholars put the adoption and design stages into a black box (at least empirically) by focusing on commissions' investigations, findings, recommendations, and consequences.

In contrast, I start with the adoption stage—really the period of violence—and the actors who made the commission possible: civil society. I advance to

[44] Lessa 2022, 6. I start with civil society, reversing the conventional story and offering a systematic, global analysis.

[45] Arthur and Yakinthou 2018; Bakiner 2014; Brysk 1993, 2013; Burt 2007; Collins 2010; Correa et al. 2020; Crenzel 2012; Della Porta and Tarrow 2005; González-Ocantos 2020; Hayner 2011; Keck and Sikkink 1998; Kim 2014; Lessa 2022; Michel 2018; Risse et al. 2013; Roht-Arriaza 2001; Rowen 2017; Sikkink 2011. To discuss just two examples, Kim (2012*b*) proposes that transnational civil society activism matters for governments' decision to implement prosecutions, and Kim (2019) suggests likewise for truth commissions. He focuses solely on new democracies, however, whereas I also consider countries emerging from armed conflict and other periods of repression and violence, bolstering the inferences we can draw about civil society's role in global TJ.

[46] As an illustration, González-Ocantos (2020) shows how domestic–international NGO partnerships have been crucial for advancing cases in the Inter-American human rights system and how this, in turn, has influenced judicialization of cases in countries including Argentina. Collins challenges the significance of international actors and dynamics. For her, "[S]trategic action by legally literate, domestic, pro-accountability actors, plus domestic judicial change over time, have been the primary drivers of the reinvigoration of domestic accountability in the Southern Cone of Latin America since the late 1990s" (Collins 2010, 3). She also challenges the importance of truth commissions in TJ, placing faith in trials, not commissions, to deliver truth and justice. While we disagree on this point (I view commissions and trials in complementary, not oppositional, terms), my theoretical framework is largely consistent with hers, in particular my emphasis on domestic civil society's influence at the commission adoption and implementation and follow-up stages.

the design stage and then to the implementation and follow-up stage. I join these stages theoretically with my model of burden sharing among domestic and international civil society groups. I also connect these stages empirically with evidence from cross-national, cross-commission, and cross-country data and analyses.[47]

Theory

We know from previous descriptive research that domestic civil society groups in different countries have placed different TJ tools on the table. For example, in Timor-Leste, the National Council of Timorese Resistance—the central coalition of political parties and civil society groups that had mobilized against the Indonesian occupation—proposed a truth commission to the UN transitional administration.[48] Likewise, the Dullah Omar Institute, established during the struggle against apartheid, helped broker the political agreement that brought democracy and TJ to South Africa, an agreement that provided for a commission.[49]

We also know from prior studies that civil society actors do not simply demand truth and justice; they are also interested in helping to make it happen. Of note, academics, activists, and others working on TJ issues have recorded and preserved a rich and extensive institutional memory of previous experiences and modalities of commissions, and they routinely advise governments attempting their own mechanisms.[50] As an example, experts from Latin America provided some of the intellectual and operational framework for the South African TRC and even served in TRC leadership, staff, and advisory roles.[51] In turn, the ICTJ—the central TJ INGO and primary steward of TJ best practices since 2001—emerged from South Africa and has advised dozens of governments on the design of strong truth commissions, among an array of TJ measures.[52]

[47] Kim (2012*a*) and I agree that, while international civil society is beneficial for commission adoption, domestic civil society is essential. But he undersells international groups' contributions. He says, for instance, that the ICTJ did not contribute to commission adoption in South Korea because local groups did not seek out its help, suggesting a fixed secondary role for international groups vis-à-vis domestic groups. But the ICTJ did not exist until after the country's first two commissions were established. The ICTJ is also not an advocacy NGO; it provides technical assistance. Where we might expect to see its involvement in a particular country—but where, admittedly, we did not see it in South Korea—is at the design stage of the later commission. Kim's work emphasizes the importance of my approach: distinguishing what groups matter at different TJ stages and analyzing a range of cases.

[48] Hayner 2011, 39.

[49] Dullah Omar Institute 2023.

[50] Ancelovici and Jenson 2013; Rowen 2017.

[51] Roht-Arriaza 2001.

Nonetheless, scholars and practitioners warn about a potential chasm between what a given TJ institution is intended (or hoped) to accomplish and what it ultimately achieves, especially in terms of contributing to measures to remedy past abuses and to prevent future abuses.[53] With regard to truth commissions, for a commission to reach its full potential or effect, its policy prescriptions must be delivered. As in international law—where NGOs operate as compliance partners for states and IOs[54]—NGOs in the TJ space support and monitor implementation of commission recommendations.[55] To provide an example, pursuant to the Guatemalan commission's recommendation to inquire into the fates of the disappeared, the Forensic Anthropology Foundation of Guatemala (FAFG) has worked with various domestic and international government agencies to collect testimonies, identify victims, exhume mass graves, match and return exhumed remains to families, and support families pursuing justice through the legal system.[56] In a similar vein, KSG has taken action with the South African Department of Justice to deliver the reparations outlined in the TRC report.[57]

So how do civil society groups, at the domestic and international levels, strategize about and realize their mutually held goals, building on one another? Below I present a new burden sharing model of advocacy, assistance, and policy delivery. Since NGOs vary in terms of their access to on-the-ground information, knowledge, resources, and expertise, burden sharing helps them to economize, exercise their comparative advantages, and make their success more likely. While I evaluate this model in the context of truth commissions, it is potentially portable to a range of public policy arenas within and beyond TJ, as I discuss later in this chapter and in the book's conclusion.

The Burden Sharing Model

To begin, at the *adoption* stage, domestic civil society groups apply pressure from below and leverage their moral authority as advocates for vulnerable and victimized populations. They document and transmit local information on abuses

[52] Ancelovici and Jenson 2013; Subotić 2012. Some view the ICTJ's approach as problematic. For instance, Nagy (2014) discusses how some local actors in Canada saw the ICTJ as providing "decontextualized technical advice" that supported a more legalistic process that detracted from grassroots efforts based in Aboriginal governance models. In South Africa, Madlingozi (2010) similarly challenges international experts and the "transitional justice industry" they have created from the so-called First World. Madlingozi contends that, in assuming a "trustee" role and championing particular models, experts reproduce colonial relations with the "Third World."

[53] Gibson 2004; Rowen 2017; Zvobgo 2020.

[54] Alter 2014.

[55] Bakiner 2014, 2015.

[56] Johnston and Stephenson 2016.

[57] Puwana and Kesselring 2018.

and express their desire for accountability to their international partners. They also engage in a diversity of contentious politics, including nonviolent protest.[58] INGOs then apply pressure from above, adapting and disseminating more broadly the information they have received, with a view to mobilizing foreign publics and their governments to also demand truth.[59] At this stage, domestic groups are in the leading role; they mobilize an appetite for truth and justice, even as they draw on ideas from abroad, including from INGOs.[60]

Next, at the *design* stage, international experts—chief among them the ICTJ—draw on their professional experience and technical expertise to encourage governments to endow commissions with strong jurisdictional and operational powers (e.g., the power to investigate a range of abuses and the power to compel testimony). With these powers, commissions are, in expectation, better positioned to conduct a rigorous investigation and produce a comprehensive report. At this stage, international groups are in the leading role; they have the experience and technical know-how.

Finally, at the *post-commission* stage, domestic civil society groups—who are essential to any country's long-term commitments to human rights and justice—take the baton once more and press governments to implement commission recommendations.[61] To do this, they first set a policy agenda. Given that commissions issue dozens, if not hundreds, of recommendations, groups must establish priorities and devise strategies for achieving them. Some focus on recommendations that match their organizational missions and fall within their existing issue portfolios. For example, some lawyers' groups focus on the implementation of legal reforms, such as changes to a country's constitution. Nonetheless, other groups diversify their portfolios, expanding their platforms and activities.

Once they have set their priorities, domestic groups engage in a range of tactics to push governments to implement their preferred agenda. These include the types of shaming and protest actions that steered governments to create commissions in the first place. Other tactics include lobbying legislators, taking governments to court, and soliciting help from foreign governments and IOs. Throughout, international groups provide support (e.g., by raising funds for their domestic partners or assisting them in legal actions against the state and suspected architects and agents of abuse). Governments are not always receptive to civil society activism, however. Thus, I also address how some

[58] Chenoweth and Stephan 2011; Cronin-Furman 2022.

[59] Franklin 2008; Hafner-Burton 2008; Loveman 1998; Murdie and Peksen 2013*a*, 2013*b*; Risse et al. 2013; Sikkink 2011; Woo and Murdie 2017.

[60] Cronin-Furman 2022; Rowen 2017.

[61] TJ processes are unlikely to emerge without the "persistent endeavors" of justice seekers, and they are also unlikely to "be sustained over time" (Lessa 2022, 141).

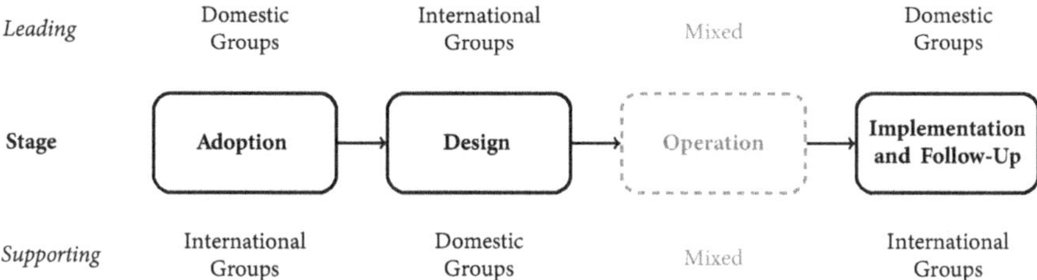

Figure 2.1 The Burden Sharing Model
Note: The figure shows domestic and international NGOs' roles—leading or supporting—at each stage of the TJ life cycle.

groups attempt to substitute for governments that are unwilling to deliver on recommendations.[62]

I do not tackle the question of commission operation (e.g., methodology, selection of participants, organization of hearings, use of different media to communicate activities, or compilation of final reports). With so many moving parts at the operational stage, single-case or small-*N* inductive and descriptive studies are more appropriate than cross-national studies. My fieldwork does indicate, if provisionally, mixed leadership and support roles for domestic and international NGOs at this stage. For example, domestic groups like KSG in South Africa can lead in supporting witnesses as they testify, while international experts like the ICTJ can lead in reviewing commissioners' work as they compile the final report and draft recommendations. Figure 2.1 illustrates the burden sharing model. At each stage—adoption, design, and implementation and follow-up—truth commissions are not simply local institutions. Rather, they are transnational, due to the global TJ network's critical work.

The burden sharing model implies that domestic and international members of the global TJ network work in effective ways and that their partnership is generally harmonious. Essentially, they have rationalized their joint strategy in keeping with conditions on the ground. Not only is this consistent with prior research on domestic–international partnerships in the human rights space, my evidence shows it. To quote a Guatemalan human rights advocate I interviewed for this project, these partnerships, between and among domestic and international groups, are "the only way that we can do our work."[63] To paraphrase another interviewee, this time an attorney for a major INGO, it is vital for international groups to have partners on the ground, not only to be able to do their work but also to frame human rights and TJ as *local ideas with local support*. It is

[62] On state abdication and legitimacy gaps in transitional states, see Kochanski (2021) and Quinn (2021).

[63] Author interview with Maya Juracán, Peace Foundation artist and curator.

important for international groups that their work is not perceived as a foreign imposition, notably by local spoilers.[64]

Of course, the burden sharing model does not suggest that effective and harmonious transnational partnerships and collaborations are universal.[65] First, not every civil society group that could be in the global TJ network participates in it—either because a group is not aware of the network, cannot reach the network, does not want to work in the network, or is not accepted into the network by existing members. Second, even within the network, members do not always adopt the same issues, nor do they always agree on goals or strategies. To be sure, groups can differ in their approaches to identifying, prioritizing, and solving problems. Moreover, they face personnel, time, and other resource constraints. Accordingly, success likely varies by where partners come together, broadly agree on goals and strategies, and have resources to support their work. Governments must also be somewhat sensitive to the interests of NGOs and the ordinary people they represent. In brief, the burden sharing model does not address selection into the global TJ network or selection into partnerships and collaborations. Rather, the model addresses *how* transnational civil society partnerships and collaborations help produce important outcomes.

My transnational politics story is not the only one that scholars have applied to TJ. Regional diffusion is another.[66] Here, the story is that governments in the same part of the world emulate each other, adopting similar practices.[67] While there is spatial clustering of TJ institutions and programs, including truth commissions, the standard diffusion story is underspecified, if not passive.[68]

In contrast, the transnational advocacy story that I propose is active: Governments create, design, and deliver and follow up on commissions because they are pressured to do so. This is not simply copycat behavior. Rather, civil society groups, at the domestic and international levels, have agency and marshal their respective resources to induce governments to deliver their preferred policies.

My theory is not antagonistic to diffusion, to be clear; transnational advocacy could be one method or driver of diffusion. Indeed, NGOs can set the trend for states.[69] Rather, my theory is more precise than the diffusion story in current TJ

[64] Name and organization omitted, per the interviewee's request.

[65] For work on domestic and international TJ actors' sometimes fraught relationships, see, among others, Madlingozi (2010). For work on disagreements among and fragmentation of domestic groups, see, among others, Rudling (2019), writing on Colombia. Also see Wiebelhaus-Brahm (2021*a*), on competition among domestic groups in Tunisia. In the larger international relations and comparative politics literature, see, for example, Carpenter (2007*a*, 2007*b*).

[66] Kim 2012*b*, 2019.

[67] Roht-Arriaza 2002; Sikkink 2011; Sikkink and Walling 2007.

[68] Finnemore 1996*a*.

[69] Finnemore 1996*b*, 64.

scholarship, and it offers greater analytical leverage by identifying specific actors engaging in specific behaviors with a view to delivering specific outcomes.

Scope and Generalizability

Though I evaluate burden sharing in the context of truth commissions, the model is portable to other TJ mechanisms and perhaps also to other human rights policy areas. Domestic civil society actors in myriad contexts have demanded trials just as they have called for commissions, and international civil society actors have helped countries design reparations programs in much the same way as they have helped countries design commissions.

To illustrate, GAM, which initiated the dialogue on a commission in Guatemala, has also helped initiate criminal investigations and advance prosecutions related to the internal armed conflict, in collaboration with domestic partners such as FAFG and international partners like the Center for Justice and International Law.[70] Meanwhile, the ICTJ, which helped implement and monitor the commission in Peru, has also aided with the implementation and oversight of the reparations program, in collaboration with domestic civil society groups.[71] There are many other examples of the dynamics we observe in transnational advocacy for commissions playing out in other arenas.

One reason we observe these patterns is that civil society groups are interested in more than just truth; they also care about justice, reparation, and nonrepetition. Another reason is that commissions recommend measures for justice, reparation, and nonrepetition—recommendations that civil society groups carry forward. Chapters 6 to 8 show domestic and international NGOs advocating before, assisting, and at times substituting for governments in implementing trials, reparations, institutional reforms, and other measures that the Guatemalan, South African, and Timorese commissions recommended. Civil society actors are possibly less influential for developing, designing, and delivering other TJ modalities than they are for commissions. Future research can investigate this empirical question.

Mechanisms of Civil Society Influence

Many political scientists, perhaps especially international relations scholars, are sure to be skeptical of civil society actors as global governors in TJ, human rights, and other policy domains. Some may think it is extraordinary for NGOs

[70] See Chapters 3 and 6 for these and other examples.
[71] Correa 2013.

to have such power. But, as numerous studies have shown, NGOs enjoy delegated, moral, and expert authority and avail themselves of a range of political strategies—including protest mobilization, lobbying, and litigation—to motivate governments to produce meaningful outcomes in world politics, perhaps especially in human rights and TJ. Still, for social scientists, it should be the evidence that counts. This book provides that evidence.

The remaining propositions address why many, though certainly not all, governments may acquiesce to, rather than refuse, civil society pressure and proposals, first by establishing truth commissions, second by endowing commissions with strong powers, and third by implementing commissions' recommendations.

Truth Commission Adoption as a Concession to Costly Advocacy

Civil society actors pose several challenges to governments that can make acquiescence to demands for truth and justice a more attractive strategy than outright refusal. Specifically, advocates can introduce political, economic, and security costs when governments do not answer their demands.

First, advocacy organizations—particularly those on the ground—can threaten a government's survival by mobilizing the mass public. They can accomplish this directly—for instance, by educating citizens about nonviolent strategies, organizing large protest crowds, and getting out the vote. They can also achieve this indirectly—for example, by bringing to communities financial, educational, and other resources that facilitate political participation.[72] Time and again, costly protest has unseated governments around the world, as have elections and other referenda. Leaders, especially of transitional governments, who are interested in surviving are both aware of this and eager to prevent it from happening, for the sake of their individual political futures and the overall stability of their countries.

Second, advocates can introduce nontrivial economic costs that governments, especially in countries emerging from long periods of violence, may not be positioned to absorb. Countries can lose access to foreign aid when international HROs name and shame their governments, including for failing to redress victims and hold perpetrators accountable. In some cases, donors respond to shaming by redirecting aid to flow through non-state channels, further strengthening advocates' power vis-à-vis governments.[73]

Third, transnational advocates can impose security and diplomatic costs that may only be lifted when governments course correct and implement some justice

[72] Bell et al. 2014; Chenoweth and Stephan 2011; Haines 1984; Mitchell 2009.
[73] Dietrich and Murdie 2017.

measures. Governments and their security apparatuses are sensitive to condemnation that can affect their power, prestige, and economic interests.[74] Domestic and international advocates can cast noncompliant governments as "pariah states" and persuade foreign governments and IOs that are interested in human rights causes to withdraw support. Among a range of sanctions, foreign governments can withhold diplomatic visits from governments that permit impunity, and they can block their participation in various IO leadership roles.[75]

Strong Truth Commission Design as a Credible Commitment

Civil society actors continue to pose a range of challenges to governments even after governments have agreed to establish a commission. Groups shift their target from institutional adoption to institutional design and quality, in particular ensuring that a commission has a clear direction and strong architecture and is able, consequently, to fulfill its role and responsibilities. Core issues at this stage include how a commission's material scope of inquiry is defined in the legal mandate and what evidence-gathering powers a commission will enjoy. As in other public policy arenas, governments can drift, sometimes intentionally but often unintentionally, from their stated commitments to a policy or idea. However, when facing the possibility of censure from civil society—which, after its initial success, is in a stronger position—leaders may elect to credibly commit and, thereby, forgo likely censure.

One way that governments can credibly commit to a high-quality commission is to invite international experts, notably the ICTJ, to advise them in designing their mechanisms. When international experts are part of the design process, a commission is more likely to have a clear direction and a strong architecture and is more likely to accomplish its mission.[76] These experts are critical for designing strong mechanisms because they are the ones who have witnessed other countries' failures and successes and can guide governments away from the former and toward the latter. And in cases where a government is uninterested in or unable to conduct a serious investigation, these same experts can decide to *not* engage in the process—to the embarrassment of that government, at home and abroad.[77] Much remains on the line for leaders who have been led to create commissions in the first place. By engaging experts and implementing expert-identified best practices, they can show they are committed to "getting things right."[78]

[74] Cronin-Furman 2022; Guest 1990.
[75] Brysk 1993, 269–271.
[76] Author interviews with Eduardo González and Priscilla Hayner.
[77] Author interview with Priscilla Hayner.
[78] Subotić (2022) warns that not all governments engage experts because they are committed to truth and justice; governments sometimes seek the assistance of fringe experts. For instance, Bosnian

Implementation of Truth Commission Recommendations as a Result of Socialization

A government that has acquiesced to civil society demands for truth at the first stage and perhaps crafted a legal mandate with strong investigative powers at the second stage may, at the conclusion of the truth commission, implement its policy recommendations. Governments may be socialized into TJ, and thus implement recommendations—for example, memorial museums, reparations packages, and personnel reforms—at the behest of civil society, which is energized by its successes to date.

Data and Methods

Until now, no systematic cross-national research has sought to explain variation in TJ emergence, characteristics, and effects and how transnational civil society actors are likely to be influential. To address these gaps, this book draws on new opportunities to study TJ in comparative and global perspective. Over the past decade, there has been impressive growth in social science research investigating the causes and consequences of various TJ tools. This work has been made possible through significant quantitative data collection projects that have widened our knowledge of the universe of TJ cases and the great diversity therein.[79] The empirical work in this project focuses on civil society actors, whose contributions to TJ have not been fully explored in prior studies.

Why Truth Commissions?

I focus on truth commissions, which are far less well understood than other TJ tools such as trials and amnesties.[80] This is due in part to the reality that commissions have been of different shapes and sizes and have been implemented in myriad sociopolitical contexts on every continent.[81] Some cases, like Chile and Peru, are exceedingly well known, while others, like Burundi and Burkina Faso, are sometimes not even counted. Yet when taken together, commissions offer rich quantitative and qualitative evidence of the extent to which TJ is shaped by and, in turn, shapes domestic and international politics.

Serb political elites have solicited Holocaust experts from Israel to deny the Srebrenica genocide was in fact a genocide.

[79] Bates et al. 2020; Dancy et al. 2019; Greenstein 2024; Horne 2012; Nalepa 2022; Olsen, Payne, and Reiter 2010.

[80] Dancy 2018; Dancy and Thoms 2022.

[81] González-Ocantos (2020, 3) affirms that "the notion of TJ has developed into a powerful legal, political, and discursive apparatus that helps victims in a much wider variety of violence-ridden contexts frame their demands, challenge the acceptability of impunity, and mobilize support."

Truth commissions also represent an ideal setting for studying civil society activism around TJ, as commissions are by nature public and participatory. They offer a range of access points for civil society actors: adoption, design, operation, and implementation of recommendations, among others. If civil society is influential for TJ processes, this is precisely where we should see it.

In addition, commissions often precede, and even enable, subsequent TJ measures. This makes commissions an important point of scholarly departure.[82] To best understand later measures—their nature, reach, and consequences—we must rigorously examine the commissions that precede them.

Relatedly, theories of socialization into human rights norms and practices would expect to find success built on success. We may observe further TJ measures precisely because civil society groups—energized by their success in influencing commission processes—demand more from governments, and, in response, governments deliver.[83]

The *Varieties of Truth Commissions* Project

The argument that I advance is not necessarily specific to particular types of regimes or political contexts, though I focus largely on countries in transition from autocracy and internal armed conflict. The cross-national samples that I employ in Chapters 3, 4, and 5 cover a range of regimes, from weak post-conflict democracies like Sierra Leone to monarchies like Morocco to consolidated democracies like Canada. And even the transitional countries that I examine in greater depth in Chapters 6, 7, and 8 vary in terms of the types of political violence preceding transition: internal armed conflict and genocide in the case of Guatemala, race-based autocracy in the case of South Africa, and foreign occupation and armed conflict in the case of Timor-Leste. Empirically, I evaluate the theory using both analysis of the *Varieties of Truth Commissions*—the most comprehensive and most granular quantitative data on truth commissions to date—and a range of qualitative data from the field. As I elaborate further, a mixed-method approach offers several advantages.

For this study, I trained and directed over a three-year period a team of seventeen research assistants at two universities to collect and code data for a unique series of datasets.[84] My research team's first task was identifying a universe of truth commissions, eighty-four in total, doubling some previous estimates.[85]

[82] Balcells et al. 2022; Bates et al. 2020; Powers and Proctor 2016.

[83] In Chapters 6 to 8, I show that we see additional measures because civil society also assists and substitutes for the state.

[84] On integrating students in research, see Becker et al. (2021), Zvobgo (2022), and Zvobgo et al. (2023).

[85] Forty-eight commissions in my data were established in transitional contexts (Boix et al. 2013; Eck and Hultman 2007; Kreutz 2010; Pettersson and Eck 2018), while the other thirty-six were

The team then proceeded to gather all available legal mandates of commissions and code dozens of investigative powers for each one. After this, my students and I located all publicly available commission final reports and coded thousands of recommendations at the paragraph level. Finally, students under my supervision coded the implementation of hundreds of recommendations from three key countries, drawing on executive orders, parliamentary records, legislation, court judgments, newspapers, and IO and NGO reports, among other sources. These efforts culminated in the *Varieties of Truth Commissions* datasets, which illuminate important variation at multiple stages: adoption, design, and delivery and follow-up.

My comprehensive yet granular data improve understanding of truth commissions and help shed light on the promise and pitfalls of TJ's proliferation. They also offer a model for measuring key aspects of other TJ modalities. While essential to rigorous research, these types of data have often been lacking in the field. Certainly, building quantitative datasets is a time- and labor-intensive endeavor, and all the more so when scholars also conduct field research, as I have done.[86] However, generating new data is necessary for answering questions of interest and urgency in world politics.

The comprehensive list of commissions from the *Varieties of Truth Commissions* enables the cross-national analysis of commission adoption in Chapter 3. I supplement these data with qualitative evidence drawn from a focus group with human rights defenders in Argentina and interviews with international advocates and experts based in Guatemala, the United Kingdom, and the United States.

The first dataset, which I use in Chapter 4, contains roughly twenty variables capturing information about commissions' mandates (notably the scope of investigation and evidence-gathering powers). I pair these data with interviews with current and former ICTJ leadership and staff and a focus group at the ICTJ's New York headquarters.

The second dataset, which I use in Chapter 5, contains approximately fifty variables capturing commissions' policy recommendations (e.g., monetary compensation for victims, rehabilitation of perpetrators, and personnel reforms) coded at the paragraph level. I build on these data with interviews,

established in non-transitional contexts. Hayner (2001, 2011) provided the first comprehensive treatment of commissions globally, drawing on an impressive database of approximately forty commissions and countless interviews with commission officials, NGO representatives, and policymakers, not to mention her field notes and reflections as a practitioner. *Governing Truth* is the most comprehensive book on truth commissions in comparative and global perspective since *Unspeakable Truths*.

[86] Irgil et al. 2021; Zvobgo et al. 2022.

including with former officials from the Canadian, Chilean, Kenyan, Peruvian, Sierra Leonean, and Timorese commissions.

The third dataset, which I use in Chapters 6, 7, and 8, codes for the Guatemalan, South African, and Timorese cases whether implementation of specific recommendations was initiated and the degree of implementation achieved (minimal, intermediate, or full). The data also capture NGOs operating across different recommendation areas. In addition, I leverage qualitative evidence from my interviews with human rights defenders, IO representatives, and government officials in Guatemala, South Africa, and Timor-Leste.

Innovations

A shortcoming of much of the existing research on truth commissions and TJ is generalizability. Studies often involve single-country or small-*N* comparative analyses that leave open questions about whether the findings conform to broad patterns in TJ regimes globally. While rich in detail, steeped in nuance, and foundational to our understanding of commissions and other TJ projects at particular times and places, this research does not help us understand them in a global sense. My project's cross-national research design is intended to address precisely this issue.

I begin by using cross-national data on transitions from internal armed conflict, mass killings, and autocracy to show that transnational civil society activism accounts for cross-national variation in commission adoption during transitions. I then use cross-commission data to demonstrate that civil society activism also accounts for variation in commission design. Meanwhile, I leverage useful cross-case variation—including in geography, social and political history, and political violence—in the chapters that focus on post-commission outcomes in Guatemala, South Africa, and Timor-Leste. Supportive evidence for my theory—that civil society actors help drive commission adoption, strong design, and implementation and follow-up—across diverse countries and contexts, using multiple types of data and social science research methods, shows my story's reach and the value of my theoretical model.

My research design further improves on existing studies in several important ways. First, I do not exclusively study transitional commissions (e.g., in Chapters 4 and 5). In other words, the sample is not limited to countries with recent experiences of political violence. Considering only transitional commissions prevents researchers from reliably concluding that civil society actors are vital, as the case selection technique is based on an outcome that likely correlates with the dependent variable. In addition, as I discuss in the concluding chapter, the book's theory should and indeed does bear out in non-transitional countries like South Korea, where policymakers have answered civil society demands to establish commissions investigating events that occurred many decades earlier.[87]

Second, and related to the first, I do not limit the sample to democracies (see again, Chapters 4 and 5, on commission design and commission recommendations). Previous studies that only encompass democracies necessarily, and quite problematically, preclude the possibility of civil society actors being active and influential in non-democratic settings. Yet we see civil society mobilization leading to commissions with robust investigations, findings, and recommendations in established autocracies like Morocco.[88]

Finally, I take care to thoroughly address alternative, but potentially complementary, explanations. For example, I account for the possibility of regional diffusion by developing fine-grained measures of truth commission precedents based on a subregional, rather than a continental, division of the world. Of note, in Chapter 4—which evaluates the influence of international experts on truth commission design—I calculate, for a given country, the number of commissions in its geographic subregion that previously possessed a given investigative power, not simply the number of previous subregional commissions. Doing so helps show that governments do not tend to endow commissions with the same powers as their regional neighbors—a finding that highlights the influence of transnational civil society actors.

[87] Kim (2014) shows committed civil society activism has been a key ingredient in South Korean TJ, especially for truth commission formation. He also emphasizes mature democracy, sympathetic elites, and strong evidence of abuses. His work suggests that context matters: We have seen much more cooperation between governments and civil society on TJ since South Korea's democratic transition than in countries like Guatemala and South Africa. This should encourage, not discourage, TJ advocates. It took Korea more than a decade to establish its first national commissions, which covered abuses dating back decades, from the period of Japanese imperial rule to the dictatorship. Faithful struggle by domestic groups, bolstered by diaspora communities and international supporters, continues to bear fruit.

[88] Hayner 2011, 42–44.

3
Research, Advocacy, and Institutional Adoption

TJ was one of the most controversial issues debated in the Guatemalan peace process, a sequence of agreements that progressed in fits and starts in the 1980s and into the 1990s.[1] Negotiators sought to address the US-backed coup that overthrew leftist Jacobo Arbenz's democratically elected government and the decades-long internal armed conflict that ensued. The conflict, fought principally between anti-communist government forces and the leftist Guatemalan National Revolutionary Unit (URNG), was rife with brutality: An estimated 200,000 people were killed or disappeared between 1960 and 1996, and more than a million were displaced.[2] Many of these abuses proceeded from General Efraín Ríos Montt's genocidal "scorched earth" campaign against the Indigenous Mayan population, which he and his associates believed provided a lifeline to the guerrillas. Hundreds of villages were razed, and multitudes were killed, tortured, and/or displaced.[3]

In the midst of these abuses, victims' relatives initiated the debate over TJ, going into the streets to protest violence and impunity.[4] The government responded with more violence. Nevertheless, these groups continued mobilizing for truth and justice. In 1984, a group of women organized to form the Mutual Support Group, better known as GAM. Like the Argentinian Mothers of the Plaza de Mayo Association and the Salvadoran Committee of the Mothers of Political Prisoners and the Disappeared (COMADRES), GAM organized nonviolent protests and gained national and international attention, both for its activism and for the government's violent reprisals against its members. In 1993, Amnesty International (hereafter, Amnesty) reported:

> Several leaders and members of GAM have been killed by death squads since it was established. There is a real need for international support for such groups and increased effort to support those for whom the dangers are too great to organize such self-help organizations.[5]

[1] Ross 2004.
[2] Oettler 2006.
[3] CEH 1999. See the section "Causas y orígenes del enfrentamiento armado interno."
[4] Impunity Watch 2008.
[5] Amnesty International 1993.

Governing Truth. Kelebogile Zvobgo, Oxford University Press. © Oxford University Press (2026).
DOI: 10.1093/oso/9780197815663.003.0003

GAM subsequently received more international support, including from the Inter-American Commission on Human Rights, various agencies and rapporteurs in the UN system, and the Friends of the Guatemalan Peace Process (Colombia, Mexico, Norway, Spain, the United States, and Venezuela). They collected evidence corroborating GAM reports of abuse and pressured the Guatemalan government and the URNG to negotiate peace and devise a means to address human rights violations.[6]

GAM's most noteworthy contribution to peace and TJ in Guatemala was, perhaps, leading civil society groups to specifically demand a truth commission, based on the Argentinian, Chilean, and Salvadoran experiences.[7] Taking a note from GAM, the government and URNG seriously debated the idea of a commission in 1994, but they struggled to agree on its details, stalling peace talks.[8] However, international pressure, including from foreign governments, moved the peace process along. A range of actors, including Amnesty, amplified civil society's pleas for truth and justice[9] and called for "a thorough and impartial investigation [to] be opened . . . and that those responsible be brought to justice."[10]

These pleas were finally answered in Oslo, Norway, in 1996, when the Guatemalan government and the URNG finalized the Agreement on a Firm and Lasting Peace, entering into force a series of ten agreements.[11] The third of these agreements established the Historical Clarification Commission (CEH), with a mandate to "clarify with all objectivity, equity and impartiality the human rights violations and acts of violence that have caused the Guatemalan population to suffer, connected with the armed conflict."[12]

The military and its supporters in government and among the public maintained power and influence, however (and continue to do so). Because of this, the CEH's investigative powers were limited, as I document in Chapter 4.[13] Civic space had also begun to close, following the murder of human rights defender, Indigenous rights advocate, and Catholic bishop Juan José Gerardi. Monseñor

[6] Author interviews with GAM director Mario Polanco and GAM legal advisor Carlos Juárez.

[7] Ross 2004.

[8] Baldwin 2009; Impunity Watch 2008; Oettler 2006.

[9] Amnesty International 1990, 1994, 1995*a*, 1995*c*.

[10] Amnesty International 1995*b*.

[11] The United Nations oversaw the peace talks, which had resumed in 1994, with Special Representative Jean Arnault leading the effort, and supported the fragile peace in its 1997 humanitarian mission, MINUGUA. See Georgetown Institute for Women, Peace and Security (2015) and Instituto Interamericano de Derechos Humanos (2005).

[12] CEH 1999. See the section "Mandato y procedimiento de trabajo."

[13] The commission lacked the power to compel testimony and other material evidence. It also lacked the power to preserve evidence. Like many others, it also could not name names (Tepperman 2002). From the start, the CEH was hamstrung so its work could not support future prosecutions (Grandin 2005). A criticism of many commissions is their inability to attribute responsibility for human rights abuses to specific individuals (Collins 2010, 9–10).

Gerardi had overseen the establishment of the Human Rights Office of the Archbishop of Guatemala (ODHAG) and the Recovery of Historical Memory (REMHI) Project, which provided fundamental assistance to the CEH.[14] In fact, Gerardi was killed two days after the publication of the REMHI report *Guatemala: Nunca Más (Guatemala: Never Again)*.[15]

Despite these challenging circumstances, which other commissions have faced, the CEH is lauded as one of the strongest truth commissions in history.[16] This is thanks in large part to the civil society groups who assisted with investigating abuses and reaching witnesses and who have carried the commission's work forward—through relentless advocacy for and involvement in implementing its recommendations, as I show in Chapter 6.

Civil society efforts to challenge the "dominant culture of impunity and silence"[17] have been obstructed at many turns, to be sure.[18] But it is notable that a truth commission—an idea that came from civil society—became policy despite forces that opposed truth and justice. It is also notable that despite lacking some useful powers and being given less than two years to do its work, the CEH conducted a thorough investigation and produced an influential report containing an important set of findings and policy recommendations. A number of these recommendations have been implemented. The commission's findings have even supported prosecutions, if belatedly. None of what has been gained would have been possible without civil society, a point that government officials who I interviewed conceded.

The Guatemalan CEH was not the first nor would it be the last such truth commission. Since 1970, scores of countries have adopted commissions to produce comprehensive histories of political violence. By documenting individual experiences of violence and connecting them to broader systems and patterns of harm, commissions have recognized personal and collective experiences of violence while confronting individual and institutional responsibility.[19] And, through their recommendations, commissions have created frameworks for a range of remedies, including memorialization projects, reparations programs, and legal and institutional reforms.[20]

[14] Author interview with Carlos Beristain, a former member of the REMHI Project.

[15] The REMHI Project had a large impact not only on the CEH but also on the International Commission Against Impunity in Guatemala and genocide trials against General Ríos Montt and other top-ranking military officials.

[16] Hayner 2001, 2011.

[17] Lessa 2022, 141.

[18] A culture of impunity and silence explains why (1) it took so long to negotiate a peace that included a commission, (2) the commission lacked key powers of investigation, (3) many rejected the commission's major finding of "genocidal acts" by the military, and (4) implementation of the CEH's recommendations has been patchy.

[19] Dancy et al. 2010; Subotić 2011.

[20] Koc-Menard 2014; Lira 2017.

Despite their prevalence and consequence, the question of why some states adopt commissions, while other similarly situated states do not, is not well understood. Not all countries with a history of political violence create them. Further, commissions are not necessarily implemented where rights violations and abuses have been most severe. Some scholars suggest regional diffusion; but while there is spatial clustering of TJ mechanisms, including truth commissions, the diffusion story is underspecified, if not passive.[21] Thus, the question remains: Why do states establish commissions? Existing elite-focused, domestic-level explanations, while vital for our understanding of certain cases, have not been developed for, let alone tested across, a multiplicity of contexts over time.

In this chapter, I consider the activism of domestic and international civil society actors who together form the global TJ network, and I present a systematic cross-national investigation of truth commission adoption. I evaluate the proposition that commissions are more likely to be adopted where TJ network members can leverage information and moral authority over governments. I do this using (1) a comprehensive dataset covering the universe of transitions from internal armed conflict, government killings of civilians, and autocracy in the period 1970 to 2018, (2) data from the *Varieties of Truth Commissions*, (3) interviews with INGO representatives, (4) interviews with Guatemalan NGO representatives, and (5) a focus group with Argentinian human rights defenders.

Consistent with my expectations, I find a strong association between domestic civil society strength and commission adoption, and between international HRO shaming and commission adoption. I also find some support for formal ties between network members enhancing prospects for a commission. The interviews and focus group corroborate the idea that international HRO advocacy strengthens domestic activism. However, in line with my burden sharing model, interviewees and focus group participants maintain that it is domestic civil society actors who are critical for commission adoption. Interviews with government officials, IO representatives, and TJ practitioners presented in later chapters of this book confirm that, without civil society, there would have been little movement on TJ in Guatemala (and other post-violence societies) from the transitional period through to the present day.[22]

My results demonstrate that the TJ network's success at this first stage, *truth commission adoption*, is shaped by its vitality within a particular country. Thus, not all advocacy is equally likely to succeed, and some advocates will fail to win

[21] Kim 2012*b*, 2019.

[22] Author interviews with María García, head of the UNDP Transitional Justice Accompaniment Programme in Guatemala, with Hilda Pineda, at the time chief prosecutor for human rights in Guatemala, and with Priscilla Hayner.

their preferred policies.[23] The analysis also makes clear that the findings are not an artifact of passive processes of diffusion. Rather, the results illuminate *specific actors* engaging in *specific behaviors* to deliver *specific policies*—similar outcomes across dissimilar contexts.

Plan of the Chapter

The next section discusses existing approaches to understanding the local and global origins of truth commissions and then describes my approach. In the section that follows, I describe the cross-national data that I use to evaluate my hypotheses regarding commission adoption. I also explain my choice of measures. I then report the results of the quantitative analysis and evaluate its robustness to alternative explanations and modeling specifications. Building on this, I delve into the qualitative evidence, which more precisely demonstrates the theory. I discuss the implications of the findings before concluding.

The Domestic and International Politics of Truth Commissions

Truth commission adoption has been portrayed in the literature as a domestic politics story[24] or as an international politics story,[25] with government and IO elites cast as the central protagonists. These explanations have typically been evaluated through single-country studies or small-*N* comparative studies. While they have been foundational to our understanding of commission adoption at particular times and particular places, these studies neither help us understand the phenomenon in a global sense nor do they explain why we observe commissions in a multiplicity of contexts across time.

A Transnational Politics Story of Transitional Justice

I theorize that transnational civil society actors are the force behind key TJ outcomes. More specifically, I propose that domestic and international civil society groups—who are connected by the global TJ network—work together to guide governments in truth commission processes, with each side leveraging its

[23] The results are robust to changes in the coding of transition periods, different transition pathways such as conflict termination via government or rebel victory, and the inclusion of potentially confounding variables.

[24] See, for example, Benomar (1993), Elster (2004), Grodsky (2010), and Huyse (1995).

[25] See, for example, Lutz and Sikkink (2001), Roht-Arriaza (2001), and Sikkink (2011).

comparative advantage in terms of access to information, resources, and expertise. At the commission adoption stage, domestic civil society groups assume a leading role, taking the crucial first steps to apply pressure from below. They document and transmit information on local conditions and express their desire for accountability to their international partners. International HROs then apply pressure from above, adapting and disseminating the information they have received, with a view to mobilizing foreign publics and their governments to also demand truth.

TJ advocates' success is not inevitable, however. Rather, success depends on TJ network members' ability to create and transmit politically salient information, both within and outside of the network, on the subject of a given country. I anticipate that commissions are more likely to be adopted where (1) domestic civil society groups are stronger, (2) international HROs more frequently name and shame, and where (3) network members have greater access to each other.

Pressure from Below and Pressure from Above

I first propose that countries with stronger civil societies are more likely to adopt commissions. Relative to a weak civil society, a strong civil society can effectively engage in contentious politics, notably protests and demonstrations, to cultivate the local interest in truth and justice. Crucially, a strong civil society can more easily transmit local information to international partners, elevate global attention to repression and violence, and increase the salience of justice measures, all while decreasing costs for international actors to monitor local conditions and get directly involved.[26]

Next, I suggest that countries where international HROs concentrate their shaming efforts are more likely to create commissions. International HROs disseminate broadly and powerfully the information they receive from domestic partners. They call for justice for those who have been harmed and demand accountability for those who have caused harm. Leaders, especially those who come to govern transitional states, are concerned with international HRO interests and, importantly, the interests of HRO allies, chiefly donor governments. Prior research shows that shaming often precedes improvements to policy and practice.[27] However, international HROs' efforts are not evenly distributed: Some countries receive more attention for abuses than others.[28] We should, therefore, expect variation in attention to correlate with variation in outcomes like commission adoption.

[26] Bob 2002; Meernik et al. 2012; Risse et al. 1999.
[27] Franklin 2008; Hafner-Burton 2008; Woo and Murdie 2017.
[28] Asal et al. 2016; Hafner-Burton 2008.

Finally, I posit that greater access between network members enhances prospects for a commission. Essentially, groups that are connected via conferences, research teams, and so on have more opportunities to share the information that I describe above and have more opportunities to coordinate strategy.

Thus, I produce the following three hypotheses:

Hypothesis 1
Countries with a stronger domestic civil society are more likely to adopt truth commissions.

Hypothesis 2
Countries where international HROs more frequently name and shame are more likely to adopt truth commissions.

Hypothesis 3
TJ network members' access to each other is positively correlated with truth commission adoption.

Data, Concepts, and Measures

I evaluate my expectations using a cross-sectional dataset covering the universe of transitions from internal armed conflict, government killings of civilians, and autocracy from 1970 to 2018. The full sample provides data for 269 post-conflict periods, 320 post-killings periods, and 87 post-autocracy periods, for a total of 676 transition periods. The unit of analysis is the transition period. This mirrors the structure of many TJ and peace and conflict studies datasets.[29] I construct my data frame using the UCDP Conflict Termination Dataset,[30] the UCDP One-Sided Violence Dataset,[31] and Boix and coauthors' data on democracy and democratic transitions.[32]

To identify the countries that adopted commissions during their transitions, I draw on data from the *Varieties of Truth Commissions*. The project records

[29] DeTommaso et al. 2017; Loyle and Binningsbø 2018; Olsen, Payne, and Reiter 2010.

[30] Kreutz 2010. For an armed conflict to be included in the data, the government must be one of the parties and each conflict year must result in twenty-five or more battle-related deaths. A conflict ends when the number of battle-related deaths goes below this threshold after an "active year." I restrict the sample to intrastate conflicts.

[31] Eck and Hultman 2007; Pettersson and Eck 2018. One-sided violence is measured similarly to armed conflict, with twenty-five deaths as the threshold. I restrict the sample to cases where state agents are the perpetrators.

[32] Boix et al. (2013) define a democracy as a political system with both high participation and contestation, where participation is defined as suffrage for the majority of men and contestation is defined as free and fair elections.

eighty-four commissions established in sixty-three countries in the period 1970 to 2018.[33] These include commissions adopted in transitional (forty-eight) and non-transitional (thirty-six) contexts. See Table A.1 ▶ in online Appendix A for the full list of commissions.

I distinguish transitional commissions from non-transitional commissions because they differ in terms of their goals, methodologies, and antecedents.[34] Thus, transitional and non-transitional commissions likely require different theories and analyses, especially regarding the question of institutional adoption. Future research should evaluate whether the relationships that I propose here also apply to non-transitional contexts.

To determine what cases are and are not transitional, I draw on previous research in the conflict and democracy literatures, in which a transition is generally conceptualized as a five- to ten-year period following an armed conflict or a period of autocratic rule.[35] Non-transitional commissions include commissions installed in consolidated democracies and autocracies.[36]

An evergreen question in scholarship on TJ, democracy and democratization, and peace and conflict is the potential sensitivity of research findings to how concepts are measured. Accordingly, I use a ten-year window to mark a transition period in the main analysis and use a five-year window as a robustness check in a supplementary analysis.

To evaluate my hypotheses, I use data on the strength of domestic civil society, international HRO naming and shaming, and network access prior to a transition to predict commission adoption during the transition. I do this while controlling for potentially confounding factors that I discuss further below.

Dependent Variable

The dependent variable *Truth Commission* is a binary variable that takes a value of 1 if a commission was adopted during a transition from internal armed

[33] The data begin in 1970, corresponding with key events connected to TJ: the start of the third wave of democratization in 1974; the entry into force of the international covenants on civil and political rights and on economic, social, and cultural rights in 1976; and the adoption of the Additional Protocols to the Geneva Conventions in 1977. Other large cross-mechanism TJ datasets also start with 1970 (Olsen, Payne, and Reiter 2010).

[34] Bakiner 2014, Zvobgo 2019*a*.

[35] See, for example, Edward Flores and Nooruddin (2009) and Walter (2002) on post-conflict countries, and Hegre et al. (2001), Kostelka (2017), and Svolik (2008, 2015) on democratic transitions and democratic consolidation.

[36] For recent research on commissions in consolidated democracies, see Posthumus and Zvobgo (2021). For recent work on commissions in autocracies, see Gillooly et al. (2024), Wiebelhaus-Brahm (2021*b*), and Winston (2021).

conflict, one-sided violence by the government against a civilian population, or autocracy; otherwise, 0.

Independent Variables

To measure the strength of a country's civil society, I draw on the Varieties of Democracy Project's core civil society index—a continuous indicator that captures the extent to which civil society is autonomous from the state and can "freely and actively pursue their political and civic goals."[37] The minimum value possible is 0, and the maximum value possible is 1.

To measure international HRO shaming, I use data from Hendrix and Wong (2014), specifically a count variable for the number of Amnesty background reports published on a given country in a given year. Background reports are "lengthy, research-based documents that are written primarily for a specialized audience of government officials, INGO officials, and academics."[38]

To measure network access, I use a count of INGOs that list a domestic membership base within a country in a given year. This measure is drawn from the Union of International Associations' (UIA) *Yearbook on International Organizations.*[39]

I use the average of the explanatory variables in the five-year period preceding the relevant transition from conflict, civilian killings, or autocracy. I do the same for the control variables. The sole exceptions are the diffusion and transition-specific control variables, which are summative. Using the years preceding a transition helps guard against reciprocal causality; it ensures that the data are not contaminated by processes already underway to create a commission following conflict, civilian killings, or autocracy—processes that may, for instance, be picked up in Amnesty reports. Taking a five-year average, in turn, captures the overall level of civil society strength, connectedness, and activism before a transition, when groups were doing the hard work in the hardest times.[40] More information on the selection of independent variables is provided in online Appendix A, as are summary statistics.[41]

[37] Coppedge et al. 2018, Codebook, 45.

[38] Hendrix and Wong 2014, 39

[39] Smith and Wiest 2005.

[40] This research design choice is appropriate for cross-sectional data. If I had panel data, I would employ single-year lags. I do not use panel data because time is not part of my theory.

[41] Kim (2012*b*, 2019) uses more coarse measures: the number of domestic HROs and the presence of a UN peacekeeping operation. The latter of these two makes it especially difficult for us to conclude that civil society matters since it does not at all relate to civil society.

Control Variables

I control for several potentially confounding factors, namely the degree to which human rights are respected, domestic political institutional constraints on and opportunities for accountability, diffusion, embeddedness in intergovernmental organizations (IGOs), wealth, aid dependence, and population size. Table A.2 ▶ in online Appendix A provides summary statistics.

First, we might be more likely to observe truth commissions where abuses have been especially severe. These are the contexts where the *need* for truth and justice is arguably the greatest. Governments may rise to the occasion and adopt commissions to acknowledge past abuses so that individual victims and society more broadly can get closure and "move on." Yet we might be less likely to observe commissions in these same contexts because the *burden* of truth and justice is arguably the greatest. Governments may estimate that this burden is simply too great to bear. To help me evaluate whether commissions are adopted where it is relatively "harder" or "easier" to address political violence within the broader context of state practice, I control for basic human rights respect using Fariss's (2014) latent measure.[42]

Second, political institutional factors, namely alternative sources of accountability and the feasibility of policy change, may moderate the effect of TJ network activism. Research has found that commissions can fill an accountability gap in places where courts cannot reliably render sound justice.[43] While courts and commissions need not be substitutes and should actually operate as complementary institutions,[44] the impetus for a commission may be reduced in countries where victims can access functional and impartial courts. To help me determine whether commissions are less likely to be adopted where there are alternative avenues for justice, I use the latent variable developed by Linzer and Staton (2015), which draws on several indicators of de facto judicial independence.

It is also possible that commissions are more likely to be adopted in contexts where creating new policy is easier. Thus, I control for veto players, using the Political Constraints III index.[45] The index interacts the number of independent branches of government with their ability to veto policy. The index also accounts for the distribution of preferences across branches of government. In brief, the index calculates the ease of changing the status quo. The more veto players and, importantly, the greater the level of inter-branch fractionalization, the greater the constraints.

[42] Having a commission does not affect a country's human rights score. Fariss's measure is derived from several datasets on physical integrity rights violations and repression.
[43] Hayner 2001, 2011.
[44] De Greiff 2012.
[45] Henisz 2002.

Third, it may be that countries with more economic resources are more likely to adopt commissions because they can afford to create new institutions. Aid-dependent countries may also be more likely to adopt commissions because aid providers expect accountability for human rights abuses. To capture wealth and aid dependence, I use gross domestic product (GDP) per capita (logged) and official development assistance (ODA) as a percentage of GDP. I also use population (logged), as truth commissions may be more costly for governments in more populous countries, where there may be more potential TJ claimants. More claimants may mean more would-be beneficiaries of government programs like reparations. These measures are drawn from the World Bank's World Development Indicators.

Fourth, to measure regional diffusion, I use a count of precedents in geographic neighbors based on the UN's subregional division of the world.[46] I also account for time (or, global diffusion) using a simple count of the number of years since 1970.

Fifth, I control for membership in IGOs, another potential source of pressure to adopt commissions and TJ. Data on IGO membership also come from the UIA *Yearbook* and the Correlates of War Project.

Finally, to ensure that no one transition type is driving the results, I estimate full population models with dummy variables for the transition type, as well as models for different samples of transitions with transition-specific controls. In the post-autocracy model, I control for the number of previous democratic breakdowns—a proxy measure for levels of historical political (in)stability. In the post-conflict model, I control for the duration (in years) and cumulative intensity of the conflict (fewer than or at least 1,000 battle-related deaths). In the post-killings model, I control for the best estimate of fatalities (logged).

Regarding the transition-specific controls, there are reasons that we might expect it is more difficult to adopt commissions after longer conflicts with a greater number of deaths, or after widespread civilian killings by the government. In these contexts, there is a wider population to whom the state would be accountable—potentially more TJ claimants than the government might deem feasible to redress. Yet there are also reasons that we might expect it is easier to create commissions in these same contexts: There may be stronger, more urgent demands for truth and justice, both domestically and internationally, that prompt commission adoption.

[46] Subregions are derived from the UNSTATS intermediate region variable, indicating, for example, "Southern Africa," which is a subset of "Sub-Saharan Africa," which is a subset of "Africa."

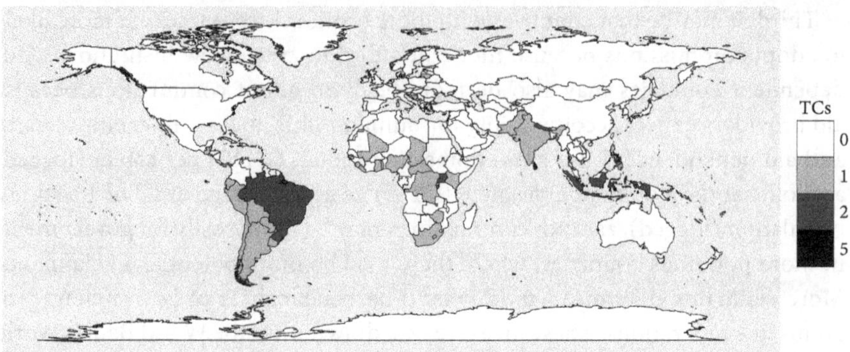

Figure 3.1 Truth Commissions During Transitions (1970–2018)
Note: The map shows in grayscale countries that implemented truth commissions during political transitions from 1970 to 2018. Darker shades represent more truth commissions.

Descriptive Statistics

While transitional commissions have spanned the globe, they have been concentrated in the Global South, as seen in Figure 3.1.[47]

Hypothesis Testing

I first evaluate my hypotheses using logit regressions, with truth commission adoption during a transition as the dependent variable and standard errors clustered by country. Figure 3.2 summarizes the results of the fully specified, full population model, re-estimated with standardized variables for ease of reading and comparison. See Table A.4 ⊙, Model 3 in online Appendix A.

At the 5 percent error level, *Strong Domestic Civil Society*, *HRO Naming and Shaming*, and *Network Access* are comparable, positive, and statistically significant predictors of commission adoption. See online Appendix A for other model specifications that produce results broadly consistent with these.[48]

Thus, I find support for a stronger civil society increasing the likelihood of commission adoption (Hypothesis 1). Across five of six models, *Strong*

[47] Note, Tunisia is not marked as having a transitional truth commission because Boix et al. (2013) did not yet count the country as a democracy.

[48] These include: Table A.5 ⊙, which assesses commission adoption in a narrower five-year transition window; Tables A.7 ⊙ and A.8 ⊙, which account for different conflict termination and regime transition types; and Table A.10 ⊙, which includes an interaction for *Strong Domestic Civil Society* and *HRO Naming and Shaming*.

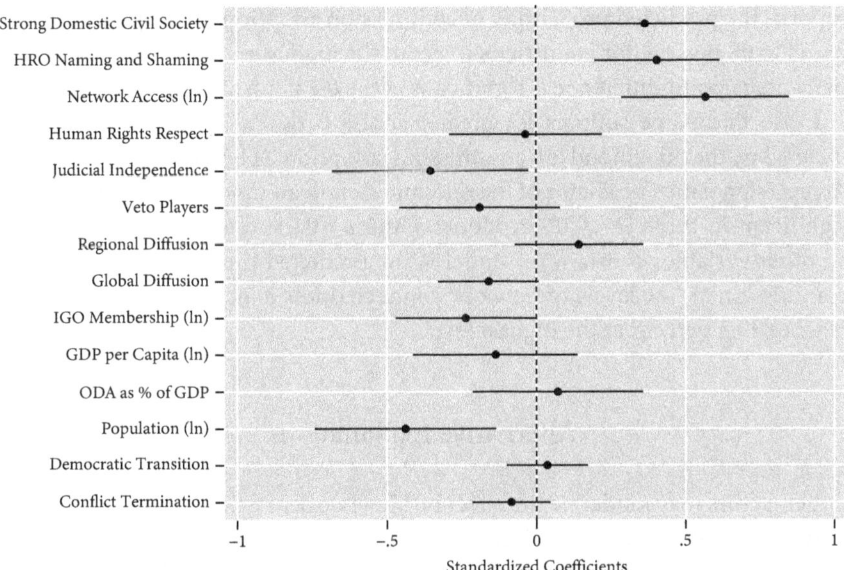

Figure 3.2 Predicted Effect of Variables on Likelihood of Truth Commissions, with 95 Percent CIs

Note: The figure shows the estimated effect of each variable on the likelihood that a country will adopt a truth commission during its transition from internal armed conflict, civilian killings, or autocratic government, with 95 percent confidence intervals (CIs). Variables to the left of the zero-line decrease the likelihood of a commission, while variables to the right of the line increase the likelihood of a commission. Variables with CIs that cross the zero-line are not statistically significant, and thus their estimated effects on the outcome may be due to chance. Because the coefficients in this figure are standardized for nonbinary variables, it is easier to compare the relative sizes and effects of the variables on the outcome.

Domestic Civil Society is a positive and statistically significant predictor of the outcome ($p < 0.01$ in Models 1–2, $p < 0.05$ in Model 3, and $p < 0.10$ in Models 4–5). Substantively, the predicted probability of commission adoption, given an increasingly strong domestic civil society, is quite large. Holding all other variables constant in Model 3, at the highest level of civil society strength, the predicted probability of the outcome is 61.6 percent, compared to 7.1 percent at the lowest level. The nearly 55 percentage point difference is significant at the 0.1 percent error level.

In addition, I find strong and consistent support for more concentrated international HRO shaming enhancing the likelihood of commission adoption (Hypothesis 2). Across five of six models, *HRO Naming and Shaming* is a positive and statistically significant predictor of the outcome ($p < 0.05$ in Model 1 and $p < 0.01$ in Models 2–5). Holding all other variables constant in Model 3, for countries subject to the lowest number of Amnesty background reports, the predicted probability of commission adoption is 10.1 percent, compared to 98 percent for countries subject to the highest number. The roughly 88 percentage point difference is significant at the 0.1 percent error level.

I also find some support for greater access between TJ network members increasing the likelihood of commission adoption (Hypothesis 3). *Network Access* is a positive predictor of the outcome across all models and is statistically significant in three ($p < 0.01$ in Model 3 and $p < 0.05$ in Models 5–6). Holding all other variables constant in Model 3, the predicted probability of creating a commission at low levels of network connectedness is nearly zero; however, it reaches 89.3 percent at the highest level.

Alternative Explanations

Other factors may moderate the effect of TJ network activism. However, I do not find consistent results for *Judicial Independence*, *Veto Players*, *Global Diffusion*, *IGO Membership*, or *GDP per Capita*. Additionally, I do not find any statistically significant results for *Human Rights Respect*, *Regional Diffusion*, or *ODA as a Percentage of GDP*. *Population* is the only control variable that is consistently significant across models. It appears that the larger the population, the less likely a commission is to be adopted. The results indicate, too, that we may be less likely to see post-conflict commissions than other commission types, though this relationship is weak in the fully specified, full population model. Most important, though, is the finding that transnational advocacy—the effect of which has been posited but not investigated systematically—appears to influence truth commission adoption.

Robustness Checks

In online Appendix A, I assess possible heterogeneous effects and produce several robustness checks. In particular, I expound on the post-conflict and post-autocracy models, controlling for different transition paths, such as conflict termination via rebel victory and democratic transition due to distributive conflict. I also evaluate the stability of the results from the main analysis by considering, via a Cox proportional hazards model, not only whether a commission was adopted but also how long it took for it to be adopted. Differences across different types of models—with different assumptions and, in the case of the Cox model, different underlying data and data structures—*are* to be expected. However, the few differences that I observe do not reduce confidence in the overall findings.

Probing Causal Mechanisms

I conducted semi-structured interviews in the spring and winter of 2019 with current and former directors, lawyers, and staff members from major INGOs to probe the mechanisms suggested by the theory, specifically Amnesty, HRW, and the ICTJ. Amnesty and HRW represent advocacy INGOs, and the ICTJ represents an operational INGO in the TJ space. I conducted the interviews over Skype or in person in New York City, with email exchanges for additional information.

I also ran a focus group in the autumn of 2019 with career human rights defenders serving in the Provincial Commission for Memory in Argentina: Sandra Raggio, the director; Yamila Zavala Rodríguez, an attorney and a daughter of the disappeared; Ernesto Alonso, a soldier during the Malvinas (Falklands) conflict; Roberto Cipriano García, a psychologist; and three of their staff, Diego Diaz, Rodrigo Pomares, and Samanta Salvatori. The commission is an independent and autonomous public body established in 1999 to promote and implement public policies of memory and human rights. The advocates' work on human rights and TJ issues precedes the commission, however, for some dating back to the junta and the transition to democracy in 1983. And in the winter/spring of 2020, I interviewed human rights NGO leaders in Guatemala, including GAM director Mario Polanco and GAM legal advisor Carlos Juárez.

The theory presents three mechanisms linking the TJ network to truth commission adoption, which I probed with interviewees and focus group participants. Recall that I first proposed that a strong domestic civil society is well positioned to create politically salient information that serves as a basis for TJ claims and contributes to governments' decision to implement TJ mechanisms, in particular commissions. Relatedly, I suggested that a strong civil society can draw attention to local concerns and mobilize external actors to also exert pressure for accountability.

The Argentinian advocates traced this dynamic from the junta to the transition to the present day, citing numerous groups, perhaps most memorably the Mothers of the Plaza de Mayo Association, that put the government's abuses in full view. The *madres* (mothers) have held vigil since 1977, both to remember their children who were disappeared and to protest impunity. The *madres* represent just one case of Argentinian human rights activists' mobilization, persistence, and savvy use of slogans and symbols—for example, wearing white scarves resembling cloth diapers to symbolize their lost children.

Accordingly, the *madres*' messages were, and continue to be, amplified by INGOs such as Amnesty and IOs such as the Inter-American Commission on Human Rights. "The government responses have had everything to do with human rights movements and civil society activism," commission director

Raggio insisted. From her and her colleagues' perspectives, TJ mechanisms implemented in Argentina—the famous National Commission on the Disappearance of Persons (CONADEP), criminal trials for leaders and agents of the junta, material reparations, and memorialization projects, among others—however flawed they may have been (are)—never would have materialized without strong, concerted, and, importantly, persistent local advocacy before, during, and after the transition.

My interviews with Param-Preet Singh, associate director of HRW's International Justice Program, and Philip Luther, Amnesty's research and advocacy director for the Middle East and North Africa region, echo many of the sentiments of the commission representatives. In particular, Singh conveyed that a strong civil society is tremendously helpful for setting up any TJ mechanism, be it a commission, a special court, or a reparations program. A robust civil society is a "constituency that can harness the local appetite for justice"—an appetite that international HROs like HRW can magnify.[49]

Priscilla Hayner added that many well-known and respected commissions such as in South Africa, Peru, and Timor-Leste would have been very different without the contributions of local civil society actors, if they would have been created at all. For his part, GAM's Mario Polanco stressed that long-term accountability depends on strong local advocacy.

Hayner in her book elaborated, "The strength of civil society in any given country—how many and how well organized the non-governmental advocacy, community-based, research, and faith-based organizations are—will help determine the success of any truth commission."[50] And this is precisely what we see in places like Argentina and Guatemala, where different presidential administrations have attempted to reverse human rights and TJ gains since their countries' commissions. They have, however, faced strong resistance from civil society, which Hayner calls the "essential ingredient" to progress.

Second, I previously suggested that more intense international HRO shaming enhances the likelihood of commission adoption because leaders, especially those governing transitional states, are concerned with HRO interests and, perhaps most importantly, the interests of HRO allies, including foreign governments. Anna Myriam Roccatello, the ICTJ's deputy executive director and director of programs, relayed the importance of international HROs' creation and transmission of reliable, consistent information.

Singh elaborated on this point, stating that documentation and dissemination of violations "underlines the imperative for reform" both at home and abroad. Likewise, representatives from the Provincial Commission for Memory

[49] Thus, there can be an "inverse boomerang," per Pallas and Bloodgood (2022, 5).
[50] Hayner 2011, 223–224.

highlighted the value of international solidarity with Argentinian causes, though they were unable to state the extent to which international HRO shaming in particular helped push the new democratically elected government to implement TJ and specifically the CONADEP.

It is important to note a recurrent concern among my interviewees, including a lawyer from a prominent INGO who requested anonymity: International pressure can be counterproductive, particularly in the absence of a strong domestic base lobbying for redress. Both this lawyer and other interviewees explained that their organizations hesitate and sometimes avoid intervening when there are no existing commitments to truth and justice. It is important for them that their work is not interpreted—however uncharitably or inaccurately—as a foreign imposition, lest there be backlash.

Third, I posited that greater access between domestic and international civil society groups enhances prospects for a commission. Essentially, formally connected groups have more opportunities to share information and coordinate strategy. Singh agreed that official ties are helpful. However, in her professional experience, it is not necessary for domestic and international groups to be in the same place and meet in person to plan and execute their objectives. She further emphasized the importance of *personal* connections between domestic and international actors.[51] Such connections, Singh said, enable communication and partnership beyond borders and across oceans, throughout the course of a career.

The qualitative data from the interviews and focus group provide strong support to the theory and add depth and nuance to the results of the statistical analysis. Critically, the interviews and focus group show both sides of the relationship between civil society actors at the domestic and international levels. Consistent with my burden sharing model, domestic groups take the lead at the commission adoption stage, with international groups in a supporting role. This is a strategic choice, as my interviewees and focus group participants underscored: International civil society advocacy is valuable, but domestic civil society advocacy is essential. This dynamic changes, however, at the commission design stage.

Implications

Both the quantitative and qualitative analyses in this chapter provide support for the argument that TJ network activism matters for truth commission adoption. While commissions are locally rooted processes, they are created within and

[51] See also Reiners (2024), on the power of interpersonal relationships in the global human rights movement.

because of the wider, global context. Truth commission adoption, therefore, represents neither a domestic nor an international politics story, but a transnational politics story.

By inquiring into the correlates of commission adoption, this chapter illuminates factors that human rights advocates and allies, including donor governments, can intervene on in countries that have yet to implement such mechanisms. Pressure from above is beneficial, but it is pressure from below that is crucial. Therefore, those with an interest in human rights and TJ should consider reinforcing domestic civil societies during periods of internal armed conflict, repression, and autocratic government.

Now that these cross-national patterns have been established, researchers can collect more fine-grained data and/or locate potential sites for natural (or quasi-) experiments that allow us to identify with greater certainty the effect of transnational advocacy on truth commission adoption. Researchers can also better engage sample selection when studying post-commission outcomes.

Conclusion

In the 1970s, the first truth commissions were established to account for political violence, notably for abuses perpetrated during authoritarian regimes and fatalities during internal armed conflicts. Since then, commissions have proliferated globally. Yet, despite their prevalence, the question of why commissions are adopted in some contexts but not in others has been poorly understood.

In this first empirical chapter, I produced a novel study that draws on a variety of original data, including the *Varieties of Truth Commissions* datasets, a series of interviews that I conducted with INGO representatives and Guatemalan NGO representatives, and a focus group that I led with Argentinian human rights defenders. I showed that domestic and international civil society actors are the force behind commissions, explaining institutional adoption across dissimilar contexts. Connected by a global TJ network, civil society actors work together to guide governments to establish commissions.

To achieve this outcome, TJ network members burden share: Domestic members assume a leading role, and international members assume a supporting role. More precisely, domestic groups take the crucial first steps to motivate governments to adopt commissions: They record and share information on local conditions with their international partners. International HROs then adapt and disseminate this information widely, mobilizing foreign publics and their governments to also demand truth.

While previous studies have often relegated civil society actors to the role of local implementers or service providers, this chapter reveals that these actors can and do spur policy around the globe. The findings motivate the next chapter's inquiry into the role of civil society actors in shaping the second stage of truth commissions: institutional design.

4
Professional Experience, Technical Expertise, and Institutional Design

In 2000 and 2001, civil society organizations, representatives of the Catholic Church, and a diversity of community leaders convened a series of meetings to discuss TJ in Timor-Leste. Among the agenda items at the first meeting in June 2000 was the idea of a truth commission, to provide an accounting of twenty-five years of foreign occupation by Indonesia and related armed conflicts following Portuguese colonization.[1]

Between 1975 and 1999, more than 100,000 East Timorese died conflict-related deaths, and hundreds of thousands more were displaced, starved, and subjected to torture and sexual exploitation by Indonesian state agents and the local armed groups they co-opted.[2] These abuses were largely hidden from the international community: For many years, Indonesia closed off most foreign access to Timor-Leste.

In this context, local resistance groups organized, developed advocacy campaigns, and forged partnerships to build support for their cause, both at home and abroad. And this support came—from HROs and foreign journalists who reported on abuses and from the local Catholic churches that sheltered activists.[3] As knowledge of the plight of the East Timorese grew internationally, a wave of solidarity crested in countries like Australia and Brazil and in IOs like the United Nations.

The growing transnational movement for Timorese self-determination ultimately drove the Indonesian government to grant an independence referendum in 1999.[4] While it was technically a vote about self-determination, the referendum represented an opportunity for accountability that many had previously thought impossible. For more than a generation, Indonesia had deprived the East Timorese of their rights to self-government, social and economic

[1] CAVR 2005, ch. 1, pg. 10. The United States green-lit the invasion, declassified documents would later show. For more information, see National Security Archive (2001).

[2] Alldén 2007; Nevins 2018.

[3] Amnesty International 1996; HRW 2000*a*, 2000*b*; Wigglesworth 2013.

[4] Hayner 2011, 39.

Governing Truth. Kelebogile Zvobgo, Oxford University Press. © Oxford University Press (2026).
DOI: 10.1093/oso/9780197815663.003.0004

development, and physical integrity.[5] Despite threats of retaliation from Indonesia and its proxies, the East Timorese voted overwhelmingly in favor of independence, and the following year, their social, religious, and political leaders met to draw the landscape of TJ.

Following the June 2000 meetings, civil society representatives recommended a truth commission to the main coalition of political parties, the National Council of Timorese Resistance (CNRT).[6] Confronted with the enormity of the task of creating a commission, the CNRT formed a dedicated steering committee to develop a full proposal. In turn, the committee—comprised of CNRT, NGO, and Catholic Church representatives and spiritual and customary legal authorities—launched two consultative processes.

The first consultative process was an international one, to help define the commission's contours. As would later be reported about the commission and other TJ modalities in Timor-Leste, domestic civil society groups, the CNRT, and the United Nations Transitional Administration for East Timor (UNTAET) "recognized the importance of responding to past abuses, but they faced significant challenges to taking action," including a lack of prior experience and expertise in TJ design and operation.[7] Given this, engaging international TJ practitioners, including Mark Freeman, Priscilla Hayner, Paul Seils, and Paul van Zyl of the newly formed ICTJ, was critical.[8] Patrick Burgess, previously the director of human rights for two UN missions to Timor-Leste and, later, principal legal counsel to the truth commission, emphasized in our interview that they drew lessons from South Africa, both good and bad, as the TRC was concluding its work. As a result, the commission was "quite well designed for [its] needs."[9]

The second consultative process was a national one. Together with the ICTJ, the steering committee sought to raise awareness, garner input, and cultivate support among the public. The process revealed a deep concern for the truth among the East Timorese, as well as an interest in reconciliation.[10] The following statements, taken during ICTJ-commissioned focus groups, are illuminating in this regard:

> I am also interested to know all of the violations that happened in other regions beside[s] mine because those incidents happened all over Timor-Leste.
>
> —Women's group member, Dili[11]

[5] CAVR 2005.
[6] Hayner 2011, 39.
[7] ICTJ 2002, 18–19.
[8] Rothfield et al. 2008.
[9] Author interview with Patrick Burgess.
[10] CAVR 2005, ch. 1, pp. 11–12.
[11] Pigou 2003, 25.

We think it is very important to know the truth of what happened during all this time so that we can tell our children and grandchildren.

—Male villager, Ossu[12]

I think the person must stand before some public meeting, explain what he did, and admit and feel sorry for his mistake in front of the victim while observed by local people. This will make the victim feel satisfied and more willing to accept him back.

—Former Resistance fighter, Baucau[13]

All of you have to know the past. It does not mean that we want revenge on our brothers who were involved in past violations. Most important, they have to realize their mistakes.

—Female student, Manatuto[14]

There should be "*naha biti boot*"—we should sit and get together to discuss the problem based on our tradition. This is the foundation for reconciliation. . . . Everyone should admit his or her past wrongdoing and be willing to introspect and clean themselves up.

—Male villager, Umatolu[15]

Some focus group participants also expressed interest in an internationally minded commission and supported continuing assistance from international experts, HROs, and others:

We are talking about human rights violations. This is not a family problem, but instead an international issue. Therefore, [we] should solve the problem internationally.

—Male political prisoner, Dili[16]

[O]rganizations that work on justice in Timor-Leste are reliable in the way they perform their job. They can channel [issues] from the people to the government.

—Male villager, Baucau[17]

[12] Pigou 2003, 26.
[13] Pigou 2003, 36.
[14] Pigou 2003, 26.
[15] Pigou 2003, 39.
[16] Pigou 2003, 29.
[17] Pigou 2003, 32.

Following these consultations, the steering committee, together with Freeman, Hayner, Seils, and van Zyl, deliberated on the commission's founding legislation and, three months later, produced a draft law for a novel commission. The proposed legislation defined for the commission a range of strong investigative powers, including the power to compel testimony and other material evidence, that would set it up for a robust inquiry.[18] Also noteworthy was the proposal's embeddedness in *lisan*—encompassing local practices of public confession, restitution, and forgiveness—and the oversight powers the proposal accorded to communities, particularly to spiritual and customary legal authorities known as *lia nain*. In this way, the draft legislation reflected the norms, interests, and priorities of both international experts and ordinary East Timorese. The steering committee submitted the draft to the CNRT and UNTAET for review, and both quickly approved. And so the CAVR was installed.[19]

As my theory predicts, civil society was not only essential to the CAVR's establishment; it was also vital to its institutional design. But to what extent are civil society actors important for designing truth commissions, in particular strong commissions, around the world? I propose that the global TJ network, through its community of experts and technical advisors, is critical to designing strong commissions and that governments that receive assistance from them are more likely to afford commissions decisive powers of investigation.

In this chapter, I study the expertise and assistance of international civil society actors, and I produce a systematic cross-national examination of truth commission institutional design.[20] I focus on investigative powers expressed in commissions' legal mandates, specifically the power to (1) investigate a range of abuses, (2) trace antecedents of abuses, (3) subpoena testimony and other material evidence, and (4) preserve evidence. While they are not the only powers or design features that can help commissions conduct an exhaustive probe, they are fundamental tools for recovering the truth and constructing a more complete narrative on the past.

I assess the proposition that these key powers are more likely to be enumerated in the legal mandates of commissions whose founding governments were advised by international TJ experts. I also consider the influence of domestic civil society actors who, according to my burden sharing model, play a supporting role in commission design. I do this using the first of three datasets in the *Varieties of Truth Commissions*, which codes various aspects of truth commission mandates across the universe of commissions from 1970 to 2018. The dataset also tracks the presence (absence) of international TJ experts, notably

[18] CAVR 2005, ch. 1, pp. 12–13; UNTAET 2000*a*, 2000*b*, 2000*c*, 2000*d*.

[19] UNTAET 2001.

[20] For a study on commission mandates that covers broader themes like reconciliation, see Kochanski (2020).

from the ICTJ, prior to and during a country's commission. I supplement these cross-national data with a series of interviews, a focus group, and a survey of current and former ICTJ leadership and staff.

I find a significant, positive relationship between the presence of international TJ experts, specifically the ICTJ, and truth commissions with strong designs, possessing in particular the power to trace antecedents and to preserve evidence. However, I do not find an equally strong relationship between TJ expert involvement and commissions possessing the power to consider a range of abuses or to compel testimony. I also find evidence that domestic civil society actors play a supporting role: A robust domestic civil society is associated with governments affording commissions the power to compel testimony.

Interestingly, the statistical analysis reveals that domestic political and institutional factors, such as transitions and regime type, can be equally if not more important for commission design than efforts by either international or domestic civil society actors. My interviews and focus group confirm the significance of experts in the design process: Numerous commissions around the world have been designed on the basis of expert advice.[21] Nonetheless, the qualitative data, like the quantitative data, indicate that experts' influence is circumscribed by domestic political and institutional factors.

My results show that the TJ network's success at this second stage, *truth commission design*, rests both on expert assistance and governments' openness to this assistance. Essentially, not all governments consult experts. And, among those that do consult experts, not all governments follow expert advice.[22] Notwithstanding, the overall results evince the continuing influence of civil society actors in diverse truth commissions and TJ processes globally.

Plan of the Chapter

The next section begins with a discussion of the relationship between certain truth commission institutional design features and commission outcomes. I detail a range of features and suggest that some are especially important for recovering the truth in post-violence societies. In addition, I chart the emergence of a TJ expert class in the 1980s and commissions' standardization in the 1990s and 2000s. I then make the link between expert assistance and commission design and offer a pair of hypotheses regarding commissions' material

[21] Author interview with Eduardo González.

[22] To be sure, experts can and do publicly announce that they will not engage in truth commission processes that they believe to be disingenuous. In addition, experts can and do disengage from frivolous processes—to the domestic and international embarrassment of offending governments. Author interview with Priscilla Hayner. See also Loken et al. (2018) for a case study on Sri Lanka, which was publicly shamed by a diversity of international groups for using commissions as a smokescreen for impunity.

scope of inquiry and their evidence-gathering powers. In the section that follows, I describe the cross-national data that I use to appraise the hypotheses. I also explain my measures. Following this, I report the results of the quantitative analysis and assess its robustness to alternative explanations. I then enrich this analysis with qualitative data from my interviews, focus group, and survey. I discuss the implications of the evidence for scholarship and policy before concluding.

The Global Transitional Justice Network and the Institutional Design of Truth Commissions

While prior research has addressed truth commission adoption, presenting it as either a domestic politics story or as an international politics story led by government elites and IOs, commission design has not been seriously queried. Scholarship does acknowledge the importance of institutional design for commissions.[23] For example, social scientists have evaluated design features to facilitate victim participation[24] and to induce perpetrator participation.[25] Surprisingly, scholars have not rigorously studied commission mandates—the founding texts from which all design features emerge and an early signal of commission quality or strength. In particular, scholars have not systematically evaluated why some governments endow commissions with strong investigative powers that enable an exhaustive inquiry while other governments do not. It is within this scholarly context that this chapter intervenes. I propose that the global TJ network, through its community of experts and technical advisors, accounts for some of the variation that we observe across commission powers and designs.

Below, I present a list of important institutional design features that I compiled based on my careful study of truth commission mandates. I distinguish some mandate characteristics as critical to assembling a more complete and accurate narrative on the past. The features that I distinguish relate to a commission's material scope of inquiry and evidence-gathering powers.

Institutional Design and Truth Commission Outcomes

Truth commission success can be measured in a number of ways, including completion, wide dissemination of the final report, and the number of testimonies collected and the number of victims identified. First, commission completion,

[23] Oduro and Nagy 2014; Stahn 2005.
[24] Ntsebeza 2000; Rana and Zvobgo 2021.
[25] Totten 2009; Zvobgo 2019*a*.

Table 4.1 Truth Commission Mandate Provisions

Provision	Desired Outcome	Example
Address women	Attention to women commensurate with violence	Timor-Leste 2002
Investigate and name perpetrators	Individual responsibility	El Salvador 1992
Outreach	Community participation	Peru 2001
Preserve evidence	Transparency, truth not mediated by outside forces	Argentina 1983
Privacy, safety, and psychosocial support	Victim participation	Sierra Leone 2002
Study range of abuses	Comprehensive narrative	South Korea 2005
Subpoena	Perpetrator participation	South Africa 1995
Trace antecedents	Contextualize abuses, make legible the pattern of violence	Canada 2009

while seemingly basic, is not a given. In Bolivia and the Philippines, for example, commissions disbanded soon after starting and produced no report. Second, dissemination of commission reports is not assured. In Haiti and Uganda, for instance, commission reports were suppressed, and in Zimbabwe, never released. Third, the degree of participation of survivors, victims' relatives, perpetrators, experts, and other witnesses can vary substantially.[26] For my part, I think of success primarily in terms of what facts a commission is able to uncover, which is linked to its design. Hence my interest in scrutinizing commissions' legal mandates—the texts from which institutional design features spring.

Table 4.1 lists important aspects of truth commission mandates, related outcomes of interest, and country examples. Take, to start, mandates that are gender-conscious, like we saw in Timor-Leste. Women's groups like FOKUPERS and institutional designers wanted the CAVR's attention to women to be commensurate with women's experiences of violence during the period of Indonesian occupation and the armed conflicts. So they made sure that the mandate explicitly addressed women and reserved 30 percent of senior commission leadership positions for women.[27] By so doing, they also encouraged recruitment of a gender-balanced staff. In addition, the commission collaborated with FOKUPERS throughout its activities, held a thematic hearing on gender violence, and dedicated a segment of the final report to women and women's

[26] Brahm 2007; Zvobgo 2019*a*.
[27] UNTAET 2001.

issues.[28] While not executed perfectly, the Timorese commission is recognized globally for its approach to and work on gender.[29]

Next, consider mandates that charge commissions with outreach, like we saw in Peru. Peruvian civil society representatives, along with commission designers, were interested in broad community participation, in particular participation of conflict-affected individuals.[30] So the mandate named outreach in conflict-affected regions as one of the commission's responsibilities. Inspired by this, the commission installed regional offices in areas that had experienced the greatest conflict intensity, in addition to the national office in Lima. In turn, regional commission coordinators organized fairs in rural areas, traveled to remote villages, and communicated with community members via Spanish–Quechua dual language speakers the commission had recruited.[31] As a consequence, the Peruvian commission attracted wide participation, gathering approximately 17,000 testimonies.[32]

Consider, also, mandates that provide for privacy of witnesses, as well as safety and psychosocial support, like we saw in Sierra Leone. As in many other countries, conflict survivors there feared being shamed, retaliated against, and ostracized if they told their stories. Civil society representatives and commission designers recognized this and, therefore, worked to include protection measures in the mandate. Ultimately, the commission organized private hearings for the most vulnerable witnesses, made available private cubicles in public hearings, and offered counseling before, during, and after statement giving.[33]

Certainly, these and other mandate features are not necessarily determining. For instance, a commission with a mandate that does not explicitly address women can, nonetheless, be gender-conscious and have this reflected in its work. However, there are some aspects of commission design that perhaps *cannot* be retrofitted into the commission, certainly not without great difficulty. There are some elements, specifically key powers of investigation, that commissions need from the outset in order to have the best chance of recovering the truth and establishing a comprehensive account of past events. These are the power to (1) investigate a range of abuses, (2) trace antecedents of abuses, (3) subpoena testimony, and (4) preserve evidence. The four powers fall into two major categories: a wide material scope of inquiry and effective evidence gathering, which position a commission to conduct a robust inquiry.[34]

[28] CAVR 2005.
[29] Hayner 2011, 39–42.
[30] Hayner 2011, 35–39.
[31] Ramírez-Barat 2011.
[32] CVR 2001.
[33] Rana and Zvobgo 2021.
[34] Just because a commission possesses particular powers does not mean it will avail itself of them or use them to the fullest extent. However, measuring commission powers on paper, rather than in

A Wide Material Scope of Inquiry

A wide material scope of inquiry is critical to an exhaustive historical narrative. And commissions that are charged with considering a range of abuses and tracing antecedents to abuses are better positioned to render such an account than commissions that are not charged with doing so. First, serious truth seeking requires consideration of multiple types of abuse. Rarely, if ever, is it the case that only one type of abuse has been perpetrated by state and/or non-state actors during authoritarian regimes, internal armed conflicts, or other periods of political violence. Commissions that are assigned to investigate some but not all abuses are, by definition, incomplete and are, by design, at odds with victims' right to truth. Second, commissions that are assigned to document instances of violence, but not to identify root causes, like social fragmentation and resource inequality, can only offer a partial understanding of the past. Such commissions are not well equipped to determine systems and patterns of abuse. Consequently, they can only recommend an incomplete set of remedies.

Consider the following example. After the death of his father, King Hassan II, King Mohamed VI of Morocco established the Equity and Reconciliation Commission, which was mandated to study arbitrary detentions and forced disappearances during his father's rule but lacked the power to interrogate root causes. Human rights advocates, both at home and abroad, criticized the monarchy for the commission's limited mandate and powers, which would obscure the full truth. Certainly, arbitrary detentions and disappearances were not the sole violation of physical integrity rights that agents of the monarchy perpetrated against civilians. Contemporaneous violations included "imprisonment, torture, and forced exile of political opponents and rights activists" as well as repression of proponents of Sahrawi independence.[35] And this is to say nothing of violations of economic, social, and cultural rights.[36] Ultimately, the limited commission produced a limited truth. The commission determined a population of 808 victims of disappearances, of which 742 had perished. The fates of the other sixty-six remained unknown.[37] These crimes were not connected to

practice, allows for more systematic cross-national data collection and analysis. It also keeps the analysis focused on transnational advocates' influence on governments. Commissions are created by, but are separate from, governments. Future research may more specifically investigate the effect of advocacy on TJ mechanisms themselves, including how they do their work.

[35] Hayner 2011, 42–43.

[36] The commission, according to Philip Luther, previously Amnesty International's research and advocacy director for the Middle East and North Africa, "managed—thanks to some progressive commissioners . . . and pressure from NGOs inside and outside Morocco—to expand the mandate in practice."

[37] Royaume du Maroc 2005, 68. Luther added that if the commission had been given stronger powers of investigation, including subpoenas on the operational side, it "could have resolved satisfactorily many more cases of enforced disappearance and political killings and revealed more details about the specific role of state organs. This could have facilitated legal action that many victims and their families wished to pursue. If the administration, military and security forces had co-operated

the broader system of abuse and the political, economic, and social factors that allowed abuse, among them the very system of monarchical government. As a consequence, the commission could not recommend the gamut of necessary remedies and reforms.

To summarize, a commission that lacks a wide material scope is effectively blocked from conducting a robust probe, producing an exhaustive report, and outlining appropriate solutions. While we might observe mandate "creep" in some instances, commissions—which are created and funded by governments—generally cannot stray too far from the path on which they are set.

Effective Evidence Gathering

Building on this, the power to compel testimony and the power to preserve evidence are each vital to a commission's ability to uncover the full range of abuses and their antecedents. First, the power to compel (or subpoena) testimony is essential, as perpetrators generally seek to avoid responsibility and, thus, tend to not volunteer their testimony. A commission's power to garner testimony and other evidence from reluctant sources positions it to produce a more exhaustive, more accurate account of past violations.[38] Second, the power to preserve evidence helps a commission conduct a more independent investigation.[39] Preserving evidence—for example, maps, organizational command charts, correspondence between perpetrators including orders from superiors, and notes on victims—is helpful for establishing key facts and enables a commission to share information directly with the public, without interference.

Consider these examples. The South African TRC issued dozens of subpoenas that forced perpetrators, including high-ranking ex-government officials and former leaders of the security forces, to testify to their responsibility for apartheid-era crimes like killings, abductions, and torture.[40] Without subpoena powers, the commission would have acquired many fewer perpetrator testimonies, and it would have missed critical leads in its investigations. Consider also Argentina, where the CONADEP was able to hand over volumes of evidence directly to the state prosecutor, ultimately leading to trials, convictions, and imprisonment of several junta leaders and agents.[41] This would have been all but unthinkable without express powers to preserve evidence.

in revealing the circumstances and fate of those subjected to enforced disappearance, this would have helped to rehabilitate these institutions and support a transition from them being organs of repression to tools for the respect of human rights."

[38] Zvobgo 2019*a*.

[39] González and Varney 2013.

[40] Zvobgo 2019*a*.

[41] Hayner 2011, 122–125.

In sum, a commission that lacks effective evidence-gathering powers in its mandate cannot reliably access and secure the information that it needs to compile and share a full and accurate historical account of violence and abuse. Critically, a commission cannot simply give itself these powers. In the case of subpoena powers, no court or magistrate would enforce subpoenas ordered by a government body that lacks the legal authority to issue them. In fact, that body would likely be accused of overreach, and its legitimacy would be called into question. In a similar fashion, a commission cannot presume control over collected evidence if its mandate does not provide for that control. To be sure, a commission would have a difficult time making this argument post hoc.

I now turn to the global TJ network and the emergence of an expert class that has helped develop, promote, and sustain high standards for governments designing truth commissions.

The Global Transitional Justice Network and the Emergence of an Expert Class

For decades, civil society actors, international TJ experts in particular, have played key roles in the institutional design of truth commissions around the world. This dates back to the early 1980s, when scholars, advocates, and practitioners began coming together at conferences and in field offices to exchange ideas and learn from each other's experiences. They learned from each other how to lobby for a commission, oversee its development and operation, and monitor implementation of its recommendations.

Foundations and other funding agencies hosted some of these conferences, where attendees developed and refined their intellectual and operational frameworks for implementing commissions—and they continue to do so.[42] Many conference participants proceeded to found TJ NGOs, taking their experiences to their home countries and beyond. To illustrate, in the early 1990s, the Ford Foundation hosted a series of conferences that served as sites of idea generation during what many considered a "justice boom," with the end of conflicts and atrocities in the Balkans, Rwanda, and elsewhere, and the establishment of international criminal tribunals and other TJ measures.

Ford conferences also served as a venue from which to recruit individuals to staff and run commissions. Of note, the ICTJ emerged from the South African TRC, which itself had relied heavily on the growing global TJ network.[43] So there was an expert network influencing important outcomes at many commissions,

[42] Roht-Arriaza 2001.
[43] Rowen 2017.

including in South Africa, even before the ICTJ was established in 2001; that part of the network was just not yet formalized.

Now the preeminent TJ INGO, the ICTJ monitors, advises, and provides operational support to governments implementing truth commissions around the world. With the support of a bevy of governmental and nongovernmental partners and supporters, the ICTJ—among a bona fide class of experts like Priscilla Hayner, an ICTJ cofounder and former UN senior mediation advisor, and Eduardo González, now an independent consultant—has worked to standardize the ideas, norms, and designs that underlie strong commissions and that help them uncover important information and contribute to meaningful knowledge and change in post-violence countries.[44]

Standardizing Truth Commissions After South Africa

Following the TRC, practitioner-experts undertook a process of standardization that involved certifying, decontextualizing, and framing truth commissions for international audiences.[45] Experts sensed growing support for commissions among supranational actors like the European Commission, leading funders like the MacArthur Foundation, development agencies such as the United Nations Development Programme (UNDP), and several Western governments. They knew that if commissions were to be installed and succeed in more post-violence countries, certain ideas from South Africa and its predecessors would have to be discarded and new ideas adopted. The ICTJ was central to these developments and, following its 2004 UN Security Council address, was styled (or *certified*) as the "guardian of 'real' truth commissions."[46]

As the ICTJ set off to promote and support commissions around the world, it secularized the South African model, decoupling truth and reconciliation.[47] While reconciliation had been a central goal in South Africa and a religious/spiritual framework had proved useful, this would not necessarily be the case in subsequent iterations of commissions.[48] Stripping away reconciliation as a central goal was important for making the sale to the widest possible cross-section of states. The process of *decontextualizing* the idea of a commission

[44] Strategic partners that offer considerable financial and diplomatic support have included the governments of Finland, Luxembourg, Sweden, and the Netherlands, and groups like Freedom House, the US National Endowment for Democracy, and the Open Society Foundations. There are also individuals who donate to the organization. I note that the ICTJ is an independent organization and does not serve specific donor interests, only the work of advancing TJ where the organization is called and needed.

[45] Ancelovici and Jenson 2013; Rowen 2017.

[46] Ancelovici and Jenson 2013, 302.

[47] VanAntwerpen 2008.

[48] VanAntwerpen 2009.

from South Africa also helped broaden the range of available discursive or argumentative frames: Commissions were *reframed* as a useful tool for peacebuilding and nation building, and not just, or necessarily, a path toward spiritual, interpersonal, and social reconciliation.[49]

Given the pioneering work of the ICTJ and the broader community of international TJ experts to standardize commissions, my argument—that these actors are influential in the design of commissions on the ground—is the logical next step. In my interview with Hayner, she conveyed that international experts have crucial roles to play. They have "learned from watching other commissions trip up." And, without them, a commission is unlikely to have a strong architecture and a clear direction. For Hayner, "if a commission isn't done well, it's not helpful."

International Experts and Truth Commission Design

I theorize that civil society actors, international TJ experts in particular, help governments design legal mandates that enumerate strong investigative powers for truth commissions. Along with their domestic partners, international members of the TJ network shift their target from the first stage, institutional adoption, to the second stage, institutional design, with a view to ensuring that commissions are robust. As we have seen in other public policy arenas, governments can drift, sometimes intentionally but often unintentionally, from their stated commitments to a policy or idea. However, when facing the possibility of criticism from civil society groups—who, after their initial success in garnering a commission, are arguably in a stronger position vis-à-vis the government—leaders may elect to credibly commit and, thereby, forgo likely criticism and censure.

One way that governments can credibly commit to a high-quality truth commission is by inviting international experts to advise them in designing their mechanisms. Eduardo González, distinguished TJ expert and former director of the ICTJ's Truth and Memory Program, conveyed to me in an interview that governments seek expert opinion precisely because they "are interested in credibility for the commission they are launching." Engaging experts helps governments characterize their process as serious and following in the tradition of South Africa, which still looms large in the global TJ imagination. While no country can have a commission like South Africa's—as González and other practitioners repeated, unprompted, across my interviews

[49] Ancelovici and Jenson 2013.

and focus group—leaders, especially of transitional states, "launch into the logic of a truth commission with a certain preconceived idea of what a truth commission is."[50]

For their part, TJ experts are interested in commission design, including investigative powers that would support a serious probe and a thorough concluding report. Besides, these individuals have a wealth of professional experience in this policy domain that governments lack. So there exists for them not only the interest but also the professional background to help set the parameters for effective truth seeking.

While TJ experts have standardized a general model of commissions—including commissions' objectives, functions, and powers—the degree to which they influence the design of commissions worldwide has not been systematically theorized or evaluated. I propose that TJ experts do in fact influence commissions' institutional design. Specifically, experts spur both a wide material scope of inquiry and effective evidence gathering.

In keeping with the burden sharing model, these international members of the TJ network are in the leading role at this second stage of the truth commission process, whereas they were in a supporting role in the first stage. Inversely, domestic members, who were previously in a leading role, assume a supporting role, echoing their international partners' messages and encouraging governments to align their mandates with international, evidence-based, practice-refined standards.

Spurring a Wide Material Scope of Inquiry and Effective Evidence Gathering

I first propose that governments advised by international TJ experts are more likely to set a wide material scope of inquiry for their commissions. In an ICTJ-commissioned "Practical Tool" for drafting a commission mandate, González affirms,

> A mandate that is incomplete, obscure, or contradictory to fundamental human rights standards can cripple a truth commission in many ways, forcing it to waste valuable time and resources in defining the parameters of its task, causing critical contradictions within the commission, and diminishing the capacity of key stakeholders to cooperate effectively with the commission.[51]

[50] Author interview with Eduardo González.
[51] González 2013, 1.

Given international experts' commitment to constructing a (more) complete account, I expect that the governments they advise are more likely to task commissions with investigating multiple types of abuse rather than a single type of abuse, as well as identifying root causes. Thus, I produce the following two-part hypothesis:

Hypothesis 1a

Governments are more likely to task commissions with uncovering a range of abuses when they are advised by international experts.

Hypothesis 1b

Governments are more likely to task commissions with tracing antecedents to abuses when they are advised by international experts.

Likewise, I expect that expert-advised governments are more likely to endow commissions with effective evidence-gathering powers, namely subpoena and evidence-preservation powers. Time and again, research and practitioner experiences show how critical the power to compel testimony and to control evidence has been to commissions' effectiveness globally—from South Africa to Timor-Leste, and beyond.[52]

González echoes these sentiments in another ICTJ-commissioned report coauthored with independent consultant Elena Naughton and Félix Reátegui, director of research at the Institute for Democracy and Human Rights at the Pontifical Catholic University of Peru. They write, "The argument in favor of such strong powers is that they may help ensure an appropriate inquiry in the face of spoilers' resistance."[53] Thus, I produce the following two-part hypothesis:

Hypothesis 2a

Governments are more likely to endow commissions with the power to subpoena testimony when they are advised by international experts.

Hypothesis 2b

Governments are more likely to endow commissions with the power to preserve evidence when they are advised by international experts.

I note that international experts, like domestic civil society actors, are not democratically elected. They advise governments on what to do and how. Far from mere technocrats, however, international experts and expert groups like the ICTJ, which I examine more closely in the quantitative and qualitative analyses below, advocate for affected communities *through* their expertise.

[52] Hayner 2001, 2011.
[53] González et al. 2014, 4.

Data, Concepts, and Measures

To evaluate these expectations, I draw on the first *Varieties of Truth Commissions* dataset, "Truth Commission Institutional Design," which codes several design features enumerated in commissions' legal mandates. The data cover commissions from 1970 to 2018, with the commission as the unit of analysis. The cross-national sample covers a range of regimes, from monarchies (e.g., Morocco), to weak post-conflict democracies (e.g., Sierra Leone), to consolidated democracies (e.g., Brazil), and includes transitional and non-transitional countries.[54] Considering only commissions in democracies or commissions in transitional countries would prevent me from reliably concluding that international TJ experts are vital, as the case selection technique would be based on an outcome that likely correlates with the dependent variable. In addition, my theory should be and indeed is borne out in transitional regimes like in Tunisia and non-transitional regimes as in Canada. To assess my hypotheses, I use information on the involvement of international TJ experts in a country prior to and during a commission to predict the aforesaid powers. I do this while accounting for several potentially confounding variables.

Dependent Variables

Each of the dependent variables—*Range of Abuses*, *Trace Antecedents*, *Subpoena*, and *Preserve Evidence*—is binary, taking a value of 1 if a commission possessed the relevant power; otherwise, 0.

Independent Variable

To measure international expert advice, I use the binary variable *ICTJ Involvement*, which captures whether the organization assisted a national government prior to and during its commission.[55] I focus on the ICTJ because it is the most prominent TJ consulting organization. Recall, the organization is said to be the "guardian of 'real' truth commissions."[56] Accordingly, it is well poised to shape commission designs around the globe. If it is influential in commission design, other experts may also be influential. However, if the organization is not effective, other experts are not likely to be effective.

[54] Seventy-four of the universe of eighty-four commissions are included in the analysis. I was unable to locate mandate documents for ten commissions, among them the three Lebanese commissions deployed in the early 2000s to investigate disappearances in the 1970s, 1980s, and 1990s. The reason why these documents are not available might not be random.

[55] For this measure, I consulted the ICTJ's website, specifically the "Our Work" section and its subsections.

[56] Ancelovici and Jenson 2013, 302.

Selection into ICTJ Involvement

Governments generally initiate a relationship with the ICTJ, though domestic NGOs are sometimes the ones to invite the organization and subsequently connect it with policymakers. But in no cases does the ICTJ get involved without an invitation. "We don't impose but we provide expertise and share knowledge," shared Rim El Gantri, head of the ICTJ's Libya, Afghanistan, and Central African Republic programs and who previously led the ICTJ's Nepal office.

Unlike its INGO peers Amnesty International and HRW, which are more on the advocacy side of the global TJ network, the ICTJ is more on the operational side. It does not get involved to shame a government or to work at cross purposes with the government; the ICTJ is interested in being an operational partner from the very beginning. So an invitation is important. This is true on both sides of the relationship, for the ICTJ as for governments, which seek the organization's critical endorsement.

Of course, the ICTJ does not always accept invitations. In particular, the organization does not enter contexts where "it seems that the government doesn't have a credible commitment to [implementing] a commission" (e.g., in Serbia).[57] So, theoretically, it is possible that the ICTJ lends its expertise to countries where having a strong commission is easier. But, in practice, as Figure 4.1 reveals, the ICTJ has been involved in a variety of contexts and countries—in places as "easy" as Brazil since 2007 and as "difficult" as Côte d'Ivoire in the aftermath of the 2011 crisis. There, the respective truth commissions resulted in drastically different results.

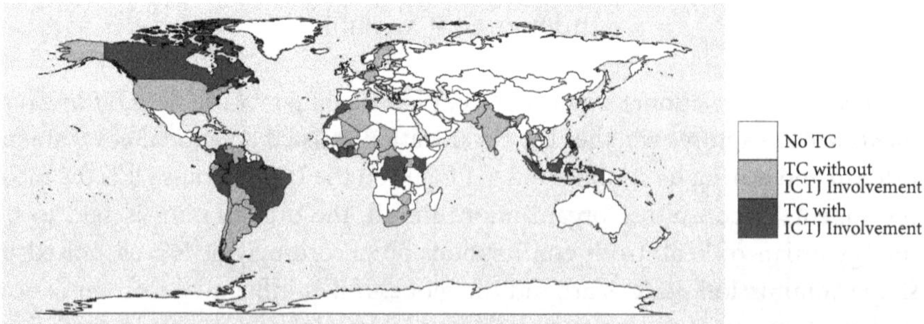

Figure 4.1 The ICTJ and Truth Commissions Around the World (1970–2018)
Note: The map shows in light gray countries that had truth commissions without ICTJ involvement and in dark gray countries that had truth commissions with ICTJ involvement.

[57] Author interview with Priscilla Hayner.

Some countries where the ICTJ has lent its expert assistance are democracies (e.g., Peru in 2001), whereas others are autocracies (e.g., Morocco in 2004). Some countries are still mired in political violence when the ICTJ becomes involved in supporting prospective TJ efforts (e.g., Kenya since 2009), while others are revisiting abuses in the recent past (e.g., Canada in 2009). Other countries, still, are confronting both historical and contemporary state violence when the ICTJ intervenes, one case being the United States since 2020.

Control Variables

I control for potentially confounding factors, including the subject of inquiry, diffusion, and regime type.

First, to account for the possibility that the subject of inquiry influences institutional design, I use two dichotomous indicators, one that captures whether a commission was created to account for abuses perpetrated during an authoritarian regime and another that captures whether a commission was created to account for abuses perpetrated during an internal armed conflict. The omitted categories are commissions created as a response to government killings of civilians, coups, foreign occupation, and so on.

Second, it may be that some design features of commissions more often appear in some geographic regions than in others. The story here would be that governments replicate their neighbors' practices. To account for regional diffusion, I calculate, for a given country, the number of commissions in its geographic subregion (e.g., West Africa) that possessed a given investigative power. I also account for time, or global diffusion, using a simple count of the number of years since 1970.

Third, transitional commissions may have stronger mandates than non-transitional commissions, as the former are likely more politically salient than the latter. Thus, I include a binary variable that takes a value of 1 if a commission was created within five years of the abuses it was tasked with investigating. This measure is a helpful proxy for political salience, including in countries that had a leadership transition but without a full regime change, like when one autocrat succeeds another.

Fourth, commissions installed in democracies may be more likely to have strong mandates. Research finds that democracies are more likely to credibly commit to a variety of human rights institutions.[58] This logic naturally extends to TJ. So I include Boix and coauthors' dichotomous measure of democracy.[59]

[58] See, for example, Simmons (2009).
[59] Boix et al. 2013.

I also account for the strength of domestic civil society. I consider this more of a control variable than an explanatory variable because my interview data indicate that when international experts are not part of the design process, a commission is unlikely to have a strong architecture and a clear direction (i.e., regardless of the strength of domestic civil society groups). Hayner emphasized that it is international experts who have the most experience; they know well the potential and pitfalls of commissions and commission designs. She emphasized, "Even the best and brightest of a country haven't grappled with a truth commission before." To put it another way, it does not follow that a strong domestic civil society is associated with the drafting of a legal mandate that includes powers that international experts consider useful to a commission's work. Nonetheless, to properly evaluate the burden sharing model, it is important for me to include domestic civil society in the analysis.

Descriptive Statistics

Figure 4.1 displays all commissions in the sample, seventy-four in total.[60] The ICTJ's work has reached every continent, though its work on commissions has been concentrated in the Global South. The organization has advised governments that established roughly one in three commissions historically.[61]

A minority of commissions in the sample possessed the power to subpoena testimony (36 percent) and the power to preserve evidence (34 percent). A small majority was empowered to trace antecedents (56 percent), while a large majority was tasked with investigating a range of abuses (77 percent). Sixty-nine percent of commissions examined abuses perpetrated under authoritarian governments, and 39 percent examined abuses perpetrated during internal armed conflicts. Approximately two-thirds of commissions in the sample were adopted in democracies. Roughly two-thirds were transitional commissions.[62]

Figure 4.2 shows the percentage of commissions that had a wide material scope of inquiry, separated by ICTJ involvement. The difference is visually striking: Approximately four in five commissions in countries with ICTJ involvement possessed both the power to consider a range of abuses and to trace antecedents. This figure is halved for commissions in countries without ICTJ involvement.

Next, Figure 4.3 shows the percentage of commissions that had effective evidence-gathering powers, separated by ICTJ involvement. The difference

[60] There are seventy-five observations in the dataset because one of the commissions was a "truth and friendship commission" created by the Indonesian and East Timorese governments. I count it for each side.

[61] The ICTJ has been involved in nearly one-half of all countries that adopted commissions since its founding in 2001.

[62] See Tables B.1 and B.2 in online Appendix B.

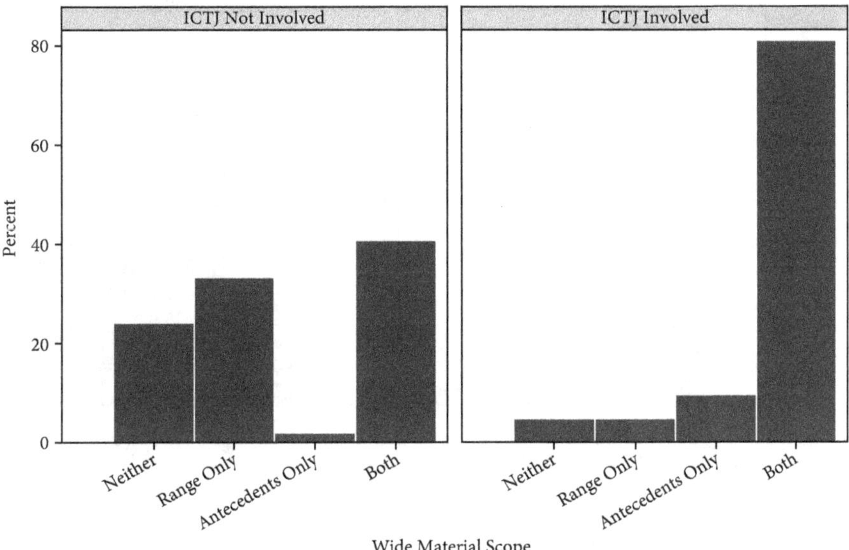

Figure 4.2 The ICTJ and Truth Commissions' Scope of Inquiry

Note: The figure shows the percentage of commissions with (1) neither the power to study a range of abuses nor the power to trace antecedents of abuses, (2) just one of the powers, or (3) both powers, separated by ICTJ involvement.

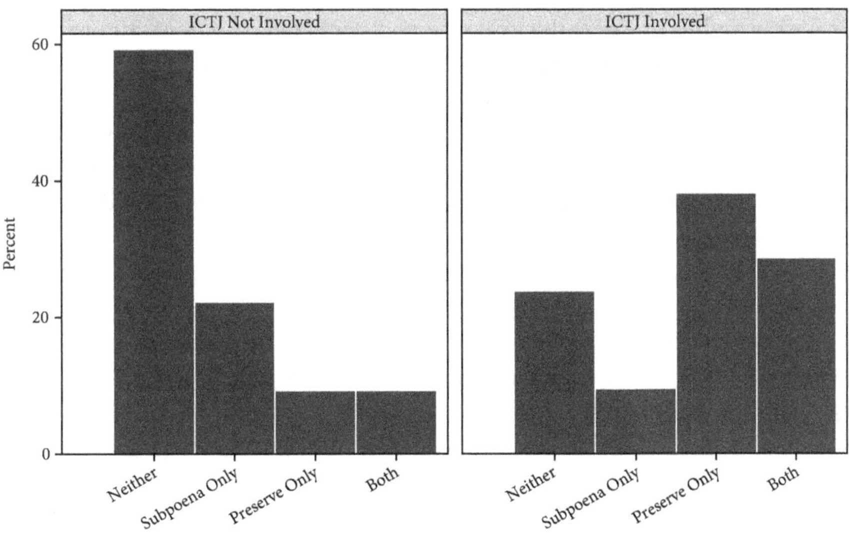

Figure 4.3 The ICTJ and Truth Commissions' Evidence-Gathering Powers

Note: The figure shows the percentage of commissions with (1) neither subpoena powers nor evidence-preservation powers, (2) just one of the powers, or (3) both powers, separated by ICTJ involvement.

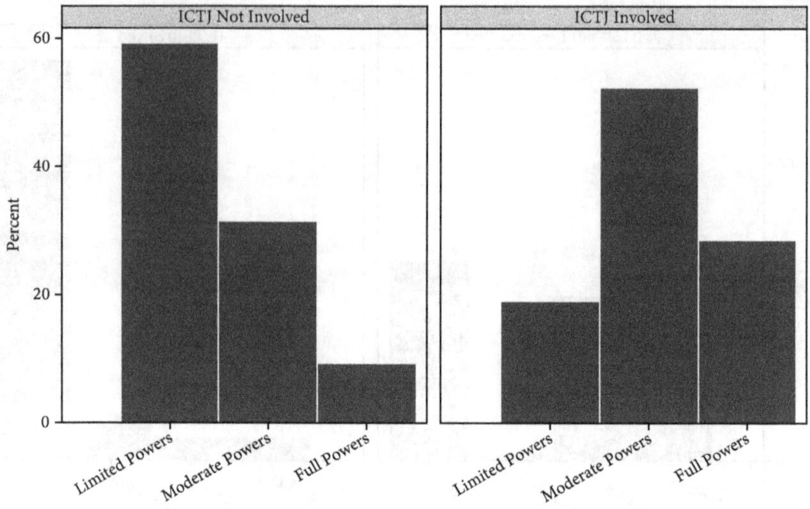

Figure 4.4 The ICTJ and Truth Commission Powers

Note: The figure shows the percentage of commissions with (1) limited powers, (2) moderate powers, or (3) full powers, separated by ICTJ involvement.

is also notable: Nearly 29 percent of commissions in countries with ICTJ involvement possessed both the power to compel testimony and other material evidence and to preserve the evidence once gathered. Less than 10 percent of commissions in countries without ICTJ involvement possessed both powers.

In turn, Figure 4.4 shows the percentage of commissions that had limited, moderate, or full powers of investigation, separated by ICTJ involvement. A commission had full powers if it had *both* a wide material scope *and* effective evidence-gathering powers; moderate powers if it had *either* a wide material scope *or* effective evidence-gathering powers; or limited powers. Here, too, the difference is clear: A greater share of commissions in countries with ICTJ involvement possessed all four powers.

The differences that I observe between commissions in countries with and without ICTJ involvement are not simply artifacts of time. Figures B.1 ▶ to B.3 ▶ in online Appendix B capture just commissions established since the ICTJ's creation in 2001. The differences remain stark.

Hypothesis Testing

For the analysis, I run logit regressions for each commission power, with standard errors clustered by country. The results of the primary analysis are presented here in Figure 4.5 and in Table B.3 ▶ in online Appendix B. The results

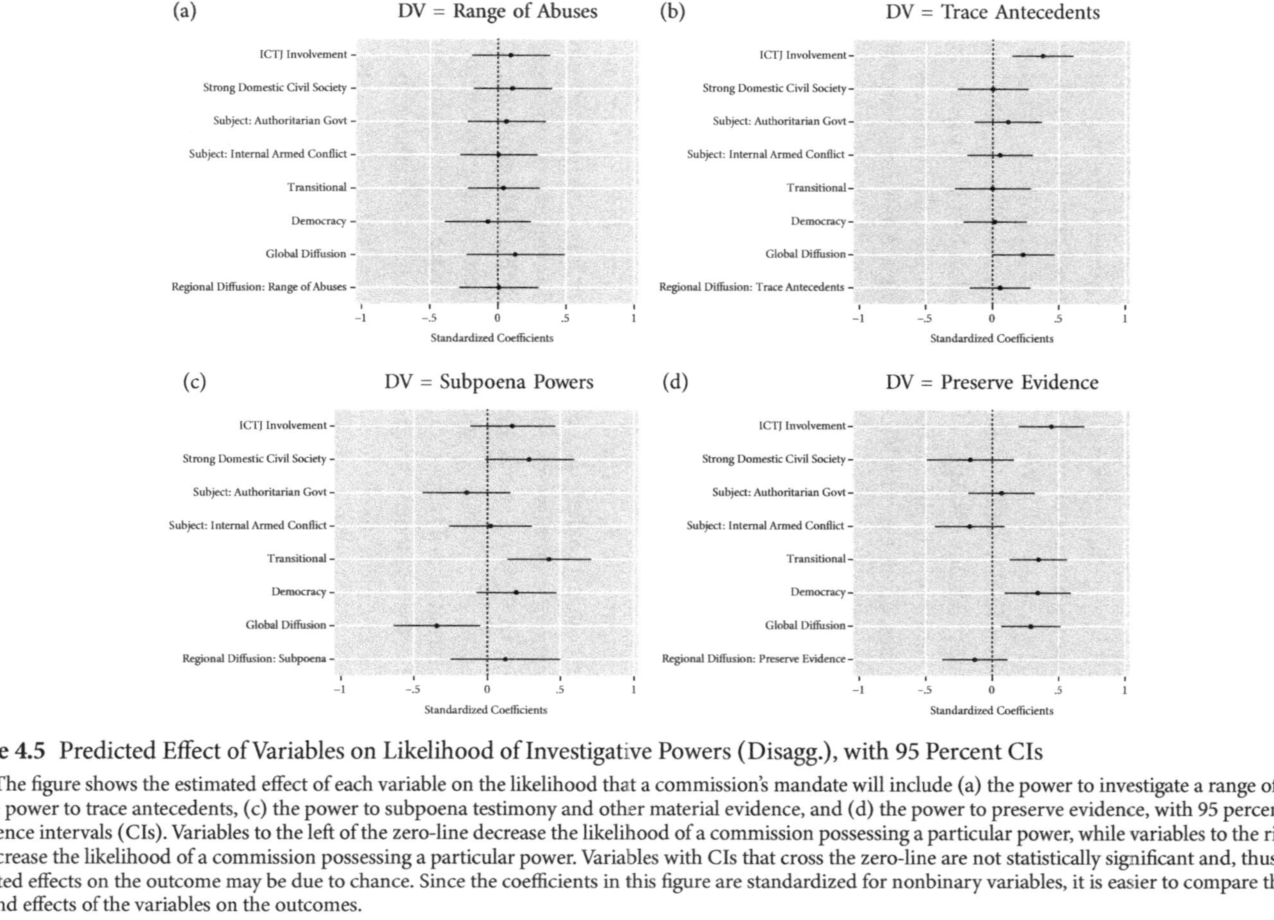

Figure 4.5 Predicted Effect of Variables on Likelihood of Investigative Powers (Disagg.), with 95 Percent CIs

Note: The figure shows the estimated effect of each variable on the likelihood that a commission's mandate will include (a) the power to investigate a range of abuses, (b) the power to trace antecedents, (c) the power to subpoena testimony and other material evidence, and (d) the power to preserve evidence, with 95 percent confidence intervals (CIs). Variables to the left of the zero-line decrease the likelihood of a commission possessing a particular power, while variables to the right of the line increase the likelihood of a commission possessing a particular power. Variables with CIs that cross the zero-line are not statistically significant and, thus, their estimated effects on the outcome may be due to chance. Since the coefficients in this figure are standardized for nonbinary variables, it is easier to compare the relative sizes and effects of the variables on the outcomes.

of a secondary analysis are presented here in Figure 4.7 and in Table B.4 ▶ in online Appendix B.[63]

Primary Analysis

I first consider TJ experts' influence on governments setting a wide material scope of inquiry; that is, whether expert-advised governments are more likely to charge commissions with uncovering a range of abuses (Hypothesis 1a) and tracing antecedents (Hypothesis 1b). While I do not find support for Hypothesis 1a, I do find support for Hypothesis 1b. *ICTJ Involvement* is a positive and statistically significant predictor ($p<0.05$) of a commission being charged with tracing antecedents. Substantively, the probability of a mandate that provides for investigating root causes, given expert advice, is quite high. Analyzing marginal effects, the estimated probability of the outcome when the ICTJ is involved is 82.9 percent, compared to 39.6 percent when the ICTJ is not involved, holding all other variables constant. The roughly 43 percentage point difference is significant at the 0.1 percent error level.

It is possible that differences in statistical significance owe to the fact that government commission designers tend to task commissions with examining a range of abuses (74 percent of commissions without ICTJ involvement possessed this power, compared to 86 percent of commissions with ICTJ involvement). This stands in contrast to designers assigning commissions to determine root causes (43 percent of commissions without ICTJ involvement possessed this power, compared to 90 percent of commissions with ICTJ involvement). There seems to be more room to move countries on investigating antecedents.

Next, I consider international TJ experts' influence on governments endowing commissions with effective evidence-gathering powers; that is, whether expert-advised governments are more likely to supply commissions with subpoena powers (Hypothesis 2a) and evidence-preservation powers (Hypothesis 2b). While I do not find support for Hypothesis 2a, I do find support for Hypothesis 2b. *ICTJ Involvement* is a positive and statistically significant predictor ($p<0.01$) of a commission enjoying the power to preserve evidence. Substantively, the estimated probability of a mandate that provides for evidence preservation, given ICTJ advisement, is also rather large. Holding all other variables constant, the estimated probability of the outcome when the ICTJ is involved is 63.6 percent, compared to 17.6 percent when the ICTJ is not involved. The 46 percentage point difference is significant at the 1 percent error level.

[63] Note, the small number of observations means that it should be harder to find statistically significant results.

Looking to domestic actors, a strong domestic civil society helps predict just one commission power—subpoena—albeit only at the 10 percent error level. The limited statistical significance notwithstanding, this is an interesting finding, given the controversy that almost always surrounds commissions with subpoena powers. Whether to aid commissions by not saddling them with an early opposition or to inhibit the extent of their investigation (and possible collaboration with courts), leaders in diverse contexts resist the advice of international experts to give commissions the power to compel testimony. Commissions with subpoena powers are also sometimes perceived as more retributive than conciliatory or restorative; so, leaders could keep this specific power off the table, depending on their goals.

Secondary Analysis

The analysis so far treats investigative powers as independent of each other. But perhaps they are not. It could be that once experts convince a government to have a commission study a range of abuses, they insist less on it tracing antecedents. That way, they might be able to secure at least one key evidence-gathering power for the commission. Similarly, if experts convince a government to have a commission preserve evidence, they might push less hard for subpoena powers. Instead, they might be able to get the commission a broader scope. Experts could also try and push for as much of everything as possible. To probe these possibilities, I run ordinary least squares regressions for three different combinations of truth commission design features.

Figure 4.6 displays the overall strength of commission designs (an index of all four commission powers), separated by ICTJ involvement. The difference is clear: The ICTJ's involvement is associated with commissions with stronger designs.[64] Before moving on to the regressions, the results of which are presented in Figure 4.7 and in Table B.4 ▶ in online Appendix B, I summarize the dependent variables.

The dependent variable in Figure 4.7(a), *Wider Material Scope*, is a three-point index that combines a commission's power to investigate a range of abuses and its power to trace antecedents. A commission receives a value of 0 if it had neither power, 1 if it had a single power, and 2 if it had both powers. To give a few examples of ICTJ-advised commissions, the Moroccan commission is coded as 0 because it possessed neither power; the Canadian commission is coded as 1 because it could trace antecedents but was limited to examining abuses in the

[64] Figure B.4 ▶ in online Appendix B captures commissions established since 2001 and the relationship persists.

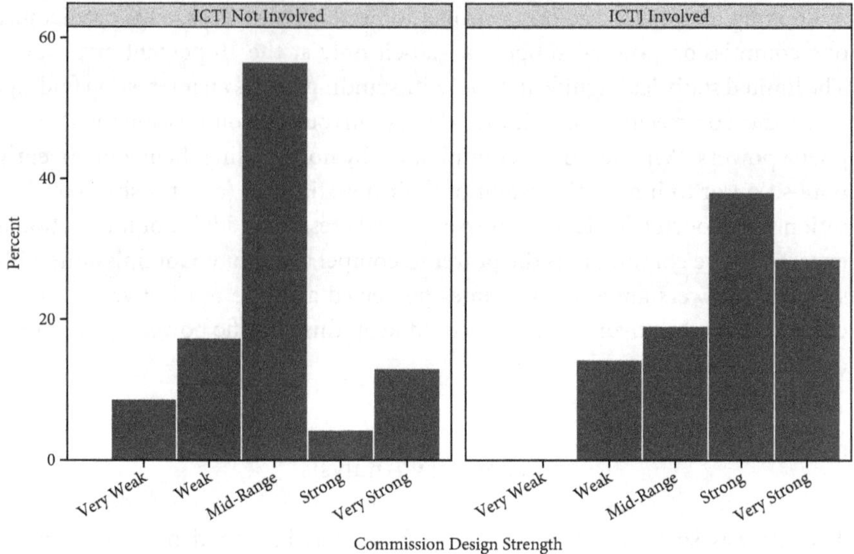

Figure 4.6 The ICTJ and the Overall Strength of Truth Commission Designs
Note: The figure shows the percentage of commissions whose designs were (1) very weak, (2) weak, (3) mid-range, (4) strong, or (5) very strong, separated by ICTJ involvement.

Indian residential school system; and both Colombian commissions are coded as 2 because they could both consider a range of abuses and identify root causes.

The dependent variable in Figure 4.7(b), *More Effective Evidence Gathering*, is also a three-point index that combines a commission's power to compel testimony and its power to preserve evidence. A commission receives a value of 0 if it had neither power, 1 if it had a single power, and 2 if it had both powers. To again give some examples of countries where the ICTJ advised governments, Côte d'Ivoire is coded as 0 because it possessed neither power; Peru is coded as 1 because it had evidence-preservation powers but not subpoena powers; and the Solomon Islands is coded as 2 because it possessed both subpoena and evidence-preservation powers.

The dependent variable in Figure 4.7(c), *Stronger Overall Commission*, is a five-point index that combines all four commission powers. The minimum value possible is 0, meaning a commission lacked all key powers, and the maximum value possible is 4, meaning a commission possessed all key powers. Among ICTJ-assisted countries, Timor-Leste is coded as 4 for *Stronger Overall Commission* because its commission possessed all powers of interest, but its later joint commission with Indonesia is coded as 3 because that one lacked subpoena powers. Nepal's 2015 TRC is coded as 2, with a wider material scope but no powers for effectively gathering evidence. Meanwhile, Morocco is coded as 1 for its

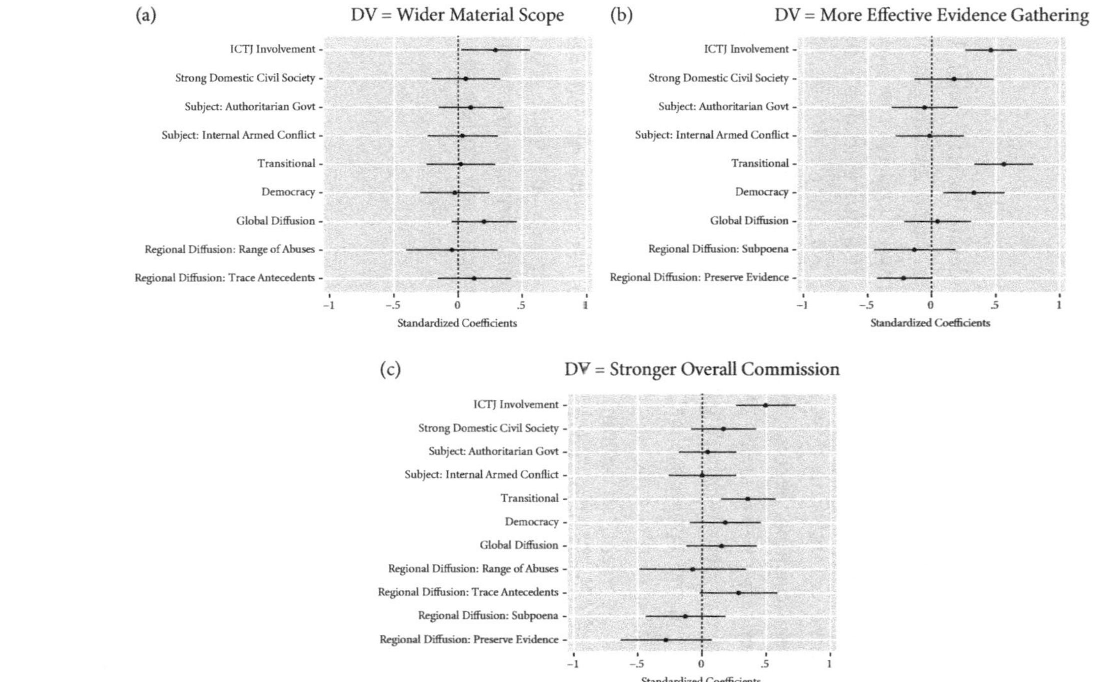

Figure 4.7 Predicted Effect of Variables on Likelihood of Investigative Powers (Agg.), with 95 Percent CIs

Note: The figure shows the estimated effect of each variable on the likelihood that a commission's mandate will have (a) a wider material scope of inquiry, (b) more effective evidence gathering, and will produce (c) a stronger overall commission, with 95 percent CIs. Variables to the left of the zero-line decrease the likelihood of a commission possessing one or more of the four component powers, while variables to the right of the line increase the likelihood of a commission possessing one or more of the four component powers. Variables with CIs that cross the zero-line are not statistically significant and, thus, their estimated effects on the outcome may be due to chance. Because the coefficients in this figure are standardized for nonbinary variables, it is easier to compare the relative sizes and effects of the variables on the outcomes.

evidence-preservation powers. No ICTJ-assisted commissions received a 0. To give an example from the broader sample of cases, the Algerian commission had none of the four key powers.

As seen here in Figure 4.7 and in Table B.4 ⊙ in online Appendix B, for every combination of powers, *ICTJ Involvement* is a positive and statistically significant predictor of the outcome.

Alternative Explanations

Domestic and international political factors may moderate international TJ experts' influence on the design of commission mandates. These include a commission's subject of inquiry, commission type, regime type, and regional and global precedents. First, while a commission's subject of inquiry accounts for some variation in some commission design features, I do not estimate statistically significant relationships. Second, regime and commission type have noteworthy positive effects in two areas. Democratic commissions are more likely to possess effective evidence-gathering powers. Transitional commissions, for their part, are more likely to possess effective evidence-gathering powers and be stronger overall. These results generally comport with the scholarship that argues that transitions represent "an opening" and, thus, can provide interested groups the opportunity to prevail on governments to design strong commissions. Similarly, scholarship demonstrates that democracies are more likely than non-democracies to credibly commit to human rights norms, instruments, and institutions. Third, while regional and global precedents can explain some variation in design features, their effects are not stable or consistent.

Practitioner Insights

I conducted interviews in the spring and summer of 2019 with current and former ICTJ leaders and staff members to discern the issues they encounter when attempting to set the parameters for effective truth seeking. I also ran a small focus group in the summer of 2019 at the ICTJ's New York headquarters. Later in the spring of 2022, I distributed a questionnaire to all current ICTJ leaders and staff members and some former personnel, approximately fifty people in total, to paint a portrait of the organization and to understand how different experts were connected to the commissions captured in the *Varieties of Truth Commissions* datasets. The questionnaire and follow-up correspondence and interviews also helped me pin down the division of labor (i.e., burden sharing) between domestic and international members of the TJ network and their engagement with governments at the commission design stage.

Who Are the ICTJ's Experts?

My survey of ICTJ leaders and staff members yielded a response rate of 36 percent. The average career length in TJ was fourteen years, with a minimum of three years and a maximum of thirty-two years. The average number of years since they first worked with the ICTJ, specifically, was ten years, with a minimum of two years and a maximum of nineteen years. Nearly all were local advocates, lawyers, government employees, and even truth commission officials in diverse countries prior to joining the organization. Most are based abroad, in the field. They have led and staffed the organization's in-country offices around the globe and supported commissions and other processes. One example is María Cielo Linares, an Argentine TJ expert, who has supported both the 2005 and 2018 Colombian commissions. Another example is Mohamed Suma, who supported the commission in his native Sierra Leone, as well as the Special Court for Sierra Leone. He heads the ICTJ's Côte d'Ivoire program, where he works with Didier Gbery, who joined as a program officer in 2013 during his country's post-conflict transition and reconstruction. In addition to the commission in Côte d'Ivoire, Gbery has supported commissions in Tunisia and leads the ICTJ's Gambia program. These profiles are not at all unusual in the dense network of international TJ experts.

How Are Experts and Truth Commissions Connected?

With few exceptions, the ICTJ personnel I surveyed have supported multiple commissions, in various capacities, with some involved in as few as two commissions to as many as thirteen, with longtime collaborators Ruben Carranza, Eduardo González, and Howard Varney tied for most commissions served, eight of them together. As discussed, many ICTJ personnel have a prior background in human rights advocacy. Carranza, González, and Varney are no exceptions.

Carranza became involved in TJ in 2003 in his native country, the Philippines, as a commissioner on the Presidential Commission on Good Government. He was also a member of the ad hoc UN committee that drafted the Convention Against Corruption. Previously, he was a faculty member at the University of the Philippines and, prior to that, assistant secretary of national defense. He has been with the ICTJ since 2007.

González got his start as an intern for the NGO Coalition for the International Criminal Court while a graduate student at the New School in 1998. After this, he returned to his native Peru in 2000 to serve as the public hearings and victim protection director of the Peruvian commission. Later, he served as a member of the editorial committee, helping to design, compile, draft, and approve the commission's final report, which was published in 2003. From there, he joined the ICTJ, serving twelve years in multiple roles, from senior associate, to deputy director for the Americas, to director of the Truth and Memory Program. He is now an independent consultant and the UN independent expert for Mali.

Varney launched his TJ career as a human rights lawyer in South Africa in the early 1990s. He consulted on the South African commission, was the chief investigator for the Sierra Leonean commission, and helped compile the final report of the Timorese commission, to give just a few highlights. He started at the ICTJ in 2008 as director of truth seeking and serves as senior expert for programs. He continues to practice constitutional, administrative, and human rights law in South Africa.

Hayner, one of the ICTJ's cofounders, transitioned after a decade to consultancy work, with private organizations like the Centre for Humanitarian Dialogue in Switzerland and UN bodies like the Office of the United Nations High Commissioner for Human Rights (OHCHR). After supporting peace negotiations in Kenya and Colombia, she was appointed a senior mediation advisor with the UN Standby Team.

So when it comes to the global TJ network, there is a great deal of overlap and coordination. Some figures move from the domestic side to the international side, and also move from NGOs, commissions, and governments to INGOs and even IOs.

Experts, Commission Design, and Effective Truth Seeking

Now, what is the relationship between experts and the design of truth commissions? While I answered this question in the quantitative analysis above, I also wanted to answer it qualitatively. I did this by conducting interviews with current and former ICTJ leaders and staff members and leading a small focus group at the organization's New York headquarters. I supplemented these interviews and the focus group with interviews with former commission officials and advisors.

Virginie Ladisch, senior expert for truth seeking and civic engagement, gave me a helpful framing of the ICTJ's efforts to support effective truth seeking. She said, "We always aim to facilitate a reflection on the full range of harms . . . whether we're doing work on truth seeking or on reparations. . . . You don't want to have a selective [mechanism] . . . so we would always encourage . . .

as robust an examination of past violations as possible. . . . And then I think it's a back-and-forth with . . . what the political context allows."

For example, the political context does not always allow for a commission to have subpoena powers. To illustrate, subpoena powers did not make it into the mandate of the Truth and Dignity Commission in Tunisia because "there was no intention to reflect that the truth commission is a revenge commission," said Salwa El Gantri, head of the ICTJ's Tunisia office. She added, "We were still in the two years after the revolution," and for local leaders, "it was important to reflect that this mechanism is there for an ultimate reconciliation." While a commission having subpoena powers need not imply vengeance or precipitate retributive justice via courts, local perceptions, concerns, and priorities matter.

This approach has limits, however. As I discussed with Ladisch, the Canadian TRC lacked subpoena powers, as there was an understanding that the government would furnish documents and other materials the commission required regarding the Indian residential school system. But the government did not always deliver on this. So this design choice was costly.

Of course, this is not to say that strong commission designs are costless—quite the opposite. Designers can waste time and momentum, González indicated, citing the Truth, Justice, and Reconciliation Commission in Kenya. This thought-provoking statement resonated with another from Senior Expert for Programs Cristián Correa. "Who are you sacrificing for the perfect?" he asked.

Certainly, mandates represent the earliest steps toward truth seeking, not the end, emphasized Senior Expert for Programs Ruben Carranza, who participated in my focus group with Anna Myriam Roccatello, deputy executive director and director of programs, and Sibley Hawkins, a programs expert. Carranza said mandates are important but not necessarily determining. For him, it does not follow that commissions that start with limited powers and expectations will necessarily be unable to conduct a robust investigation. Roccatello similarly conveyed, "More power does not mean better results," and commissions with less power "can [still] make a huge difference."

The Guatemalan commission is an excellent case in point. While the commission *did* have a mandate to investigate a range of abuses and trace antecedents, it lacked the power to compel testimony and to preserve evidence. The military strongly opposed anything that could one day lead to criminal prosecutions. Based on the mandate alone, this commission was not exactly "set up for success." Yet, despite these limitations, the Guatemalan commission is one of the strongest commissions in history, thanks in large part to civil society groups who shared in investigating abuses and reaching witnesses, and kept records.

That said, some commissions "have it all" on the design front but do not exercise all of their powers because they do not need to do so. Pat Walsh—an

Australian human rights advocate who worked with East Timorese leaders for many years and helped establish and advise the CAVR—shared with me:

> CAVR had all the powers required to fulfill its mandate but did not need to exercise all of them, including its full suite of inquiry-related powers, because it received the full cooperation it needed, at least within Timor-Leste . . . the commission's inquiry-related powers did not extend to governments or institutions outside Timor-Leste that were widely believed to have been actively complicit with the Indonesian military's violence and excesses in Timor-Leste . . . this undercut the international impact of the commission.

There are also the commissions that possess key powers but fail to engage in effective truth seeking, either through under-use, as was the case with subpoenas in Sierra Leone, or because leaders lack a serious commitment to the process, as in the Democratic Republic of the Congo, Côte d'Ivoire, and others.[65] Roccatello described the Ivorian commission as a "humongous, obscene waste of money" that yielded virtually "no victim testimony." For her and other experts, "The key is not to judge inputs with outputs; they don't always go hand in hand."

I was surprised when one of my research participants said they actually *did not* expect expert-supported commissions to be more likely to possess strong powers. Coming from someone with a long professional relationship with the ICTJ and a deep personal commitment to its success, this was a jarring statement. However, as our conversation progressed, it became clear that this statement was shaped less by doubts about the organization's abilities and more by evergreen challenges in the contexts in which it operates. Rather than suggesting that expert advisement is the definitive factor, the interviewee suggested instead "deep political factors" that influence the strength of mandates as well as commissions' subsequent success. Indeed, there are significant domestic political and institutional factors that circumscribe the organization's influence, as the quantitative analysis also shows.

Likewise, I was struck by González's warning that, though a wide material scope of inquiry is consistent with human rights principles and victims' right to truth, a commission given this charge runs the risk of disappointing people if it does not succeed in establishing key facts across the range of abuses or if it is unable to elucidate root causes and identify solutions. In a similar vein, while it is useful to have strong powers enumerated in the mandate, González commented that this is no guarantee that they will be used or be effective. Hawkins urged remaining circumspect after the commission design stage, especially for victims' sake. Echoing Roccatello, she remarked that how a commission

[65] Rana and Zvobgo 2021; Zvobgo 2019*a*; Zvobgo and Crawford 2023.

starts is not necessarily how it finishes. Thus, the commission process must be monitored. Further, for a commission to reach its full potential or effect, its recommendations must be implemented.

Rim El Gantri, González, Hayner, and Ladisch revealed an additional element of commission design that I did not initially consider but that I have come to realize is quite important: the selection of commission officials. Based on their professional experience, presidential or parliamentary appointments to commissions are not ideal; public nominations are preferable, as merit, not political connections, becomes the selection criterion. While not directly anticipated by my theory, the increasing use of merit-based selection of commission officials has been made possible by international consultants, namely the ICTJ. Hayner relayed, "That level of international experience and technical input is valuable."

Burden Sharing Among Domestic Civil Society and International Experts

I followed up with several ICTJ representatives to pin down burden sharing within the global TJ network at the institutional design stage. I also wanted to better understand their engagement with governments. Rim El Gantri is one of the participants I followed up with. She first got involved in TJ in her native Tunisia in 2011, starting as a program associate in the ICTJ's Tunisia office and then serving as head of program from 2013 to 2016. She revealed to me the inner workings of the global TJ network and how the ICTJ, in consultation and collaboration with local civil society organizations, was able to influence policymakers as they crafted the Tunisian commission's mandate.

Together with the UNDP and the OHCHR, the ICTJ advised the committee that drafted the Organic Law on Establishing and Organizing Transitional Justice, which created the commission. The drafting committee comprised twelve members (two from the Ministry of Human Rights and Transitional Justice and ten representatives of five civil society organizations). Much like in Timor-Leste, which I covered at the beginning of this chapter, the founding law on TJ was drafted after a national consultative process, the National Dialogue on Transitional Justice, which the ICTJ helped design and implement with the ministry and civil society. "Our role was mainly to build the capacities of the members of the [various] committees so they [had] a better understanding and knowledge on comparative experiences, lessons learned and best practices so they could draft the law," Rim El Gantri affirmed. The ICTJ then commented on the draft legislation and helped sensitize members of the National Constituent Assembly (Tunisia's post-Ben Ali government) "so they could understand the law they were voting [on]."

Rim El Gantri's colleague, Salwa El Gantri, shared that the "internationals," including the ICTJ, "brought on board their expertise but it was necessary to do [everything] in consultancy with the locals to ensure a minimum of ownership for the whole operation." The idea of local ownership over TJ mechanisms' design and operation is something that came up in multiple conversations.

Correa described the Timorese commission as "a foreign truth commission," precisely because the UNTAET and other international actors who oversaw key TJ efforts did not adequately engage locals, both in the NGO community and in the future government. This has negatively affected the Timorese commission's impact and implementation of its recommendations, as I will elaborate on in Chapter 8. Alas, cases like Timor-Leste are more common than cases like Tunisia in terms of how much (or, more accurately, how little) local civil society groups are included at the commission mandate drafting stage, in Virginie Ladisch's experience.

Still, the ICTJ aims to conduct assessments "of all the different actors, in the capital, and also outside the capital, recognizing that [local organizations] that are capital based might have one set of demands . . . and then you go out to the rural areas and they're like, 'Those people don't represent me.'" In this way, the ICTJ helps bring in local civil society perspectives to their own governments. "As an international NGO, sometimes we have access that [they] wouldn't have," Ladisch summarized.

The ICTJ generally works within a tight time frame when negotiating mandates with governments and other local stakeholders. Sometimes they receive a draft and the government wants feedback in two weeks or a month at most. So they must work quickly, playing a leading role, as my model of burden sharing indicates for this stage of the truth commission process, while local groups play a supporting role.

Implications

Both the quantitative and qualitative analyses in this chapter demonstrate how commissions are not created equally; they are not similarly positioned to uncover and help safeguard against harm. In other words, commissions' expected capability varies, at least from an institutional design perspective. I documented considerable variation in commission mandates, notably between commissions in countries that were and that were not advised by international TJ experts, between democracies and non-democracies, and between transitional and non-transitional commissions. These results bear special relevance for scholars, practitioners, and donor governments and agencies.

For scholars, variation in commission design may help explain perennially mixed results in studies of truth commission "impact." For donors, this chapter indicates specific areas to place benchmarks. Historically, international donors have invested resources in commissions without estimating a return on investment based, at least in part, on implementing established best practices.[66] Thus, donors, in cooperation with civil society organizations, may consider ways to guide differently situated governments toward the same goal (e.g., by conditioning funding support on implementing particular design features, like the power to compel testimony).

Importantly, this chapter reveals that civil society's influence is not limited to commission adoption. It extends to shaping commissions' substance, including specific powers of investigation conferred in commissions' founding texts.

Conclusion

Over the past five decades, truth commissions have proliferated globally in response to the growing TJ norm. However, little attention has been paid to commission design and variation in design features across political contexts. While we might expect that commission design is a function of the subject of inquiry, regional politics, or global diffusion, scholarship has lacked a comprehensive assessment.

In this second empirical chapter, I presented a study that draws on a range of original data, including the first *Varieties of Truth Commissions* dataset, interviews with current and former ICTJ leaders, and a focus group with current ICTJ leadership and staff. I demonstrated that members of the global TJ network are not only critical for truth commission adoption; they are also important for commission design. I found support for my argument that international TJ experts, notably the ICTJ, influence governments' commission design choices.

Examining truth commissions in diverse political contexts, with diverse subjects and occurring in different regions and at different times in history, I found a positive and significant association between ICTJ involvement and governments charging commissions with tracing antecedents, not solely documenting instances of abuse. I also found a positive and significant association between ICTJ involvement and governments affording commissions evidence-preservation powers. However, ICTJ involvement was not a significant predictor of commissions possessing the power to investigate a range of abuses or enjoying subpoena powers. In follow-on analyses, ICTJ involvement was a consistently significant predictor of commissions' overall powers and strength.

The qualitative data provided support to the results of the quantitative analysis and helped sharpen the initial propositions. Interviews disclosed that advice from experts is valuable and consequential; nonetheless, it comes second to

[66] Quinn 2011; Gillooly et al. 2024.

domestic political considerations. Interviews and a focus group also instructed that commission design represents just the first step and does not always predict success. Some commissions appear strong at the outset but are ultimately ineffective, while others at first seem weak but are nevertheless effective.

Crucially, I found further support for burden sharing among members of the global TJ network. While domestic and international groups respectively played leading and supporting roles at the truth commission adoption stage, international groups assumed a leading role and domestic groups took on a supporting role at the design stage. The findings motivate my exploration in the remaining chapters of civil society's role in shaping commission outcomes, namely implementation of recommendations.

5

Policy Entrepreneurship and Truth Commission Recommendations

Chapters 3 and 4 provided strong evidence for my theory that truth commissions are a transnational institution that is governed by domestic and international NGOs. These transnational actors engage in costly advocacy that makes acquiescence to demands for truth and justice a more attractive strategy for governments than outright refusal. Specifically, domestic NGOs record information on abuses and disseminate this information among their networks. They also cultivate local interest in truth and justice, including through protests and demonstrations. For their part, INGOs publicize the information they collect, both independently and from their domestic partners, and lobby target governments directly and indirectly, including via foreign governments and IOs that can impose a variety of sanctions on target governments. Together, domestic and international NGOs' efforts enhance the prospects of a commission being established.

NGOs then shift their target from institutional adoption to institutional design and quality. In particular, they work to ensure that the prospective truth commission has a clear direction and strong architecture so it can fulfill its role and responsibilities. Governments that wish to credibly signal their commitment to such a commission, lest they face censure at home and abroad, engage international experts as they design their commissions. This consultation process improves the odds of governments endowing commissions with strong investigative powers.

But, once commissions are installed, what do civil society actors do next? Prior research teaches us that civil society helps implement commissions. Concretely, groups help vernacularize the truth-seeking and truth-telling process within their national contexts (e.g., by embedding the process in customary legal and spiritual frameworks and practices as we saw in Chapter 4 with *lisan* in Timor-Leste). Civil society actors also serve as statement takers, trauma counselors, and program evaluators.[1] Existing scholarly accounts are very valuable—first, for their attention to domestic civil society during truth commission processes and, second, for the questions they provoke about what else domestic and international advocates do. Can they—and do they—propel commissions

[1] Backer 2003.

Governing Truth. Kelebogile Zvobgo, Oxford University Press. © Oxford University Press (2026).
DOI: 10.1093/oso/9780197815663.003.0005

beyond historical inquiries to instruments of policy change? I propose that the answer is "yes."

In this chapter, I argue that civil society organizations use truth commission outputs, namely recommendations, to produce normative and policy frameworks for governments. Using a range of political strategies, civil society groups push governments to implement additional TJ measures based on a commission's results. These measures include public education on historical violence, human rights prosecutions, material reparations, and personnel reforms, among others. And where governments are unwilling or unable to implement further measures, domestic organizations, with the material and political support of their international partners, attempt to substitute for governments and implement commission recommendations themselves. I demonstrate this argument across Chapters 6, 7, and 8 using the cases of Guatemala, South Africa, and Timor-Leste.

But, to understand what NGOs advocate for in the post-commission period, we must first know the menu of options. In other words, we need to identify the population from which NGOs select their advocacy priorities—that is, the universe of truth commission recommendations. Thus, I present, for the first time in the empirical study of TJ, the global landscape of commission recommendations.[2] This exercise grounds the rest of the book and situates my three main study countries in broader perspective.

The second *Varieties of Truth Commissions* dataset codes at the paragraph level nearly 6,000 recommendations made by fifty-five commissions from 1970 to 2018. The data are unusual, both for their broad inclusion of commissions and their granularity: Each recommendation was coded across approximately fifty variables, many of which I showcase in this chapter and in the three that follow.[3]

Only with data like these can we systematically evaluate civil society's influence in post-commission, post-violence countries. Moreover, only with data like these can scholars explore in a disciplined and rigorous way commissions' impact on post-violence politics—or the lack thereof. I supplement the

[2] I do not advance a theory of recommendations. This is a just-emerging area of scholarship. The first volume to seriously investigate recommendations, with a focus on thirteen Latin American cases, *Exploring Truth Commission Recommendations in a Comparative Perspective: Beyond Words Vol. I*, does not advance a theory of what recommendations are likely to be made and under what conditions. Skaar et al. (2022*a*) suggest several factors that may influence the formulation of recommendations, including organizational factors (e.g., commission mandates and work strategy), commissioner backgrounds, commission findings, the sociopolitical context in which a commission operates, and the work of previous commissions. But they do not generate and evaluate any particular theory and its alternatives. The main contribution of their chapter on formulation of recommendations is rich description. The present chapter follows in this vein but for the universe of cases with available data, rather than a selection of cases from a single world region.

[3] This data structure permits greater uniformity in coding and facilitates comparisons across commissions. It also reveals variation in the level of detail that different commissions afford to recommendations.

description of the quantitative data in this chapter with insights from my interviews with former commission officials, international TJ experts, and representatives of NGOs in Argentina, Canada, Chile, Costa Rica, Guatemala, Indonesia, Kenya, Sierra Leone, Timor-Leste, and the United States. The interviews help explain the content and scope of the dozens, and sometimes hundreds, of recommendations that commissions make.

I find that commission recommendations represent but a small share of the issues that commission leaders and staff members encounter during the course of their inquiry and that they believe governments must address. Of note, the interview data reveal yet more evidence of civil society's influence on truth commissions and TJ: NGOs, together with survivors and victims' families, help shape the content of commission recommendations. Importantly, NGOs use commission recommendations to push governments to implement additional TJ policies.

But how do they accomplish this? I lay out at the end of the chapter the argument and data that I evaluate in Chapters 6 to 8: NGOs attempt to set governments' post-commission agenda by selecting, among the numerous recommendations that commissions make to policymakers, a core set of policies to champion. Having established their advocacy goals, they prevail on governments to implement recommendations through diverse strategies like traditional lobbying and more provocative actions like protest. The theory predicts that (1) domestic groups, with the support of their international partners, advocate for recommendations that match their organizational interests, (2) governments are more likely to implement recommendations when they are pressured to do so by civil society groups, and (3) governments are more responsive to broader civil society coalitions than they are to narrower ones.

Plan of the Chapter

In the next two sections, I make the case that recommendations are the most straightforward way that we can assess NGOs' influence on post-truth commission TJ politics and the impact of commissions on post-violence societies. My approach is a rejoinder to prior work, in particular how scholars have defined and interpreted commissions' potentially positive impacts and the political actors that support them. I then introduce my data, which show how different recommendations relate to different political contexts, including whether they were made by transitional commissions, commissions investigating authoritarian governments or internal armed conflicts, and early and later commissions. I also address questions that emerge from the data using my interviews. Finally, I present my argument concerning NGOs' influence over governments' post-commission TJ policies and the research design for Chapters 6 to 8.

Why Should We Study Truth Commission Recommendations?

Prior scholarship lacks a clear understanding of what measures truth commissions have prescribed to policymakers in diverse contexts and countries, and which of these measures policymakers have moved to implement. The relative paucity of systematic studies on recommendations and implementation suggests a lack of scholarly interest in the topic.[4] This is troubling from a theoretical and empirical point of view.

On the theory side, recommendations provide a framework for policy change based on a commission's investigation and findings—a framework that civil society actors can and do use to move governments beyond their initial TJ commitments. On the empirics side, studying post-commission government policy without knowing the full range of options that were available to governments is, essentially, selecting on the dependent variable. Yet we must study both the "zeros" and the "ones." The implementation of recommendations likely correlates with democracy, human rights, and peace—outcomes of great interest and concern to scholars, governments, practitioners, and affected communities.

Persistently mixed results regarding the potential benefits, and even harms, of commissions (among a portfolio of TJ measures) may be an adverse consequence of the field's inattention to commission recommendations.[5] Indeed, an enduring question is whether and to what extent TJ mechanisms support democracy, human rights, peace, and the rule of law.[6] Regarding truth commissions in particular, scholarship is divided on their impact on human rights and democracy.[7]

Besides failing to produce consistent findings, a fundamental flaw in much of this work is that it does not explain exactly *how*, *why*, and *with whose help* commissions might contribute to democratization and democratic consolidation,

[4] Collaborative research by Martín et al. (2022), Skaar et al. (2022*a*, 2022*b*, 2025), and Wiebelhaus-Brahm et al. (2023) examining implementation of recommendations across a set of Latin American cases is an exception, as is work by Byrne et al. (2024) on implementation of memorialization projects.

[5] Mendeloff 2004.

[6] Some studies find that trials, either on their own or when combined with other TJ tools, support peacebuilding, democracy, and human rights (Akhavan 2001; Kim and Sikkink 2010; Lie et al. 2007; Olsen, Payne, and Reiter 2010; Olsen and Reiter 2010). Yet a substantial body of research finds the exact opposite. For the negative relationship between trials and peace and peacebulding, see Meernik (2005, 284). For the negative relationship between trials and human rights respect, see Snyder and Vinjamuri (2003/2004). Other research, still, finds limited and mixed results: Sikkink and Walling (2007) and Wiebelhaus-Brahm (2010) suggest that trials have limited effects on democracy, peace/stability, and human rights. For their part, Stromseth et al. (2006) do not find that tribunals increase support for the rule of law or enhance capacity building.

[7] While some work indicates limited or negative effects (Wiebelhaus-Brahm 2010, ch. 7), some research suggests a positive effect (Dancy and Thoms 2022; Nalepa 2022), including when commissions are combined with trials and amnesties (Kim and Sikkink 2010; Olsen, Payne, Reiter, and Wiebelhaus-Brahm 2010).

respect for the rule of law and human rights, and the durability of peace.[8] While commissions are often established in contexts where one or more of these outcomes is a goal, past work is not clear on how commissions themselves are positioned to produce them. Per Vinjamuri and Snyder, "Studies so far have rather loose connections between the logic of the theory and measurements of its core concepts."[9]

What *is* clear is that commissions are empowered to conduct an investigation—which often involves gathering and analyzing state documents, witness testimonies, and other evidence—and to prepare a report that synthesizes the findings and presents policy prescriptions. Notwithstanding, social scientists have not systematically examined truth commission reports, which, in addition to detailing commissions' research findings, contain recommendations.

Truth commissions make recommendations with a view to supporting additional efforts toward truth, justice, reparation, and institutional reform—issues for which domestic and international civil society groups advocate following commissions. If implemented, these measures can help foster the conditions that propel and sustain democracy, human rights, peace, and the rule of law. And, if analyzed, variation in implementation of commission recommendations may resolve the problem of mixed results. Just as civil society influences governments to implement recommendations, implementation of recommendations may contribute to and help sustain the aforementioned macro outcomes.

To summarize, understanding the *direct* effects of truth commissions and other TJ mechanisms (e.g., implementation of recommendations) may help us better understand their *indirect* effects (e.g., improved democratic representation, reduced repression, and decreased crime).[10]

Linking Truth Commissions with Political Outcomes via Recommendations

Truth commissions generally recommend additional steps toward truth, justice, reparation, and institutional reform, and sometimes propose services like rehabilitation and counseling. To underline their political significance and to emphasize why we should study them, I lay out below a few ways that different types of recommendations might contribute to good governance. In succeeding

[8] Research by Monika Nalepa, Geoff Dancy, and their collaborators is an exception. I highlight especially Nalepa (2022) and Dancy and Thoms (2022).

[9] Vinjamuri and Snyder 2015, 320.

[10] Ang and Nalepa 2019, Dancy et al. 2019, Trejo et al. 2018.

chapters, I show in detail how discrete recommendations have a positive impact on post-violence countries via civil society.

Truth and Peace

To begin, if implemented, recommendations about further truth revelation may support peace. For example, information disclosure, such as declassification and dissemination of state documents, can "reduce the number of lies that can be circulated unchallenged in public discourse"[11]—lies that can foment discord and jeopardize newly won peace. Likewise, education on the past, and on human rights more generally, can contribute to a well-informed and, consequently, more peaceful public. As an example, an educated public will likely be vigilant about ideas that enabled or precipitated violence in the past—for instance, the manufacture of an ethnic or religious "Other." As a result, such a public may reject politicians and parties that traffic in "othering" behaviors, race-baiting, and fearmongering. In a similar vein, memorialization—such as the installation of museums on the disappeared, statues in memory of individuals executed by a regime, and national days of remembrance of conflict victims—can keep the tremendous costs of political violence at the fore of the collective memory and encourage atrocity-prevention measures.[12]

Justice and Human Rights Respect

Next, if implemented, recommendations related to justice and the judiciary could improve human rights respect in a given country. Recommendations about procedural justice—for example, due process protections and efforts to support the independence of judges—may support human rights by helping protective institutions function well. Similarly, recommendations pertaining to retributive justice, notably criminal investigations and prosecutions, may support human rights via punishment for past abuses and deterrence of future abuses.

Reparations and Human Rights Respect

As with the procedural and retributive justice measures just described, distributive and restorative justice measures, namely material and symbolic reparations, may bolster human rights respect. Material reparations made to survivors and

[11] Ignatieff 1998, 178. See also Tepperman (2002).
[12] Byrne et al. 2024.

victims' families—through, for example, cash payments or the allocation of land in contexts where governments have previously expropriated this resource—can help remedy past actions, develop a culture of redress for harm, and engender a norm of harm prevention. Besides, symbolic reparations (like an apology by a head of state) can cultivate state responsibility and accountability norms and affirm the fundamental rights and dignity of all people.

Institutional Reforms and Democracy

Finally, if implemented, recommendations about institutional reforms may improve the chances that countries will attain and maintain democracy. For instance, legal reforms, including amendments to a country's constitution[13] and criminal codes,[14] can support the institutions needed to achieve and safeguard democracy. In addition, recommendations about personnel reforms—such as vetting, lustration and purges, training of civil servants and security personnel, and regulations for the conduct and operation of government agents—can help ensure that the people working within democratic institutions will not undermine those same institutions.[15] The relationship between democracy and recommendations about electoral reforms (e.g., term limits, simpler systems for voter registration and identification, and election monitoring) is perhaps the most straightforward. Such measures improve citizens' ability to hold governments electorally accountable.

Recommendations in Global and Comparative Perspective

The second *Varieties of Truth Commissions* dataset, "Truth Commissions and Policy Entrepreneurship," captures 5,710 recommendations[16] made by fifty-five truth commissions[17] from 1970 to 2018.[18]

My aim in constructing such rich, detailed data was to bring first-of-its-kind rigor to the study of truth commissions. I had encountered scholarly works

[13] For example, reshaping the powers of the executive, legislature, or judiciary.

[14] For example, repealing repressive laws and enacting protective laws.

[15] Horne 2014, Nalepa 2022.

[16] This sample was determined on the basis of availability of commission final reports, which my research team gathered in 2017 and 2018 in electronic formats and physical formats where electronic formats were not available. Most reports were in English, even for countries whose official language is not English. Where reports were in another language, I engaged student research assistants who were proficient in the language. Where I could not find a research assistant proficient in a particular language, I instructed research team members to use digital translation software.

[17] Recommendations were entered twice for the "truth and friendship commission" created by the Indonesian and Timorese governments in 2005. This was done to enable the data comparisons presented later in this section.

[18] Note, the commissions in Tunisia, Mali, Nepal, Bolivia, Venezuela, Colombia, and the Gambia had not yet concluded their work as of the 2018 cutoff.

that indicated that few, if any, recommendations issued by one commission or another were initiated or implemented fully. However, there was a troubling lack of precision that raised a stream of questions in my mind: How many recommendations do commissions typically make? What issues do they seek to address? Are some issue areas over- or under-represented across commissions? Are some types of recommendations implemented at greater rates than others? And, if so, why? My data were constructed to help answer these and related questions.

The data enable me to describe the global landscape of recommendations and explore how they relate to different political contexts. These data then make possible the analyses in Chapters 6 to 8, in which I investigate civil society's attempts to set governments' post-commission agendas and civil society's subsequent pursuit of implementation via lobbying, protest, and other tactics.

How Are Recommendations Produced?

Recommendations are produced collaboratively by commission leaders and staff members. In many instances, this is done with input from the public, including survivors and victims' relatives via oral and written testimonies, among other submissions. Civil society also plays an important role. As an example, the Human Rights Office of the Archbishop of Guatemala (ODHAG), which works with INGOs like Amnesty International and IOs like the United Nations to defend human rights in Guatemala, submitted its historical memory recovery project (known by its acronym in Spanish, REMHI) to the truth commission. The report documented state terror and its impact on individuals and communities, and contained many recommendations for the commission to pass on to policymakers.[19] The REMHI Project thus laid important groundwork for the CEH.[20]

ODHAG's outreach to the CEH is illustrative of the value that civil society actors place in truth commissions.[21] Commissions, as government-sponsored bodies, offer a unique and useful means to advance civil society goals from

[19] Author interview with ODHAG's Historical Memory Program director Patricia Ogaldes, Carolina Rendón, director of ODHAG's Monseñor Gerardi Memory Center, and Carlos Beristain, who worked with the REMHI Project.

[20] The CEH was also helped by declassified US intelligence files (McConnachie 2004).

[21] The REMHI Project further suggests that "unofficial" truth projects led by civil society can be powerful complements to "official" truth projects and, per Carlos Beristain, civil society-led initiatives can be more community based and engaged. Unofficial truth projects are sometimes the best available option when governments prefer silence and impunity to truth and justice. Unofficial truth projects can be a (temporary or partial) substitute for government action. The 2004 Greensboro Truth and Reconciliation Commission in North Carolina is an example. *Gukurahundi in Zimbabwe: A Report on the Disturbances in the Matabeleland and the Midlands*, first published in 1997 by the Catholic Commission for Justice and Peace, is another.

inside, not just outside, the traditional halls of power. More generally, TJ helps civil society move from the margins of power to the center. I have demonstrated this already in the chapters on commission adoption and design. Recommendations bolster civil society demands in the post-commission period, even if they are not substantively different from existing demands. What matters is that they are now articulated by an official body and can be subsequently used by civil society as a focal point and a justification for their advocacy.

Throughout my research interviews, especially in Guatemala, I was captivated by advocates who referenced recommendations by memory, sometimes verbatim. And I stood in awe as I witnessed a commemoration in downtown Guatemala City, where performers in different corners of a cultural center's courtyard recited portions of the CEH report. Never was it so clear to me how meaningful commissions have been to affected communities and how useful many of their reports have been for advocates seeking to advance various TJ measures—from reparations, to human rights litigation, to legal reforms, and more.

To adapt Simmons's argument to the TJ context, commissions, their findings, and recommendations are meaningful to the extent that they empower previously disempowered groups, namely NGOs and their constituency—that is, survivors and victims' families.[22] What's more, these groups can guide governments toward which recommendations to implement first. "The more they learn about transitional justice . . . [the better they] frame their work," said Patrick Burgess, previously principal legal counsel to the CAVR in Timor-Leste.

Commissions are expected to make recommendations based on their investigations and are often explicitly tasked with doing so, though not always. To give an example from a "negative case," in Argentina, the decree establishing the CONADEP did not enjoin the commission to make recommendations. Rather, it simply instructed the commission to write "a report that offers a detailed explanation of the facts investigated that [would] help educate the national and international public."[23] The CONADEP's inclusion of recommendations in its report indicates that some commissions exceed the technical requirements (and even the limits) of their founding documents. This resonates with a point raised by senior ICTJ personnel as recorded in Chapter 4: Commissions can overcome limited powers and expectations, in some cases by writing them in for themselves.

Some commissions make fewer than a dozen recommendations, while others make hundreds. The latter group of commissions surprised me. I did not expect at the beginning of this project that my research team would read and

[22] Simmons 2009, 125.
[23] Author translation of Spanish of Decreto 187 (Congreso de la Nación de Argentina 1984).

process nearly 6,000 recommendations. Based on the reports I had read from early-period commissions, from India (1977) to the United States (1980) and Argentina (1983), I initially thought recommendations would be few in number (say, a dozen), concise, and practical.[24] As data collection progressed, however, my team discovered that this was not the case in many countries.

To illustrate, the commissions that I study in greater detail in Chapters 6 to 8 jointly made 647 substantive recommendations. Specifically, the Guatemalan CEH made 87 recommendations, the South African TRC offered 313, and the Timorese CAVR proposed 247. While certainly on the higher end, these commissions are not so unusual. The first and second Canadian commissions respectively enumerated 155 and 231 recommendations, the Kenyan commission 116, and the Sierra Leonean commission 343.

Figure 5.1 contextualizes these numbers by showing the distribution of recommendations across the fifty-five truth commissions in the sample. Note, report structures were standardized to aid comparability across commissions and recommendations. Where possible, a recommendation was coded down to the level of the article-paragraph-clause. So the *Varieties of Truth Commissions* numbering scheme may differ slightly from commissions' numbering schemes.

But are recommendations equivalent, both within and across commissions? Yes and no. Much like human rights treaty obligations, there is variation in the degree to which recommendations are demanding (i.e., strong, precise, and

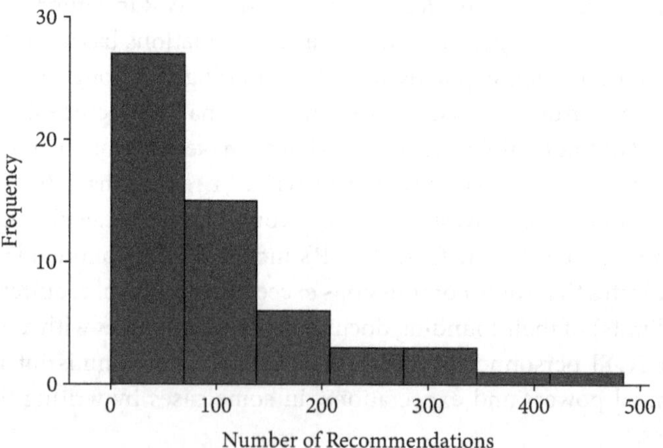

Figure 5.1 Distribution of Truth Commission Recommendations
Note: The figure shows the distribution of recommendations across commissions.

[24] In my interview with CONADEP expert Emilio Crenzel, he suggested that a small number of well-articulated, actionable recommendations is preferable to a large number of less well-defined, less actionable recommendations. But not all experts agree, as this chapter will show.

actionable). This is true within and across commission reports.[25] While some reports simply state the rules of the game, like we see in the analogous case of the concise, very demanding Genocide Convention, commission reports can also serve as focal points, as with the longer, less demanding Convention on the Rights of the Child.

Truth commissions can make recommendations that are at once practical (e.g., disband a security services unit) and aspirational (e.g., promote a culture of human rights respect across society). To the extent that they give themselves more space in their reports (i.e., issue more recommendations), commissions can include more of both, integrating "the big things" and "the small things,"[26] both the low- and high-hanging fruit.[27] The best cases for comparison may, therefore, be commissions that issue similar numbers of recommendations.

Types of Recommendations

Recommendations in the dataset were first coded as either pertaining to truth, justice, reparation, institutional reform, or services.[28] Figure 5.2 displays the distribution of recommendations by type. Commissions' emphasis on institutional reforms is intriguing. While scholars tend to think of truth commissions as historical projects that attempt to stitch together people, places, times, and events in the past, through witness testimonials, document analysis, and other research, the data suggest that commissions view themselves as policy entrepreneurs, with an express interest in contributing to reforms.

Below, I elaborate on my typology of recommendations, which I developed after an extensive reading of multiple commission reports.

Truth

The recommendation area *truth* has six main components that are displayed in Figure 5.3: *identify victims*, *identify perpetrators*, *exhumations*, *memorialization*, *education*, and *disclosure*, all of which are dichotomous indicators. While many of these are self-explanatory, I will elaborate on a few.

[25] Mulesky et al. 2024; Zvobgo et al. 2020.

[26] Author interview with Zoe Dugal, research officer for the Sierra Leonean TRC and international advisor to the Kenyan Truth, Justice and Reconciliation Commission.

[27] Author interview with Patrick Burgess.

[28] While TJ traditionally has four pillars—truth, justice, reparations, and guarantees of nonrepetition (operationalized as institutional reforms)—my research team encountered many instances of recommendations about services that did not neatly fit under the four pillars, so a fifth category was added. There is also an "other" category that future research may analyze.

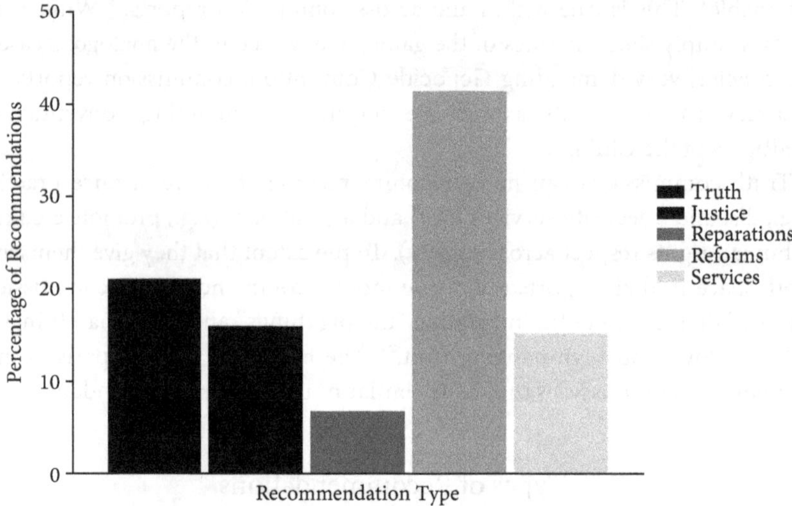

Figure 5.2 Types of Recommendations
Note: The figure shows the percentage of recommendations across five substantive areas: truth, justice, reparations, institutional reforms, and services.

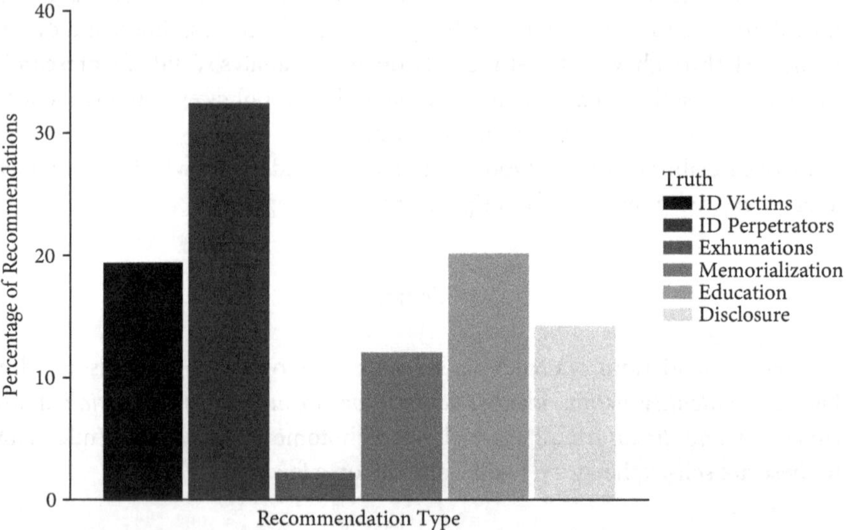

Figure 5.3 Types of Proposed Measures for Truth
Note: The figure shows the percentage of different types of recommendations about truth.

The variables about victim and perpetrator identification refer to post-commission efforts to determine victims' and perpetrators' identities and/or whereabouts. In the case of victims, the identification variable encompasses ascertaining the abuses they sustained and, in the case of perpetrators, ascertaining the abuses they are suspected of committing. Of note, these identifications are not necessarily related to criminal proceedings; rather, they relate to advancing the cause of truth and memory. Next, the memorialization indicator encompasses the establishment of memorials, museums, official days of remembrance, and the like. For its part, the education variable captures formal (i.e., primary, secondary, and/or tertiary) or popular (e.g., public service announcements and national sensitization campaigns) education related to historical violence and/or human rights. Regarding information disclosure, see, for example, the CONADEP's first recommendation:

> That the body which replaces this Commission speeds up the procedures involved in bringing before the courts the documents collected during our investigation.[29]

Commissions' emphasis on efforts to identify perpetrators (compared to efforts to identify victims), as presented in Figure 5.3, is striking. The data suggest that while they may be somewhat satisfied with the degree to which they have been able to uncover the identities and fates of victims, commissions perceive much unfinished business with respect to perpetrators. This makes intuitive sense: While survivors and victims' families are often interested in testifying before commissions and having their experiences documented and preserved for the historical record, perpetrators are much less forthcoming. Indeed, perpetrators represent but a fraction of commission participants.[30] Education is another key area of interest, with information disclosure and memorialization following just behind. The weak emphasis on measures to exhume and return the remains of victims to families is interesting.

Justice

The recommendation area *justice* comprises three binary variables: *trials*, *judicial reforms*, and *amnesty*. The trials indicator captures whether a commission proposed criminal investigations and prosecutions of individuals suspected to have committed abuses studied by the commission. The judicial reforms variable encompasses measures to change the operation and function of the judiciary, such as efforts to secure due process protections and to cultivate the norm

[29] CONADEP recommendation no. 1.
[30] Zvobgo 2019*a*.

and practice of judicial independence.[31] Consider, for instance, the Timorese commission's recommendation about the tenure of judges:

> The Commission recommends that . . . measures necessary to ensure the independence of the judiciary are put in place, including . . . development of career paths for judges, including a system of proper remuneration and tenure in order to reduce the risk of corruption or political pressure on judges.[32]

Finally, *amnesty* is an umbrella variable that captures whether a commission recommended in favor of or recommended against amnesties—whether general or conditional—or commuted or vacated sentences. For example, the 2005 South Korean commission recommended pardons and rehabilitation for individuals convicted of crimes who gave a full and truthful disclosure of their actions.[33]

Figure 5.4 presents the three justice measures by region. While countries in the Americas, notably in Central and South America, are well known for the many

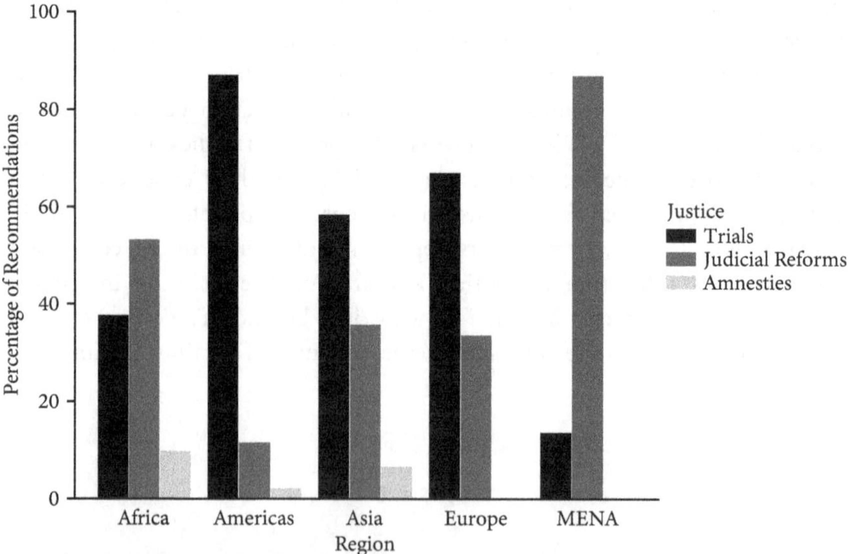

Figure 5.4 Types of Proposed Justice Measures by Region

Note: The figure shows the percentage of different types of recommendations about justice, separated by geographic region.

[31] Judicial reforms are a type of institutional reform, but because reforms to the judiciary are so closely linked to the (potential) provision of additional TJ measures, including trials and reparations, and because the judiciary reviews institutional and legal reforms, I separate judicial reforms and put them under *justice*.

[32] CAVR recommendation no. 105.

[33] South Korea TRC recommendation no. 8. This is different from the South African commission, which itself granted amnesty to perpetrators who confessed fully to politically motivated crimes they committed during apartheid.

criminal investigations and prosecutions that followed their respective commissions, and often on the basis of commissions' research, the figure also shows an interest in trials among commissions in Asia and Europe. This is less true in Sub-Saharan Africa and the Middle East and North Africa (MENA) region, where judicial reforms have been the preferred proposal. Commissions around the world have been less likely to opine on amnesties and other forms of judicial relief, relative to other justice measures, with commissions in Europe and MENA not discussing these measures at all.

Reparations

The recommendation area *reparations* has two subcategories, *symbolic* and *material*, both of which are coded as binary. For an example of a symbolic reparation recommendation, consider the Sierra Leonean commission's urging that the president apologize for sexual and gender-based violence (SGBV):

> The Commission recommends that the President, as the "Father of the Nation" and as the Head of State, should acknowledge the harm suffered by women and girls during the conflict in Sierra Leone and offer an unequivocal apology to them on behalf of the government and preceding governments in Sierra Leone. This is an imperative recommendation.[34]

Figure 5.5 shows reparation recommendations by region. Material measures have been much preferred to symbolic measures in Europe and MENA than in other world regions.

Institutional Reforms

Institutional reforms covers seven classes of recommendations: *legal reforms, human rights reforms, democracy reforms, electoral reforms, domestic institutions, international institutions,* and *personnel reforms.* The legal reforms class of recommendations encompasses changes to the constitution, criminal law, civil rights law, and human rights law more generally, as well as accession to international legal instruments. The human rights reforms variable concerns such measures as the state committing to protect the rights of racial and ethnic minorities, or to cultivating cultures of inclusion and respect within state institutions. The democracy variable encompasses democracy promotion and cultivating political tolerance. The electoral reforms variable records such changes as leader term limits. The domestic institutions variable captures calls

[34] Sierra Leone TRC recommendation no. 151.

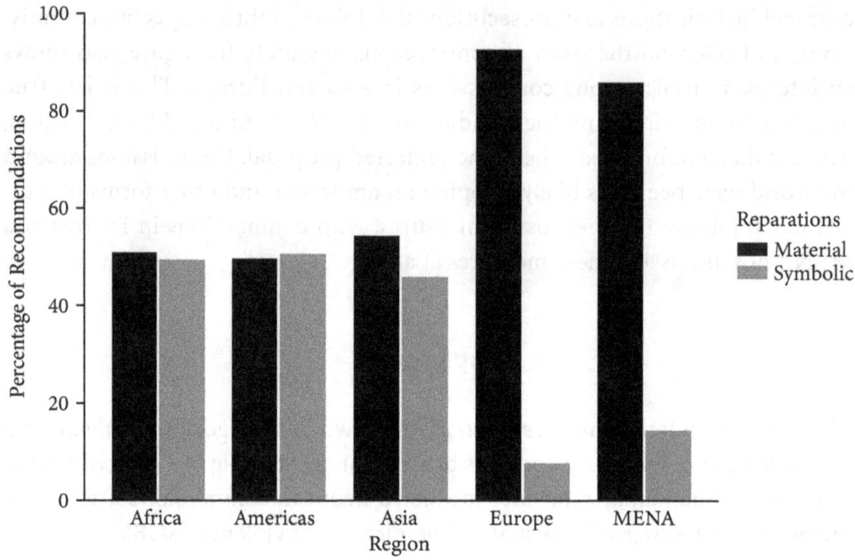

Figure 5.5 Types of Proposed Reparations by Region
Note: The figure shows the percentage of different types of recommendations about reparations, separated by geographic region.

to create new institutions, while the international institutions variable captures calls to join or strengthen participation in IOs. For their part, personnel reforms generally consist of exclusion rules[35]—such as vetting and purges—education and training, and regulation of structures, conduct, and operation. This category of reforms targets two classes of individuals: public officials and civil servants, and state security agents such as the military, police, and intelligence officers. These are captured by the variable *personnel group*. As an example, consider one of the Guatemalan CEH's proposals to reform the conduct and operation of the military:

> That a new Military Code be drafted and put into effect based on legal, moral and doctrinal criteria in accordance with the Constitution of the Republic and the reforms to the same derived from the Peace Accords.[36]

As seen in Figure 5.6, the plurality of proposed institutional reforms are legal reforms, followed by personnel reforms and the creation of new domestic institutions, like a national human rights institution or a victims' advocacy unit in the police or judiciary.

[35] Nalepa 2022.
[36] CEH recommendation no. 46.

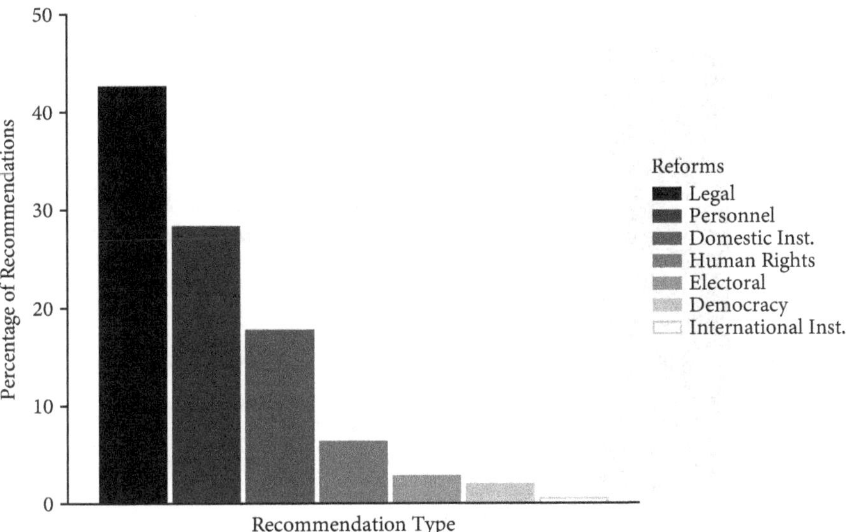

Figure 5.6 Types of Proposed Institutional Reforms

Note: The figure shows the percentage of different types of recommendations about institutional reforms.

Services

Finally, *services* has three main components, which are coded as binary indicators: *victim rehabilitation*, *perpetrator rehabilitation*, and *social welfare*. The rehabilitation variables encompass a range of services for physical health (e.g., prostheses and physical therapy) and mental health (namely, counseling and psychological services). The social welfare variable captures proposals about programs like public assistance. Consider one of the South African commission's first recommendations:

> The commission recommends that government accelerate the closing of the intolerable gap between the advantaged and disadvantaged in our society by, *inter alia*, giving even more urgent attention to the transformation of education, the provision of shelter, access to clean water and health services and the creation of job opportunities. The recognition and protection of socio-economic rights are crucial to the development and sustaining of a culture of respect for human rights.[37]

[37] South Africa TRC recommendation no. 2.

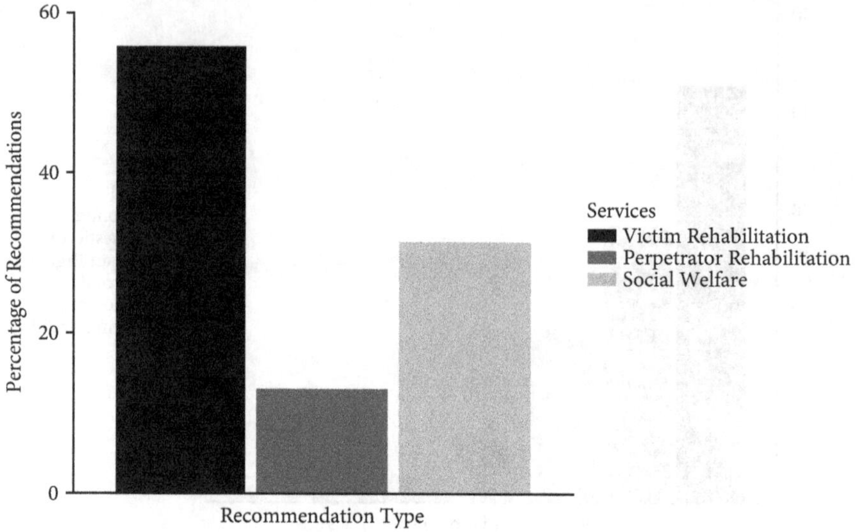

Figure 5.7 Types of Proposed Services
Note: The figure shows the percentage of different types of recommendations about services.

Figure 5.7 shows that the most recommended post-commission service is victim rehabilitation. This makes intuitive sense: Commissions are principally victim-oriented TJ institutions. While there may be some concern for the health of perpetrators and the wellness and resiliency of the broader society, survivors of violence remain at the fore.

Recommendations over Time

With thousands of recommendations issued by commissions globally, one question is their temporal distribution: Are commissions offering more proposals over time? Figure 5.8, which shows the number of recommendations per commission over time, indicates that the answer is "yes." This suggests, albeit preliminarily, that commissions' perceived role and responsibilities are expanding. More than investigative bodies, they seek to guide governments toward public policies that address past harm and safeguard against future harm.

Recommendations by Type and Time

I consider next the relationship between types of recommendations and time. Figure 5.9 presents types of recommendations and the share of each type by decade. The data suggest that measures for truth, reparation, and services

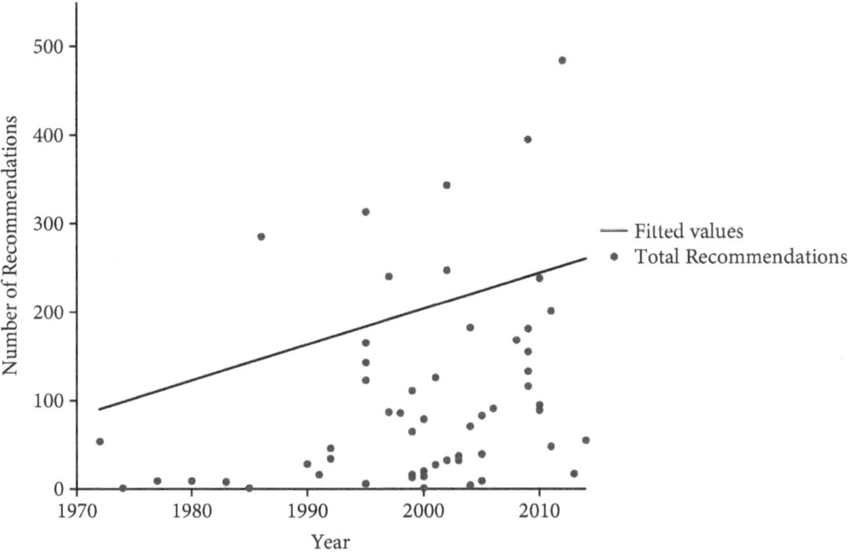

Figure 5.8 Recommendations over Time

Note: The figure shows the number of recommendations made by different commissions over time.

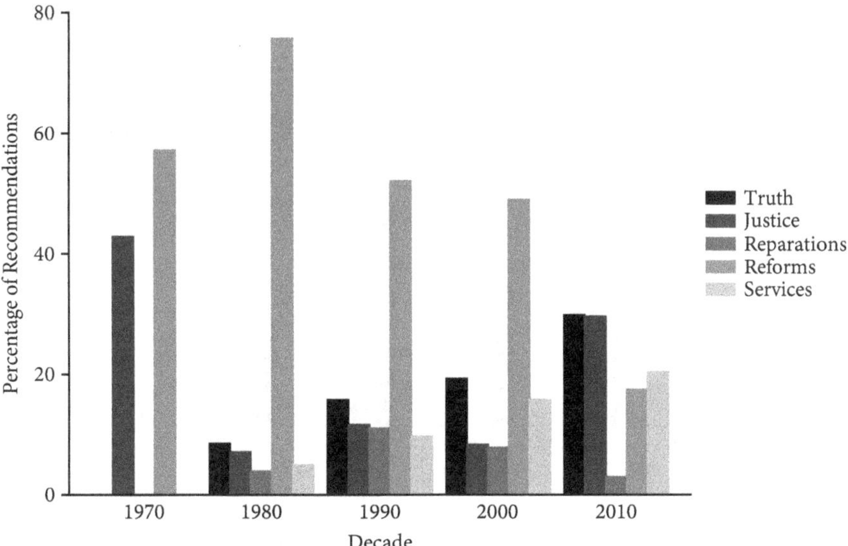

Figure 5.9 Recommendation Types by Decade

Note: The figure shows the percentage of recommendations in different substantive areas, separated by decade.

were not priorities in the 1970s and 1980s, while institutional reforms were high-priority items. And, whereas commissions in the 1990s and 2000s closely resemble each other in terms of the policies they prescribed, commissions in the 1970s and 2010s differ considerably, reflecting, respectively, the least and the most holistic approaches to policy proposals. Indeed, there has been a marked increase over time in recommendations regarding truth, justice, and services. Meanwhile, recommendations for reforms, as a proportion of all recommendations, have been declining since the 1980s. Commissions, and TJ tools more generally, are getting more complex with time.[38]

Recommendations by Type and Region

A related question is about the geographic distribution of recommendations. Figure 5.10 shows the proportion of recommendation types by region. Institutional reforms represent an exceedingly large share of recommendations in all regions, save for the Americas. One possible explanation is that measures for

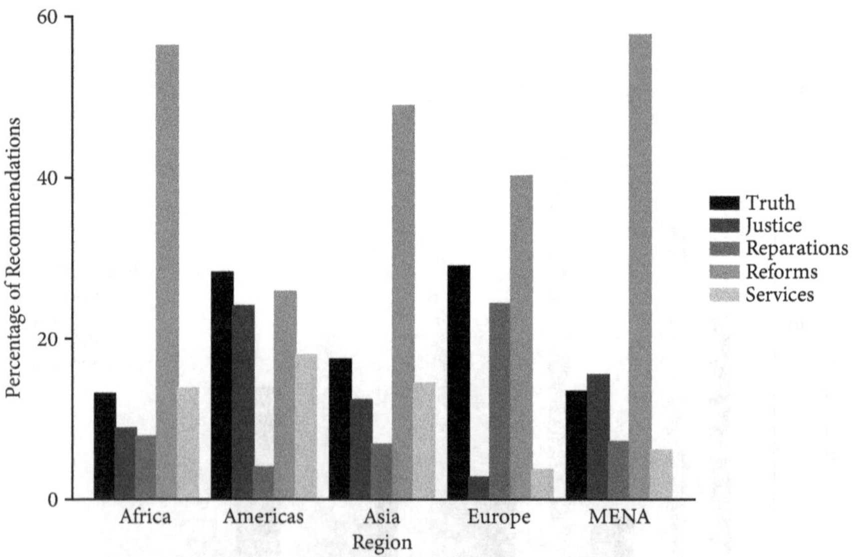

Figure 5.10 Recommendation Types by Region

Note: The figure shows the percentage of recommendations in different substantive areas, separated by geographic region.

[38] Per Gready (2010, 6), as TJ has matured, there has been "a growing tendency to adopt holistic understandings."

truth, justice, and reparation are already unfolding as commissions begin to conclude their work and draft their recommendations. Another possible explanation is a concern in Africa, Asia, Europe, and MENA with broader structural changes, in contrast to the Americas, where many truth commissions were created in contexts where former authoritarian elites retained influence (Central and South America) and democratic elites did not perceive a need for an overhaul to existing institutions (North America).

In online Appendix C, I include additional figures and discussion, notably on the relationship between types of recommended reforms and commission subject matter (authoritarian governments or internal armed conflicts) and types of recommended reforms and commission timing (transitional or non-transitional).[39] The upshot from the data presented here in the main text and in the appendix is isomorphism. There is noteworthy similarity in recommendations across regions, countries with diverse conflict histories, countries conducting commissions in different political moments—the list goes on. This evinces again the transnational nature of truth commissions.

Truth Commission Officials' Perspectives on the Content and Scope of Recommendations

To better understand the content, and especially the scope, of truth commission recommendations, I went directly to the source: former truth commission leaders and staff members. In my interview with Karine Duhamel, director of Canada's second commission, the National Inquiry into Missing and Murdered Indigenous Women and Girls (NIMMIWG), she explained that one reason commissions issue so many recommendations is that they receive in the statement-taking process hundreds, if not thousands, of suggestions from survivors, victims' families, and civil society actors—something we have seen in other contexts, including in Guatemala with ODHAG and the REMHI Project. Thus, the several dozen or few hundred recommendations that are articulated in a given commission's concluding report represent just a fraction of the issues and concerns that commissioners and commission staff encounter in the course of their work and that they believe must be addressed.

In the case of the NIMMIWG, the commission received between 7,000 and 8,000 recommendations from survivors and victims' families, but itself issued just 231. Duhamel shared a second reason for presenting many prescriptions: creating a framework that is empowering to communities and their advocates as *they* pursue implementation. In many ways, recommendations

[39] See Figures C.1 ▶ to C.4 ▶ in online Appendix C.

clarify and affirm what communities deserve. As the products of an official body, recommendations hold much value.

The process in Timor-Leste was more technical in terms of producing recommendations based on testimonies. In my interview with Pat Walsh, a key advisor to the CAVR, the post-CAVR Technical Secretariat, and its successor organization, the Chega! National Center, he shared:

> The commission invited victims, local communities, and those who testified directly or in public hearings, including leaders, to nominate recommendations. As the report was being written, it also convened a series of listening and dialogue sessions on recommendations with victims groups, women, and political parties.

In my interview with Zoe Dugal, a research officer for the Sierra Leonean commission and international advisor to the Kenyan commission, she offered a third reason. At both commissions, she and her colleagues considered it a rare moment in time—perhaps the only real opportunity they would ever have—to say something meaningful to the public, something official, as they sought to respond to what they had seen and heard about people's experiences of violence. Cristián Correa, who served as legal secretary for Chile's second truth commission, the National Commission on Political Imprisonment and Torture (also known as the Valech Commission), echoed these sentiments in our interview, underlining, "You have a responsibility to victims but also you have a responsibility for the rest of society."

Returning to Dugal, she expressed a desire among the teams at the Kenyan and Sierra Leonean commissions to make recommendations that were at once aspirational and practical. Hence, the large number of recommendations made by both the Kenyan and Sierra Leonean commissions. Dugal also conveyed a concern about issuing a narrow set of recommendations and, in the process, ignoring a group of victims and opening up the commission to criticism. This is something we saw in Guatemala, where the commission marginalized, if unintentionally, SGBV survivors. So much of the commission's emphasis was on victims of disappearances, who were predominantly men, that women's experiences of harm went largely unacknowledged.[40] In some ways, commissions that suggest a wide range of policies do so to prevent further pain and conflict. They likely also do so to protect the institution's integrity and legacy.

But, of course, there is the 6,000-pound elephant in the room: implementation. What do commission officials think are the prospects of implementation,

[40] Author interviews with Juana Tipaz, founder of the Guatemalan National Victims' Movement, and Rosalina Tuyuc, head of the National Coordinator of Guatemalan Widows.

especially when there are so many recommendations? Burgess indicated, "You don't expect for them all to be implemented, and particularly not immediately." Dugal added that implementation, immediate or otherwise, is not the only consideration when drafting recommendations. Speaking of her work in Sierra Leone and in Kenya, she said, "We were thinking twenty-five years down the line. . . . Something that is not possible now may be possible later." This is certainly what we have observed all around the globe. For instance, while trials were not possible immediately following democratization in the 1980s and 1990s in Central and South America, many countries, including Argentina and Guatemala, were later able to conduct human rights trials—and are continuing to do so. Duhamel added that recommendations are also about acknowledgment and recognition: "They are meaningful to victims and their families, even without implementation."

Duhamel conceded the trade-off between a broad and narrow set of recommendations. A narrow set is, in expectation, much easier to implement and monitor, while a broader set is more difficult. However, she, along with the other authors of the NIMMIWG report, was concerned that the Canadian government would limit the scope of action if only a few recommendations were made. Commissions, as policy framers and entrepreneurs, negotiate. If they ask for too little to start, they may receive even less. Duhamel and her colleagues also wanted to spell out exactly what needed to be done, by whom, for whom, how, and in what time frame. While this might mean that fewer recommendations are ultimately implemented, those that are implemented will be implemented well and their delivery will be more meaningful. Lengthier, more detailed recommendations may indeed leave less wiggle room for implementers.[41] Dugal added that partial or incomplete implementation of recommendations is also not something that is unique to truth commissions or TJ. She cited the example of election observation missions that make recommendations to governments, some of which are implemented and some of which are not. In many contexts, the important thing is that recommendations are made and that there is *some* progress.

Correa, as a senior expert for programs at the ICTJ, had a somewhat different perspective, shaped by his time working in the Valech Commission and, later, serving in the Chilean government and helping to implement the commission's reparation recommendations. He shared with me what he describes as a struggle when working with commissions: how to "work with victims and civil society and government to try and come up with something that is reasonable

[41] This idea resonates with Huber and Shipan (2002).

but meaningful enough, and that could be, also, simple enough to be implementable, and that could be accessible to all." Being a bit more moderate, he suggested, is one way to be loyal to victims.

Do commission officials think that different types of recommendations are more likely to be implemented than others? Yes. As Dugal indicated, some recommendations represent lofty ideals and goals (e.g., the recurring recommendation across commission reports for countries to develop a "human rights culture" and for governments to act in "full observance" of human rights norms, principles, and instruments). Simply, more abstract recommendations are less likely to be fully implemented. But, again, implementation is not the only objective. Dugal also discussed the policy adjustment costs that different recommendation types entail. Certainly, structural changes—to the law, to institutions, and to governance—are difficult, especially in countries that are politically fragile.

Andy Javalois, attorney and legal analyst at the Myrna Mack Foundation in Guatemala, noted that reforming the judiciary is especially challenging: It requires addressing norms, laws, people, and institutions, all of which are slow to change. Yet again, this is not TJ or human rights specific; these same challenges are widespread in other political arenas. For his part, Walsh expected recommendations on justice and reparations to have the lowest rates of adoption. He shared, "For this reason, and in response to anticipated objections, each of these sets of recommendations [in the CAVR report] was prefaced with an extensive explanation of its background, rationale and benefits."

Speaking of the financial costs of different recommendations, Duhamel suggested that if a recommendation is more expensive, it will be more difficult to realize. For example, she said she expects that symbolic reparations, such as apologies, are more likely to be implemented than material reparations. Correa agreed; reparations programs are costly to build and operate, to say nothing of the funds to be disbursed. Duhamel went further, suggesting, "Symbolic reparations will always be implemented first; it's an easy win." She proposed that this would also be the case for recommendations relating to healing, commemoration, and legacy. Burgess added education to this list but, based on his experience, education, especially as it relates to still-influential groups like the military, is contentious and a challenge to implement. While the question of implementation is perhaps one that policymakers and the civil society actors who lobby them are best poised to answer, these insights are illuminating.

Speaking from his unique position—as a member of the nonviolent resistance movement against torture during the Pinochet regime, then a truth commission leader, then a government official, and now an international TJ expert and advocate—Correa thinks the design of recommendations "is very important for the likelihood of the implementation." But he added:

> I see beautiful reports . . . well written . . . that tick all the [boxes] . . . that say the right thing . . . but are either foreign to the country or that fail . . . [to] make people, who could carry these issues, get involved and own them. And this is something that I am critical of many truth commissions, on the way they define their recommendations. . . . Maybe by going slower, more timidly, but involving more people, more organizations, and those entities that you don't like in government . . . could [make it] more likely that they will own those recommendations . . . and support them and implement them.

When they tell governments what to do, rather than collaborate with governments, commissions run the risk of alienating them and making recommendations feel like an imposition. "The tendency of governments is not to listen," Correa synthesized, so it is important to "approach government in a way that encourages [them] to listen."[42]

I now turn to address (1) how NGOs attempt to influence government TJ policy following commissions and (2) why NGOs are successful in many instances. The next section discusses the first part of this argument. To influence post-commission government TJ policy, NGOs, domestic ones especially, advocate for recommendations. Since their resources are scarce, they are likely to advocate for some, but not all, recommendations. I turn to the extant literature for guidance on how NGOs might decide their post-commission advocacy priorities.

Some prior work suggests that existing issue portfolios shape NGOs' advocacy efforts: Organizations "stay in their lane," playing to their strengths in order to get policy "wins." In a post-commission context, this would mean pursuing recommendations that correspond with organizational histories and prior experience. Other work suggests, by contrast, that NGOs can step out of their lane, broadening their policy portfolios as new issues and opportunities arise. In a post-commission context, this would mean pursuing recommendations that do not correspond with organizational histories and prior experience, alongside recommendations that do. Either or both of these may operate in a post-commission context.

Though I will reason through how NGOs might establish their preferences—a task I undertake to bridge my work with past work and to set up my last empirical tests using evidence from Guatemala, South Africa, and Timor-Leste in Chapters 6 to 8—I am agnostic on the question of NGO advocacy preference formation. My argument is that NGOs shape important TJ outcomes, including

[42] I will return to these points in succeeding chapters, especially Chapter 8 on Timor-Leste. Simply, there has not been enough government ownership over TJ in the country, in part because many processes, the truth commission included, were launched by the UN transitional administration and few strides were made toward getting the incoming government deeply interested and seriously invested in further measures, including the commission's recommendations.

implementation of truth commission recommendations. And I expect that the recommendations that NGOs prefer, and thus advocate for, will be implemented at higher rates than the recommendations that NGOs do not prefer.[43]

This is a general expectation, to be sure. With guidance from previous research, I will explain along the way why this expectation might not always be met. Throughout, domestic NGOs will play a leading role, and INGOs will play a supporting role, per the burden sharing model.

Defining the Post-Commission Agenda: NGO Priorities and Strategies

While from a normative perspective, civil society groups may value truth commission recommendations equally—for example, recommendations about reparations, trials, and memorials—groups cannot, from a practical point of view, pursue them equally. NGOs contend with limited resources to pursue issues of interest and urgency, including the range of recommendations that commissions make in their concluding reports.[44] Thus, civil society groups at the domestic level begin the journey toward implementation by selecting proposals to bring to policymakers.[45] This section describes how they do this.

Advocacy Priorities: Maintaining vs. Expanding Issue Portfolios

NGOs, domestically and internationally, inside and outside the TJ space, operate strategically, establishing agendas that can secure and extend their power as well as provide societal benefits.[46] Organizations need "wins," and a body of existing research suggests that the main way they can attain them is to select issues—for our purposes, advocate for truth commission recommendations—that match their existing issue portfolios.[47] Indeed, it is here that they can leverage their professional experience, and existing access to influential allies and policymaking bodies, to advance their missions.[48]

I offer a brief illustration to animate these ideas. The Guatemalan commission made a range of recommendations that were substantively diverse and complex. Many comprised different subelements, thus requiring area experts with the

[43] Here, I echo Wong (2014, 3), who maintains that NGO activism helps certain issues gain prominence.

[44] On NGO resource-maximizing behavior and "principled instrumentalism," see Mitchell and Schmitz (2014).

[45] Capella 2016; Schnattschneider 1960.

[46] Light 1982; Mihr and Schmitz 2007; Prentice and Brudney 2017.

[47] Prentice and Brudney (2017) would call this lobbying strategy "concentration."

[48] Kellow and Murphy-Gregory 2018.

relevant knowledge resources, contacts, and operational tools. For instance, regarding disappeared children, the commission called for (1) the establishment of a national commission for the search for disappeared and illegally adopted children, (2) legislative measures relating to access to information, and (3) an international information campaign. While the International Center for Human Rights Research (CIIDH)—an organization whose founding mission was to search for victims of forced disappearance—was, ex ante, well positioned to advocate for and monitor implementation of this recommendation, the Central American Regional Research Center (CIRMA)—a cultural and historical preservation organization—was not. Rather, it was better suited to advance, for example, the recommendation calling for the establishment of a national day of remembrance, monuments, and memorial markers.

So we might expect that if NGOs engage in post-commission advocacy, they will choose to advocate for some recommendations and not others because of their backgrounds and expertise. Thus, I derive the following hypothesis:

Hypothesis 1a

If NGOs attempt to set governments' post-commission agenda, they will advocate exclusively for truth commission recommendations that match their existing issue portfolios.

Still, NGOs can engage in "mission creep," opportunistically expanding the issues in their advocacy portfolio. This may be because new issues emerge, their constituents want them to address issues outside their portfolio, or groups think they can grow their power and influence by taking on more issues. Organizations may also think they must change in order to survive. Each of these possibilities is consistent with, for example, Amnesty International's development from an organization concerned exclusively with the condition of political prisoners to an organization concerned with the rights of racial and ethnic minority groups, migrants, LGBTQIA+ individuals, and others.[49] Consider also the Coalition for the International Criminal Court, which transitioned from advocating for the creation of the ICC to doing work on the court's behalf.[50] Accordingly, I derive the following hypothesis:

Hypothesis 1b

If NGOs attempt to set governments' post-commission agenda, they will advocate for truth commission recommendations beyond their existing issue portfolios.

[49] Hopgood 2013.

[50] Haddad 2013, 2018; Struett 2008. Prentice and Brudney (2017, 938) find that in the United States, "nonprofits lobby across multiple policy domains, rather than restricting their focus only to their particular mission area."

Advocacy Strategies: Framing, Navigating Political Conditions, and Leveraging Networks

Once NGOs have determined their advocacy priorities, they elaborate on what should be done, how, by whom, and why. This is also known as agenda setting and it proceeds in three important steps that I expect NGOs interested in implementation of commission recommendations will take in their dealings with governments: framing issues, contending with prohibitive political conditions, and making use of mobilizing structures.

First, framing "render[s] events or occurrences meaningful," and "function[s] to organize experience and guide action."[51] Joachim identifies three complementary types of framing: diagnostic, prognostic, and motivational.[52] Diagnostic framing involves identifying a problem, while prognostic framing involves outlining possible outcomes of different actions, or inaction, given a particular problem. For its part, motivational framing "provides a reason for why people should take action with respect to a particular issue."[53]

Second, political conditions shape what is possible in terms of policy production.[54] Evergreen challenges include low levels of political will among policymakers and scarce human, material, and political resources to implement particular initiatives.[55] To raise the salience of social and political problems, and propose solutions to them, interest groups like NGOs require access to and allies in policymaking bodies.

Third, mobilizing structures (i.e., groups' resources and networks) sometimes help groups overcome political barriers. Key aspects include organizational entrepreneurs, international constituency, and knowledge and expertise. So I offer the following hypothesis:

Hypothesis 2
If NGOs attempt to set governments' post-commission agenda, they will advocate for truth commission recommendations through a process of framing, navigating prohibitive political conditions, and leveraging mobilizing networks.

Observable Implications of NGO Agenda Setting

This section lays out how we might observe NGOs' post-commission TJ agenda-setting attempts.

[51] Snow et al. 1986, 464.
[52] Joachim 2007, 19–22.
[53] Joachim 2007, 20.
[54] Joachim 2007, 22–31. See also Cronin-Furman (2022).
[55] Hertel 2006.

Issue Portfolios

If NGOs attempt to set governments' post-commission agenda, we should see them advocating for specific truth commission recommendations.

Framing Truth Commission Reports

Next, we should see NGOs producing frames around a truth commission's work. This process of meaning making and illuminating the path forward will involve diagnosing problems (e.g., the plight of disappeared and illegally adopted children and their families), echoing a commission's findings. And, as groups lay out their diagnoses, we should see them presenting prognoses—essentially, the consequences of action and inaction. Prognoses should be paired with prescriptions (e.g., an international search for disappeared and illegally adopted children), elaborating on a commission's recommendations. Having diagnosed a problem or set of problems, and having offered prognoses and prescriptions, we should then see NGOs offering motivations for action (e.g., arguing that searching and pursuing justice for the aforesaid children is a moral and legal imperative).

Navigating Prohibitive Political Conditions

Building on this, we should see NGOs determining how to overcome obstacles. As discussed in previous chapters, post-violence governments face significant non- and anti-TJ interests. Beyond concerns about political stability, governments also consider the human and material costs, as well as the political capital, required to implement public policies like a national reparations program or memorial museum. Given prohibitive political conditions such as scarce resources and low levels of political will in government, we should see civil society groups seeking to cultivate alliances with people in government.

Mobilizing Structures, Mobilizing Action

Finally, NGOs must leverage the full range of their resources and networks, including domestic and international partnerships. Per my burden sharing model, we should see domestic and international NGOs exercising their comparative advantages. For instance, domestic groups may share on-the-ground information, professional networks, and practical experience, and international groups may lend material resources. International groups may also exert political pressure on governments (e.g., by broadcasting domestic groups' demands widely). Indeed, INGOs can introduce nontrivial costs that governments, especially in countries emerging from violence, may not be in a position to absorb.[56]

[56] Dietrich and Murdie 2017.

Why Are Governments Responsive?

But why would governments provide TJ beyond a truth commission? And why would they be responsive to NGOs' post-commission policy ideas? I again turn to the extant literature for guidance. Theories of socialization in human rights suggest why governments might implement commission recommendations and be more likely to deliver on those supported by civil society coalitions. I formulate testable implications of socialization and evaluate them in Guatemala, South Africa, and Timor-Leste in Chapters 6, 7, and 8, respectively.

Implementing the Post-Commission Agenda: NGO Advocacy Success, Challenges, and Innovations

NGOs are said to be the engine of the global human rights regime, in particular those organizations that compose a transnational network.[57] However, few scholars have extended this important argument to TJ which, as I discussed in Chapter 1, is part of the human rights regime but is distinct from other better-studied areas like environmental protection, economic development, and the movement to improve respect for physical integrity rights.[58] I propose that after establishing a set of advocacy priorities based on commission recommendations, civil society groups move governments beyond the truth commission. More precisely, I expect that NGOs motivate governments to implement specific recommendations and that broader coalitions of NGOs are more influential. Essentially, larger movements likely represent larger threats to noncompliant governments. Thus, I offer the following hypothesis:

Hypothesis 3a
Governments are more likely to implement recommendations when they are pressured to do so by civil society groups.

Hypothesis 3b
Governments are more responsive to broader coalitions of civil society groups than they are to narrower coalitions.

With this dual expectation, I aim to refine the influential research program in international relations and comparative politics that argues that norm and policy entrepreneurs like NGOs help socialize governments into pro-human rights

[57] Haddad 2018; Keck and Sikkink 1998; Risse et al. 1999; Struett 2008.
[58] Similar to these areas, TJ is about shaming, punishing, and preventing harms. But, dissimilar to these areas, it is also about holistic redress for historical wrongdoing.

behaviors. Socialization is a top candidate for explaining government actions and reactions in the post-commission period because the TJ policy a government initially "budgeted for," the truth commission, has completed its work, leaving a long list of to-dos that NGOs capitalize on. Perhaps a government does more than it initially planned or agreed to because of socialization. Below, I review socialization in the human rights literature and describe how it might operate in the TJ realm.

What Is Socialization?

Socialization, led by domestic NGOs and supported by INGOs, may explain how and why a government that has adopted a truth commission and, in certain cases, endowed that commission with strong investigative powers may go a step further and implement the commission's recommendations. Socialization is a "process by which principled ideas held by individuals become norms in the sense of collective understandings about appropriate behavior which then lead to changes in identities, interests, and behavior."[59]

Risse and coauthors' spiral model is perhaps the best known and most influential model of socialization into human rights norms and practices, and domestic and international civil society actors play an important role.[60] The spiral model specifies five phases: (1) repression and activation of a transnational network, (2) denial by the rights-violating state, (3) tactical concessions, (4) attainment of prescriptive status, and (5) rule-consistent behavior. I touched on the first three phases in previous chapters, albeit with different language and from a slightly different perspective. In this chapter, I focus on the third, fourth, and fifth phases, as they are the most germane to the post-commission period.

To begin, governments make *tactical concessions*—essentially small, usually short-term, changes—to pacify domestic and/or international critics.[61] To illustrate, an executive may, at the prompting of civil society, create an agency to receive human rights complaints. However, the new agency might only be temporarily useful, if at all, because the executive's commitment to human rights is shallow.

Next, *prescriptive status* refers to when a government accepts in discourse and in practice the validity of particular human rights ideas conveyed or underlined by civil society groups. Continuing with the example already given, an executive may publicly state that she accepts citizens' right to be heard by the new human

[59] Risse et al. 1999, 11.
[60] Risse et al. 1999.
[61] Gillooly et al. 2024, Winston 2021.

rights agency. She may even accept adverse findings from the agency. However, her responses are not consistent or reliable. She is practicing human rights but is not necessarily committed.

Finally, *rule-consistent behavior* reflects a government's internalization, not just practice, of the aforesaid ideas and principles. To round out the example, at this stage, an executive will trigger fewer complaints to the human rights agency because she and her administration are complying with human rights rules. And, where complaints do arise and the agency finds in favor of the complainants, the executive will accept the finding and repair the harm (e.g., through compensation). At this stage, the executive's pro-human rights orientation and actions are consistent and long-term.

Now, there are two main pathways for civil society groups to socialize governments into human rights norms like TJ. The first pathway is pressure by protest—either domestic, international, or both—to which a government may initially respond strategically with tactical concessions. The second pathway is rhetoric and argumentation. Essentially, civil society groups produce discursive frames about what actions are morally correct and required. This is also known as consciousness raising. Groups define and assess appropriate and inappropriate behaviors and reward good conduct and punish bad conduct. (Groups may pursue both pathways to enhance the likelihood of their success.)

To be clear, neither the use of the language of human rights nor behavioral changes on their own provide evidence of socialization. Rational choice arguments about utility maximization could also explain this behavior. However, pro-human rights discourse and adaptation represent points of departure from which governments may "entangle themselves in a moral discourse which they cannot escape in the long run."[62] Instrumental adaptation and argumentative discourses can come together to produce institutionalization and habituation, which, in turn, can yield internalization of norms in identities, interests, and behaviors. In this way, governments may be moved from the instrumental to the ideational. But whether changes in language and behavior are the result of socialization is an empirical question.

Translating the Spiral Model to Understand Post-Commission Transitional Justice

If the spiral model extends to truth commissions and TJ more broadly, ideas about redress for historical wrongdoing, initially advanced by domestic and international civil society groups, would be adopted by policymakers, shifting their preferences and actions. Essentially, what began as instrumental adaptation—in our case, establishment of a truth commission—and a discourse

[62] Risse et al. 1999, 16.

of appropriateness—in our case, stated commitments to robust TJ—may culminate in governments finding themselves in a corner. Essentially, governments that "talk the talk" may eventually have to "walk the walk." Habits can be regularized and institutionalized and ultimately internalized.

To echo Sandra Raggio's[63] sentiments, which I first recorded in Chapter 3, post-commission actions by governments, much like pre-commission actions, have much to do with civil society activism. But whether socialization is the vehicle is an open question. Thus, I probe whether governments' delivery of further TJ measures is due to changes in their normative orientation and commitments.

I also explore the extent to which civil society actors effectively abandon socialization and pursue, instead, substitution, where they, and not governments, become TJ providers. On this last point, I want to be clear that NGOs cannot always substitute for the state. There are some things, like a national reparations program, that cannot materialize without the government. So when I talk about NGOs substituting for the state, it is in those areas where they can plausibly do so (e.g., victim identification, exhumations, osteology and DNA testing, and reburials with families, as groups like the Forensic Anthropology Foundation of Guatemala have done for decades).

Socializing the State or Socializing the Public?

Readers may wonder whether civil society seeks to socialize the state or the public into human rights norms and behaviors like TJ. Domestic and international NGOs, among other groups, can do both. But for the purposes of this book, I focus on civil society's attempts to socialize the state. I have two reasons for this. The first is conceptual/theoretical, and the second is methodological/empirical.

First, the state is the duty bearer in human rights and TJ; ordinary people are the rights holders. Civil society actors work to get the state to fulfill its duty to them. Second, state socialization is easier to examine; we can see the specific policies that states do and do not produce, and we can evaluate whether they advance or undermine human rights in general and TJ in particular. And we can do this over time, year to year, decade to decade. This is much harder to do with the public.

In any case, and as I have discussed extensively elsewhere, in this story, civil society organizations act as representatives of and advocates for the public, in particular individuals and communities affected by political violence. To be sure, these individuals and communities themselves play important roles in furthering TJ, together with and separate from civil society groups. They can act independently (e.g., by exercising their vote in support of human rights-minded

[63] Director of the Provincial Commission for Memory in Argentina.

politicians). They can also work in coordination with civil society groups, implementing powerful political tactics (e.g., mass protests) to realize their preferred policies.[64]

So does civil society attempt to socialize citizens? Certainly—through education, training, and mobilization. And is citizen socialization a potential pathway to government socialization? Also, yes. But this is not the focus of the present exercise.

Observable Implications of Socialization

This section lays out how we might observe government socialization into TJ norms—a development that would produce additional commitments to TJ, in particular implementation of commission recommendations. I do not assume that governments are necessarily socialized; rather, I delineate the types of behaviors and actions that we would see if governments were more socialized or less socialized into TJ.[65]

Less Socialized: Government Implementation as Strategy

If additional TJ measures are being delivered tactically—that is, due to civil society pressure rather than due to norm adoption (prescriptive status) or norm internalization (rule-consistent behavior)—we should see a government implementing truth commission proposals as a reflex. Civil society pressure could involve lobbying, petitions and lawsuits, and contentious politics like protest. At this lowest level of socialization, we would also expect to see civil society groups substituting for the state in delivering commission recommendations.

More Socialized: Government Implementation as Habit

If TJ attains prescriptive status in a country, we should see a government accepting the validity of civil society frames and making stronger efforts to provide additional measures. This could involve installing a national reparations program pursuant to recommendations in a truth commission report. Unlike at the tactical-concessions phase, a government at the prescriptive-status phase would implement recommendations semi-independently because leadership believes that this is a necessary course of action. At this moderate level of socialization,

[64] Chaudhry Forthcoming; Chenoweth and Stephan 2011.

[65] I recognize that in transitional settings, there is a degree of volatility. What is learned by one government can be unlearned by another. And one administration can make commitments that another reverses. But this is something that socialization accounts for theoretically and that I assess empirically; because it is a process, multiple governments are needed to evince socialization.

we would also expect to see civil society groups minding the gap in TJ policy areas that the government has not yet reached but may reasonably still reach.

Fully Socialized: Government Implementation as Identity

If a government implements further TJ measures because it is self-motivated to abide by—and, indeed, has internalized—the "rules of TJ," as promoted over the years by civil society groups, we should see the government implementing measures independently and robustly. Unlike at the tactical-concessions and prescriptive-status phases, a government at the rule-consistent behavior phase would implement truth commission recommendations not because it "has to" but because it "wants to"; leadership believes that this is the right thing to do. At this highest level of socialization, we would also expect to see civil society groups playing more marginal roles in TJ and shifting to new policy arenas. Essentially, they could "afford" to move on.[66]

Recommendations, Advocacy, and Implementation in Guatemala, South Africa, and Timor-Leste

Chapters 6, 7, and 8 explore civil society organizations' post-commission policy priorities, agenda-setting strategies, and advocacy success in Guatemala, South Africa, and Timor-Leste. I study how these actors, who have inspired and helped design and deliver truth commissions, use commission outputs, namely recommendations, to push governments beyond their initial TJ pledges. Below, I elaborate on my case selection rationale, situate the three-country data within the global data, and present my research design for the remaining empirical chapters.

Case Selection Justification

Successive governments in Guatemala, South Africa, and Timor-Leste have contended with domestic and international attention and pressure to deliver redress for past violence, making the three countries well suited to evaluate my argument that NGOs matter not only for TJ adoption and design but also for delivery

[66] I do not suggest that socialization and implementation necessarily rise together. While we could observe greater implementation because of greater socialization, we could also observe greater implementation over time simply because civil society groups continue to hold governments' feet to the fire and governments respond through additional TJ implementation. What is key for making a determination about socialization is *both* rising levels of implementation and decreasing levels of civil society effort to realize TJ.

and follow-up. On the domestic side, civil society organizations in each country played key research and advocacy roles during the period of repression and violence and later transition, including demanding that the respective governments establish commissions. For their part, international groups lent governments their expertise in designing the commissions. And both domestic and international groups helped carry out the commissions. If we see NGOs using truth commission outputs in contexts like these, we may see them doing the same in other contexts. However, if we do not detect this work here, it is unlikely that we will observe it elsewhere.

In addition, the three countries are significant for the space they occupy in the global history of TJ. They launched their processes at the height of the justice boom of the 1990s and early 2000s,[67] and their commissions are internationally respected and renowned[68]—highly regarded for their strong designs and rigorous investigations that culminated in thorough, authoritative reports of historical political violence.[69] These reports included a vast array of policy recommendations that NGOs took up in their advocacy. A leading truth commission expert, Priscilla Hayner, whom I was fortunate to interview for this project, has described Guatemala, South Africa, and Timor-Leste as having three of the five strongest commissions in history.[70] The commissions also jointly made 647 recommendations—more than 11 percent of all recommendations in the *Varieties of Truth Commissions*—despite representing just 5 percent of commissions. This underlines their significance in the global TJ landscape.

Moreover, Guatemala, South Africa, and Timor-Leste offer useful variation in terms of the types of political violence that their commissions investigated—internal armed conflict, race-based authoritarian government, and foreign occupation and conflict—and geographic region—Central America, Southern Africa, and Southeast Asia. This variation helps me rule out alternative explanations like regional diffusion and similar post-violence political trajectories. Additionally, because the countries all had their commissions in the aftermath of violence, I am able to hold constant the singular window of opportunity that political transitions represent for policy adoption. To put it another way, the three countries had comparable chances for their governments to deliver on truth commission recommendations. So, if I find similar outcomes, they cannot be caused by factors that differ across the cases.

[67] This was a time of great activity and optimism in the international human rights movement, with international criminal tribunals and truth commissions on the rise.

[68] The TRC and CAVR had all four key investigative powers that I studied in Chapter 4. The CEH had two.

[69] Hayner 2001, 2011.

[70] Future research should evaluate whether the relationships proposed here are portable to the other two commissions Hayner spotlights (Peru and Morocco) and yet others still. The Moroccan case would be especially interesting to scholars studying TJ under authoritarian governments.

The three countries are also valuable for the lessons they offer for what we might see in different contexts. The Guatemalan case gives insight into what we might see in post-conflict contexts, the South African case offers a glimpse into what we might see in post-authoritarian contexts, and the Timorese case provides a perspective into what we might see in formerly occupied countries. Conversely, if I find dissimilar outcomes, they cannot be caused by factors that are constant across cases—that is, a key role for NGOs in commission adoption, design, and operation.

Supportive evidence from each case will bolster my argument that domestic NGOs attempt to set the post-commission agenda and that they do so through a process of selecting and framing issues, navigating political opportunity structures, and leveraging mobilizing structures like their international networks.[71] The analysis will also help us better understand the process through which NGOs in other parts of the world may place some issues on the table while leaving other issues off the table, as well as the barriers they may encounter and the strategies they may employ to overcome them. With this information in hand, I will then be able to explain why governments might implement some recommendations but not others, preferring those endorsed by NGOs in general and broad coalitions of NGOs in particular.

Truth Commission Recommendations in Guatemala, South Africa, and Timor-Leste

The third and final *Varieties of Truth Commissions* dataset, "Truth Commissions and Implementation of Recommendations: Guatemala, South Africa, and Timor-Leste," captures 87 CEH recommendations, 313 TRC recommendations, and 247 CAVR recommendations. Figure 5.11 displays relative percentages of recommendations across five substantive areas: truth, justice, reparations, institutional reforms, and services. Despite their countries' political, historical, and cultural differences, the three commissions made remarkably similar types of recommendations and broadly reflect the global sample.

Institutional and policy isomorphism is to be expected in the TJ realm. Take, for instance, institutional reforms, which, as Figure 5.11 shows, was a key area of concern for each commission. Bad actors thrive in, or in the shadow of, bad institutions. Accordingly, commissions designed to investigate entities like armed groups and authoritarian governments may be similarly interested in legal, personnel, and other reforms. Measures for truth were another focal point for the

[71] Bennett and Checkel 2015.

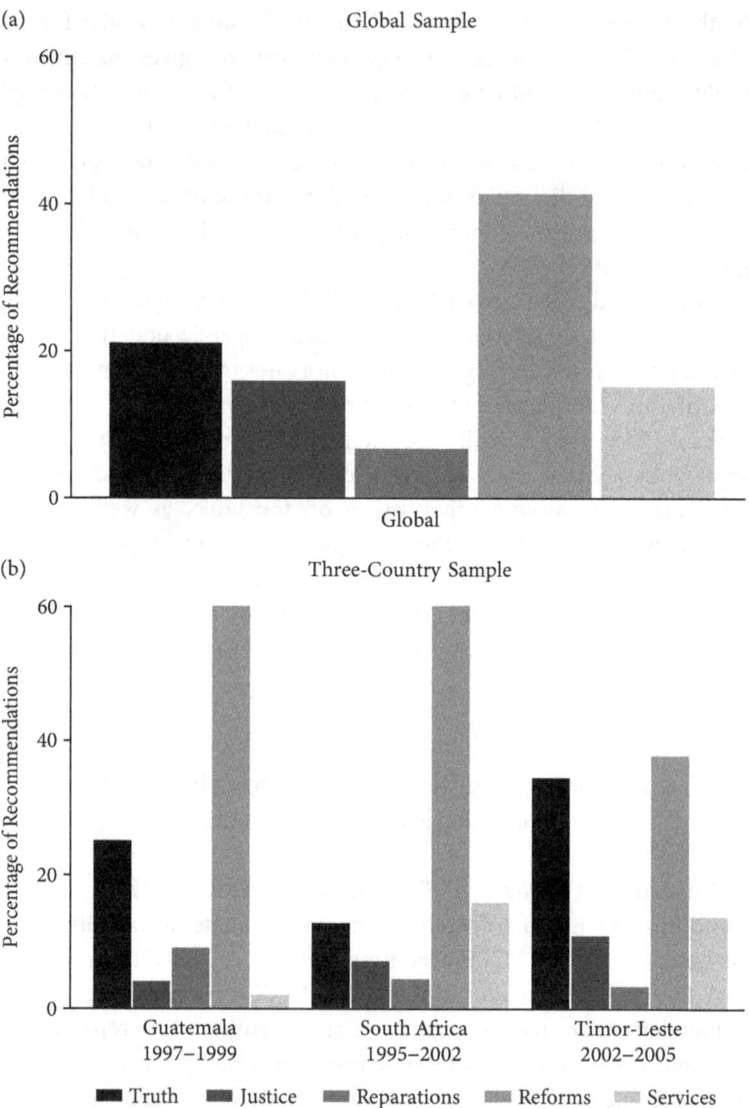

Figure 5.11 Recommendation Types: Guatemala, South Africa, and Timor–Leste vs. Global Sample

Note: The figure shows the percentage of recommendations across five substantive areas—truth, justice, reparations, institutional reforms, and services—in Guatemala, South Africa, and Timor-Leste, compared to the global sample.

Guatemalan and Timorese commissions, as were services for the South African and Timorese commissions. See online Appendix C for further breakdowns of the three-country data.

Research Design

To make the case that NGOs attempt to set the post-commission agenda, I produce in Chapters 6, 7, and 8 a structured comparison of post-commission Guatemala, South Africa, and Timor-Leste. Each chapter is divided into two parts.

The analysis in Part One of each chapter is descriptive. I begin by showcasing NGO agenda-setting attempts across the 647 CEH, TRC, and CAVR recommendations, with the recommendation as the unit of analysis.[72] The *Varieties of Truth Commissions* additionally capture the presence and size of NGO coalitions active in different substantive areas (e.g., exhumations and forensic anthropology, trials, judicial reforms, memorialization, and education) and the truth commission recommendations they raised before policymakers. These data were constructed using NGO documents (e.g., annual reports), government documents (e.g., minutes from parliamentary sessions), IO documents (e.g., UN treaty body reports), newspapers, and secondary analyses. Each list of NGOs was assembled in a snowball fashion. See online Appendix C for details.

This descriptive analysis provides insight into the "what" and suggests the "why" of civil society post-commission advocacy priorities. To better understand the "why" and the "how," I examine NGO issue prioritization and advocacy. Drawing on materials from my interviews with representatives of human rights groups, governments, and IOs, I follow the multistep process of framing commission recommendations, contending with prohibitive political conditions, and mobilizing structures.

The analysis in Part Two of each chapter is quantitative and qualitative. I perform statistical analyses of recommendations uptake and recommendations fulfillment by the Guatemalan, South African, and Timorese governments, evaluating the influence of NGO advocacy and advocacy coalition size on the likelihood of recommendations being initiated and completed. My data capture whether implementation of a given recommendation was initiated and the degree of implementation achieved (minimal, intermediate, or full), first within five years and then ten years of a commission's conclusion. Qualitative evidence from my fieldwork enriches these quantitative data.

Process tracing combined with statistical analysis is useful when the relationship between the explanatory variable(s)—here, NGO interests and advocacy—and the outcome variable(s)—here, policy selection and implementation—is plausible but the exact mechanisms are not clear.[73] Evidence from crucial cases

[72] Tables 6.1, 7.1, and 8.1 in Chapters 6, 7, and 8, respectively, present information on the substantive issue areas the CEH, TRC, and CAVR addressed, which I discuss alongside information on involved NGOs.

[73] Gerring 2007.

is exceedingly valuable.[74] It is in settings like Guatemala, South Africa, and Timor-Leste that we would expect to see policymakers acquiescing to demands for continued efforts toward truth, justice, reparation, and institutional reform, and doing so because they have become accustomed to human rights principles advanced by transnational civil society actors.

Measuring Implementation

The first dependent variable in the implementation analysis is *Implementation Initiated*. It is binary, taking a value of 1 for a given recommendation if there was any evidence of efforts to realize the recommendation; otherwise, 0. Evidence of initiation can include a parliamentary debate on the subject of a given recommendation or set of recommendations, a memo from an executive agency, a speech from a policymaker, and so on. The second dependent variable, *Implementation Level*, is a three-point variable that captures whether a recommendation reached minimal, intermediate, or full implementation. I construct measures capturing implementation within five years and within ten years of a commission's conclusion.

Implementation was automatically coded as *minimal* if implementation was initiated. To borrow an example from South Africa, the TRC proposed trials for South African Police Service (SAPS) agents who faced credible accusations of assault, torture, and extrajudicial killings and who had failed to testify before the commission. While the National Prosecuting Authority received hundreds of referrals for prosecution and began investigations in 2003 (five years after the initial release of the TRC report in 1998), prosecutors did not seriously pursue SAPS agents within the following five years and have not done so in a serious way in the years since.[75] As I will discuss more in Chapter 7, there has even been government interference in these and other TRC cases.

Implementation was coded as *intermediate* if further steps were taken toward full implementation within the respective five- and ten-year windows of analysis. For instance, in Guatemala, the CEH recommended an internal accountability and inspection unit for the National Civil Police. While a national commission for security was established in 2001, following the dissolution of the ambulatory military police, the council's exact functions were not fully defined or publicly reported.[76] There were reports, too, of security commission members working *against* provisions of the peace accords relevant to the security sector. Internal control mechanisms such as this one have been largely ineffective, if not counterproductive.[77]

[74] Bennett 2010; Bennett and Checkel 2015; Collier 2011; George and Bennett 2005; Gerring 2007; Mahoney 2010.

[75] Burke 2016; Farbstein 2015.

[76] Salvesen 2002, 10.

[77] Salvesen 2002, 10; Aeby and Barrachina 2007.

Implementation was coded as *full* if all elements of the recommendation were achieved. To borrow another example, this time from Timor-Leste, the CAVR recommended that the government ratify the UN Convention Against Corruption. Timor-Leste did so within five years.

Measuring NGO Advocacy

The first independent variable in the implementation analysis is *NGO Advocacy*. It is binary and captures, for a given recommendation (e.g., to conduct an international search for disappeared children), whether at least one domestic NGO advocated for it; otherwise, 0. The second independent variable, *NGO Coalition Size*, is a count of domestic NGOs advocating for recommendations in a particular issue area (e.g., victim identification). The third independent variable, *INGO Coalition Size*, is also a count and is measured like *NGO Coalition Size*. Organizations did not have to explicitly cite a recommendation by name or number. For example, if there was a recommendation to disband a particular branch of the security services and groups organized protests where participants called for that security services branch to be disbanded, this was counted as recommendation-specific advocacy.

In Guatemala, 71 of 87 recommendations (82 percent) were represented by at least one domestic NGO. Domestic NGO coalition sizes ranged between 5 and 41 organizations, while INGO coalition sizes ranged between 1 and 9 organizations. In South Africa, 213 of 313 recommendations (68 percent) were represented by at least one domestic NGO. Domestic NGO coalition sizes ranged between 1 and 47 organizations, while INGO coalition sizes ranged between 1 and 17. In Timor-Leste, 162 of 247 recommendations (66 percent) were represented by at least one domestic NGO. Domestic NGO coalition sizes ranged between 2 and 121 organizations, while INGO coalition sizes ranged between 1 and 53.

Managing Limitations

One limitation of the data collection is that there may be cases of NGO collaboration, domestically and internationally, that my research team missed because we did not find published, electronically available information attesting to it. Another limitation is that there may be instances where NGOs do not want to be seen as collaborating, perhaps especially along the domestic–international axis, amid shrinking civic space.[78] For this reason, I do not "hang my hat," as the saying goes, on the quantitative data but rely heavily on qualitative evidence from the field involving civil society, government, and IO stakeholders.

[78] Chaudhry Forthcoming.

6
Post-Commission NGO Advocacy: Success, Challenges, and Innovations in Guatemala

In 1992, the Association of Relatives of the Detained and Disappeared of Guatemala (FAMDEGUA) was founded to press the government to investigate the whereabouts of approximately 45,000 people and to return them to their communities. Tragically, for many, this would not come to pass. While their fates—and the fates of thousands of others disappeared during the 1960–1996 internal armed conflict—have never officially been determined, it is all but certain that they perished at the hands of the state. In some cases, this is a known fact.

During my fieldwork in Guatemala in early 2020, I had the privilege of visiting FAMDEGUA's headquarters in downtown Guatemala City, a building secured by a wrought-iron gate designed to protect the organization's members, visitors, and a trove of documents painstakingly assembled with all available information on disappeared, detained, and executed persons. I met with Manuel Farfán, the director and son of renowned human rights activist and FAMDEGUA cofounder Aura Elena Farfán. Manuel is also the nephew of Rubén Amílcar Farfán, who was disappeared on May 15, 1984, and confirmed dead in the infamous *Diario Militar*, a military death squad diary leaked to the public in 1999. The confirmation? The number "300" added to the entry on Rubén.

Prior to, during, and after the truth commission (known by its acronym in Spanish, CEH), FAMDEGUA and its partners agitated for truth and justice for victims and their families[1]—(1) making appeals to the government for information on the fates of the disappeared; (2) calling for resources to be allocated to families to pursue judicial remedies; and (3) pressing for exhumations, the return of remains to families, and reburials.[2] FAMDEGUA helped bolster the CEH investigation and report, and the CEH, in turn, helped bolster FAMDEGUA's work. The organization has advocated for more than a dozen

[1] I highlight especially the Working Group Against Enforced Disappearance of Guatemala, which includes the International Center for Human Rights Research, the Human Rights Commission of Guatemala, the Mutual Support Group, and the Forensic Anthropology Foundation of Guatemala.

[2] ODHAG 1998. Author interview with Manuel Farfán.

Governing Truth. Kelebogile Zvobgo, Oxford University Press. © Oxford University Press (2026).
DOI: 10.1093/oso/9780197815663.003.0006

discrete CEH recommendations, and has even integrated CEH-recommended legal reforms into its advocacy portfolio.

Never one to rely on the state to deliver on its obligations, FAMDEGUA has led in the search for disappeared persons, participated in exhumations of clandestine cemeteries, and supported families with reburials.[3] Along with many others, the organization has worked with the Office of the Human Rights Ombudsman on a range of issues, including remedies for victims' families.

Equally noteworthy has been FAMDEGUA's legal representation and support of families in national and international courts, one of the most famous being *"Las Dos Erres" Massacre v. Guatemala*, which the Inter-American Court of Human Rights (IACtHR) heard a decade after the CEH recommended criminal accountability for killings, torture, and forced disappearance. In 2009, the court determined that Guatemala had violated the American Convention on Human Rights, the Inter-American Convention on the Prevention, Punishment, and Eradication of Violence Against Women, and the Inter-American Convention to Prevent and Punish Torture. Accordingly, the court ordered Guatemala to deliver a range of remedies, including bringing individual perpetrators to justice, identifying and returning victims' remains to their next of kin, making reparations, promoting education, and constructing a memorial.[4]

This landmark judgment and order for remedies echoed back to the CEH report. One of my interviewees, Carlos Beristain, an investigator with the Inter-American Commission on Human Rights (IACmHR) and a former member of the Recovery of Historical Memory (REMHI) Project, emphasized that civil society groups like FAMDEGUA and Indigenous movements are the reason TJ processes have advanced for Guatemala at both a domestic and international level.

The case of FAMDEGUA prompts us to query why and how NGOs lend their advocacy to some TJ issues, represented by truth commission recommendations, and not others in the post-commission period. Do they focus on the issues they know best in order to leverage their technical expertise and professional experience, or do they expand their focus and take on new issues? And is NGOs' representation of particular issues and recommendations connected to governments' delivery of further TJ measures?

In this chapter and the two that follow, I study how civil society governs post-commission TJ. Per the theory, at the earlier adoption stage, civil society promotes the norm and practice of truth telling following political violence, pressuring the government to create a truth commission and, at the design stage, purveys the norm and practice of effective truth telling, prompting the

[3] Wandita et al. 2006.
[4] IACtHR 2009.

government to design a commission with strong powers in order to uncover as much of the truth as possible. Now, at the post-commission stage, civil society advances the norm and practice of responding to the now-revealed truth, driving the government to implement commission recommendations. But how?

Groups first determine their advocacy priorities and strategies, selecting some issues and recommendations but not others. Groups then execute their advocacy strategies, converging on the government to deliver on specific recommendations via a process of framing, overcoming political barriers, and taking advantage of professional networks and network resources. Lastly, groups assist the government with implementation, increasing the state's capacity,[5] and, in some instances, they substitute for it.

Each of these three chapters is divided into two parts in which I leverage qualitative data from my fieldwork and quantitative data from the *Varieties of Truth Commissions*, which capture NGO advocacy and government implementation of truth commission recommendations. In Part One, I study post-commission *advocacy effort*, which entails setting priorities and determining strategies for advocacy. Evaluating advocacy effort is important for understanding why governments might follow up on some recommendations but not others.

In terms of *advocacy priorities*, I assess two competing propositions from Chapter 5. The first proposition is that organizations advocate exclusively for recommendations that match their organizational interests and prior professional experience. Civil society groups have limited resources, so this is a straightforward way for them to economize on resources and realize important policies. This is one way to burden share, with groups doing their part in their areas of expertise. The second proposition is that civil society groups evolve and transform their missions under the guidance of outgoing truth commissions and with the infusion of resources from international partners. This is another way to burden share, with groups partnering on more issues and projects than those they know best.

In terms of *advocacy strategies*, I anticipate that domestic civil society groups and coalitions produce frames around a commission's work—diagnosing outstanding TJ problems, prescribing solutions, prognosticating the consequences of action and inaction, and offering motivations for governments to act. I also foresee them navigating prohibitive political conditions, like low political will in government, by forging alliances with sympathetic decision makers. Finally, I expect groups to mobilize their resources and networks, notably international civil society partners who, per my burden sharing model, participate in post-commission activities from a supporting position.

[5] González-Ocantos 2020. Author interview with Cristián Correa, based on his experience as a human rights advisor to Chilean President Michelle Bachelet.

In Part Two, I assess a further proposition, this time related to *advocacy success*. I propose that, once domestic groups have determined their advocacy strategies—that is, how they will frame issues, contend with prohibitive political conditions, and mobilize networks and resources—they execute that strategy, engaging in tactics like lobbying and protest to push governments to implement recommendations. Essentially, they repurpose at the post-commission stage some of the methods they employed at the pre-commission stage. Where needed, domestic groups assist governments with recommendations delivery or do so themselves. Throughout, international groups provide operational and political support (e.g., by educating their domestic partners on how to design a reparations program).

In Part One of this chapter, I find that the Guatemalan CEH's recommendations have been very important to NGO advocacy over the past two, almost three, decades. My interviews revealed that the text of the commission report is front-of-mind and at the fingertips of NGO workers, in particular the commission's eighty-plus recommendations. In terms of advocacy issue selection, I find that instead of focusing solely on recommendations related to their previous work and experience, as some prior research would lead us to expect, NGOs in Guatemala diversified their portfolios at the CEH's prompting. While their pre-commission portfolios have remained at the core of their work and identity—for example, investigating forced disappearances for FAMDEGUA and GAM, whose story I told in Chapter 3—groups have also made strides into other issue areas. This has spurred knowledge and resource sharing within the human rights community, tightening links between and among NGOs. INGOs like Impunity Watch and even IOs like the United Nations have also shared the burden of post-commission TJ, lending domestic groups financial, logistical, and political support.

In Part Two, I find that NGO advocacy has yielded remarkable success in Guatemala, especially when we consider the many roadblocks that successive administrations have set on the path to progress. This is due in large part to the fact that Guatemalan civilian governments since the end of the internal armed conflict have operated in the shadow of the military, which has remained a veto player despite the peace accords and the CEH. Still, I find positive post-commission policy outcomes tied to TJ network members, in particular domestic NGOs, advancing different CEH recommendations. The data suggest that wherever NGOs have been influential, their advocacy for specific measures has been as important as, if not more important than, the size of their coalitions. Statistical analyses indicate a strong role for NGOs in spurring the government to *make progress* on TJ policies but a weak role in driving the government to *select particular issues* over others. The Guatemalan government *has not* prioritized implementing recommendations supported by domestic NGO coalitions, even large ones. But, among those that it has elected to implement, the government has ultimately made better progress on NGO-supported recommendations. Case analysis then shows that in situations where the government has been unwilling or unable to provide additional remedies, NGOs have intervened, assisting the government with implementation in some instances and substituting for it in other instances.

These findings provide evidence for the third part of the burden sharing model: Domestic groups, who are fundamental to any country's long-term commitments to human rights and justice, have played a leading role. They have selected issues, framed problems and solutions, navigated prohibitive political conditions with the help of influential allies, and mobilized their resources and networks, including international partnerships, to set the post-commission TJ agenda. They have also assisted with, and in some cases led, the delivery of this agenda. International groups, with commitments in Guatemala and elsewhere in the world, have played a supporting role.

Plan of the Chapter

Part One starts with a brief history of the internal armed conflict in Guatemala. It also discusses the truth commission's development, operation, findings, and recommendations. I then present the descriptive analysis of NGO advocacy. Specifically, I describe the presence and size of NGO coalitions across different substantive issue areas. Following this, I trace the presence of the observable implications of the causal process that I have proposed, from defining issue portfolios, to framing, to navigating prohibitive conditions, and, finally, to mobilizing resources and networks. I do this across five areas of note: (1) searching for the disappeared and finding justice, (2) exhumations, forensic science, and reburials, (3) reforming the judiciary, (4) holistic reparations, and (5) education and memorialization.

Part Two starts with an overview of Guatemala's TJ policies following the CEH, describing the initiation of different policies across four key areas—truth, justice, reparations, and institutional reforms—and the level of implementation reached—minimal, intermediate, or full. After this, I present the quantitative analysis, which estimates the likelihood of governments in Guatemala initiating and implementing recommendations fully, given NGO support and especially broad NGO support. This is supplemented by a qualitative analysis, again drawing on my fieldwork interviews. This analysis indicates the extent to which civil society has been responsible for post-commission government TJ policy progress and reveals in some areas civil society's substitution for the state.

Part One: *Memoria del Silencio* (Memory of Silence)

Between 1960 and 1996, an estimated 200,000 people were killed or disappeared, and more than a million others were displaced, during Guatemala's internal armed conflict, fought between government forces and the leftist Guatemalan National Revolutionary Unit (URNG). The conflict was precipitated in part by the 1954 CIA-orchestrated coup against Jacobo Arbenz's democratically elected government. After nearly four decades of conflict, the Government and the URNG signed in Oslo, Norway, the Agreement on a Firm and Lasting Peace, entering into force a set of ten agreements, the third of which created the CEH.

Initially proposed by civil society groups, the truth commission conducted a nearly two-year investigation into conflict-related abuses and released its report in 1999. Bolstered by the civil society-led REMHI project, which I discussed in the previous chapter, the CEH produced a robust report establishing a concrete record of abuses. The CEH determined that the military and its affiliates committed 93 percent of violations and that the Indigenous Mayan population suffered 83 percent of the abuses. The report provided a point of reference to raise awareness of the excesses of state violence. The finding of "genocidal acts" in particular spurred on the movement for additional TJ measures in the country.[6] The report also contained dozens of recommendations that, per my theory, NGOs used—and, significantly, continue to use—to affirm the validity and necessity of their work and to advance TJ beyond the commission.

This has not been an easy process. The post-commission period in Guatemala has been rife with contestation between civil society and the government, with some administrations even attempting to "end" TJ. For example, at the time of my field research in early 2020, President Alejandro Giammattei threatened to terminate several institutions created by the peace accords, including the Secretariat for Peace, the executive agency responsible for monitoring implementation of the 1996 accords, as well as the National Reparations Program. Dozens of organizations protested this action, but by the end of the year, Giammattei had shut down the Secretariat.

These actions undermined the ongoing process of peace and justice and contravened victims' rights. But these actions also affirm my broader argument: TJ is not primarily, and certainly not exclusively, led by governments but, rather, by civil society. Interestingly, the Giammattei administration did not dissolve the National Reparations Program, suggesting some sensitivity to criticism and NGOs' ability to limit, if not altogether stop, TJ backsliding. All of

[6] The CEH report, like the REMHI report, continues to serve as evidence at the IACtHR. Because of these reports, "It is now impossible to negate the truth, that there was violence and genocide of Maya," Carlos Beristain said.

this is to say, TJ measures in Guatemala—however flawed, incomplete, interrupted, or dismantled—only materialized because of strong, focused, persistent NGO activism. And the CEH's investigation, findings, and recommendations have been at the heart of this activism.

NGOs by Commission Recommendation Area

Table 6.1 shows the seventeen substantive areas the CEH addressed in its recommendations, grouped by TJ theme. The data show at least one domestic NGO working in each area prior to the CEH. However, the number of groups varied. For example, thirty-six organizations, including the National Victims' Movement, were advancing memorial projects; fifty-one organizations were promoting education, among them the Human Rights Office of the Archbishop of Guatemala (ODHAG); and twenty-nine organizations were identifying victims. The Center for Forensic Analysis and Applied Sciences (CAFCA) and the Forensic Anthropology Foundation of Guatemala (FAFG), specialized organizations that require the intermediation of local organizations to establish contact with families, took leading roles in this area.[7]

Table 6.1 Substantive Recommendations from the Guatemalan CEH

Recommendation Areas	
Truth	**Reforms**
Education	Democracy
Exhumations	Human rights
Information disclosure	International institutions
Memorialization	Legal
Victim identification	New domestic institutions
	Personnel
Justice	
Judicial reforms	**Services**
Trials	Social welfare
	Victim rehabilitation
Reparations	
Material	
Symbolic	

[7] See Chapter 5 and online Appendix C for more information on how the lists of NGOs by recommendation and recommendation area were assembled.

NGOs by Commission Recommendation

Given the breadth of pre-CEH NGO activity, it should come as no surprise that most of the commission's proposals were adopted by one group or another. Notwithstanding, some recommendations fell through the cracks. Take, for instance, personnel reforms. The CEH recommended diversifying the newly created National Civil Police and training police candidates in human rights, intercultural competence and communication, and nonviolent conflict resolution. While there were several organizations that advocated for CEH-recommended personnel reforms, including police reforms, my research team did not find documentation indicating that groups explicitly pressed for these two measures. NGOs concerned with personnel reforms focused heavily on the military, giving special attention to its reconfiguration and submission to civilian oversight and control. This makes intuitive sense: The military was the major aggressor during the conflict, and so, among institutions needing reform, it drew the most attention.

Now, just because members of the Guatemalan human rights community adopted most recommendations does not mean they represented recommendations uniformly. For instance, while there were nearly forty organizations promoting symbolic reparations, we only found evidence of four organizations—including the Mayan-led National Victims' Movement—that asked the government to reclaim and restore sacred Mayan sites that had been targeted during the internal armed conflict. Later in the chapter, I evaluate whether the breadth of lobbying coalitions has influenced the likelihood of the government initiating implementation of particular recommendations and implementing them fully.

Qualitative Analysis: Agenda Setting

For the descriptive qualitative analysis of post-commission agenda-setting attempts in Guatemala, I rely on nearly two dozen semi-structured interviews that I conducted in early 2020. I interviewed executive directors, managers, lawyers, and staff members of fifteen leading NGOs. I also interviewed government officials, notably in the Office of the Human Rights Ombudsman, the Office of the Prosecutor for Human Rights, and the Secretariat for Peace. I also had the opportunity to speak with the head of the UNDP Transitional Justice Accompaniment Programme (PAJUST) and, in March 2022, a former IACtHR judge. I conducted all but the last interview in person in Guatemala City.

Issue Portfolios

The first observable implication of NGOs attempting to set governments' post-commission TJ agenda is issue selection. Some prior research indicates that NGOs will draw governments' attention to issues (in our case, truth commission recommendations) that are already part of their platforms. This is not what we see in Guatemala. Instead, we see mission creep, with NGOs evolving their missions and activities.

Rather than focus solely on recommendations relating to their previous work and organizational expertise, Guatemalan NGOs diversified their portfolios. As an example, the Myrna Mack Foundation (FMM), which had a long history advocating for legal and judicial reforms, incorporated into its portfolio memorialization projects and reparations for survivors and victims' families. Likewise, GAM, which had been focused on searching for victims of forced disappearance, began advocating for legal reforms highlighted by the CEH (e.g., to promulgate new laws to criminalize genocide and torture). GAM also lobbied for legislation to define forced disappearance as an ongoing crime, thereby overcoming the problem of retroactivity and making the crime of forced disappearance justiciable in Guatemala. In sum, there was notable crossover into different issue areas. This is evidence of burden sharing; if groups already working in a particular advocacy area could do it on their own, we would not see crossover. Further, we would not see so many organizations active across recommendations and recommendation areas.

The NGO representatives I interviewed, including GAM legal advisor Carlos Juárez, expressed that their pre-commission portfolios were a function of what they knew, their piece of what they would later understand to be "transitional justice." During the conflict, organizations like GAM did not operate under the full TJ framework because they did not really know about it, Juárez reported. The language of TJ and knowledge of the TJ toolkit came in phases.

GAM's executive director, Mario Polanco, elaborated that in the 1980s, GAM leaders and members simply wanted to know the truth, in particular the fates of the disappeared. In the 1990s, the organization (and the broader human rights community) became interested in justice, prompted in part by the CEH's finding of genocidal acts by the military. So their portfolio grew to encompass truth *and* justice. Relatedly, with the CEH's validating account, GAM and other organizations sought remedies for survivors and victims' families, including reparations, and measures for nonrepetition like judicial and legal reforms. These measures included the Law for Postulation Commissions, to make merit the central criterion for judicial appointments. A reformed judiciary, they believed, would help combat impunity and deter would-be human rights violators. So GAM's portfolio now included truth, justice, reparations, and institutional reforms.

These findings are consistent with the proposition that civil society groups transform their missions under the guidance of outgoing truth commissions. Below, I trace NGOs framing issues, navigating challenging political environments, and capitalizing on their networks, including international actors.

Framing

The second observable implication of the theory is that NGOs frame the outputs of a TJ process to make them more actionable for governments. In the case of truth commissions, we should see NGOs re-articulating commission findings and recommendations. And this is exactly what happened in post-commission Guatemala. NGOs diagnosed the problem of the past in somewhat different but complementary ways. This reflects their distinct but nevertheless overlapping post-commission portfolios and evinces burden sharing between and among organizations. With each diagnosis came a clear prognosis, a prescription for policymakers, and a compelling motivation for action. Below are a few examples.

Searching for the Disappeared and Finding Justice

Knowing that there was still so much to be known about the past, even with the CEH's investigation and hefty report, GAM, along with FAMDEGUA, the Association for Justice and Reconciliation (AJR), and the Center for Legal Action in Human Rights (CALDH), among others, diagnosed the problem of insufficient truth and justice for victims. Consequently, the groups prescribed a national and international search for the disappeared, as specified in the CEH report, and legal assistance for families to pursue criminal cases against suspected perpetrators. The groups motivated their demands by warning about the possibility of a relapse into violence should the recommendations not be delivered. They also held that without a robust search resulting in information for families and, in some cases, contributing to trials, Guatemalan society would never have closure and could never truly move on from the past.[8]

Exhumations, Forensic Science, and Reburials

Likewise, organizations, including CAFCA, FAFG, the International Center for Human Rights Research (CIIDH), the National Victims' Movement, and the Truth and Life Civil Association, identified the problem of not knowing the fates of many of the disappeared, including children. However, this second group of organizations zeroed in on the issue of too-few forensic investigations that

[8] Author interviews with Mario Polanco, Carlos Juárez, Manuel Farfán, and CALDH communications director Fabiola García.

could, in the first instance, provide families answers and potentially closure and, in the second instance, serve as evidence in criminal trials. They prioritized and presented the truth commission's recommendations to identify clandestine cemeteries, including on military bases, and conduct exhumations, match and return remains to families, and assist with reburials. Groups were motivated by the idea that without forensic evidence, families would be left without answers and could not seek judicial remedies and other forms of redress. Moreover, perpetrators would enjoy impunity.[9]

Reforming the Judiciary

By contrast, FMM discerned a broader problem plaguing Guatemala: a broken judiciary. FMM pinpointed corruption in the judicial appointments process and a lack of judicial independence. Indeed, many judges were appointed not due to merit but, rather, because of their ties to the military. This impeded their ability to mete out justice for victims. What's more, judges lacked proper training and professionalization, making them even less able to adjudicate on difficult cases. FMM and partners, including GAM and CALDH, consequently urged legal and judicial reforms outlined by the truth commission. The organization motivated its petitions as fundamental elements of a functioning democratic state subservient to the rule of law.[10]

Holistic Reparations

While many conceive of reparations as monetary compensation for harms suffered, the National Coordinator of Guatemalan Widows (CONAVIGUA) and the Community Studies and Psychosocial Action Team (ECAP) affirm that reparations are—and, indeed, must be—so much more. CONAVIGUA and ECAP identified a lack of holistic reparations in the government's post-conflict response. And, as with the commission, these organizations and their local partners called for a comprehensive approach, encompassing apologies, psychosocial support, mental health care, and restoration of cultural heritage. In addition, CONAVIGUA, as a Mayan women's organization, raised the issue of acknowledging and repairing the harms suffered by victims of SGBV, who were in many ways marginalized in the CEH's investigation. Undergirding the groups' focus on holistic reparations has been the idea that a multipronged approach is essential to restoring communities.[11]

[9] Author interviews with CAFCA director Rafael Herrarte, CAFCA forensic anthropologist and historian Erwin Melgar, CIIDH president Carlos Fernández Pérez, FAFG special assistant to the executive director Erica Henderson, National Victims' Movement founder Juana Tipaz, and Truth and Life coordinator Dora Mirón.

[10] Author interview with Andy Javalois.

[11] Author interviews with CONAVIGUA founding member and head Rosalina Tuyuc, ECAP cofounder Felipe Sarti, and ECAP coordinator for special programs for survivors of human rights violations Elizabeth Pedraza.

Education and Memorialization

Together with ODHAG, the Central American Regional Research Center (CIRMA), and its offshoot, the International Institute of Learning for Social Reconciliation (IIARS), noted the lack of formal education about the internal armed conflict, especially outside the rural areas. In line with the CEH's recommendations, ODHAG pleaded for a national sensitization program, and CIRMA and IIARS proposed a national educational curriculum on "recent history," human rights, interculturalism, and democracy.

The Peace Foundation and Memorial for Peace, newer entrants in this space, have expressed related concerns about the loss of memory, especially without physical sites of memory. Together with CIRMA, IIARS, and ODHAG, they have warned of the risks that this poses for future repetition of abuses and they have advocated for both physical and virtual sites of memory.[12] The Sons and Daughters for Identity and Justice Against Forgetting and Silence (HIJOS), a collective of orphans of the disappeared who engage in contentious politics, has similarly urged public commemorations.

Navigating Prohibitive Political Conditions

The third observable implication of the theory is that NGOs contend with prohibitive political conditions by gaining access to policymaking bodies and cultivating allies in government. Here, I present Guatemalan NGO leaders' perspectives on post-CEH barriers to TJ, with a focus on four recurring themes: low political will, corruption, government turnover, and fluctuating economic resources. I then chronicle how groups in different areas have exercised the law, their expertise, and their respected position among domestic and international publics to overcome (some of) these obstacles to agenda setting.

NGOs have faced a range of obstacles when advocating for TJ measures since the CEH. The first is low levels of political will within and across governments since 1999. "No one is interested in finding [more of] the truth; they are scared of justice," GAM's Mario Polanco declared. CONAVIGUA head Rosalina Tuyuc similarly conveyed that there has been "zero political will" on the part of the state to realize a public policy of reparation that is holistic and effective. "They have never supported us," she relayed. Echoing Tuyuc nearly verbatim, Juana Tipaz

[12] Author interviews with ODHAG's Historical Memory Program director Patricia Ogaldes, ODHAG's Monseñor Gerardi Memory Center director Carolina Rendón, Peace Foundation artist and curator Maya Juracán, IIARS manager César García, and Memorial director Julio Solórzano Foppa.

of the National Victims' Movement expressed, "It is really sad that the State has not supported us . . . especially with the search for the children."[13]

FMM attorney Andy Javalois concentrated on the problem of corruption and the ubiquity of "influencers" in Guatemalan politics. Linked to the military, these "bosses" have interfered in investigations and legal proceedings. With every two steps forward, there has been at least one step backward. A related problem is the diversion of funds from institutions like the National Reparations Program into the pockets of elites. To cite an example, members of the program's board, said to be volunteers, have not-so-secretly drawn handsome salaries from the money intended for reparations to survivors and victims' families.

Then there has been the challenge of government turnover. IIARS manager César García recounted, "Every four years, there is a new government, a new set of public policies. We have to adapt all the time." In a similar vein, Emir Mejía, director of information and documentation in the former Secretariat for Peace, judged that each successive government "does not see ahead to the future"—a position shared by ODHAG's Patricia Ogaldes, who communicated that progress, like regress, depends on who is in government. Some administrations have been somewhat helpful, but most have been exceedingly unhelpful. When CAFCA director Rafael Herrarte told me that "there has never been a leader who is strong enough, who has the courage to [truly] support civil society [and our goals]," I did not appreciate that this extended to not supporting the very institutions the government established to achieve peace.

Related to government turnover is fluctuating resources accorded to those few government bodies responsible for dealing with human rights complaints like the Human Rights Ombudsman. Alejandro Reyes, head of special investigations, reported that his unit, along with the larger ombudsman office, has had its funding cut regularly, in some years by as much as 20 percent. FAFG's Erica Henderson also raised funding and bureaucratic red tape as key obstacles to FAFG's forensic investigations.

Despite, or perhaps because of, these barriers, NGOs in Guatemala have been savvy to find allies inside and outside government and have gained access to key institutions, notably the Human Rights Ombudsman and Public Ministry. This has facilitated implementation of the CEH's recommendations.

[13] This finding is not unique to Guatemala. Examining the Southern Cone, Lessa (2022, 141) writes, "Strong pro-impunity pressures from the cronies of old regimes and their sympathizers, as well as weak or appeasing new democratic regimes and political leaders, frequently define the years following a transition. . . . Later on, other challenges persist, including the residual power of former perpetrators, the predominance of passive judiciaries and public prosecutors, and the lack of political will to probe a contested past." Cronin-Furman (2022, 7) has observed similar dynamics in Bahrain, Sudan, and Sri Lanka, where "there is a range of relevant actors with decision-making power . . . [that] disrupt . . . accountability."

Searching for the Disappeared and Finding Justice

NGOs whose primary focus is searching for victims of forced disappearance and finding justice have gained access to the Public Ministry, Human Rights Ombudsman, and national courts through a novel legal personality, *querellante adhesivo*, created in the 1992 Guatemalan code of criminal procedure.[14] Private individuals and organizations with a demonstrated stake in a criminal matter may be designated a *querellante adhesivo* (auxiliary or third-party prosecutor). For example, Helen Mack—sister of slain forensic anthropologist and human rights defender Myrna Mack—is competent to serve as a *querellante adhesivo* in human rights cases related to the internal armed conflict, as is FMM. This legal personality has brought individuals and groups with an interest in accountability for conflict-related abuses directly into state institutions.[15] NGOs help realize private prosecution's potential as a societal check.[16]

Exhumations, Forensic Science, and Reburials

Forensic anthropology groups like CAFCA, CIIDH, and FAFG have earned access to key government institutions because of their expertise and respected position among domestic and international publics. To quote Alejandro Reyes from the Human Rights Ombudsman's office, "We [the government] need them [civil society] and they need us." Because of the strong partnerships that it has forged, CAFCA in particular has helped to improve the competence and capacity of the Human Rights Ombudsman and the Public Ministry (e.g., by developing a standard protocol for forensic work, supplying operational assistance for exhumations, and offering workshops and trainings for prosecutors). Meanwhile, CIIDH has formed alliances with select members of the legislature and lobbied them to respectively vote up and vote down pro- and anti-human rights legislative proposals.

Reforming the Judiciary

FMM has enjoyed special access to the courts of Guatemala because of its designation as a *querellante adhesivo*. Beyond this, the organization has had access to some members of the National Congress, who have relied on the organization's assistance in drafting legislation.

[14] See Michel's (2018) analysis of private prosecutors in Chile, Guatemala, and Mexico.

[15] Michel (2018) explores the influence of private prosecutors as a quality-control mechanism and finds that they help the state keep cases open, win justice for victims, and improve perceptions of the judicial system.

[16] Michel 2018, 16.

Holistic Reparations

Because of their intimate relationships with survivors and victims' families, CONAVIGUA, ECAP, and others were invited to work directly with the National Reparations Program to implement reparations. CONAVIGUA's Rosalina Tuyuc even headed the program from 2004 to 2008—said to be its most productive years. Yet, despite this noteworthy access, working with the government has been an experience fraught with grief for NGOs and their members. Tuyuc remarked that it is difficult to have a collaborative relationship with the government because "we are [still] victims and they are [still] perpetrators."

Education and Memorialization

ODHAG, whose central mission for decades has been educating domestic and international publics on conflict-related abuses in Guatemala, has had one of the human rights community's longest partnerships with the Ministry of Education and teachers' groups. It has also been designated a *querellante adhesivo* in cases relating to the internal armed conflict. And, as I relay in the coming analysis of implementation, ODHAG has entered its research materials as evidence in criminal trials.

Mobilizing Structures

The fourth and final observable implication of NGOs attempting to set governments' post-TJ agenda is using mobilizing structures to overcome prohibitive political conditions. Per my burden sharing model, civil society groups in Guatemala have mobilized action by exercising their comparative advantages.

As I indicated earlier, Guatemalan NGOs diversified their well-defined issue portfolios after the CEH concluded its investigation and published its report. While their pre-CEH portfolios have remained at the core of their work and identity—for example, forced disappearance investigations for GAM, litigation for CALDH, judicial reforms for FMM, reparations for CONAVIGUA, and psychosocial support for ECAP—the truth commission prompted them to expand their platforms and activities.

This expansion has tightened links in the human rights community. As two cases in point, GAM and FMM have teamed up on legislative proposals to assist the search for the disappeared and strengthen the judiciary, and CONAVIGUA and ECAP have worked at the nexus of reparations and mental health to provide holistic care. Each organization has increasingly lent a hand to its partners and brought them into institutions to which they have access. For instance, the Judicial Bureau of Human Rights, a nonprofit lawyers collective, has represented victims groups as a *querellante adhesivo*, and FMM has accompanied petitioners to the IACtHR.[17] Rather than work in silos or compete, they have chosen to collaborate. I remarked about how everyone seemed to know each other, professionally and personally, to the Peace Foundation's Maya Juracán, and she responded, "It is the only way that we can do our work."

Organizations' pre-CEH work has mattered a great deal, in particular for sharing knowledge and expertise. ECAP has always been at the forefront of mental health and has practical experience that is invaluable to the others; CONAVIGUA, FAMDEGUA, and the National Victims' Movement have an ear to the ground as victim-led organizations; CAFCA and FAFG have globally renowned technical expertise in forensic science; and AJR, CALDH, FMM, the Judicial Bureau of Human Rights, and others enjoy status as *querellantes adhesivos* because of their legal training, expertise, and demonstrated stake in criminal proceedings related to the internal armed conflict.

The importance of international partnerships in Guatemala cannot be overstated. As an example, the Due Process of Law Foundation and Impunity Watch have collaborated with FMM and other organizations to lobby the Guatemalan government to protect rule of law principles like judicial independence.[18] IOs, notably the United Nations, have also been important operational partners. The UNDP has helped finance and monitor progress on TJ issues through the PAJUST program.[19] UNICEF, in turn, has worked with NGOs in the education sector to develop a blended methodology for teaching about human rights and the armed conflict, involving on-site and online activities.[20] For its part, the OHCHR has advised on legal matters.

International agencies and groups have had the advantage of a larger, global platform and a broader audience from which to solicit financial support for their Guatemalan colleagues. They have helped to bring in resources from Germany, Norway, Spain, Sweden, Switzerland, and the United States, among others. While the amount of support has varied by donor country and by year, it has proved vital for Guatemalan civil society organizations' ongoing work. Groups like GAM even use some of the funds they raise to support government bodies like the Human Rights Ombudsman.[21]

[17] Michel discusses how private prosecutors take advantage of international human rights courts like the IACtHR, especially when states strongly resist justice and when the risk of repression for victims is high. Michel (2018, 9) affirms, "Private prosecutors turn to these courts when judicial proceedings stall or when remedies have been exhausted."

[18] Author interview with Andy Javalois.

[19] Author interview with PAJUST head María García.

[20] Author interview with Patricia Ogaldes.

[21] Author interview with Mario Polanco.

Discussion

Part One adds to scholarship's understanding of truth commissions, and TJ more generally, by considering what happens *after* such processes conclude. Commissions are not only retrospective; they are also prospective.[22] They make recommendations to policymakers about how to respond to the results of the truth-seeking and truth-telling process. Instead of cutting off the story at commissions' conclusion, the chapter so far has carried the story forward, striving to make sense of commissions' reach into the future.[23] The chapter has also sought to understand civil society's post-commission work.

Where some scholars might expect governments to set the agenda, with civil society groups standing in the wings or offstage altogether, I have instead argued that civil society attempts to set governments' post-commission agenda. Far beyond being statement takers and counseling trauma victims during commissions, I have suggested that these groups help make TJ policy after commissions, prioritizing and advocating for recommendations that advance their interests.

Through an extensive analysis of Guatemala since the CEH, I have shown that NGOs diversified their issue portfolios and activities while preserving much of their pre-commission organizational identity. Per the burden sharing model, domestic groups played a leading role in this first half of the implementation and follow-up stage—framing problems and solutions, navigating prohibitive political conditions, and mobilizing their networks. For their part, international groups played a supporting role, using their global platforms and access to financial and other resources to bolster their domestic colleagues' work.

This part of the chapter also advances our understanding of transnational advocacy and advocacy networks. While much work has focused on partnerships and collaboration during periods of repression and political transitions, my research extends the timeline to after violence has ended and an initial set of TJ measures, specifically a truth commission, have been carried out. The analysis reveals that past need not be prologue; NGO missions can expand with guidance from commissions themselves and with resources from international partners. Importantly, the partnerships that mattered early on matter still. But domestic groups lead while international groups follow.

The burden sharing model indicates and the empirical analysis shows that TJ at the post-commission agenda-setting stage is not simply a domestic politics story. If it were, then we would not see INGOs playing key support roles, as we have seen in Guatemala with groups like Impunity Watch. In fact, the

[22] Ang and Nalepa 2019; Nalepa 2022.
[23] Bakiner 2014, 2015.

organization began its work in Guatemala in response to local human rights groups seeking support in the fight for redress. And just as TJ at the post-commission agenda-setting stage is not a domestic politics story, it is also not an international politics story. If it were, we would not see domestic civil society groups staking out different truth commission recommendations to integrate into their advocacy platforms. We also would not see local groups changing the domestic politics landscape by calling in INGOs like the Due Process of Law Foundation and IO agencies like the UNDP, UNICEF, and OHCHR for operational assistance, as we have also seen in Guatemala.

Part Two: *Después de la Verdad* (After the Truth)

I now study how civil society's attempts at agenda setting in the post-commission period have influenced government implementation of CEH recommendations. I examine the extent to which and reasons why governments implement recommendations, and I query the degree to which implementation is tied to civil society activism and the size of lobbying coalitions. I also explore how domestic groups effectively substitute for governments that are unwilling or unable to implement recommendations.

The results are mixed. Despite robust NGO advocacy, the quantitative analysis suggests that the Guatemalan state has not been socialized into TJ norms—a result that contradicts previous research. Rather, successive governments have chosen a piecemeal approach to implementing remedial and preventive TJ measures. The qualitative data likewise indicate unrealized socialization into TJ norms. These data also show NGOs substituting for the state in implementing TJ measures.

Descriptive Statistics: Implementation

My data capture the implementation status of all 87 substantive policy recommendations made by the CEH, showing us the degree to which proposed policies were initiated by policymakers within five and ten years of the CEH and, significantly, the level of implementation achieved. Implementation was initiated for 65 of 87 recommendations (75 percent) within five years of the commission's conclusion. Just two others were initiated within ten years (for a total of 77 percent). Thus I focus on the five years following the commission. Figures 6.1–6.4 display the frequency of recommendations and the percentage initiated by TJ area and sub-area—a picture we could not paint without the *Varieties of Truth Commissions* data.

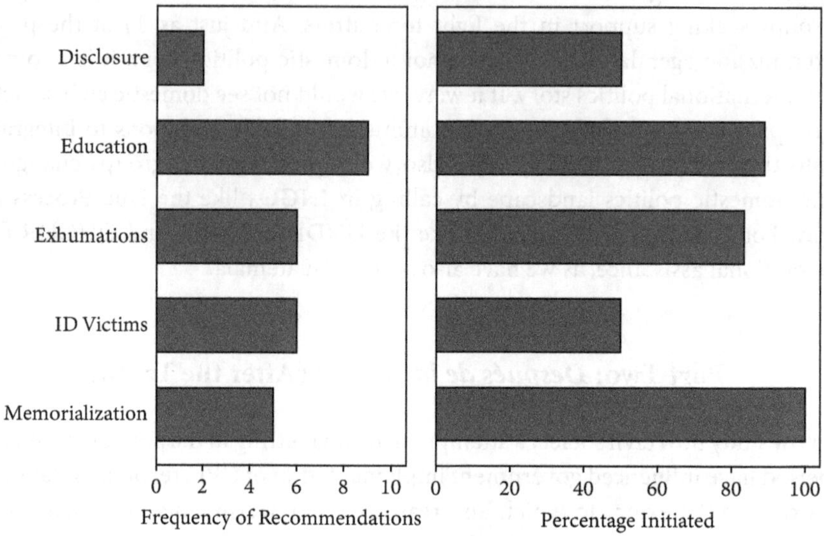

Figure 6.1 Guatemala: Initiation of Measures for Truth

Note: The figure shows the frequency of recommended measures for truth (left panel) and the percentage initiated (right panel).

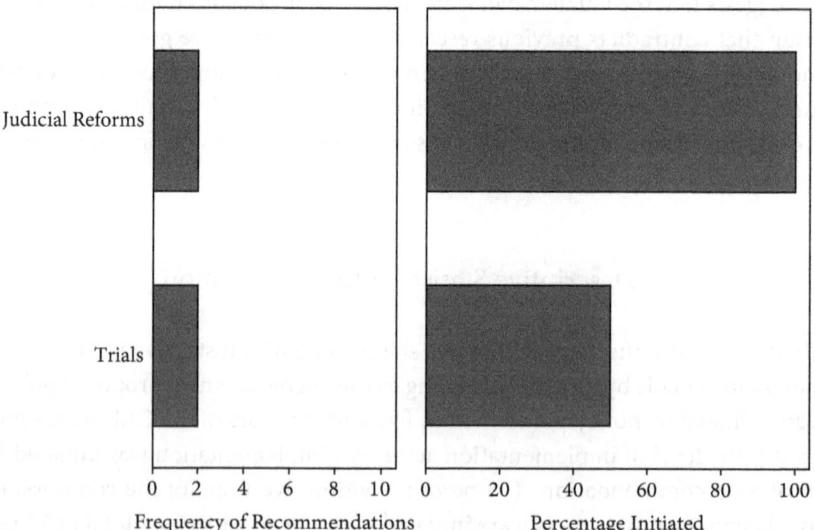

Figure 6.2 Guatemala: Initiation of Justice Measures

Note: The figure shows the frequency of recommended justice measures (left panel) and the percentage initiated (right panel).

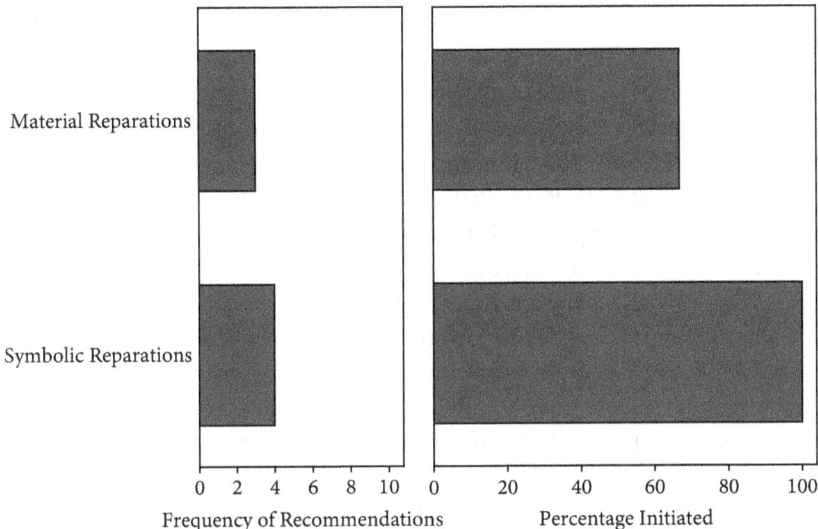

Figure 6.3 Guatemala: Initiation of Reparations

Note: The figure shows the frequency of recommended reparations (left panel) and the percentage initiated (right panel).

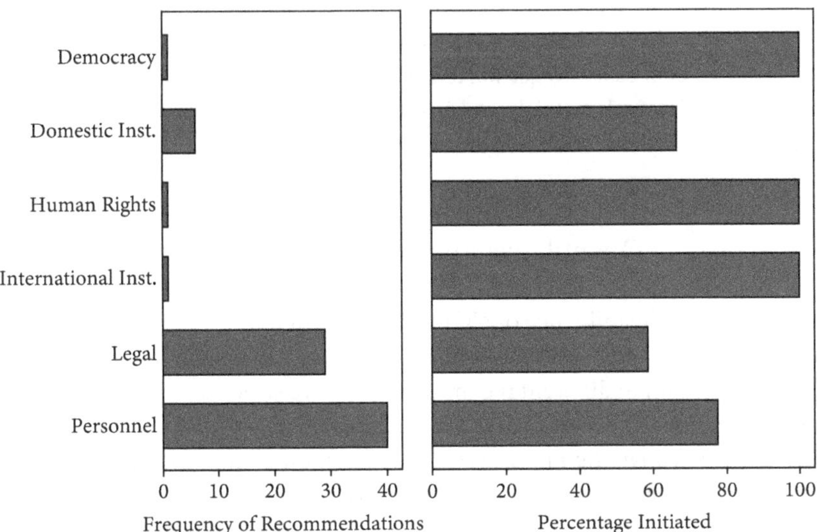

Figure 6.4 Guatemala: Initiation of Reforms

Note: The figure shows the frequency of recommended reforms (left panel) and the percentage initiated (right panel).

To begin, education represents the largest share of recommended measures for truth (36 percent), while information disclosure represents the smallest share (8 percent). Victim identification and exhumations each made up 24 percent, and memorialization made up 20 percent.[24] Of measures for truth, uptake was highest for memorialization and education. Next, in terms of recommended justice measures, there was an even split between judicial reforms and criminal investigations/trials. But initiation of implementation was stronger for the former than the latter. For their part, symbolic and material reparations were recommended at similar rates, but symbolic measures fared better when it came to initiation. Finally, personnel reforms made up two-thirds of recommended institutional reforms and fell in the middle of the pack in terms of initiation.

But we are interested not only in whether implementation of a given recommendation was initiated but also the level of implementation that was attained. Five years after the CEH, 32 of 65 initiated recommendations (49 percent) reached minimal implementation, while 15 others (23 percent) reached intermediate status, and yet another 18 (28 percent) reached full implementation.[25] Figure 6.5 shows the percentage of recommendations at each level of implementation across the four big TJ areas. A plurality of measures for truth were fully implemented, while a majority of reparation measures and a minority of reform measures were fully implemented. No justice measures were fully implemented.

The descriptive data presented in Figures 6.1–6.5 comport with qualitative evidence from my interviews with commission officials in Chapter 5: Measures relating to truth, in particular education and memorialization, and symbolic reparations seem easier to get started and get delivered in full. By contrast, measures for justice such as trials and institutional changes like personnel reforms appear more difficult to launch and fully implement.

Quantitative Analysis: Implementation

I now evaluate the influence of NGO advocacy on implementation of CEH recommendations. I focus on advocacy for specific recommendations and NGO coalition breadth in different recommendation areas. For the analysis, I run four logit regressions and four ordered logit regressions, with *Implementation Initiated* and *Implementation Level* as the respective outcome variables. Models 1, 2, and 3, respectively, estimate the effects of *NGO Advocacy*, *NGO Coalition Size*,

[24] Note, the percentages of recommended measures by TJ area (e.g., truth) may exceed 100, as some recommendations fall under more than one category in a given area (e.g., victim and perpetrator identification).

[25] These numbers track well with Martín et al. (2022), whose sample of Latin American countries includes Guatemala.

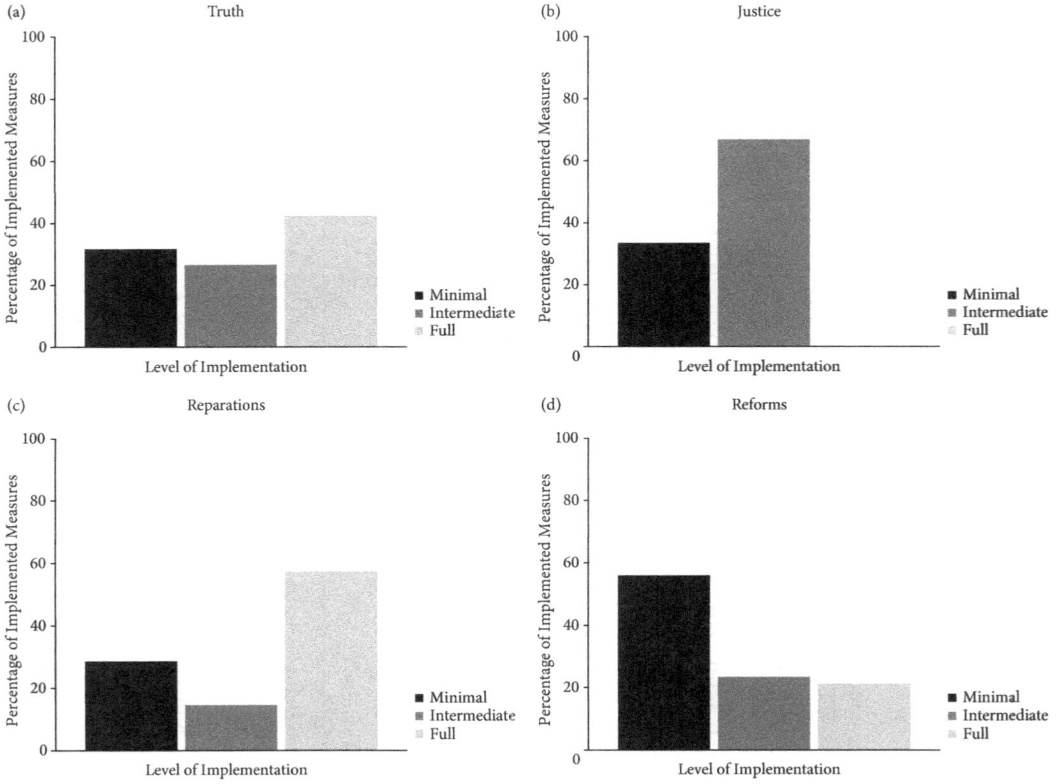

Figure 6.5 Guatemala: Level of Implementation of Recommendations

Note: The figure shows the percentage of recommendations that reached different levels of implementation across the four main TJ areas.

Table 6.2 Analysis: NGO Advocacy and Implementation of Recommendations in Guatemala: Initiation

	Implementation Initiated			
	(1)	(2)	(3)	(4)
NGO Advocacy	0.72 (0.59)			0.91 (0.63)
NGO Coalition Size		0.00 (0.03)		0.04 (0.04)
INGO Coalition Size			-0.20^{*} (0.10)	-0.26^{*} (0.11)
Observations	87	87	87	87

Logit models. Standard errors in parentheses.
$^{+}p < 0.10$, $^{*}p < 0.05$, $^{**}p < 0.01$

Table 6.3 Analysis: NGO Advocacy and Implementation of Recommendations in Guatemala: Level

	Implementation Level			
	(1)	(2)	(3)	(4)
NGO Advocacy	1.61^{+} (0.83)			1.47^{+} (0.84)
NGO Coalition Size		0.05^{+} (0.03)		0.03 (0.03)
INGO Coalition Size			0.13 (0.10)	0.07 (0.12)
Observations	65	65	65	65

Ordered logit models. Standard errors in parentheses.
$^{+}p < 0.10$, $^{*}p < 0.05$, $^{**}p < 0.01$

and *INGO Coalition Size*. Model 4 includes all three explanatory variables. See Tables 6.2 and 6.3. The small number of observations means that it should be harder to detect statistically significant results.

While *NGO Advocacy* is positively associated with initiation of implementation, it is not a statistically significant predictor of the outcome. Similarly, *NGO Coalition Size* is not statistically significant and is estimated around zero. Interestingly, there appears to be a negative relationship between *INGO Coalition Size* and initiation of implementation, and the relationship is significant at the 5 percent error level. There are several possible explanations for this result.

INGO coalitions may be more likely to form in "hard cases" (i.e., in places where governments are likely to resist implementation). Yet the average INGO coalition comprised between four and five groups across each of the TJ areas. A second explanation is that the government has de facto devolved many of its TJ responsibilities to other actors, including INGOs and even IOs, which are still working on TJ issues in Guatemala nearly thirty years since the end of the internal armed conflict and more than twenty-five years since the commission concluded. A third explanation is that the government may resent external advocacy and has therefore resisted it. My interviews lend some credence to the second explanation especially. Interviewees representing domestic and international NGOs noted the government's effective abandonment of implementation in many instances.[26]

By contrast, with regard to the level of implementation, *NGO Advocacy* is a positive and statistically significant predictor of the outcome, albeit at the 10 percent error level. *NGO Coalition Size* is also positively correlated with the outcome but is small and not significant in the fully specified model. *INGO Coalition Size* is likewise positive but not significant. Consistent with the burden sharing model at this stage of the TJ life cycle, domestic actors' efforts seem more important than international actors' efforts.

Potentially Conflicting Mechanisms and Mixed Results

Two conflicting mechanisms may explain some of the null results. The first mechanism is the one proposed in my theory, that NGO advocacy has a positive causal effect on recommendation uptake and completion. The second is that NGOs, and especially INGOs, advocate for recommendations that are not on track for adoption or that they fear will not be fully implemented (i.e., hard issues). This would generate an effect in the opposite direction of the first mechanism.

I tried to address hard issues through additional tests, recognizing, of course, that what is considered "hard" may vary from country to country. Little changed. Across the Guatemalan, South African, and Timorese cases, the results are largely stable to controlling for general issue areas (i.e., truth, justice, reparations, and reforms, with the services and "other" categories omitted) and even specific issue areas (e.g., personnel reforms). My interviews also did not indicate that NGOs pursue either the "easy things" or the "hard things," but a range of issues, consistent with their historical advocacy portfolios and the new opportunities for advocacy that truth commissions create. These findings are broadly consistent

[26] For example, Juana Tipaz shared her profound disappointment at the government's lack of robust action to find and reunite disappeared and illegally adopted children with their families.

with work by Martín et al. (2022), who do not find that recommendation type is strongly related to implementation, specifically time to implementation.

Martín et al. (2022) find for a sample of Latin American countries that implementation of recommendations is quicker when truth commissions are created by executive order rather than by legislation or in peace agreements. The reasoning here is that executives who have a greater sense of ownership over a commission should deliver on the commission's proposals—reasoning that the ICTJ's Cristián Correa also gave in our interview. This would predispose Guatemala (and South Africa and Timor-Leste, if Martín et al.'s findings generalize beyond Latin America) to have slower recommendations uptake, if any.

The Guatemalan commission was created through peace accords; the South African commission was agreed to in a democratic pact between the outgoing apartheid government and the incoming Mandela government; and the Timorese commission was established through UN administration. So, in comparison to cases where commissions were created by executive order, groups advocating for implementation of recommendations in Guatemala, South Africa, and Timor-Leste faced a steeper, uphill battle. In addition, in the Guatemalan context, the conflict did not end with the total defeat of the military, predisposing the CEH's recommendations to not be fulfilled. Meanwhile in South Africa, there was external and internal pressure to not change too much or change too quickly.[27] Timor-Leste, for its part, had to build itself up from scratch, after centuries of colonial rule and decades of occupation and conflict.

Related work by Skaar et al. (2022*a*, 190–204) probes the relationship between implementation and (1) the number of recommendations, (2) the scope of recommendations (systemic vs. non-systemic), (3) national resources, and (4) time across a sample of Latin American countries. The analysis, based on descriptive statistics, first suggests a negative relationship between the number of recommendations and implementation rates. The implication for my three cases would be that we should see higher rates of implementation in Guatemala, where the commission made 87 recommendations, than in Timor-Leste, where the commission made 247 recommendations, or in South Africa, where the commission made 313 recommendations.

[27] While Mandela had a sizable electoral mandate and a parliamentary majority, Western trade partners of the former regime would only throw their political and financial support behind his government if it committed to power sharing and the traditional economic system; hence, de jure and de facto amnesties, waning socialist rhetoric and commitment to redistributive politics, and continuing societal divisions. A criticism more specific to the TRC is that it "put apartheid, a crime against humanity itself, as background context rather than subject of scrutiny. The ordinary violence of apartheid was never addressed; only the extraordinary violence used to maintain and contest it was. In addition, more attention was paid to physical repression than to bureaucratic and economic repression—the consequences of which still make South Africa a racially stratified and unequal society, even with Black political power" (Murphy and Zvobgo 2023, 423). See, too, Bowsher (2020), Hamber (2001), and World Bank (2018).

To reiterate the findings in this chapter and to preview those to come in the next two chapters, I find five-year initiation rates of 75 percent, 56 percent, and 49 percent in Guatemala, South Africa, and Timor-Leste, respectively. So, Skaar et al.'s finding at first seems to hold up. But the extent of difference narrows when one considers not only initiation but also the level of implementation. Twenty-eight percent of recommendations in Guatemala, compared to 33 percent in South Africa and 29 percent in Timor-Leste, reached full implementation.

Second, Skaar et al. find some evidence that non-systemic recommendations (i.e., reparations, criminal prosecutions, and follow-up institutions) are less likely to be implemented than systemic recommendations (i.e., institutional and legal reforms). But, using similar data and cases, Martín et al. do not find that recommendation type is a statistically significant predictor of timely implementation.[28] In my own research, I have not found stable, statistically significant results for recommendation type's effect on implementation.

Third, Skaar et al.'s descriptive statistics indicate richer or more developed countries have higher implementation rates than poorer countries. Looking at gross domestic product (GDP) per capita in the year their commissions concluded, 1999, 2002, and 2005, respectively, Guatemala, South Africa, and Timor-Leste had a GDP per capita (in US dollars) of approximately $1,600, $2,700, and $500. So, Skaar et al.'s trend might not travel to other regional contexts: South Africa should have done the best, having had a leg up on the other two countries. Still, variation in resources might not be sufficiently large across my three cases to produce differences.

Last, Skaar et al.'s data suggest greater implementation over time. The role of time is not something that I can evaluate, as I measure implementation in the first five and ten years after the Guatemalan, South African, and Timorese commissions. This was a deliberate research design choice; I wanted to hold the implementation period I studied constant across cases.

The bigger story of implementation, I believe, has to do with civil society advocating before the state—a story for which I find evidence in this chapter and in the two that follow. Still, this discussion supports the idea that scholars have a great deal of work to do, expanding beyond particular cases and regions to the universe of cases. At this stage, because we lack a global baseline of implementation, it is hard to say what is or what would be a "good" or "high" level of implementation. And we must always think about the counterfactual. What would the TJ landscape look like in a country if there never were a truth commission or if civil society did not advocate for implementation of the commission's recommendations? With this in mind, what might appear as "low" implementation is still an achievement.

[28] Martín et al. 2022.

We must also always remember that additional progress may yet be made. Carlos Beristain noted that, sometimes, it can look like civil society is not having an impact. He referenced Argentina, where amnesty laws and presidential pardons prevented prosecutions of junta-era human rights abuses for two decades. But change came with Néstor Kirchner's presidency. Kirchner, in response to civil society demands, asked Congress to annul the amnesty laws, which it did in 2003, and the Supreme Court confirmed the laws and presidential pardons were unconstitutional in 2005, paving the road for prosecutions. Kirchner also answered civil society's pleas to transform detention centers into memory museums. TJ progress continued under Cristina Fernández de Kirchner's presidency.

Qualitative Analysis: Implementation

The Guatemalan state's decision to implement additional TJ measures could in theory be the result of socialization into TJ norms—a process prompted by civil society. I operationalize and assess socialization at three levels. First, at a low level of socialization, a government's decision to establish further TJ measures is purely strategic. Implementation of recommendations, here, is reactive, even haphazard—triggered by pressure from civil society. Second, at a moderate level of socialization, a government's decision to supply additional TJ is the result of an emerging practice—not a one-off policy concession intended to co-opt or demobilize critics. In this case, implementation of commission recommendations is undertaken somewhat independently. Though implementation may not be a government's preference, it is seen as appropriate. Third, at a high level of socialization, a government's decision to implement additional measures reflects a transformed identity, with a new set of ideas and interests. Implementation of recommendations at this stage is part of this new identity and occurs more or less independently of forces external to the government, NGOs among them.

Guatemala since the CEH, and really since the internal armed conflict, has been stuck at the lowest level of socialization: tactical concessions. Successive governments have only implemented TJ measures strategically, as a concession to political pressure. Despite the optimism and enthusiasm conveyed in the Global North, including in scholarship, no post-1999 government has internalized the TJ norm. My best qualitative evidence of this actually comes from people who were working in different agencies within the government and who were frustrated by overly positive accounts of the government's approach to TJ.

The head of special investigations in the Human Rights Ombudsman's office, Alejandro Reyes, confirmed, "The government does not want to talk about the past. Previous ombudsmen have not been very engaged or interested in the topic." His candor was remarkable. Additionally, the work of advancing human rights remains dangerous, even for government employees like Reyes. "We are investigating military power," he said, "and governments have had the military behind them. . . . [Almost] every member has a boss that can ask for information to be blocked." Therefore, any success in investigations and prosecutions is *despite* interference. Statements like these stand in contrast to claims like the following from Risse and coauthors:

> [T]here can be little doubt that some minimal progress toward rule-consistent government and human rights behavior has been made in Guatemala. *At this moment Guatemala seems poised between prescriptive status and rule-governed behavior.* How the government, the international community, and domestic civil society responds to the challenges in *the next few years will determine whether Guatemala stays stalled or moves ahead to genuine change.*[29]

Scholarly accounts like this show us two things. First, there may have been programmatic changes in Guatemala but not substantive progress. To say it another way, the conflict may have ended, plans put on paper, and formal institutions set in place, but the underlying commitment was not actually there. I grant that TJ delivery is not an exact measure of the overall domestic human rights situation—in Guatemala or elsewhere.[30] But TJ is concerned with truth, justice, reparation, and nonrepetition. The decision to deliver or not deliver TJ after a truth commission, and how much, is indicative of the degree of commitment to redress for the past and preventive action for the future. Whether and to what extent a government delivers additional TJ reflects the domestic human rights situation. The intensity with which human rights groups wage their uphill battles for TJ in post-commission contexts shows us this.

Second, even if we accepted the premise that there was a time when Guatemala attained a level of socialization beyond tactical concessions, somewhere between prescriptive status and rule-consistent behavior, it regressed from this within just a few years of signing the peace accords. Put differently, socialization is not an inevitable, forward-moving process, as the original spiral model indicates, especially after political transitions.[31]

In fact, since Efraín Ríos Montt's genocide conviction was overturned on procedural grounds, human rights defenders have seen regression in cases relating

[29] Risse et al. 1999, 197, emphasis added.

[30] Neither is a simple reduction in repression a measure of the human rights situation; it does not on its own mean that a country is governed by human rights norms. Practicing human rights à la carte does not fulfill human rights norms.

[31] Risse et al. (2013, 16) acknowledge, "The original spiral model was developed and applied only to states with authoritarian and repressive regimes."

to the internal armed conflict and the justice system in general. In addition, military "bosses" have tried, and in some cases succeeded in, buying influence with judges, weakening reforms, and undermining judicial proceedings. At the time of my field research, Reyes's colleagues at the Public Ministry were collecting evidence to present accusations against a group of these individuals while at the same time fearing for their futures. Moreover, Congress had passed laws to (re)produce impunity. Emir Mejía at the now-dissolved Secretariat for Peace poignantly shared, "If we had implemented the accords holistically, we would have had such a change in Guatemala; it would be a different country. We have made progress, yes. But not as much as we hoped."

Chief Prosecutor for Human Rights Hilda Pineda's assessment was slightly more optimistic than that of her colleagues in the Human Rights Ombudsman's office and the Secretariat for Peace, certainly as she looked to the future. She completely agreed that there was previously little interest in cases related to the conflict. That is one of the reasons why, in response to civil society criticism, the government created the Office of the Prosecutor for Human Rights within the Public Ministry in 2005—to handle select cases related to the conflict. Despite this, the Public Ministry still seemed to not be committed to trying cases. This changed with Pineda's arrival as chief prosecutor in 2016. Civil society groups commended her efforts, which built on her previous prosecutions, including in Ríos Montt's genocide trial. The prosecution, it is worth noting, leveraged the CEH report and civil society outputs, such as the REMHI report, to build the case against Ríos Montt and other top-ranking military officials.

Referring to state-led abuses during the internal armed conflict, Pineda shared with me, "We know what happened. We work as hard as we can so that victims have the opportunity to come before a judge. . . . We work to learn every day. We cannot fail the victims. They have been waiting a long time."

Pineda noted her division's limited resources and the importance of being strategic with prosecutions, addressing crucial or "emblematic" cases that speak to general trends and that acknowledge different types of victims' suffering. Pineda's plans were unfortunately cut short. In 2021, Attorney General María Consuelo Porras removed Pineda and seven other human rights prosecutors from their posts—a move that followed the "arbitrary ousting and harassment of several independent judges and prosecutors since Porras first took office in 2018," HRW reported.[32]

These accounts from government officials and external observers demonstrate that the Guatemalan government has neither adopted nor internalized the TJ norm. Even policy concessions like the creation of Pineda's office were made with great reluctance and inadequate support, and were ultimately reversed. Low

[32] HRW 2022.

socialization is also evident when we consider the civil society side. Recall, at the lowest level of socialization, NGOs, to the extent they can, take on the state's responsibility to further implement TJ.

Searching for the Disappeared and Finding Justice

Querellantes adhesivos have played essential roles in criminal investigations and trials since the CEH. Several NGOs whose representatives I interviewed enjoy this designation, among them CALDH, FAMDEGUA, FMM, and GAM. While they do not have the power to independently open a criminal investigation, bring charges, or make arrests, they can prompt state investigators to do so. At the time of my field research, *querellantes adhesivos* were trying to expedite criminal investigations and proceedings related to the internal armed conflict. Given how many decades have passed since thousands upon thousands were tortured, disappeared, and killed, this work is critical.

After an investigation has been opened, *querellantes adhesivos* work with the Public Ministry and Human Rights Ombudsman on research, trial strategy, and preparing survivors and victims' families for court. Of note, they bring petitions and other information from survivors and families to judges, ensuring that their interests and wishes are represented throughout the judicial process. *Querellantes adhesivos* also provide sentencing recommendations as well as reparation recommendations.

A standout example of NGO burden sharing in this area is the Marco Antonio Molina Theissen case. Members of the military disappeared fourteen-year-old Marco Antonio in 1981, and raped and tortured his sister Emma Guadalupe, a young activist. On behalf of Marco Antonio's family, GAM filed a complaint with the Supreme Court of Justice in January 1998, forcing an investigation. Later that year in September, GAM and the Center for Justice and International Law (CEJIL) in Washington, DC, also filed a complaint with the IACmHR, which the IACtHR later took up.[33]

In 2004, IACtHR judges decided in favor of the complainants, finding Guatemala responsible for violating Marco Antonio's and his family's human rights and enjoining legal action against the perpetrators. In 2018, judges in Guatemala's high-risk crimes court convicted a group of ex-military officers of Marco Antonio's disappearance and Emma Guadalupe's rape and torture. This court victory would not have materialized without transnational NGO advocacy, which will likely be critical in upholding the decision.[34]

[33] IACtHR 2004.

[34] In 2023, a Guatemalan appeals court ordered three of the officers' release, rejecting the 2018 decision and defying the IACtHR (Al Jazeera 2023).

Another emblematic case of NGO partnerships in litigating conflict-era abuses is *Sepur Zarco*, named after the Indigenous Q'eqchi' community where the military disappeared and killed many of the men and enslaved and sexually abused the women who remained. CONAVIGUA's Rosalina Tuyuc, on behalf of the surviving *abuelas* (grandmothers) of Sepur Zarco, filed a denunciation in 2011, triggering judicial action.[35] FAFG provided forensic evidence in the trial, ECAP gave the *abuelas* psychosocial support, and the National Union of Guatemalan Women helped them navigate the proceedings. The Alliance to Break the Silence and Impunity designed the litigation strategy, with the support of national and international women's groups and multiple UN agencies.[36]

In 2016, Guatemala's high-risk crimes court in a landmark judgment found two ex-military officers guilty of crimes against humanity on counts of sexual violence and sexual and domestic slavery—a global first—as well as homicide and forced disappearance. Judges also enjoined reparations for the women and their community.[37] Amid these many obstacles, we see that *NGOs burden share to govern elements of the judicial process.*[38]

Exhumations, Forensic Science, and Reburials

Guatemalan forensic anthropology organizations have been international standard bearers in evidence gathering for decades, collaborating regionally and internationally with groups like the Argentine Forensic Anthropology Team (EAAF). Together, they have located numerous clandestine graves and cemeteries, and through osteology and DNA analysis, they have matched remains to families and returned them for burials and funerals.[39] They have also delivered expert testimony that would otherwise have been missing. FAFG alone has rendered testimony in an estimated 200 criminal proceedings, including Ríos Montt's genocide trial.[40]

Forensic anthropology groups also accompany families through the legal process and liaise between them and the Public Ministry and Human Rights Ombudsman. Concretely, NGOs reduce the Public Ministry's and Human Rights Ombudsman's workload by making sure that families and communities have their information recorded, are present at meetings, and have interpreters.

[35] Burt 2016*b*.
[36] SáCouto et al. 2022.
[37] Burt 2016*a*.
[38] Speaking to a broader set of cases in Latin America (Chile, Guatemala, and Mexico) and homicides constituting both human rights cases (where state agents are implicated) and "ordinary" cases (where private persons are implicated), Michel (2018, 16) emphasizes that "although state actors (judges or prosecutors) are often key agents in the pursuit of justice, their work always builds upon the preceding efforts of private prosecutors."
[39] EAAF 2018.
[40] Author interview with Erica Henderson.

In addition, NGO liaisons work to ensure that families and communities understand and develop trust in the process and are prepared for it. NGO liaisons help prepare them to testify and they provide psychosocial support.

While groups like EAAF have been on-the-ground collaborators, other INGOs, including Amnesty International, have supported Guatemalan groups' work through other means—disseminating information on abuses, keeping an eye on teams' safety, spreading the word about their accomplishments, and raising funds.[41] Through burden sharing, *NGOs guide and manage aspects of the investigative process.*

Reforming the Judiciary

Organizations promoting, assisting with, and monitoring legal and judicial reforms, like FMM, have helped shape new laws to protect citizens from abuses, including in the judicial system, as well as laws to indemnify citizens in cases of violations. The Due Process of Law Foundation, based in Washington, DC, is one important international partner in FMM's work to build up the rule of law in Guatemala.[42] Some highlights of FMM's work with partners like GAM include developing laws on access to information and transparency in the judicial appointments process. These statutes boosted, at least for a time, the independence, capabilities, and professionalism of judges, and facilitated the search for victims and the pursuit of justice in their memory. Helping promulgate anti-SGBV laws is another highlight.[43] Accordingly, *NGOs contribute to and provide oversight for the legal system.*

Holistic Reparations

NGOs with a focus on reparations for survivors, victims' families, and injured communities have been committed to a multipronged approach that involves material, symbolic, psychological, and cultural reparations—an approach the CEH endorsed. Impunity Watch, a Dutch organization, has tracked the distribution of victim reparations. Local groups such as ECAP and CONAVIGUA have not been satisfied with the reparations overall, and Impunity Watch data helps them make their case.[44] The government's focus on material reparations to individuals has been especially problematic. ECAP director Felipe Sarti and special programs coordinator Elizabeth Pedraza ruminated that administrations have focused on individual material reparations because they want to keep communities weak by cultivating inequality and disunity. They suggested that this approach is insensitive to the reality that "everyone suffered."

41 Amnesty International 2008.
42 Author interview with Andy Javalois.
43 Author interviews with Mario Polanco, Carlos Juárez, and Andy Javalois.
44 Impunity Watch 2023.

Sarti expounded that governments were aware of communities' potential power and believed that an individualized approach would hinder community solidarity and revitalization. To make matters worse, "influencers" and "bosses" have lined their pockets with resources slated for survivors, victims' relatives, and communities. These powerful actors have also taken a lot of the credit for the National Reparations Program when, in fact, it is civil society actors who are responsible for its success. As mentioned earlier, the program's most productive and effective years were under Rosalina Tuyuc's leadership.

Part of civil society organizations' response to this grim state of affairs has been to assume the responsibility of advancing the other components of reparation. For instance, ECAP has taken on the task of providing survivors and families mental health care and psychosocial support, including and especially throughout the judicial process, where those on trial and their supporters attempt to harass and intimidate them. "Anything that has been accomplished has been due to civil society," Tuyuc underscored. As for her organization, they have revived Mayan customs and healing practices that involve dialogue, music, traditional medicine, fire, water, and more. In these ways and more, *NGOs are helping to rehabilitate and secure reparations for individuals, families, and communities.*

Education and Memorialization

Finally, in the memory and education area, CIRMA and IIARS have supplied the Ministry of Education and educators with trainings and materials for teaching the "recent past," interethnic relations, and citizenship. For its part, ODHAG has adapted its research materials for children, people with low levels of literacy, non-hispanophones, and others. This has been a direct response to government inaction.

For an illustration of burden sharing, consider ODHAG's research, in particular the REMHI report, which has been admitted as evidence in human rights trials in which local partners have served as *querellantes adhesivos*. International partners such as the Washington Office on Latin America (WOLA) have amplified ODHAG's and other local groups' advocacy for the preservation and protection of access to information on human rights violations (like the National Police Historical Archive).[45]

Beyond supporting the CEH's legacy, ODHAG through the REMHI Project has proved crucial for the peace process, including, very significantly, contributing to the dismantling of many illegal security groups and clandestine security organizations—a change enacted in cooperation with the now-concluded International Commission Against Impunity in Guatemala.

[45] WOLA 2019.

For their part, the Peace Foundation and Memorial for Peace have made no inroads with the government and thus operate independently, though they hold out hope for the future, ideally a collaboration toward a national memory museum. As in other sectors, civil society organizations are leading memory work in Guatemala. HIJOS, as an explicitly anti-state group, has not engaged the government directly but, rather, helps with consciousness raising, notably through *escraches*—public shamings of government officials through chants, demonstrations, and postings of photographs of victims of forced disappearance in prominent locations. With social movement actors, *NGOs are leading education and memorialization.*

A Legacy of Progress

So, we see NGOs governing, with domestic groups leading in the search for victims of forced disappearance; directing various aspects of criminal investigations and the judicial process; overseeing the judiciary and shaping legal reforms; helping to repair affected communities materially, mentally, and spiritually; and disseminating information on the recent past through education and memorialization. International groups have supported their domestic partners, through material resources and message amplification. As easy as it may be to see what has not been done by the government in Guatemala (and other countries), it is important to recognize what has been achieved, thanks to civil society.

I must note here a limitation of this book's overall theory and analysis: It lacks a counterfactual of what Guatemala and other cases might have been like without a truth commission and without domestic and international NGO engagement over the decades. These countries are likely much better off than they would have been without a commission or without an active civil society. Statements from my interviews with victims' groups and other civil society organizations, as well as from my interviews with government officials, indicate as much. But could governments have done more? *Should* governments have done more? The quantitative and qualitative data marshaled here and elsewhere suggest so. TJ, like human rights, is a struggle—a struggle that continues.

Implementing Like a State? The Phenomenon and Problem of Civil Society Substitution

Julio Solórzano Foppa, director of the Memorial for Peace, expressed to me a deep frustration: Truth commission recommendations are intended for governments, not civil society. It is governments, not NGOs, who are obligated to deliver them. Anything less is a dereliction of duty and contravenes victims' rights and international TJ norms. Indeed, since the UN Human Rights Committee approved the 1997 Joinet Principles on Combating Impunity and since paradigm-shifting cases from the Inter-American and European regional human rights courts, states have been charged with providing survivors and victims' families truth, justice, reparations, and guarantees of nonrepetition.[46] So when an institution like a commission—based on its collection of evidence and analysis of the facts—lays out what measures are required next, it is troubling that a government's responses would be episodic and piecemeal. But, as I have shown, NGOs do not rely solely on governments to implement further measures; they work with governments and, in many instances, substitute for governments.

I asked other interviewees on the NGO side what they thought of civil society fulfilling the state's obligations. GAM's Mario Polanco admonished that the persistent failure to provide comprehensive TJ is itself a violation.[47] CONAVIGUA's Rosalina Tuyuc assented and elaborated on a triple-trauma that she and others have experienced. The first trauma is the violence they suffered during the internal armed conflict. The second is inadequate measures for redress since the conflict. The third is the burden placed on them to compensate for the state's failings.

Relatedly, Polanco reported that NGOs sometimes find themselves fundraising for themselves as well as for government agencies like the Human Rights Ombudsman, just to keep things moving. This was a shocking revelation: NGOs, which have limited resources to start, dedicate some of their own funds so that the government can do *its* job. Truth and Life's coordinator Dora Mirón shared, "It is a huge responsibility for us." CAFCA's Rafael Herrarte flatly stated, "It is just the way it is. We have to continue no matter what."

I also asked interviewees on the government and IO side for their take. María García, the head of UNDP PAJUST and a Mayan woman herself, shook her head, sighed, and said, "It is a burden for civil society to implement. But it is very important. *Without them, we would not have been able to do anything at all.* They are organized. They have the data. They are committed." Chief Human Rights Prosecutor Pineda ratified these sentiments: "Without civil society, things would be much more complicated and much slower. . . . I am not sure if many cases would have been possible. *Civil society listened to the victims before the State did. Civil society has their history, their truth, their trust.*"

Carlos Beristain echoed Pineda's sentiments, saying, "Having victims' trust is the most important thing." Margarette Macaulay, an IACmHR commissioner,

[46] See, for example, *Velázquez Rodríguez v. Honduras* (Inter-American Court of Human Rights, 1988) and *McCann v. United Kingdom* (European Court of Human Rights, 1995).

[47] As Michel (2018, 3) powerfully writes on prosecutions, "Impunity is ultimately the result of state failure. When a state fails systematically in its duty to investigate and prosecute a crime, the human right to a judicial remedy is violated."

also shared Pineda's sentiments, acknowledging that the commission needs NGOs, their data, and their connections to victims to do their work effectively. Prior to joining the commission, Macaulay was an IACtHR judge. During her tenure, the court heard several cases related to the Guatemalan internal armed conflict, including the famous "*Las Dos Erres*" case.[48] As mentioned at the beginning of the chapter, victims' families, represented by such groups as FAMDEGUA, won an important victory: The court determined that Guatemala violated multiple human rights treaties, and ordered accountability for perpetrators, identification and repatriation of victims' remains, and reparations, among other items.

My interviews, with civil society actors and government and IO officials, demonstrate that NGOs are governors in TJ and that they are governing well. Governments do not produce post-commission TJ on their own, let alone systematically and comprehensively. The TJ network, domestic NGOs in particular, are the driving force and, really, the reason there is TJ at all. Even in challenging contexts, where there are few gains, whatever is gained is because of civil society.

It is possible that in other contexts, governments may be interested in providing additional TJ measures but are unable to do so themselves. This would be different from Guatemala, where administration after administration has often been *unwilling* to provide additional TJ. Given the possibility of governments that are "willing but unable," scholars and practitioners would do well to develop frameworks for how governments in this position might support civil society's work to advance TJ.

Governments could, for example, improve the legal and regulatory environment for civil society activity, making it easier for organizations to do their work. Governments could also provide financial assistance through grants and other initiatives. I note that this would go against global trends, as Chaudhry shows.[49] Governments, in democratic and non-democratic countries alike, have in recent decades been on an upward trajectory for cracking down on civil society, not only through physical repression but also through administrative controls that stymie organizations' work.

Normalizing the devolution of state responsibility to the third sector could, nonetheless, be harmful for TJ norms and efforts.[50] Therefore, we should proceed with extreme caution. Importantly, there are some TJ modalities that civil

[48] See also *Tiu Tojín v. Guatemala* (2008), *Chitay Nech et al. v. Guatemala* (2010), *García and Family Members v. Guatemala* (2012), *Río Negro Massacres v. Guatemala* (2012), and *Gudiel Alvarez et al. (Diario Militar) v. Guatemala* (2013).

[49] Chaudhry 2022, Forthcoming.

[50] Quinn 2021. Kochanski (2021, 131) affirms, that "'letting state[s] off the hook' can embolden government actors . . . [to] politicise [TJ] by taking credit . . . even when their involvement has been nominal." He admonishes scholars to scrutinize state irresponsibility, even as we consider public–private partnerships or, indeed, private actor substitution.

society simply cannot deliver. Civil society cannot conduct trials nor can it ratify international agreements. Neither can it require security institutions to change or single-handedly pay out reparations to thousands of would-be beneficiaries. Civil society—while vital to policy delivery and a potential substitute for governments in some areas—is not a replacement for governments.

Discussion

Part Two explored how Guatemalan NGOs have helped realize the CEH's recommendations. I probed the strategies they employ to motivate government implementation. I found that groups have pressed for policy issues through a variety of efforts, including protest, lobbying legislators, filing lawsuits, and drafting legislative proposals. Of note, I interrogated whether recommendations supported by NGO coalitions are more likely to be initiated and implemented fully.

Statistical analyses revealed no significant effect of NGO representation or NGO coalition breadth on policy initiation, but indicated an effect on policy progress. Qualitative analysis uncovered that where the government has been unwilling or unable to provide additional remedies, NGOs have intervened, assisting the government in those areas where there is some commitment to a positive outcome and substituting for the government where there is not such a commitment. While INGOs and IOs have lent financial and logistical support, this has not been a panacea for low political will among decision makers, corruption, government turnover, and fluctuating economic resources.

Consistent with the burden sharing model, domestic advocates were in the leading role at this stage of the TJ life cycle. Their resources are finite, however, so there have been limits on what they can achieve (to say nothing of limits on their authority to realize certain types of TJ on their own). Given this, those with an interest in redress for historical wrongdoing—private persons, INGOs, foreign governments, and IOs—should invest in domestic civil societies before, during, and after truth commissions.

7

Post-Commission NGO Advocacy: Success, Challenges, and Innovations in South Africa

In 1995, survivors of apartheid violence formed Khulumani Support Group (KSG) to provide psychosocial support to witnesses at the South African TRC. The group's founding members encouraged, "*Khulumani*" (Let us speak). They believed testifying would be therapeutic for them as individuals and educational for the public. A former political prisoner, Oupa Ishmael Tsotetsi, disclosed, "If I hadn't been with Khulumani, I could have been mad by now."[1] Thousands of South Africans like him, the vast majority of them Black or non-white, testified before the commission.

During the three-year statement-taking period, the TRC collected approximately 23,500 testimonies.[2] Much like FAMDEGUA in Guatemala, examined in Chapter 6, and FOKUPERS in Timor-Leste, which I will examine in Chapter 8, KSG's work in the memory politics space did not end with the commission. Rather, its advocacy extended into the post-commission period and, indeed, reaches into the present.[3]

KSG seized the opportunity to redefine itself and its work—to complete "the unfinished business of the TRC." This has included pressing the South African government to deliver reparations—one of the commission's most important policy prescriptions.[4] When the government attempted to limit reparations awards to just 16,000 people, KSG mounted a forceful resistance.[5] More concretely, the organization helped many eligible individuals claim the reparations they were due.[6] And, on behalf of those deemed ineligible including due to late

[1] Duke 1998.
[2] Hayner 2011, 28–29. The figure captures 21,000 victims and witnesses and 2,500 eligible amnesty applicants.
[3] ICTJ 2011*b*.
[4] Hayner 2011, 176–177.
[5] Thousands of victims, including even those whom the TRC named in its report, were shut out of the reparations program because they did not successfully file within the government's very narrow application window.
[6] New Tactics in Human Rights n.d.

Governing Truth. Kelebogile Zvobgo, Oxford University Press. © Oxford University Press (2026).
DOI: 10.1093/oso/9780197815663.003.0007

filings, KSG has taken action with the Department of Justice (DOJ). Likewise, KSG and other domestic civil society organizations have advocated for a series of memorialization projects, including the renaming of streets, the establishment of museums, the installation of memorials, and the removal of apartheid monuments.[7]

The case of KSG motivates us to examine the extent to which NGOs have been influential for the implementation of TRC recommendations in South Africa. In this penultimate empirical chapter, I investigate how South African NGOs have helped implement policies specified in the truth commission report. I am interested in how organizations determine their advocacy priorities: Do they stick to what they know, or do they adopt new issues? For the analysis, I take advantage of data from the *Varieties of Truth Commissions*, which capture NGO advocacy and government implementation of commission recommendations, and qualitative data from my fieldwork.

Part One focuses on NGO advocacy effort and finds noteworthy variation in the assembling of NGO issue portfolios, as well as variation in NGO agenda-setting attempts. Some organizations worked on a range of issues in the pre-commission period and have continued to do so in the post-commission period. For example, the Dullah Omar Institute advocated for legal and institutional reforms and government programs to address economic and other structural inequalities. Accordingly, there were not many additional TJ advocacy areas for the organization to enter. To win its preferred policies in this context, the institute has built and fortified collaborative relationships—with domestic groups like the Centre for the Study of Violence and Reconciliation (CSVR), INGOs like HRW, and IOs like the European Union. Other NGOs have grown their mission. As an illustration, the Institute for Justice and Reconciliation (IJR), which had worked on issues like reparations prior to the commission's conclusion, has taken on additional, complementary issues like memorialization and education. Other organizations, still, have remained squarely within their existing missions. Take, for instance, the South African History Archive Trust (SAHA), which has kept its eyes trained on information—from disclosure, to preservation, to education.

Part Two focuses on NGO advocacy success and documents progressive post-TRC outcomes connected to TJ network activism. Statistical analyses reveal the overall positive effect of NGO advocacy on policy uptake in South Africa, but not on ultimate policy progress. Though the government made a better start on NGO-backed recommendations in the years following the TRC, it did not make better progress on them. In this way, South Africa is different from Guatemala, where NGOs were influential for policy progress, but not initial uptake. This is

[7] CSVR 2004.

in large part the result of the South African government not wanting to change too much—an issue that goes back to the democratic transition, the formulation of the TRC, and the decision to not directly confront apartheid and, in so doing, transform South African society.

While there are reasons to think that a new government might do better in terms of post-commission TJ than a government working in its predecessor's shadow (as in Guatemala), there are also reasons to expect a new government to focus on other issues besides TJ. In fact, administrations since the TRC have preferred to "move on" from apartheid. They have therefore prioritized other matters, including building political and economic power regionally and internationally, all while not disrupting racial and economic inequality at home. The new South African state seems to have let itself "off the hook" for remedying violations by the old apartheid state.

Qualitative case analysis then illuminates innovation in South African NGOs' strategies in situations where the state has been unwilling or unable to provide additional remedies. NGOs have often intervened, supporting the government's implementation of recommendations in some cases and substituting for the government in other cases.

Together, my findings provide support to the third part of the burden sharing model. In the post-commission period, domestic NGOs have played a leading role—pursuing, and realizing, various items in their post-TRC agenda. Meanwhile, INGOs and IOs have played a supporting role.

Plan of the Chapter

Part One begins with an overview of apartheid, South Africa's democratic transition, and the establishment of the truth commission. I also discuss the commission's operation, findings, and recommendations. After this, I offer a descriptive analysis of NGO recommendations advocacy, addressing the presence and size of NGO coalitions across different issue areas. I then evaluate my theory of agenda-setting attempts by domestic organizations using qualitative data from my fieldwork interviews to trace evidence of the causal chain that I have proposed. These steps include selecting recommendations, framing recommendations, navigating difficult political circumstances, and mobilizing resources and networks. I do this across four areas of note: (1) ethically recovering narratives of harm, (2) healing trauma, (3) preventing crime and rehabilitating offenders, and (4) fighting for legal accountability and equal justice.

Part Two presents descriptive statistics of implementation of the TRC's recommendations, first with respect to initiation and second with respect to the level of implementation reached. Following this, I conduct the quantitative analysis, which reveals the extent to which the government has been likely to start and finish implementing recommendations endorsed by NGO coalitions, larger ones especially. A qualitative analysis of my fieldwork interviews supplements the quantitative analysis, illuminating how NGOs have achieved their wins, both in cooperation with and separate from the state.

Part One: *Iqiniso: Indlela Yokulungisa*? (Truth: Road to Redress?)

From 1948 to 1994, millions of South Africans, the vast majority of them Black or non-white, were subjected to unspeakable abuses under apartheid. A legacy of British and Dutch colonization, apartheid was an autocratic system of government predicated on white supremacy, racial separatism, and the political and economic subjugation of non-white people. Black, Asian, and mixed-race South Africans were denied basic rights like free movement and free speech, and were harassed, assaulted, abducted, tortured, and killed in their fight for freedom and democracy—all in an effort to contain their power to produce political change.[8] Their white allies were also violently punished.[9]

The major institutional vehicle for resistance was the African National Congress (ANC), which at first espoused the Gandhian approach of nonviolent civil protest.[10] But, when nonviolence did not produce significant results, the ANC became more militant.[11] Anti-apartheid revolutionary Nelson Mandela and his comrades Oliver Tambo and Walter Sisulu, among others, called for an armed uprising to run parallel to the nonviolent resistance.[12] The white-minority government used the ANC's attacks as an excuse to repress non-white South Africans and their allies even more severely.

The freedom movement—which crested in the 1980s, with growing violence as its backdrop—drew significant international attention and support, including a concerted campaign of isolation, boycotts, and sanctions that had "tremendously detrimental effects on all aspects of South African life" and put the government "under considerable pressure to change its politics."[13] As we saw in Guatemala, internal and external forces converged on South Africa, forcing President F. W. de Klerk and his National Party to negotiate peace with Mandela and the ANC.

8 TRC 2002, vols. 5 and 6.
9 Presbey 2006.
10 Presbey 2006.
11 Kurtz 2010.
12 Benneyworth 2011.
13 van Zyl 1999, 649. See also Klotz (1995, 2002).

The South African peace process advanced in fits and starts—something we also saw in Guatemala. The process officially began in 1990 with Mandela's release from prison and the lifting of the ban on opposition movements and parties. Next, in March 1992, two-thirds of white South African voters approved a negotiated end to the apartheid regime.[14] But, in June 1992, dozens of civilians were massacred at Boipatong by supporters of the National Party-backed Inkatha Freedom Party. The ANC broke off talks but later returned to the negotiating table.[15]

As in Guatemala, defining TJ's contours proved contentious. Government negotiators proposed blanket amnesties for state officials and agents, while some ANC members wanted criminal trials. Ultimately, the parties agreed to a truth commission that would offer *conditional* amnesties to perpetrators of politically motivated crimes in exchange for a full and truthful accounting of their actions.[16] Thus proceeded the transition to democracy. In April 1994, South Africa held its first multiracial, one-person-one-vote elections. Mandela and the ANC won in a sweeping victory.[17]

The TRC—whose idea had been proposed in 1992 by Kader Asmal, an Indian-South African human rights scholar and anti-apartheid activist—was officially established under the Promotion of National Unity and Reconciliation Act No. 34 of 1995,[18] with a mandate to establish "as complete a picture as possible of the causes, nature and extent of the gross violations of human rights" under apartheid.[19]

CSVR, which I mentioned earlier, brought domestic and international civil society groups together to influence the commission's design and operation, contributing to hundreds of hours of debate and providing input on drafts of the act.[20] CSVR has also played a major role since the commission. I spoke with CSVR senior research specialist Hugo van der Merwe who described their post-commission advocacy as "almost an obligation."

The TRC received testimonies from approximately 21,000 victims and witnesses, about 2,000 of whom participated in public hearings. Of the 7,112 amnesty applications it received, the commission assessed that approximately 2,500 cases were eligible. Ultimately, the commission granted amnesties to 849 perpetrators. A five-volume report was presented to President Mandela in October 1998. However, the TRC's mandate was extended so that the Amnesty

[14] Kurtz 2010.
[15] Simpson 2012.
[16] Mamdani 2002; van Zyl 1999.
[17] Lodge 1995.
[18] Asmal 1992.
[19] Parliament of the Republic of South Africa 1995.
[20] Ancelovici and Jenson 2013; Asmal 1992; Hayner 2011; Roht-Arriaza 2001.

Committee could proceed for an additional two and a half years. In 2002, the commission presented its revised report, with a new sixth volume.[21]

The report produced a comprehensive account of abuses by government officials, agents, and affiliates, as well as by Resistance fighters—a record that NGOs would later invoke to underscore the legitimacy, necessity, and importance of their work. The determination of "crimes against humanity," especially, propelled the movement for further TJ measures in the country.[22] In addition, the report contained hundreds of recommendations that, per my argument, civil society used—and, importantly, still uses—to advance TJ beyond the TRC.

NGOs by Commission Recommendation Area

The *Varieties of Truth Commissions* data capture for a given TRC recommendation whether there was at least one domestic NGO with prior professional experience in the recommendation's substantive issue area—for example, education—and, if so, how many NGOs. The data also capture whether and how many groups lobbied for specific recommendations. Table 7.1 shows the twenty substantive areas that the TRC addressed in its recommendations, grouped by TJ theme.

The data show that there was at least one domestic NGO with prior professional experience in each of the twenty substantive areas, though the number of groups varied. For instance, twelve organizations, including CSVR, were advocating for information disclosure; ten organizations, among them KSG, were fighting for criminal investigations and trials; eight groups were promoting personnel reforms, with the National Institute for Crime Prevention and the Reintegration of Offenders (NICRO) and the Foundation for Human Rights (FHR) taking leading roles; and twenty-one groups, among them IJR, were lobbying for human rights reforms, including anti-racism initiatives.[23]

NGOs by Commission Recommendation

The breadth of pre-TRC NGO activity helps explain why a large majority of the commission's prescriptions were picked up by one group or another.

[21] Hayner 2011, 27–32. A seventh volume, released in 2003, was a tribute to victims and included narratives not presented elsewhere in the report.

[22] Mamdani 2002.

[23] See Chapter 5 and online Appendix C for more information on how the lists of NGOs by recommendation and recommendation area were assembled.

Table 7.1 Substantive Recommendations from the South African TRC

Recommendation Areas	
Truth	**Reforms**
Education	Democracy
Exhumations	Electoral
Information disclosure	Human rights
Memorialization	Legal
Perpetrator identification	New domestic institutions
Victim identification	Personnel
Justice	**Services**
Amnesties	Perpetrator rehabilitation
Judicial reforms	Social welfare
Trials	Victim rehabilitation
Reparations	
Material	
Symbolic	

Nonetheless, there were recommendations that were left behind. Consider, for example, personnel reforms. The TRC recommended that members of the justice system, from law clerks to judges, receive intensive training on the new constitution, notably with respect to human rights, and that prosecutors in particular consider victims' interests as they perform their duties. While several NGOs advocated for TRC-prescribed personnel reforms, including in the criminal justice sector, the evidentiary record does not indicate groups explicitly lobbying for these two measures. Organizations with an interest in personnel reforms focused primarily on the police and prisons. This is understandable: The lion's share of apartheid-era abuses were perpetrated by the police and in prisons. Thus, addressing these two institutions was essential and drew the specific attention of groups such as CSVR and the Centre for Conflict Resolution.

As in Guatemala, South African NGOs' wide adoption of recommendations did not mean uniform representation. To illustrate, while there were more than a dozen groups advocating for legal reforms, my research team only found evidence of one, the Dullah Omar Institute, that specifically lobbied for a ban on holding individuals in police custody without specific charges, even in states of emergency. Likewise, our research revealed only Africa Criminal Justice Reform (ACJR) and the Legal Resources Centre (LRC) advocated for a prohibition on scientific research on interrogation and torture techniques.

Qualitative Analysis: Agenda Setting

For my descriptive qualitative analysis of NGO agenda-setting attempts in post-commission South Africa, I make use of semi-structured interviews that I conducted remotely in the summer of 2022, with participants representing seven notable organizations.

Issue Portfolios

According to the theory, to set a government's post-commission agenda, NGOs must select a set of issues to champion. While some South African NGOs continued with their pre-commission issue portfolios, others expanded their missions and activities. To give a few examples, since the late 1990s, FHR has advocated for criminal accountability for perpetrators of political violence and remedies for survivors and victims' families. FHR, with such groups as CSVR, has also pressed for measures that would combat discrimination (i.e., racism, sexism, xenophobia, and homophobia) in South Africa. The organization is also concerned with civic education, so South Africans of all racial and ethnic backgrounds know the violence the apartheid regime wrought and also learn about democracy, human rights, and justice. FHR's partners, CSVR and the Trauma Centre for Survivors of Violence and Torture (hereafter, the Trauma Centre), have maintained this advocacy from the pre-commission period into the post-commission period. The Human Rights Media Centre (HRMC), established while the TRC's work was ongoing, has likewise pursued this diverse issue set.

HRMC was founded in 2000 by Shirley Gunn, a survivor of state torture who I had the honor to interview for this project. She was an anti-apartheid activist, initially recruited into the ANC in 1980 and, later, into its armed wing uMkhonto we Sizwe (MK) in 1984. The next year, 1985, she was arrested by the security police and placed in solitary confinement. The renowned human rights defender Dullah Omar represented Gunn at her trial and ultimately secured her release. Still, she remained a target, constantly surveilled and harassed by state security agents. She took refuge in Botswana and, not long thereafter, was sent for military training in Cuba and was then dispatched to an MK training facility in Angola.

When Gunn returned to South Africa, she was still a target. In 1989, she was accused by Adriaan Vlok, the minister of law and order, of bombing the South African Council of Churches headquarters the previous year. Vlok would later confess to the Goldstone Commission, a commission of inquiry that preceded the TRC, that he had been part of the plot to frame her for the security police's crime. At the time of her wrongful arrest in 1990, she refused to be separated from her then-infant son Haroon. So the security police detained them both. In the end, Haroon was taken away and, only through an emergency court order, was he handed over to Gunn's mother. After two months in detention, Gunn was released. She later sought legal remedy and received a settlement from the minister of law and order.[24]

Gunn was one of the white victims of apartheid crimes who testified at the TRC.[25] Her testimony was aired on radio and television, and she was asked to give numerous media interviews. Regrettably, her interviewers were not properly trained to engage her and other trauma survivors.[26] Gunn created HRMC to ethically document and disseminate fellow survivors' stories via a range of media and to advocate for their rights to acknowledgment, justice, and reparation.[27] In addition to HRMC, she leads the South African Coalition for Transitional Justice (SACTJ), which convenes NGOs to share ideas and resources, agitate together, and give and receive mutual aid.[28]

Thus, we see burden sharing. If groups could pursue and win their preferred TJ policies on their own, we would not see such a complex of organizations—from Gunn's HRMC to human rights lawyers and researchers at the Centre for Applied Legal Studies (CALS) to the watchdog group Open Secrets, among others—coalescing to form the SACTJ to advance TJ issues within and adjacent to their expertise.

Framing

Per the theory, NGOs next frame the results of truth commissions so they are legible and actionable for the state. More precisely, groups re-present commission findings and recommendations. This is what we see in South Africa as in

[24] Author interview with Shirley Gunn. See also Gillespie (2013), Handlarski (2009, 48–50), Healy (2008, 739–740), Sarkin-Hughes (2004, 112–113), South African History Online (2020), and South African Press Association (1996).

[25] TRC 2002, vol. 4, 304.

[26] See de la Rey and Owens's (1998) discussion on private hearings at the TRC, which were introduced when commissioners realized public hearings potentially violated witnesses' right to privacy. This explained in part why women often did not speak of their own suffering, but of their relatives' suffering. See also Hamber's (1998) discussion of the TRC's ambivalence about providing psychosocial support: There were internal debates about whether this was part of the commission's mandate. Ultimately, the TRC decided to narrowly interpret its mandate as a quasi-legal institution and less a counseling institution. This resulted in commission staff—including statement takers, briefers, and debriefers—with varying degrees of training in counseling psychology to support witnesses. Byrne (2004) argues the importance of robust psychosocial support services and draws attention to a range of issues commissions should be aware of and be prepared to handle, including witness age and gender. Because of shame, embarrassment, or a desire to not burden others with their trauma, some witnesses may not feel comfortable speaking to someone who is younger than they are or who is of a different gender, especially in cases of sexual abuse.

[27] For more, see HRMC (2023).

[28] SACTJ 2022.

Guatemala. NGOs framed the core problem of the past in different ways; yet, the frames complemented each other. This is because their post-commission portfolios overlapped. Prognoses, prescriptions, and prompts for action accompanied their diagnoses for policymakers. The following represent but a few examples.

Ethically Recovering Narratives of Harm

TRC commissioners affirmed that their work collecting narratives of apartheid crimes needed to continue, and NGOs like KSG and HRMC reaffirmed this. But things had to change. Recalling her experience testifying before the TRC, Gunn said, "It was quite a strange experience.... I didn't know the majority of people in that room and it was a massive auditorium ... the lights were blazing ... because of all the cameras." Sharing her story, she told me, was the opposite of cathartic—an idea that runs counter to many popular perceptions of the TRC, especially outside South Africa. The TRC was also not the last time or place she would tell her story. Gunn elaborated:

> [Everyone] wanted to interview me ... psychiatrists or psychologists ... [people] studying politics, or sociology, anthropology or history—or God knows. Everyone was interested in our TRC ... interested in research, but they [didn't] know how to deal with trauma.[29]

Trained in trauma response herself, Gunn and her associates diagnosed the problem of media professionals and other stakeholders in narrative recovery being ill-equipped to engage survivors. Even social workers, Gunn noted, were not all trained in trauma. Capturing stories of profound harm, they believed, had to be done in an ethical way, where participants knew their rights, how the process would go, how their story would be used and by whom, and what they would or would not receive in exchange. It was also important that they received mental and emotional support throughout. In brief, the story-gathering and story-telling process needed to dignify victims. Otherwise, their trauma would compound.

Healing Trauma

Organizations like the Trauma Centre, whose board chairperson Glenda Wildschut served as a TRC commissioner, zoomed in on the issue of healing and preventing violence, in particular torture. They held—and continue to hold—that every part of the individual must be addressed. Acknowledgment, recompense,

[29] See also Handlarski (2009) describing how the TRC did not adequately represent women's (including Gunn's) narratives and sometimes minimized their trauma.

and justice must accompany counseling. Trauma Centre director Marguerite Holtzhausen explained to me that concern for individuals' primary trauma, and the secondary trauma that would likely arise from not addressing it, underlies her organization's commitment to a holistic approach. A comprehensive approach was needed to rehabilitate people and restore communities. South African NGOs' analysis echoes in a remarkable way Guatemalan NGOs' analysis of this same issue.

Preventing Crime and Rehabilitating Offenders

Preventing crime and rehabilitating offenders has been another major NGO target since the TRC. One of the biggest predictors of crime is poverty, a painful legacy of the apartheid system, NICRO chief executive officer Betzi Pierce shared with me. Non-white South Africans are more likely than white South Africans to live in poverty and experience violence, both by private individuals and state agents. With this in mind, NICRO and its partners have advocated for diversion, which entails offenders accepting responsibility, making amends, and going through rehabilitation, as opposed to going to trial and receiving a criminal record. Diversion seeks to address root causes of crime and makes crime less likely.

NGOs have also advocated for noncustodial sentencing to address less-serious crimes. Due to the systemic and cyclical nature of poverty, violence, and injustice, individuals with a criminal record are more likely to commit crimes in the future, as are individuals who are incarcerated. Diversion is a means of preventing the former, and noncustodial sentencing is a means of preventing the latter.

Last, NICRO and its allies have sought to improve the conditions of incarcerated persons—from juvenile safety and protection from police violence, to adequate healthcare, to literacy building and skills training, to civil and human rights education. NGOs have also promoted post-release counseling and reintegration programs. Groups have argued that, collectively, these practices would help break vicious cycles.[30]

Fighting for Legal Accountability and Equal Justice

As discussed, perpetrators made up roughly one-tenth of TRC participants and were promised legal amnesty in exchange for a complete disclosure of their responsibility for and participation in political violence.[31] Of course, receiving 2,500 eligible amnesty applications (and the state conducting just a few trials in

[30] Author interview with Betzi Pierce.
[31] Zvobgo 2019*a*.

parallel to the commission) was a far cry from holding accountable the thousands upon thousands who architected and carried out the system and crime of apartheid. Consequently, FHR, alongside such groups as CALS, CSVR, and LRC, diagnosed the problem of inadequate accountability. In articulating their demands, groups argued that survivors and victims' families had a fundamental right to see offenders in the defendant's box and, ultimately, behind bars. They warned that de facto or "backdoor" amnesty for apartheid crimes would undermine the rule of law.

Beyond legal accountability, organizations like CALS identified problems in the criminal justice system. For one, it was, and remains, a racialized system, shared Thandeka Kathi and Sithuthukile Mkhize, both CALS attorneys and researchers. Non-white South Africans and the poor are more likely to be harassed and brutalized by the police, arrested, found guilty, and given harsh penalties, even for nonviolent offenses. They are also less likely to gain access to justice as victims. NGOs pleaded that all South Africans have a right to equal treatment before the law.

Taking this twin set of issues together, groups warned that weak adherence to the rule of law and unequal treatment would threaten South Africa's budding democracy. For CALS, FHR, and other groups, there was work yet ahead when it came to TJ, not only in terms of litigation against perpetrators who had not received conditional amnesties from the TRC but also in terms of developing policies and programs around education and reparation, as well as anti-discrimination.[32]

Navigating Prohibitive Political Conditions

Next, the theory holds that NGOs navigate prohibitive political conditions by gaining access to policymaking and policy-implementing bodies. In this section, I present NGO leaders' thoughts on post-TRC barriers to TJ, focusing on three themes that hearken back to Guatemala: low political will, corruption, and meager budget allocations. I then track how groups in different fields have used the law, their professional expertise, and soft power as victim advocates on the domestic and international stage to transcend these obstacles to agenda setting, if only in part.

To begin, NGOs in South Africa have faced low levels of political will in government to make progress on TJ. As the data in Part Two will show, approximately one-fifth of all the TRC's recommendations were fully implemented

[32] Author interviews with Thandeka Kathi, Sithuthukile Mkhize, and FHR senior researcher Katarzyna Zdunczyk.

within five years. As previously discussed, in the area of legal accountability for apartheid crimes, there had only been a handful of successful prosecutions when the TRC concluded its work. Based on the statements it received, the commission "handed over several hundred cases to the [National Prosecuting Authority] for further investigation and prosecution," FHR senior researcher Katarzyna Zdunczyk reported. These were "cases where amnesty was refused or where perpetrators did not apply for amnesty." From then, families were routinely told that the cases were in progress. But this was not so in most cases. Zdunczyk revealed:

> There was basically an instruction coming from [a] high level of the government not to deal with TRC cases.... This instruction was made by the executive and was directed at the [NPA] and the police... the suppression of the TRC cases.... They didn't want these cases to proceed.

I was shocked to hear this. From Mandela's successor Thabo Mbeki, to Kgalema Motlanthe, to Jacob Zuma, it seems the executive's political will to prosecute apartheid cases was not so much low or absent. Rather, there *was* political will, but it was to obstruct, not advance, accountability. And that is only if we consider historical cases. Speaking of contemporary cases of the government committing infractions and abuses, and its defiance even of court orders, Kathi said, "We are dealing with a government that cannot be held accountable."

Gunn zeroed in on the complementary but nevertheless distinct problem of corruption and its pervasiveness among the now-political elite of South Africa. Corruption, according to Gunn, explains in part the slow movement on reparations and, frankly, why the state has been so tightfisted, trying to pay as little as possible to as few people as possible. Gunn lamented:

> Your comrades, who you were shoulder to shoulder in the trench with... there's [now] this huge divide between them and us... because of all the rot and all the inappropriate expenditure and corruption ... paying reparations to apartheid survivors of gross human rights violations is really [at] the bottom of their list.

Related to corruption is insufficient funds dedicated to government agencies and NGOs like the Trauma Centre and NICRO that are working on trauma response and violence prevention.

Nevertheless, NGOs have deftly gained access to institutions like Parliament, government ministries and departments, the police, and the courts. Organizations have accomplished this by positioning themselves as experts, aiding implementation of TRC recommendations.[33]

[33] Author interview with Hugo van der Merwe.

Ethically Recovering Narratives of Harm

"I have never understood or believed that our solutions [would be] offered on a golden platter that … after we voted in 1994, that South Africa would be a bed of roses," Gunn disclosed. "[But] I've always believed in the power of people." Consequently, HRMC, KSG, and other NGOs in the narrative recovery field have maintained a liberation struggle-like approach to their advocacy, with the hope of reaching people in power and, importantly, their constituents. Gunn said proudly:

> What makes us tick is we've got truth on our side, we've got justice on our side … our agenda is legitimate. It is … what the world expects us to defend. … It's a battlefield, this area of transitional justice.

NGOs in this area have produced public service announcements, led demonstrations, and taken various parties to court.

Healing Trauma

The Trauma Centre has taken a similar approach. There is a notable physical aspect to their work. Yes, they deploy traditional tactics like filing paperwork with the police and the Department of Social Development (DSD). But they also deploy less traditional tactics, like marching on police stations when there are problems. Holtzhausen recounted to me a case in Delft, where the Trauma Centre organized various groups to descend on the police commander's office and put direct pressure on him for failing to address the high level of SGBV in Delft (one of the highest in all South Africa), not training officers in trauma response, and further traumatizing women in the case intake process as a consequence. As I will elaborate in Part Two, because of the Trauma Centre's professional experience and expertise, the police and others rely perhaps too much on the organization to do the *government's* job. CSVR, for its part, has been commissioned by the government on an ad hoc basis to do research on violence and trauma, among other topics. CSVR has also run trainings for government workers like healthcare professionals, so they understand trauma management and care.

Preventing Crime and Rehabilitating Offenders

Pierce shared that NICRO has a largely "soft diplomacy" approach, where the organization leverages its contacts in and partnerships with different government departments (e.g., the NPA, DOJ, and Department of Education). Pierce, herself, worked for the DSD prior to joining NICRO in 2006. She said candidly that she made sure to leave on good terms so that she would be as effective as possible in her new role. Referring to her colleagues in the department, she said,

"People trusted me," and she has used this to NICRO's benefit. In addition, because of its expertise, NICRO actually trains social workers throughout their careers as public employees, as part of a national professional development program. The organization also offers pro bono services to the government, positioning itself as "here to help." Also, due to frequent turnover in government departments with which organizations like NICRO work, they in some ways have a longer institutional memory and, thus, have opportunities to capitalize on their knowledge and experience, serving as the ones to help officials "get up to speed."[34]

Fighting for Legal Accountability and Equal Justice

CALS, FHR, and groups working toward legal accountability for apartheid-era crimes have accessed the courts through litigation assistance, both to families and to the NPA. Not only that, they monitor cases at all stages, from the decision to charge, to the investigation, to the trial, to the verdict. Beyond monitoring is direct participation. Notable in South Africa is the possibility for groups like FHR to participate in inquests into suspicious deaths, similar to *querellantes adhesivos* in Guatemala, which I examined in Chapter 6. In many cases, groups like FHR and victims' families have forced the DOJ to reopen cases like the falsely reported 1971 suicide of anti-apartheid activist and trade unionist Ahmed Timol in police custody. The record was only corrected in 2017, a whopping forty-six years later, and only after FHR and Timol's family compelled a re-examination of the case and presented previously suppressed evidence that it was actually the Security Branch that killed him.[35] Groups have also used litigation to challenge such issues as state infringements on free expression. They also regularly provide amicus briefs to the courts and legal comments and other submissions to Parliament.[36] CALS's professional expertise helps it say, "We can help you carry out your mandate," Mkhize confirmed.

A Two-Way Street?

To be sure, it is not always NGOs that want governments to do something. Sometimes it is governments that want NGOs to do something. CSVR's van der Merwe informed me that NGOs can "get a lot of collaboration from government . . . if you can position yourself to make them look good, to do the work that they are supposed to do . . . then you become their darling." He gave here the example of general human rights monitoring reports on compliance with UN treaties. But the idea extends to other areas where the government is willing and able but would still like to farm out the work.

[34] Author interview with Betzi Pierce.
[35] Author interview with Katarzyna Zdunczyk.
[36] Author interviews with Thandeka Kathi and Sithuthukile Mkhize.

Mobilizing Structures

Last, the theory submits that NGOs deploy mobilizing structures to overcome the aforementioned prohibitive political conditions and, more generally, to meet their mandates. In keeping with the burden sharing model, NGOs have prompted the South African government to implement recommendations by making use of their collective power and comparative advantages.

As already discussed, South African NGOs largely retained their diverse issue portfolios following the TRC, although some that possessed a narrower remit expanded them. Consequently, many groups, if not a majority, were already connected. Still, they have strengthened their ties, including via the SACTJ, which has been active since 2008. At the time, President Mbeki was considering pardoning an estimated 100 individuals who had been tried and found guilty of politically motivated crimes during apartheid. Among the first groups to fight this possibility were CSVR, HRMC, IJR, KSG, SAHA, the ICTJ, and the Freedom of Expression Institute. With help from the LRC, the SACTJ sought aid from the Pretoria High Court and stopped the process.[37] And so, a new collective, a new player, was on the scene.

To speak to the theme of comparative advantages, Holtzhausen offered a useful example. One of the Trauma Centre's partners in responding to SGBV is the organization Mosaic, which is expert at obtaining protection orders for survivors. So the Trauma Centre turns to them to help clients who need such an order. Rape Crisis is another partner. Recall, the Trauma Centre seeks to address many different types of violence, so having colleagues with expertise in a particular type is tremendously valuable. The same is true of Molo Songololo and Masithembele, which work primarily with children.[38]

NICRO, which works with all these groups, also collaborates with businesses to create employment opportunities for individuals with criminal records and individuals who have been released from prison. NICRO has also worked with multinationals like Heineken, which has supported alcohol and drug rehabilitation services. CSVR, for its part, has been part of the South African delegation at UN meetings. It is such a valued organization, domestically and internationally, that it almost *has to* be included.[39]

Global partnerships with INGOs, foreign governments, and IOs have also been invaluable. For example, the Trauma Centre has received support from the Julia Taft Fund, administered by the US Department of State. The US Agency for International Development has been another key funder. The European Union,

[37] SACTJ 2022.
[38] Author interview with Marguerite Holtzhausen.
[39] Author interview with Hugo van der Merwe.

United Nations, and World Bank have also supported a slate of South African NGOs promoting TJ, through research, funding, and technical support. The same is true of the ICTJ all these years later. "As a collective, we can really move mountains," Gunn declared.

Discussion

The analysis in Part One has substantiated the argument that civil society helps set governments' post-commission TJ agenda. Through a comprehensive analysis of South Africa following the renowned TRC, I have demonstrated that domestic NGOs developed broad issue portfolios, some before and some after the commission. In keeping with the burden sharing model, domestic groups played a leading role in this first part of the implementation and follow-up stage. They framed and offered policymakers solutions to sociopolitical problems, traversed conditions prohibitive for policy change, and lined up their collective resources. International groups played a supporting role, chiefly as funders. Similar to Guatemala, South Africa demonstrates that TJ—first at the adoption stage, then at the design stage, and now at the implementation and follow-up stage—is a transnational politics story. Domestic and international members of the global TJ network alternate between who leads and who follows, depending on their comparative advantages at different stages. At this stage, groups in South Africa staked out different TRC recommendations, incorporating them into their advocacy, with INGOs backing them.

Part Two: *Uhambo Olude Oluya Enkululekweni* (Long Walk to Freedom)

Part Two provides an overview of South Africa's post-TRC TJ policies. The quantitative analysis follows. In it, I show the extent to which the government has been more likely to initiate and implement fully recommendations backed by NGO coalitions, especially large coalitions. As with Guatemala in the preceding chapter, the results are mixed. Concerted NGO advocacy notwithstanding, the analysis indicates that the South African state has not been socialized into TJ norms—a finding that challenges the conventional wisdom outside the country. Instead, administrations have sparingly and haphazardly implemented TJ measures intended to remedy past violence and injustice and prevent future violence and injustice. Following this, I offer qualitative evidence of unsuccessful socialization into TJ norms and NGOs taking the initiative to assist and substitute for the state in delivering further TJ measures.

Descriptive Statistics: Implementation

The *Varieties of Truth Commissions* capture the implementation status of all 313 substantive recommendations made by the TRC. Within five years of the commission's conclusion, 174 recommendations were initiated (56 percent). Thirty-five others were initiated within ten years (for a total of 67 percent). To aid comparability with Guatemala, I analyze implementation five years post-TRC.

Figures 7.1–7.4 visualize the frequency of recommendations and the percentage initiated by TJ area and category. First, information disclosure and education made up the largest shares of recommended measures for truth (45 and 38 percent, respectively).[40] Uptake was also higher for information disclosure and education than most of the other categories, save for memorialization. Second, judicial reforms made up one-half of recommended justice measures, compared to trials at roughly 19 percent and measures pertaining to amnesties at 31 percent. The TRC urged the government to fight impunity by being selective

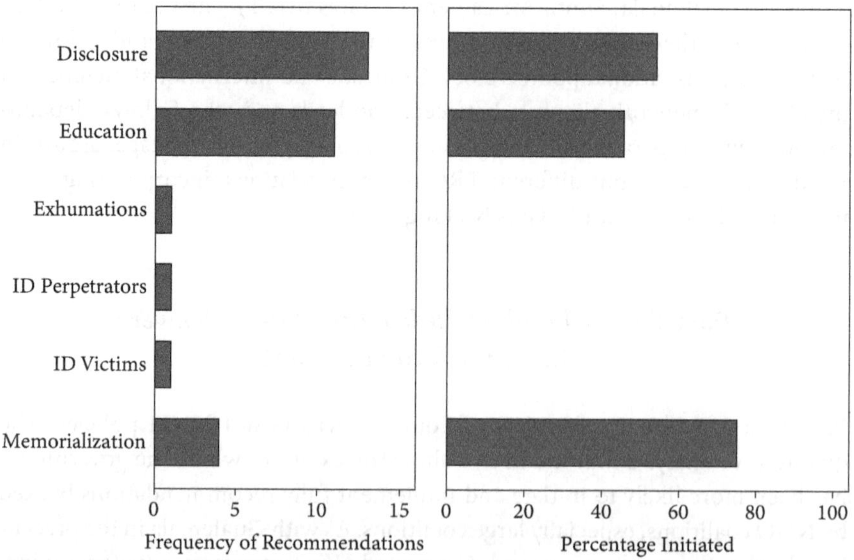

Figure 7.1 South Africa: Initiation of Measures for Truth

Note: The figure shows the frequency of recommended measures for truth (left panel) and the percentage initiated (right panel).

[40] Note, the percentages of recommended measures by TJ area (e.g., truth) may exceed 100, as some recommendations fall under more than one category in a given area (e.g., victim and perpetrator identification).

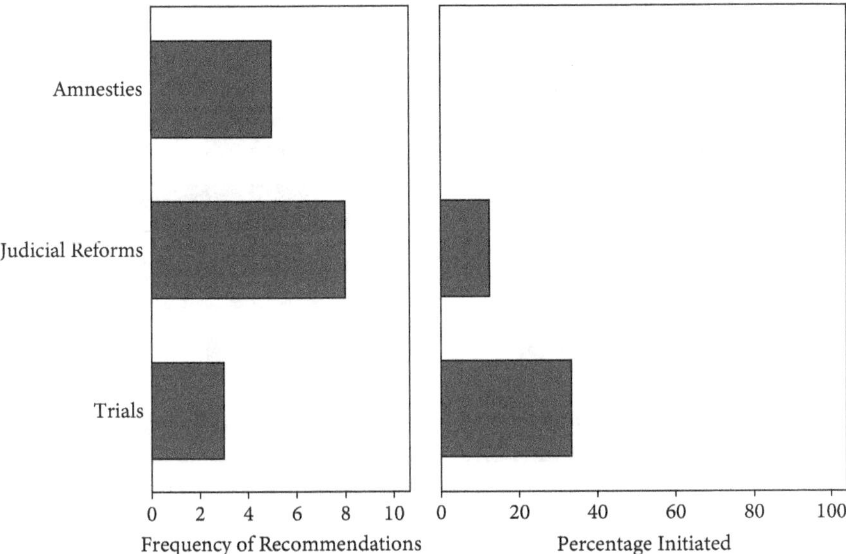

Figure 7.2 South Africa: Initiation of Justice Measures

Note: The figure shows the frequency of recommended justice measures (left panel) and the percentage initiated (right panel).

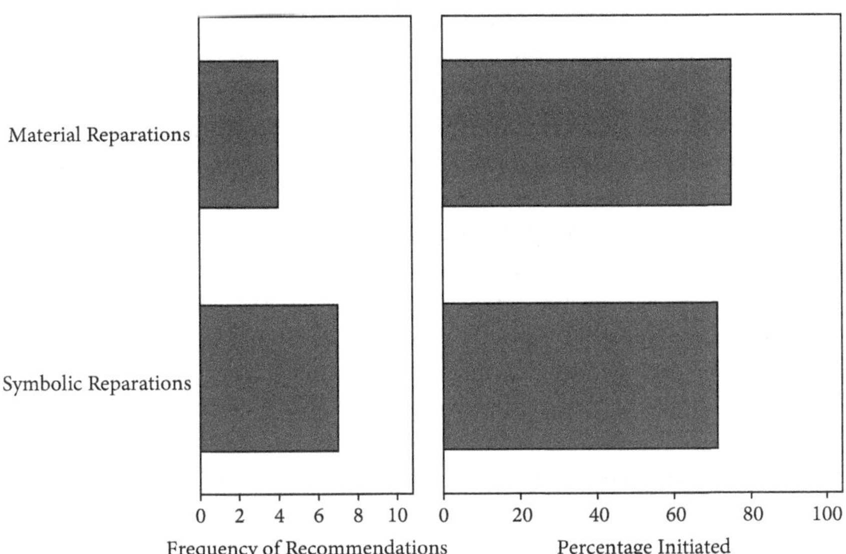

Figure 7.3 South Africa: Initiation of Reparations

Note: The figure shows the frequency of recommended reparations (left panel) and the percentage initiated (right panel).

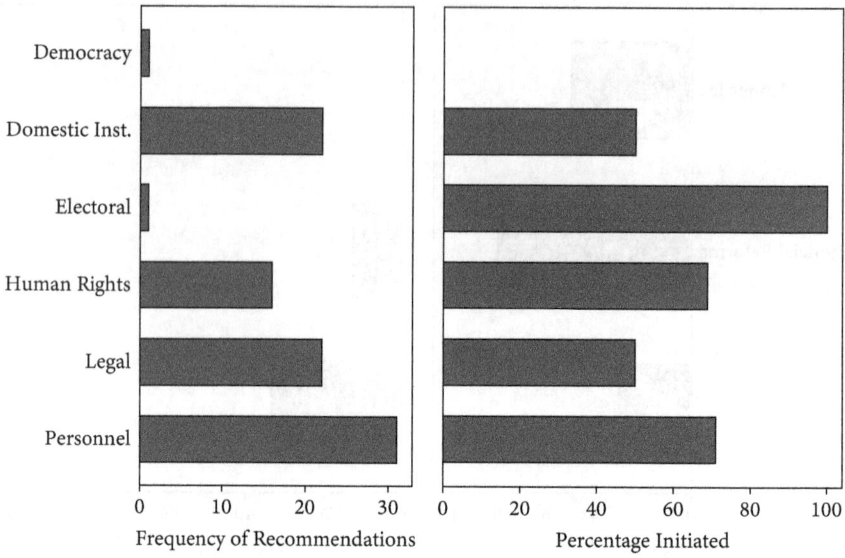

Figure 7.4 South Africa: Initiation of Reforms

Note: The figure shows the frequency of recommended reforms (left panel) and the percentage initiated (right panel).

with amnesties (beyond those the commission offered in exchange for perpetrator testimony), all while taking victims' needs into consideration. The government was not able to walk this fine line and did not initiate the recommended measures pertaining to amnesties. The government went farther with investigations/trials than with judicial reforms. Third, symbolic and material reparations were recommended at a rate of nearly two to one, but they were initiated at similar rates (both above 70 percent). Fourth, personnel reforms were a major focus for the TRC and a large majority were initiated.

I now turn to the level of implementation. Five years after the TRC, 55 of 174 initiated measures (32 percent) reached minimal implementation while 61 others (35 percent) reached intermediate status and yet another 58 (33 percent) reached full implementation. Compared to CEH recommendations, a greater proportion of TRC recommendations reached intermediate status (35 percent in South Africa, compared to 23 percent in Guatemala) and full status (33 percent in South Africa, compared to 28 percent in Guatemala). Figure 7.5 shows the proportion of recommendations at each level of implementation across the four TJ areas. A strong majority (nearly 60 percent) of measures for truth and a plurality of reforms (nearly 40 percent) reached full implementation. A minority of reparation measures (13 percent) reached full implementation. No justice measures were fully implemented—just as in Guatemala.

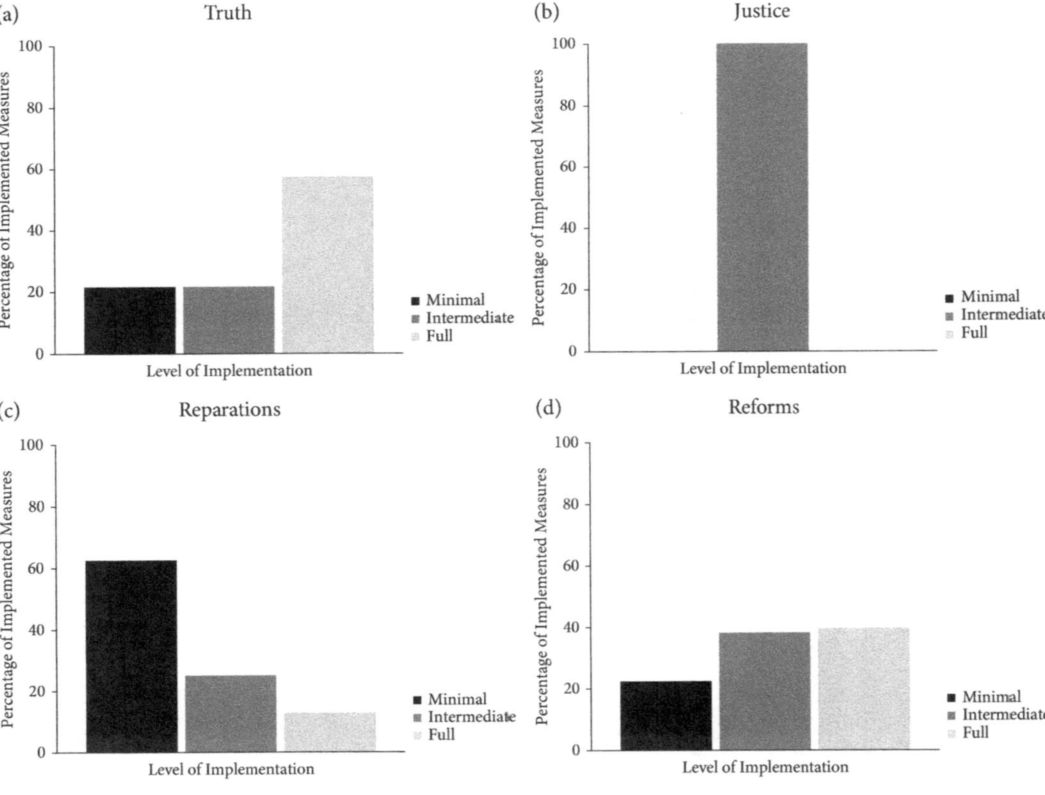

Figure 7.5 South Africa: Level of Implementation of Recommendations

Note: The figure shows the percentage of recommendations that reached different levels of implementation across the four main TJ areas.

The descriptive data presented in Figures 7.1–7.5 square with the findings from Guatemala in Chapter 6, as well as interviews with commission officials in Chapter 5: It is often easier to begin and complete policies relating to truth such as education. Conversely, it is often more difficult to realize policies relating to justice. An interesting point of difference between the Guatemalan and South African cases, however, is levels of implementation for reparations and reforms. Whereas most reparation measures were fully implemented and most reform measures only minimally implemented in Guatemala, the opposite was true in South Africa. Most reparation measures only achieved minimal implementation, and most reform measures reached intermediate or full implementation. The abiding strength of the military and ex-members' continuing influence over politics in Guatemala, compared to the diminished National Party in South Africa, help explain this difference.

An important implication of this research thus emerges: Where transitions in governance are less clear-cut, reforms may be more difficult to deliver because they threaten powerful interests. Meanwhile, where transitions in governance are more clear-cut, reparations may be more difficult to deliver because the government in power is not the one that is culpable for the harms that are to be repaired.

Quantitative Analysis: Implementation

I now examine the relationship between NGO advocacy and implementation of TRC recommendations. Tables 7.2 and 7.3 present the results of the logit and ordered logit regressions, with *Implementation Initiated* and *Implementation Level* as the outcome variables.

Table 7.2 Analysis: NGO Advocacy and Implementation of Recommendations in South Africa: Initiation

	Implementation Initiated			
	(1)	(2)	(3)	(4)
NGO Advocacy	0.51*			0.64*
	(0.24)			(0.25)
NGO Coalition Size		−0.01		−0.01
		(0.01)		(0.01)
INGO Coalition Size			−0.02	0.00
			(0.02)	(0.03)
Observations	313	313	306	306

Logit models. Standard errors in parentheses.
$^{+}p < 0.10$, $^{*}p < 0.05$, $^{**}p < 0.01$

Table 7.3 Analysis: NGO Advocacy and Implementation of Recommendations in South Africa: Level

	Implementation Level			
	(1)	(2)	(3)	(4)
NGO Advocacy	−0.08 (0.32)			−0.04 (0.34)
NGO Coalition Size		0.01 (0.01)		−0.02 (0.01)
INGO Coalition Size			0.11* (0.03)	0.14** (0.04)
Observations	174	174	170	170

Ordered logit models. Standard errors in parentheses.
$^{+}p < 0.10$, $^{*}p < 0.05$, $^{**}p < 0.01$

In terms of initiation, *NGO Advocacy* is a positive and statistically significant predictor of the outcome ($p < 0.05$). South Africa is thus different from Guatemala, where the relationship was not significant at a conventional error level. *NGO Coalition Size* hovers around zero in Models 2 and 4 and, likewise, *INGO Coalition Size* in Models 3 and 4. These latter results suggest that it is not the sheer force of advocacy (i.e., the breadth of coalitions) that matters but the specificity of advocacy.

Neither *NGO Advocacy* nor *NGO Coalition Size* is a positive and statistically significant predictor of the level of implementation, however. It appears that while South African NGOs may have pushed the government to initiate specific recommendations, they were not determining for their fulfillment. This is not to say that civil society groups have not worked mightily to hold the state to its commitments; they certainly have.[41] Rather, it reflects unresponsiveness on the state's part. Hayner confirms a "lack of political commitment" to implement many recommendations in the years following the TRC.[42] Yet the results suggest the helpfulness of international partners. *INGO Coalition Size* is both a positive and statistically significant predictor of the level of implementation ($p < 0.01$).

Now more than twenty years later, it is clear that while the TRC played an important role in post-apartheid South Africa, bringing to light what had for so long been obscured, its legacy has been frustrated by government inaction. In particular, the government's "lack of commitment to a more serious reparations program [has been] a source of great bitterness and anger, and for some [is] an

[41] Risse et al. 1999.
[42] Hayner 2011, 31.

indictment of the entire truth commission process."[43] Indeed, there is a strong feeling that post-commission TJ efforts have been "too little, too late."[44]

Qualitative Analysis: Implementation

The South African state's implementation of TRC recommendations could theoretically be the product of socialization into TJ norms—a process catalyzed by civil society. South Africa is arguably the most famous TJ case, one that has inspired dozens of others around the globe. So I now probe evidence of socialization. If the level of socialization is low, implementation is a reaction to civil society pressure. If the level of socialization is high, implementation is a government initiative, arising independently of civil society pressure.

South Africa since the TRC seems to have stalled at a low level of socialization, acting on calls for further TJ by fits and starts, after substantial delays, for a limited set of issues, and almost entirely because of NGO advocacy. In this respect, South Africa is similar to Guatemala. South Africa, the emblem, model, and ambassador of global TJ has not reached its potential to finish the unfinished business of the TRC—far from it.

The end of apartheid and the dawn of multiracial democracy did not produce a bed of roses, to echo Shirley Gunn. There has not been a stable, sincere, inherent commitment to truth, justice, reparation, and reform, potentially owing to the fact that the ANC did not create the harms that civil society is now asking it to remedy. Administrations have spent much more time and effort trying to make the country a political and economic leader regionally and internationally. A low level of socialization is also clear when we consider the NGO side. Indeed, groups have not only assisted the state to meet its duty in some areas but they have also assumed the state's duty in other areas.

Ethically Recovering Narratives of Harm

Recovering trauma narratives has proved to be slow and challenging work. For all the attention that South Africa received during its "transitional justice moment," most of the progress since the TRC is due to civil society groups like KSG and HRMC. Not everyone who could have testified or provided written statements to the commission had the opportunity to do so. Others, still, were not yet ready. So KSG has compiled testimonies from survivors and witnesses of apartheid violence, building on the TRC's record.

[43] Hayner 2011, 177.
[44] Chapman and Merwe 2008, 285.

KSG boasts an impressive database of more than 90,000 victim accounts of apartheid-related abuse. To put this number in context, that is more than four times the number of victims from whom the TRC received oral and written statements. And it is a victim-led NGO, with limited resources, that has accomplished this feat. While mainly a technical assistance provider, the ICTJ has supported KSG's work, including endorsing its campaign for a national advisory committee to "develop policy to deal with the gaps in dealing with the past."[45]

Meanwhile, HRMC has trained media practitioners, oral historians, and others to capture and disseminate more broadly the narratives of survivors and victims' relatives. From public service announcements and podcasts, to documentary films and books, HRMC has been a trainer, co-producer, and co-publisher, helping to preserve the national patrimony that is the stories of those who lived, suffered, and died under apartheid.[46] The ICTJ has been supportive here, too, amplifying HRMC's and local partners' work to seek, find, and preserve the truth, in support of victims' dignity and reconciliation in the broader society.[47] So we see that *NGOs govern narrative recovery.*

Healing Trauma

Organizations with their eyes trained on healing and preventing violence have been dedicated to a holistic approach that not only involves counseling but also acknowledgment and redress through perpetrator accountability and victim reparation. Alas, the government's approach has been limited, fragmented, and scattered in all these areas.

Additionally, Holtzhausen shared with me that the government's approach seeks to be curative, not preventive. It does not address deeper structural issues like poverty. Neither is the government's approach tailored to communities. Basically, the government has offered an underfunded, one-size-fits-all, reactive, rather than proactive, policy. As I foreshadowed in Part One, if left unaddressed, primary trauma can be compounded by secondary trauma. Both can produce—and have for many produced—chronic stress, a sense of hopelessness, even depression, and interpersonal and community violence, sometimes resulting in a violent response by state actors.

Holtzhausen attributed many of South Africa's current social ills to a lack of remedy for the past. So the Trauma Centre, KSG, NICRO, and others have intervened to provide counseling and support individuals' and families' pursuit of the justice they both need and deserve. Regional groups such as the Civil Society Prison Reform Initiative, which happens to be based in Cape Town, have shared

[45] ICTJ 2014.
[46] Author interview with Shirley Gunn.
[47] ICTJ 2011*a*.

the burden, monitoring and reporting on reforms[48] and lobbying Parliament for legislation on harm prevention.[49] Groups have also secured important legislative wins, including the Children's Act of 2005 and, more recently in 2021, a stronger version of the 1998 Domestic Violence Act.[50] Thus, *NGOs are leading trauma response.*

Preventing Crime and Rehabilitating Offenders

Groups working on crime prevention and offender rehabilitation have made important strides toward their missions since the TRC, often working with the state. Courts regularly refer individuals in trouble with the law to NICRO. Schools do likewise. NICRO also accepts self-referrals and family referrals.

One highlight in burden sharing is NICRO's development of minimum standards for diversion for the South African government—work it undertook in collaboration with local and international partners such as the Human Sciences Research Council (HSRC) and the Open Society Foundation (OSF). This is actually work the government formally contracted NICRO and the HSRC to do based on their expertise. OSF, for its part, has provided funds and research collaboration.[51]

Beyond its criminal justice work with courts, NICRO offers counseling workshops as well as workshops on parenting and family life. It also has a drug and alcohol program. Moreover, it works to reduce the stigma around people who have come into contact with the criminal justice system, people who desperately need assistance—to find and keep jobs, be reintegrated into their families and communities, and regain their dignity.

This work is not easy. It is "a fight every day for your survival," Pierce shared on the subject of securing the resources needed to do all this work. In sum, *NGOs are at the helm of efforts to prevent crime and rehabilitate offenders.*

Fighting for Legal Accountability and Equal Justice

Organizations interested in the law and accountability like FHR have taken a number of steps to deliver on the TRC's recommendations: They have shared the fruits of their investigations with the NPA to assist with criminal trials and inquests. In addition, they have coordinated and provided technical and financial resources to survivors and victims' families whose cases the TRC turned over to the NPA but that have yet to be taken forward. FHR conducts its own investigations, working with pro bono lawyers wherever possible and covering

[48] Civil Society Prison Reform Initiative 2020.
[49] Civil Society Prison Reform Initiative 2022.
[50] Author interview with Marguerite Holtzhausen.
[51] Berg 2012.

expenses when this is not possible. As the Ahmed Timol case shows, they have increased the NPA's capacity and improved its performance.

FHR and its partners' steadfast activism has also recently contributed to Parliament's Justice Portfolio Committee's biannual reviews of the NPA, so the body has more direct supervision and is held accountable for its disappointing performance to date. Take the example of student activist and MK member Nokuthula Simelane's 1983 kidnapping and murder: Between 2003 and 2015, there was not only a lack of will to investigate and prosecute her killers but, indeed, political interference as well. Only in 2016, after decades of her family and FHR fighting for accountability, did the NPA announce it would prosecute the men suspected of her kidnapping and murder. At the time of my field research, the process was still ongoing. Since then, the trial has been postponed because one of the two living suspects is reportedly unfit to stand trial due to dementia.

With all this said, the situation has improved since President Ramaphosa appointed Shamila Batohi as national director of public prosecutions in 2019.[52] With her strong credentials, Batohi, like Hilda Pineda in Guatemala, could be a reformer. Prior to her appointment, she served for ten years as senior legal advisor at the ICC's Office of the Prosecutor. At the outset, she seemed more serious about holding accountable perpetrators of apartheid-era crimes and working with NGOs like FHR. But challenges persist, and TRC cases have not been at the top of her agenda. Still, the situation is better than before.

INGOs, including the ICTJ through the SACTJ network, have shone a spotlight on cases like Simelane's, with the hope of spurring progress,[53] and shamed the government when it has acted against victims and rule of law principles, including by pardoning convicted criminals.[54]

It is histories and experiences like these that highlight the indispensability of NGOs in the justice space. Still, as Mkhize said to me, in the strongest of terms, "We don't want to be in a position where we do their [the government's] job." To summarize, *NGOs have led the charge in the fight for legal accountability and equal justice.*

A Legacy of Progress

Taken together, we observe NGOs governing the process of recovering and disseminating narratives of abuse; heading the response to primary and secondary trauma; at the vanguard of crime prevention and offender rehabilitation;

[52] Author interview with Katarzyna Zdunczyk.
[53] ICTJ 2015.
[54] ICTJ 2012.

and at the front of the fight for legal accountability and equal justice. This is consequential work and is exemplary of civil society actors as TJ governors.

Implementing Like a State: Civil Society Substitution in Post-TRC South Africa

One of the liveliest parts of each of my interviews was when I raised the issue of civil society substitution for the state, in those words. In South Africa, more than anywhere else I have done research, my interlocutors lit up hearing their reality so parsimoniously described. Yes, they were frustrated, but it was also clear that they were gratified to have their work recognized in this way. At this point in the interviews, many would elaborate on other areas where their organizations mind the gap between TJ promises and policies.

Adding to the earlier analysis, areas of NGO assistance to and substitution for the state include funding forensic expert reports, tracking down suspected perpetrators and fugitives of the law, providing legal opinions to the DOJ and NPA, and training prosecutors on litigating apartheid as a crime against humanity. FHR would not and could not do this work if the government did not recognize the organization as an expert and a valuable, if not always valued, partner in the fight for legal accountability and equal justice. To this point, the South African government has at times appropriated NGOs' work as its own. Pierce recounted to me how, in some provinces, the government has taken over NICRO's diversion programs, essentially pushing them out of the space they were responsible for creating—additional evidence that supports NGOs as governors and that contradicts the state's socialization into TJ norms.

In terms of reparations as a means of addressing trauma and providing justice, HRMC has been a leader in developing a framework to guide state policy. Gunn shared that she believes the state's reading of the TRC reparation recommendations was the wrong one. The state narrowly interpreted reparations beneficiaries as just the 16,000 people listed in the TRC report. They have been "close-minded" and have demonstrated "little imagination," she criticized. HRMC and its partners are offering a new reading, a fundamental rethinking of who deserves recompense. They want victims to be identified by the violation, not by whether they testified or applied for reparations on time.

I mentioned earlier that state institutions like the police may rely too heavily on NGOs like the Trauma Centre to do their jobs. Holtzhausen informed me that the police will send survivors to the Trauma Centre to complete their intake forms—this, despite the fact that it is the police's job to help these individuals against whom a crime has been committed. In some cases, survivors will just go to the Trauma Centre, not the police or a local DSD office. They trust the people at the center, not the people working for the state. "We are there, we are accessible," Holtzhausen explained, but added, "We have to push the government to do their work." The organization also engages lawyers, usually for a fee but sometimes on a pro bono basis, to confront police detectives for their inaction or slowness on certain cases, including domestic violence cases. "We do it because it works," she said in resignation.

Another area of NGO work that I have not yet mentioned is assessing the status of reconciliation, now some twenty years since the TRC concluded. IJR runs the South African Reconciliation Barometer, drawing on a nationally representative sample of South Africans, to understand intergroup relations and social cohesion. The 2021 survey revealed across a wide cross-section of the population that reconciliation is still needed, with respondents indicating "everybody has a part to play in the process."[55]

Despite NGOs substituting for the state in key ways, Mkhize expressed, "That's not what we [CALS] want to do . . . [or] be seen to be doing. . . . We honestly use litigation as a last resort." She emphasized that NGOs should not seek to replace the role of a democratically elected government—essentially advancing one cluster of norms, TJ, at the expense of another, democracy. CALS wants to see more accountability, more reparations, and less corruption. CALS also wants the government to be proactive, not simply reactive, in matters of truth and justice.[56]

Beyond potentially corroding norms of democratic representation, the state's devolution of responsibility to the third sector, as discussed in Chapter 6, and/or the third sector's assumption of responsibility could undo TJ norms, domestically and internationally.[57] But Pierce pushed back on this idea, saying she sees some civil society substitution in a positive light. She told me it is important for civil society to stay a trailblazer, not only to do important work that otherwise would not get done but also to show the government how to do it.

Van der Merwe had a similar view. He sees CSVR's and civil society's role as piloting various approaches that the government can take. Still, as he made clear, "We cannot let them off the hook." He mentioned that for survivors and victims' families, implementation *by the government* is meaningful. Implementation is also linked with nonrecurrence; it provides a mechanism to incentivize human rights respect today and in the future.

South Africa has a "vast, well-funded state," van der Merwe also shared. "When it chooses to do something, it can do it really well. . . . There *is* a capable state." Echoing van der Merwe nearly verbatim, Kathi expressed, "When they want to

[55] IJR 2021, vi.
[56] Author interviews with Thandeka Kathi and Sithuthukile Mkhize.
[57] See Kochanski (2021) and Quinn (2021), who make similar arguments.

make something [happen], they are able to do it . . . [if] it benefits them." Regrettably, certain parts of the bureaucracy are corrupt or the people do not care or they are not set up for the job because they are political appointees, not civil servants.[58]

Taken together, the body of qualitative evidence that I have amassed—against the South African government's socialization into TJ and in favor of South African NGOs' advocacy before, assistance to, and substitution for the state—confirms that NGOs are governors.

Discussion

Part Two investigated South African NGOs' efforts to turn truth commission proposals into policy. I followed the strategies they employ to propel government implementation of commission recommendations. I found that organizations lobby for their desired policies and programs through litigation, legislative and executive branch monitoring, demonstrations, and designing and helping to carry out trauma response, rehabilitation, and crime-prevention programs.

Statistical analyses of recommendation implementation showed a significant effect for NGO representation on policy uptake, but not policy progress. In this way, South Africa is different from Guatemala, where NGO representation was important for policy progress but not for initial uptake.

Qualitative analysis then revealed NGOs intervening in post-TRC TJ policy, assisting the government in areas where it was willing but perhaps unable to enact some measures on its own, and substituting for the government where it was unwilling. INGOs and IOs have lent support, chiefly funds, but this has not been an antidote for low political will and interference in government, corruption, and paltry budget allocations. In keeping with burden sharing, domestic advocates led in this final stage of the TJ life cycle.

[58] Author interviews with Thandeka Kathi, Sithuthukile Mkhize, and Hugo van der Merwe.

8

Post-Commission NGO Advocacy: Success, Challenges, and Innovations in Timor-Leste

In 1997, a group of women formed the East Timorese Women's Communication Forum (known by its acronym in Tetum, FOKUPERS), the first women's rights NGO in Timor-Leste. FOKUPERS documented women's experiences of the Indonesian occupation and related armed conflicts, gave them psychosocial support, carried messages to and from their detained relatives, and advocated for them before domestic and international audiences.[1] The group collaborated with a broad swath of human rights and women's groups in Timor-Leste and Indonesia, throughout Southeast Asia, and around the globe, transmitting to them its records of violence against women.[2] In turn, FOKUPERS' international partners disseminated its research and echoed its calls for an end to violence and justice for victims.[3]

As the human rights situation worsened in 1998—what would be the occupation's penultimate year—FOKUPERS invited the UN special rapporteur on violence against women, Radhika Coomaraswamy, to visit Timor-Leste and hear from conflict-affected women directly.[4] Asma Jahangir, the special rapporteur on extrajudicial, summary or arbitrary executions, and Nigel Rodley, the special rapporteur on torture, joined Coomaraswamy on the investigative mission. Their observations led the United Nations to call for an independence referendum and a range of TJ measures. Indonesia's hands were tied; it acquiesced to a referendum, however begrudgingly.[5]

Once the referendum date was set, FOKUPERS partnered with the main coalition of political parties, the National Council of Timorese Resistance (CNRT) to get out the vote. Their combined efforts resulted in a 98.5 percent voter turnout and a 78.5 percent super-majority vote for Timorese self-government.[6]

1 Niner 2016.
2 FOKUPERS 1999.
3 Amnesty International 1998, 1999.
4 UNCHR 1999.
5 Hunt 2016; UNCHR 2001; UNSG 1999.
6 Wigglesworth 2013.

Governing Truth. Kelebogile Zvobgo, Oxford University Press. © Oxford University Press (2026).
DOI: 10.1093/oso/9780197815663.003.0008

With this success in hand, FOKUPERS contributed to policy debates, including by convening hundreds of women from across Timor-Leste to develop the Platform for Action for the Advancement of Women in 2000, which guided the UN transitional administration's gender policy. FOKUPERS also promoted, consulted on, and offered technical support to a variety of social, economic, and TJ initiatives, including the truth commission (known by its acronym in Portuguese, CAVR).[7]

FOKUPERS went from strength to strength. Its leaders and staff members played many important roles in the commission, among them their cofounder Galuh Wandita, who I had the privilege to interview. Wandita served on the steering committee that drafted the commission's founding legislation and mandate, sat on the panel to nominate commissioners, and even worked for a time as the commission's deputy director. Other FOKUPERS members assisted the CAVR with staff recruitment for the women's research team and those with professional experience in psychology facilitated healing workshops. In addition, the organization contributed its database of approximately 300 interviews with women victims and witnesses of abuse. FOKUPERS even helped design and carry out the commission's collective reparations program.[8]

Consistent with my burden sharing model and the evidence provided in the preceding chapters, FOKUPERS—in tandem with other domestic and international civil society groups—called for an end to violence, demanded truth and justice for abuses, and helped design and implement appropriate measures, not least among them the commission. But, like this book, the organization's story does not end there. Rather, it continues on to the post-commission period, where the government has implemented some commission recommendations but not others. Since the CAVR's conclusion in 2005, FOKUPERS—in partnership with AJAR, the Hak Association, the ICTJ, UN Women, and others—has played a vital role in advancing the commission's recommendations. Focusing on its areas of expertise, FOKUPERS has promoted the CAVR's proposals relating to women.

This case encourages us to investigate whether and to what degree Timorese NGOs have lent their advocacy effort to some TJ issues suggested by the CAVR due to organizational histories and professional experience. In the two preceding chapters, we saw domestic groups in Guatemala and South Africa come together around the respective commission reports and recommendations—diversifying their issue portfolios, learning from and disseminating information among themselves, pooling resources, and sharing the burden of post-commission

[7] Hunt 2016. The commission followed up on the principle of reconciliation discussed by the CNRT in Portugal in April 1998.

[8] Wandita et al. 2006.

TJ advocacy. They did this with their international partners' financial, logistical, and political support. This chapter explores the extent to which this has also been the case in Timor-Leste. The chapter examines the relationship between NGO advocacy effort and NGO advocacy success in Timor-Leste, specifically whether and to what degree the state has prioritized implementing NGO-backed CAVR recommendations, especially those supported by broad coalitions. For the analysis, I analyze data from the *Varieties of Truth Commissions*, which capture NGO advocacy and government implementation of recommendations, alongside qualitative data from my fieldwork.

In Part One, which centers on NGO advocacy effort, I find notable variation in Timorese NGO issue prioritization and agenda-setting attempts. Some NGOs had very diverse issue portfolios in the pre-commission period, not just the post-commission period. For instance, the HAK Association advocated for victim identification, memorialization, reparations, legal reforms, and other issues, from its founding in the mid-1990s onward. So there were not many more new TJ advocacy realms for the organization to explore. Organization leaders in this context developed and strengthened partnerships—with domestic groups like FOKUPERS, INGOs like Amnesty International, and IOs like the Asian Development Bank—to push for their desired policies. Other NGOs expanded their work. As an example, Timor Aid, a development NGO, made strides into the legal sector, partnering with groups like FOKUPERS and the HAK Association to lobby for CAVR-recommended legal reforms, including greater compliance with international human rights treaty obligations. Other NGOs, still, stayed the course, retaining their existing issue portfolios. To illustrate, Juristas focused on law-related CAVR recommendations.

In Part Two, which centers on NGO advocacy success, I uncover positive post-CAVR outcomes linked to TJ network members promoting a variety of commission recommendations. Similar to Guatemala and South Africa, the data from Timor-Leste confirm that NGO advocacy matters. I also find in Timor-Leste that advocacy coalition size matters. Statistical analyses show the positive effect of both NGO advocacy and advocacy coalition size on policy adoption, though not policy completion—similar to the pattern in South Africa.

While the Timorese government did prioritize initiating recommendations supported by domestic NGO coalitions in the five years following the CAVR, the government ultimately did not make better progress on them. This is due in large part to: multiple security crises since Independence; leaders' rapprochement with Indonesia and thus, at times, attempts to distance themselves from civil society's agenda; and the challenge of being "on the hook" for remedying abuses the post-Independence government did not itself perpetrate. This is what TJ requires, to be clear, but marshaling the political will and material resources to meet this obligation is not easy.

Qualitative case analysis reveals NGO intervention where the government has effectively abandoned its obligations to deliver further TJ. Taken together, the findings support the third part of the burden sharing model. Domestic NGOs have played a leading role since the CAVR, attempting to and, in some instances, succeeding in setting and implementing the post-commission agenda, with and without the government, and with international partners' help.

Plan of the Chapter

Part One starts with a brief history of Indonesia's occupation of Timor-Leste, the armed conflicts, the transition, and the CAVR's founding. I also discuss the commission's proceedings, findings, and recommendations. Next, I produce a descriptive analysis of NGO recommendations advocacy, addressing the presence and size of NGO coalitions in different issue areas. I then assess my theory of agenda-setting attempts by domestic NGOs against the empirical record using data from my fieldwork interviews to detect the steps in my proposed causal chain—from developing issue portfolios, to framing, to navigating opposition, to resource and network mobilization. I do this across four areas of note: (1) building the legal and judicial system, (2) securing the security sector, (3) responding to violence against women and children, and (4) remembering and teaching the past. Part Two surveys CAVR-recommended TJ policies that were initiated and, in some cases, fulfilled by the Timorese government. Following this are quantitative and qualitative analyses of the influence of NGO advocacy and advocacy coalition size on the initiation and fulfillment of the CAVR's recommendations.

Part One: *Chega*! (Enough!)

During Indonesia's occupation of Timor-Leste and the resulting armed conflicts, from 1975 to 1999, an estimated 100,000 people were killed and hundreds of thousands more were displaced. Following nearly three decades of violence, and at the prompting of domestic, regional, and international movements for Timorese self-determination, the Indonesian government agreed to an independence referendum in 1999. The referendum produced incontrovertible evidence that an overwhelming majority of Timorese wanted self-government. So Indonesia acquiesced, but not until after mass post-election violence that resulted in the deaths of approximately 1,400 people and the displacement of still others to Indonesian-controlled West Timor. Given the volatility of the political environment, the United Nations administered Timor-Leste's transition, from

1999 to 2002. Among the first orders of business for the transitional administration was creating the CAVR.[9]

First advocated by domestic civil society actors—and later shaped with the assistance of the newly formed ICTJ, the United Nations, and other international experts—the truth commission examined over a three-year period nearly three decades of violence and abuse. Approximately 85 percent of reported violations were attributed to Indonesian security forces and their proxies, with the remainder attributed to pro-independence forces.[10] The CAVR determined that Indonesian security forces perpetrated crimes against humanity, including starvation, arbitrary executions, and torture of Timorese combatants and civilians alike. The CAVR report raised awareness among members of the international community of abuses that had for so long been concealed. However, the Indonesian government has declined to accept many of the findings, and Indonesian–Timorese history remains a highly sensitive topic in the country. Critically, the CAVR report provided both a normative and evidentiary basis for further efforts toward truth, justice, reparation, and institutional reform, and issued hundreds of recommendations. Per the theory, civil society organizations in Timor-Leste adopted many of these prescriptions as part of their post-commission advocacy agenda, effectively extending TJ beyond the CAVR.

NGOs by Commission Recommendation Area

The *Varieties of Truth Commissions* data capture for a given CAVR recommendation whether there was at least one domestic NGO already active in the recommendation's key issue area—for instance, material reparations—and, if so, how many NGOs. The data also capture whether and how many groups lobbied for particular proposals. Table 8.1 shows the nineteen substantive areas that the CAVR addressed in its recommendations, arranged by TJ theme.

The data show that there was at least one domestic NGO already active in each of the nineteen recommendation areas, though the number of groups in each area varied. To illustrate, six organizations, including the Hak Association, were rallying for material and symbolic reparations; nineteen organizations, among them FOKUPERS and Timor Aid, were advancing education; eight groups were fighting for information disclosure, including the names of disappeared children, with the Judicial System Monitoring Programme (JSMP) and La'o Hamutuk playing key roles; and fifteen groups, among them the Timor-Leste NGO Forum (FONGTIL), were lobbying for human rights reforms like

[9] Hayner 2011, 39–40.
[10] Hayner 2011, 41.

Table 8.1 Substantive Recommendations from the Timorese CAVR

Recommendation Areas	
Truth	**Reforms**
Education	Democracy
Exhumations	Human rights
Information disclosure	Legal
Memorialization	New domestic institutions
Perpetrator identification	Personnel
Victim identification	
Justice	**Services**
Amnesties	Perpetrator rehabilitation
Judicial reforms	Social welfare
Trials	Victim rehabilitation
Reparations	
Material	
Symbolic	

policies to ensure equitable distribution of the benefits of development among the East Timorese—without respect to gender, age, ability, or region.[11]

NGOs by Commission Recommendation

As in Guatemala and South Africa, the diversity of pre-commission NGO activity in Timor-Leste suggests why groups adopted the majority of the CAVR's proposals. Yet not all recommendations were adopted. Take, as an example, legal reforms. The CAVR recommended that Parliament enact legislation to institutionalize reporting on compliance with human rights treaties that Timor-Leste had ratified. While multiple NGOs lobbied for CAVR-prescribed legal reforms, like the incorporation of UN human rights treaties into domestic statute, this particular proposal does not appear to have been pursued. Consider, also, memorialization. The CAVR proposed that the government institute a national day of remembrance for victims of the 1978–1979 famine and conduct research and outreach on food insecurity in Timor-Leste. While several organizations rallied for commission-recommended memorial projects, like placing

[11] See Chapter 5 and online Appendix C for more information on how the lists of NGOs by recommendation and recommendation area were assembled.

historical markers at significant sites of killings, my research team did not find documentation of groups lobbying for that specific measure.

Also similar to Guatemala and South Africa, broad adoption of recommendations by members of the Timorese human rights community did not result in uniform representation. For example, while our research revealed nearly twenty organizations working on education after the CAVR, only four—including the Chega! For Us Association (ACbit)—demanded that the government recognize, document, and disseminate through various platforms women's contributions to the Timorese liberation struggle. Yet, in other recommendation areas, we did not see attrition. In fact, we saw the opposite. For instance, in the area of criminal investigations and trials, sixteen groups were active in the pre-commission period, but twenty-three ultimately lobbied for recommendations related to investigations and trials. Likewise, in the domain of legal reforms, four organizations, including Juristas, were active in the pre-commission period; however, the number of groups grew to forty-four. The expansion of lobbying coalitions and "crossover" of NGOs between recommendation areas tracks with trends in Guatemala and South Africa.

Qualitative Analysis: Agenda Setting

For the descriptive qualitative analysis of NGO agenda-setting attempts in post-commission Timor-Leste, I draw on semi-structured interviews that I conducted virtually in the spring and summer of 2022, with participants representing ten prominent domestic, regional, and international NGOs. I also interviewed officials from the CAVR and Post-CAVR Technical Secretariat, the Timorese–Indonesian Commission of Truth and Friendship (CTF), the Chega! National Center (CNC)—the main public institution tasked with following up on the CAVR's recommendations—and the United Nations Transitional Administration for East Timor (UNTAET) and United Nations Mission of Support to East Timor (UNMISET).

Issue Portfolios

Issue selection is the first observable implication of civil society attempting to set a government's post-commission agenda. As the chapters on Guatemala and South Africa show, some organizations direct focus to commission recommendations that correspond with their existing issue portfolios, while many others engage in mission creep, evolving their policy platforms and activism. We see both of these stories playing out in Timor-Leste, the second one especially.

Some NGOs, like FOKUPERS, focused on their historical areas of expertise. As an example, pursuant to the CAVR's recommendation for Timor-Leste to adhere to the Convention on the Elimination of All Forms of Discrimination Against Women, FOKUPERS has monitored the state's compliance with its obligations under the treaty and submitted periodic reports to the OHCHR.[12] The organization has also pressed the government to grant material and symbolic reparations to SGBV survivors.[13] Other groups have substantially expanded their issue set, and in some instances they have spurred on new groups. JSMP is just one organization that is demonstrative of this development.

JSMP was established in 2001 by Nélson Belo, with whom I had the privilege to speak. He served in the Timorese Resistance during Indonesia's occupation, playing many roles. He was a student activist, a recruiter for clandestine forces, and a key conduit between guerrillas and the outside world, smuggling international journalists in and out of the country as they met with commanders to report on the violence the East Timorese were suffering. Belo was arrested and detained several times but persisted. When the independence referendum succeeded in 1999 and members of the Resistance began pivoting their attention to governance and justice issues, Belo decided to launch JSMP to monitor the Special Panels for Serious Crimes in Timor-Leste and the Ad Hoc Human Rights Tribunal in Indonesia.

As these judicial processes unfolded and the quasi-judicial CAVR conducted and concluded its work, JSMP advocated for the commission's recommendations related to the criminal legal system. This was all consistent with the organization's existing issue portfolio. But the group also set its sights on other issues, advocating for civic and human rights education, demanding reparations for conflict-affected communities, and urging memorialization of victims. JSMP took on women's issues, too, joining organizations like ACbit and FOKUPERS to fight domestic violence and support women's leadership initiatives. This is clear evidence of burden sharing: If groups advocating for women's issues could go it alone, we would not see issue crossover. In addition, we would not see organizations like JSMP operating across such a wide array of recommendation areas.

Framing

NGOs framing commission outputs is the second observable implication of the theory. Groups seek to make recommendations more legible and actionable for policymakers—identifying problems, offering solutions, and motivating action.

[12] OHCHR 2009; Rede Feto Timor Leste 2015.

[13] Working Group on Reparations 2008.

We see this in post-commission Timor-Leste, just as we saw it in post-commission Guatemala and South Africa. Timorese NGOs pinpointed the core problem of the past in slightly different but still complementary ways. This is emblematic of their distinct yet overlapping post-commission portfolios and evinces burden sharing in the NGO community.

Building the Legal and Judicial System

As one of the first independent countries of the twenty-first century, "everything [had to be] started from scratch" in Timor-Leste, including the legal and judicial system, JSMP's program manager Casimiro dos Santos shared with me. Recall, the country was colonized by Portugal from the eighteenth century to 1975, then occupied by Indonesia until 1999, and administered by the United Nations until 2002. It was vital, dos Santos continued, that the new country complied with international standards in developing and practicing its laws. This would give it the foundation it needed to be stable and prosperous. Establishing the independence of judges, conducting free and fair trials, rendering perpetrators of violence criminally accountable, and meting out justice for victims—these would all be key elements of the new country's progress. Accordingly, JSMP has advocated for these and other rule of law issues.[14] The organization consistently emphasizes that the rule of law is "an integral component that underpins the other democratic pillars of the Timor-Leste State and Constitution." Without it, it is difficult to "guarantee and protect people's rights and ensure national stability, and . . . contribute to a sustainable development process."[15]

Securing the Security Sector

The earlier discussion on issue selection showed groups either sticking to their core issues or expanding them. But it is also important to address new organizations coming out of old ones, as a part of problem identification and issue framing. In 2009, JSMP's Belo cofounded, with peace and development specialist Edward Rees, the Guardian Foundation (hereafter, Mahein) to address the security sector—a key area the CAVR addressed in its recommendations. So we have advocates like Belo not only expanding their organizations' missions and activities but also creating new ones altogether to specialize in new issues.

Belo told me that from Independence to 2005, there was no civilian oversight over the security sector. Neither were there mechanisms for dispute resolution in security institutions. Belo cited these twin problems as creating the conditions for the 2006 crisis, which almost led the young country to collapse.

[14] Author interviews with Casimiro dos Santos and Jose Pereira, coordinator of JSMP's National Parliament Monitoring Programme.

[15] JSMP 2015, 1.

Initially a dispute over discrimination in the armed forces, the crisis grew into an attempted coup and ignited violence across the country. Mahein sought to create avenues for dispute resolution within the security community and make space for the public to be informed about and participate in decision-making related to the security sector. Connected to the work of its sister organization, JSMP, Mahein also wanted everyone to be subordinate to the rule of law, with no exceptions for the powerful and well connected. Indeed, impunity for abuses creates the conditions for more abuse. Last, the group sought to build early warning systems to prevent and mitigate against conflict within the military and the police.

Responding to Violence Against Women and Children

ACbit, FOKUPERS, the National Victims' Association, the Organization for Legal Services for Women and Girls (ALFeLa), and other groups that work on women's and children's issues identified the interwoven problems of a lack of acknowledgment, redress, and relief for survivors of conflict-related sexual violence (CRSV). The groups believed that if these issues were left unaddressed, they would perpetuate cycles of discrimination and violence. As a consequence, NGOs have prioritized and lobbied for the CAVR's recommendations to raise public awareness of, reduce the stigma around, combat, and provide reparations for CRSV and discrimination and violence against women more generally. In addition, they have fought for recognition of women's contributions to the Resistance, both at home and abroad. Last, groups have devoted themselves to children's issues, including identifying thousands of "stolen children" and having them returned from Indonesia to Timor-Leste.[16]

Remembering and Teaching the Past

FONGTIL, the Hak Association, La'o Hamutuk, and Psychosocial Recovery & Development in East Timor (PRADET), among other groups, identified the absence of a formal educational curriculum on historical political violence in Timor-Leste. Together with groups like ACbit, FOKUPERS, and JSMP, they were concerned about memory being lost, especially absent physical sites of memory, and they signaled the risks that this posed for repetition.[17] Consistent with the CAVR's recommendations, Timorese NGOs in the memory space have advocated for educating the East Timorese—in public and private schools, government institutions, and public discourse—on the recent past, human rights,

[16] Author interview with Galuh Wandita.

[17] Author interviews with Casimiro dos Santos, Jose Pereira, Galuh Wandita, Hugo Fernandes (currently the CNC executive director and, previously, head of research and investigation at the CAVR and research coordinator for the CTF), and Pat Walsh (a CNC advisor and, previously, a key advisor to the CAVR and the Post-CAVR Technical Secretariat).

and democracy and citizenship. They have also promoted memorials and historical markers at significant sites of killings and detention centers, as well as restoration of cultural heritage sites. In addition, they called for the preservation of archives and a national human rights center.[18]

Navigating Prohibitive Political Conditions

NGOs contending with prohibitive political conditions is the third observable implication of the theory. NGOs do this by gaining access to policymaking and policy-executing bodies. Here, I relay civil society leaders' perspectives on barriers to TJ following the CAVR, with special attention given to three persistent themes: low political will, sociopolitical issues, and geopolitical issues. I also document how groups across different fields have overcome, if only in part, these obstacles to agenda setting.

The first obstacle NGOs in Timor-Leste have encountered when advocating for post-commission TJ measures is low levels of political will in government, much like in Guatemala and South Africa.[19] Cristián Correa, the ICTJ's visiting expert in Timor-Leste, imparted, "This is a commission that had a challenge in terms of ownership from the start. . . . It was not a commission created by a government . . . that feels that it owns it." Indeed, Xanana Gusmão's administration inherited the CAVR and other TJ institutions and programs from the UN transitional administration. To be sure, the Timorese government was not against the CAVR per se. But it was something that people in government saw as "imposed on the agenda by Sérgio [de Mello]. . . . I think that's . . . a clue," Correa continued, "to understand the CAVR and its long-term impact. It's a foreign commission. . . . What I heard from people there is the Timorese commissioners were not the most active."

This came up with another interviewee who, for the purposes of this discussion, requested anonymity. They said some of the local commission staff "felt like they couldn't do anything" without the approval of the "internationals." Correa speculated about this: "That's the thing that happens when you are a foreigner or you are a Westerner or maybe when you are white, that you just silence people." Patrick Burgess, former legal counsel to the CAVR, also relayed to me feedback he received from some in civil society who felt the CAVR, not just its leadership, was taking up a lot of space in the post-Independence political environment. Yet, despite the somewhat exclusive nature of the commission's leadership, NGOs like FOKUPERS still managed to play significant roles in its operation, and

[18] ICSC 2022.
[19] La'o Hamutuk 2005*a*.

groups like JSMP were "quite satisfied" with the substance of its report.[20] It is a document that "can be used by civil society for years and years to come."[21]

Sociopolitical issues represent the second obstacle, specifically how victims are defined and deemed worthy of reparation and remembrance. The CNC's Pat Walsh and JSMP's Jose Pereira explained that many in government who were freedom fighters have a narrow view of who counts as a victim and who should be prioritized: fighters. This is despite the fact that non-fighters, including women and children, also resisted and also suffered during the occupation and armed conflicts.

Galuh Wandita—now director of the regional NGO AJAR, with several other affiliations and board member roles—also raised this problem. She affirmed that it is the violation that should define the victim,[22] not whether they picked up arms or what political party they joined or what views they held.[23] The first awarded reparations and the first memorialized, however, have been military veterans and very few others beyond them. Correa described this "guys club" approach to reparations as very frustrating. "It proved that it was possible when there was willingness." Pereira also holds this view: Political will is the issue, not the budget. Similar to the South African case, if the political will is there, there will be a budget; if it is not, there will not be.

Geopolitical issues have been the third major obstacle, especially in terms of recommendations about accountability for Indonesia and its enablers like Portugal and the United States.[24] Eduardo González, who supported the writing of the CAVR report, shared that there was a *realpolitik* mentality when President Gusmão came to power in 2002. When the commission concluded its work in 2005, Gusmão dismissed its report and did not publish it. In fact, it was the ICTJ that published a copy that had been leaked to them. This negative reception of the report by Timorese elites would have far-reaching consequences for its dissemination and, importantly, implementation of its recommendations.[25] González had this to say:

> The government of East Timor was an extreme case of that phenomenon, when enemies become friends, and then suddenly . . . it's a complete turnaround politically. . . . Their future was with Indonesia—and that was it. And, so, the political rapprochement between the Timorese leadership and the Indonesian leadership was very, very clear from day one. I remember Xanana met with

[20] Author interview with Casimiro dos Santos.

[21] Author interview with Patrick Burgess.

[22] NGOs such as La'o Hamutuk have also recommended taking victims' vulnerability into account (La'o Hamutuk 2010*b*).

[23] Note, some Timorese, albeit a minority, supported Indonesia.

[24] Author interview with Pat Walsh.

[25] Author interview with Pat Walsh.

> General Wiranto himself . . . one of the persons most responsible for the worst moments of repression in East Timor. . . . They saw the commission as part of a project that had to do with putting Indonesians in jail, and they simply didn't like that.[26]

Nevertheless, NGOs in Timor-Leste have been expert at finding allies, both inside and outside government, gaining access to such institutions as the courts, Parliament, the police, and executive offices like the Ministries of Education and Justice, to move the needle on CAVR recommendations.[27]

Building the Legal and Judicial System

NGOs whose main focus is developing the legal and judicial system have gained access to government institutions and influenced decision-making via two key pathways: personal connections and technical expertise. In our conversation, Nélson Belo shared very plainly of policymakers, "They all know me." Indeed, he served as a key liaison during the Resistance, connecting the outside world with then-military leaders and now-political leaders. He was one of them; their paths simply split after Independence. From Gusmão to Taur Matan Ruak and, now, José Ramos-Horta, all these presidents have asked for and benefited from Belo's advice, first when he was at JSMP and, now, at Mahein.

Legally and judicially focused organizations like JSMP have also engaged directly with Parliament and the courts, leveraging their technical expertise. They draft memos, helping parliamentarians to digest the vast amount of information they need to make key votes, and offer legal commentary, helping judges to comply with international standards and monitoring their adherence to national and international laws. JSMP's legislative analysis and court monitoring is exemplary, making it "well recognized as *the* oversight organization to the justice sector. . . . Parliament, they always ask us to provide our comments . . . [and] the Court . . . they say JSMP's presence [helps] them improve their work."[28]

Dos Santos attributed success to the organization's diplomatic approach, or "soft advocacy." They do not generally lead demonstrations; they prefer direct meetings with officials. They also tend to not name names in their press releases and, instead, refer in more general terms to government agencies or committees. Their cooperative relationship with state institutions, as dos Santos described it, means that "what we propose is mostly considered by the government."

[26] For this criticism from domestic civil society actors, see, for example, La'o Hamutuk (2005*a*, 2010*a*, 2013).

[27] Author interview with Pat Walsh.

[28] Author interview with Casimiro dos Santos.

Securing the Security Sector

Groups working on security sector issues like Mahein have likewise used informal and formal relationships with government officials, and leveraged their technical expertise to meet their missions. Timor-Leste is a very small country, with few degrees of separation between civil society actors and people in government. Whether it is a government official's "wife or their brothers or sisters, [they] can get someone to put [Mahein's reports] in their hands."[29] Mahein has also negotiated regularly scheduled meetings with the minister of justice, the president's office, the executive committee in charge of security, national defense, and foreign affairs, and military and police commanders. In addition, Mahein uses television, radio, university seminars, and other avenues to raise public awareness of rule of law issues among parliamentarians' constituents and motivate them to also apply pressure on the government.

Responding to Violence Against Women and Children

ACbit, ALFeLa, FOKUPERS, the National Victims' Association, and other groups in the gender and youth justice space have reported that the government has largely turned a blind eye to CRSV survivors. Much of this has to do with the intense stigma around CRSV, including the wrong belief that these survivors were either prostitutes or "slept with the enemy." Those who had children as a result of their abuse are doubly stigmatized because of the social taboo of having children out of wedlock. Wandita also shared, "We are finding that the discrimination and stigma can be inherited," affecting not only the women but also their children. To overcome these obstacles, NGOs have practiced "gymnastics," as Wandita describes it, couching their advocacy for remedies for historical violence against women and girls in their advocacy for remedies for contemporary violence against women and girls, where there is some government interest (like in the social services ministry). There is also the interest of, and importantly funding from, external actors like UN Women. Civil society groups attend village, district, and national government meetings and, as part of their survivor-focused, grassroots strategy, they have the women tell their stories in their own words.[30]

Remembering and Teaching the Past

As in other issue areas, NGOs working in the memory space have availed themselves of both formal and informal access to and relationships with decision makers to make progress on the CAVR's recommendations pertaining to memorialization and education. Parliament, the Ministry of Education, and the prime

[29] Author interview with Nélson Belo.
[30] ACbit and AJAR 2017.

minister's office have been key institutions they have engaged.[31] A notable obstacle to their progress, however, has been defining victims. As I raised earlier, the state has prioritized Resistance fighters for acknowledgment and memorialization because they are who many members of the government see as *the* victims of the occupation and conflicts. This perception has been difficult to overcome and has limited the level and scope of implementation of recommendations.

Mobilizing Structures

Using mobilizing structures to overcome prohibitive political conditions is the final observable implication of NGO attempts to set the post-commission agenda. Consistent with the burden sharing model, Timorese NGOs have prompted government action by playing on their comparative advantages.

As previously indicated, civil society organizations substantially expanded their issue portfolios following the CAVR. Some maintained their core set of issues—for instance, law and justice for JSMP; security issues for Mahein; reparation and healing, with a focus on women, for FOKUPERS; and acknowledgment, education, and dignification of victims for ACbit. But, similar to groups in Guatemala and South Africa, the commission spurred them on to broaden their agendas.

This broadening has strengthened connections in the human rights community. To give just a few examples, ACbit and FOKUPERS have joined forces to produce participatory action research on gender violence. Wandita shared that getting gender violence survivors involved in the identification of problems and solutions is not only operationally smart but is also a way to empower them. Mahein—together with JSMP, the Hak Association, and others—has also shared the burden of advocating for an improved, safety-oriented, human rights-respecting security sector.

NGOs that have formal access to government institutions like Mahein also act as conduits for NGOs that lack this formal access. When the government needs help with an issue that is outside Mahein's expertise, Mahein gets groups that do have this expertise in contact with the relevant ministry.

I will also take the opportunity to highlight here domestic and international NGO advocacy for criminal justice, separate from the examples given above. Organizations like the National Alliance for an International Tribunal (ANTI), the East Timor and Indonesia Action Network (ETAN), the International Federation for East Timor (IFET), and TAPOL (previously known as the British Campaign for the Release of Indonesian Political Prisoners) continue to agitate

[31] Author interviews with Casimiro dos Santos, Hugo Fernandes, Jose Pereira, and Galuh Wandita.

not only for criminal accountability at the domestic level but also at the international level. ETAN cofounder John Miller and Charles Scheiner, who has been a member of ETAN and IFET since the 1990s and a researcher for La'o Hamutuk since 2001, stressed the international community's obligation to support Timor-Leste with TJ and hold external actors like Indonesia, Portugal, and the United States accountable for their role in the occupation and armed conflicts.

International partnerships and solidarity with Timor-Leste have been vital.[32] For instance, AJAR has collaborated with ACbit and FOKUPERS on women's issues and with Hak, JSMP, and Mahein on security issues. CIVICUS, for its part, sends monitoring reports on behalf of the East Timorese to the UN's Universal Periodic Review. TAPOL coordinator Adriana Sri Adhiati shared that her organization does likewise and makes submissions to UN Security Council members, in addition to publishing press releases.

The International Coalition of Sites of Conscience has also worked with Timorese NGOs to strengthen history education and violence prevention. And, to take the book's broader story full circle, FAFG, the Forensic Anthropology Foundation of Guatemala, which I examined in Chapter 6, is another collaborator on these issues.[33] IOs, in particular the European Union and United Nations,[34] have been key funders and logistical partners in much the same way as we saw in Guatemala and South Africa. Funding is always an issue, Belo, dos Santos, Pereira, and others shared with me. Small private donors, large INGO and external state donors, and everyone in between provide crucial lifelines to human rights and TJ advocacy in Timor-Leste.

Discussion

Part One has offered evidence of and increased our confidence in civil society groups' TJ agenda setting. Through an analysis of Timor-Leste since the momentous CAVR, I have shown that Timorese NGOs transformed their issue set while retaining their core missions. Consistent with my model of burden sharing, domestic groups led these efforts in the first half of the implementation and follow-up stage. They framed problems and offered solutions to policymakers, navigated challenging political and social conditions, and marshaled network resources. International groups took on a supporting role, assisting their domestic partners, including with funding. Like Guatemala and South

[32] Author interview with Pat Walsh.

[33] AJAR 2018.

[34] I highlight here the UNDP, UN Women Asia-Pacific, and the UN Trust Fund to End Violence Against Women.

Africa, Timor-Leste shows us that TJ is a transnational politics story. Domestic and international NGOs exchange leadership and support roles, depending on their comparative advantages at different stages of the TJ life cycle.

Part Two: *Em Direção a um Futuro de Esperança?* (Toward a Hopeful Future?)

This section gives a broad overview of Timor-Leste's TJ policies after the CAVR. I lay out the initiation of numerous policies relating to truth, justice, reparation, and institutional reform, as well as the level of implementation reached. This is followed by a statistical analysis that shows the influence of NGO coalitions on policy uptake and policy completion. While mixed, the results cohere with those from South Africa: NGO issue representation and coalition breadth appear to matter for policy uptake but not for final policy completion. After this, I explore unmet state socialization into TJ norms and NGO efforts to mind the gap for the state and themselves provide additional TJ measures.

Descriptive Statistics: Implementation

The *Varieties of Truth Commissions* capture the implementation status of all 247 substantive recommendations made by the CAVR: 120 (49 percent) were initiated in the first five years, and 13 others were initiated within ten years (for a total of 54 percent). For an even comparison with Guatemala and South Africa, I concentrate on the first five years post-CAVR. The level of initiation in Timor-Leste is lower than in Guatemala, where 75 percent of recommendations were initiated within five years, but more or less on par with South Africa, where 56 percent of recommendations were initiated within five years.

Figures 8.1–8.4 show the frequency of recommendations and the percentage initiated by TJ area and category. First, information disclosure and education made up the largest shares of recommended measures for truth (51 and 34 percent, respectively) and fell in the middle of the pack in terms of initiation.[35] Second, trials and judicial reforms dominated recommended justice measures (57 and 39 percent, respectively), while recommendations related to amnesties trailed (just 4 percent). The CAVR admonished the government to not amnesty war crimes and crimes against humanity involving sexual violence

[35] Note, the percentages of recommended measures by TJ area (e.g., truth) may exceed 100, as some recommendations fall under more than one category in a given area (e.g., victim and perpetrator identification).

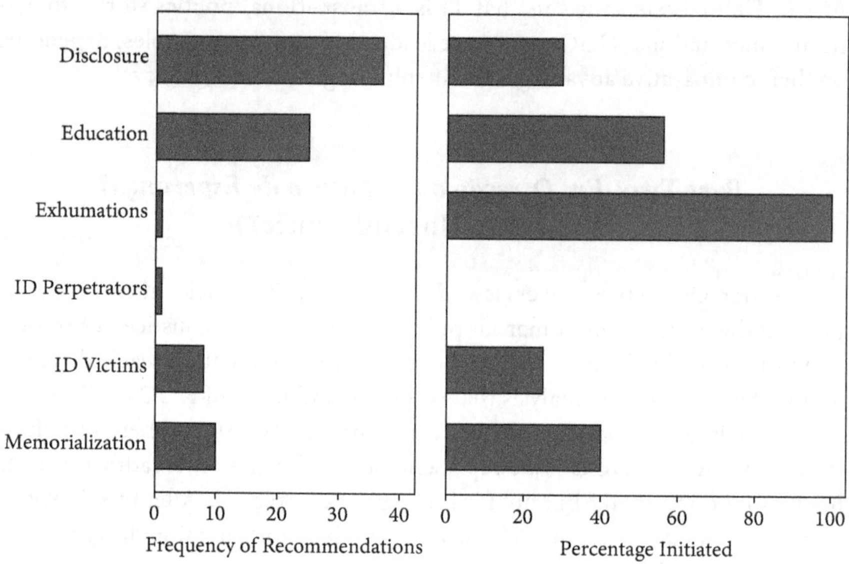

Figure 8.1 Timor-Leste: Initiation of Measures for Truth

Note: The figure shows the frequency of recommended measures for truth (left panel) and the percentage initiated (right panel).

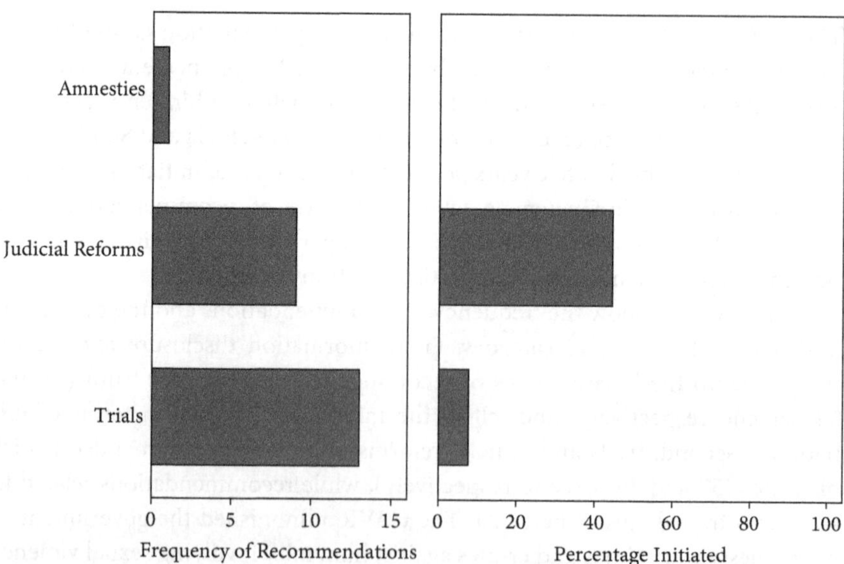

Figure 8.2 Timor-Leste: Initiation of Justice Measures

Note: The figure shows the frequency of recommended justice measures (left panel) and the percentage initiated (right panel).

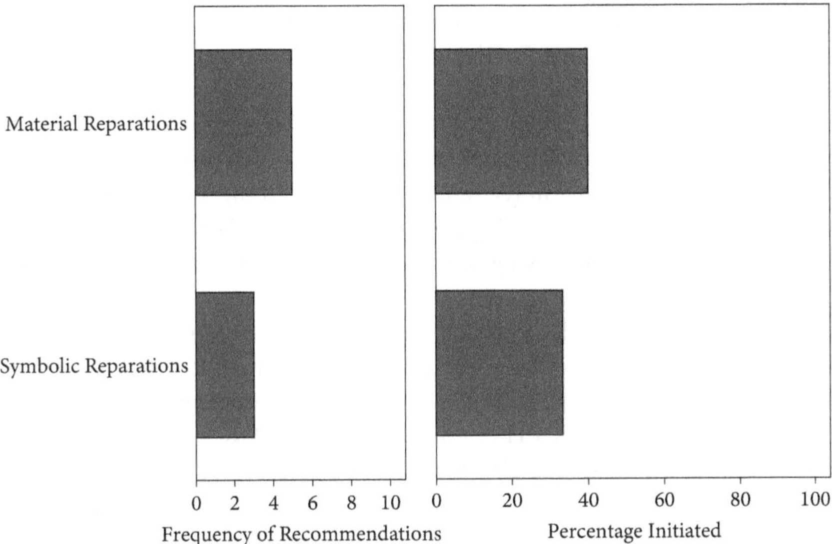

Figure 8.3 Timor-Leste: Initiation of Reparations

Note: The figure shows the frequency of recommended reparations (left panel) and the percentage initiated (right panel).

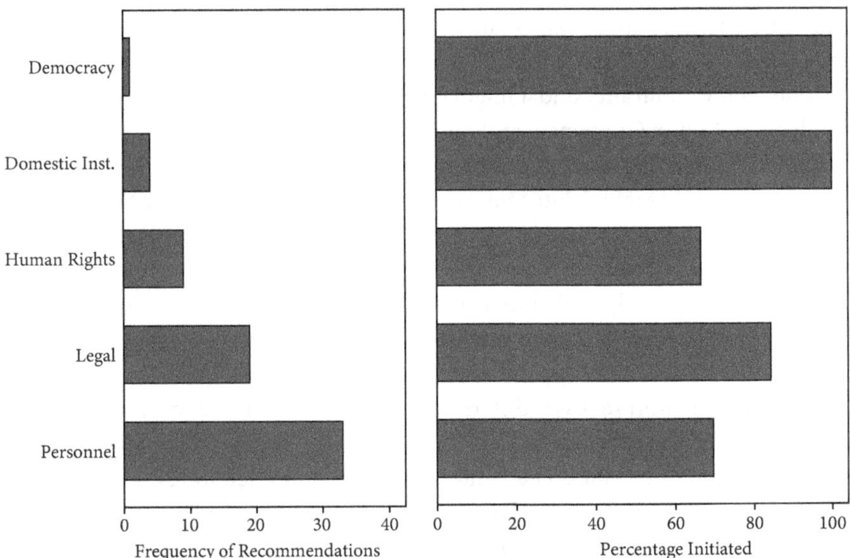

Figure 8.4 Timor-Leste: Initiation of Reforms

Note: The figure shows the frequency of recommended reforms (left panel) and the percentage initiated (right panel).

against women and girls. But the government de facto amnestied many perpetrators, especially Indonesians. On the initiation side, the government went farther with judicial reforms. Third, material reparations made up a greater share of recommended reparations, but they were initiated at similar rates as symbolic reparations. Fourth, personnel reforms were a major focus for the CAVR (representing 41 percent of reform recommendations), and the government initiated most of the recommendations. Legal reforms, which ranked second among recommended reforms (composing 24 percent), were initiated at a higher rate than personnel reforms.

Next is the level of implementation. Five years after the CAVR, 66 of 120 initiated measures (55 percent) were minimally implemented, 19 (16 percent) were mostly implemented, and 35 (29 percent) were fully implemented. Compared to both the Guatemalan CEH's and South African TRC's recommendations, a smaller proportion of the CAVR's recommendations attained intermediate status—16 percent, compared to 23 percent in Guatemala and 35 percent in South Africa. The proportion of CAVR recommendations that reached full implementation (29 percent) is nearly identical to the proportion of CEH recommendations (28 percent) but is somewhat smaller than the proportion of TRC recommendations (33 percent) that reached this status.

Figure 8.5 shows the proportion of recommendations at each level of implementation. There are notable differences between the Timorese, Guatemalan, and South African cases across TJ areas. First, whereas no justice measures were fully implemented in either Guatemala or South Africa, a plurality of justice measures were fully implemented in Timor-Leste (approximately 40 percent). Second, while a plurality and a majority of policies relating to truth reached full implementation in Guatemala and South Africa, respectively, a minority of such measures reached this level in Timor-Leste (28 percent). Third, while some reparation measures reached intermediate or full implementation in South Africa and most reparation measures reached intermediate or full implementation in Guatemala, no reparation measures were moderately or fully implemented in Timor-Leste. The only real similarity is with Guatemala in the area of institutional reforms, where less than one-quarter of measures that were started were completed.

Thus, the Timorese case differs considerably from the other two cases. A major reason for this difference is the succession of crises that have occurred in Timor-Leste since 2006. The United Nations intervened to restore peace, but then in 2007, in the lead-up to the presidential elections, violence reignited. And in 2008, there was an attempt to assassinate both Prime Minister Gusmão and President Ramos-Horta. While Gusmão was not injured, Ramos-Horta barely survived.

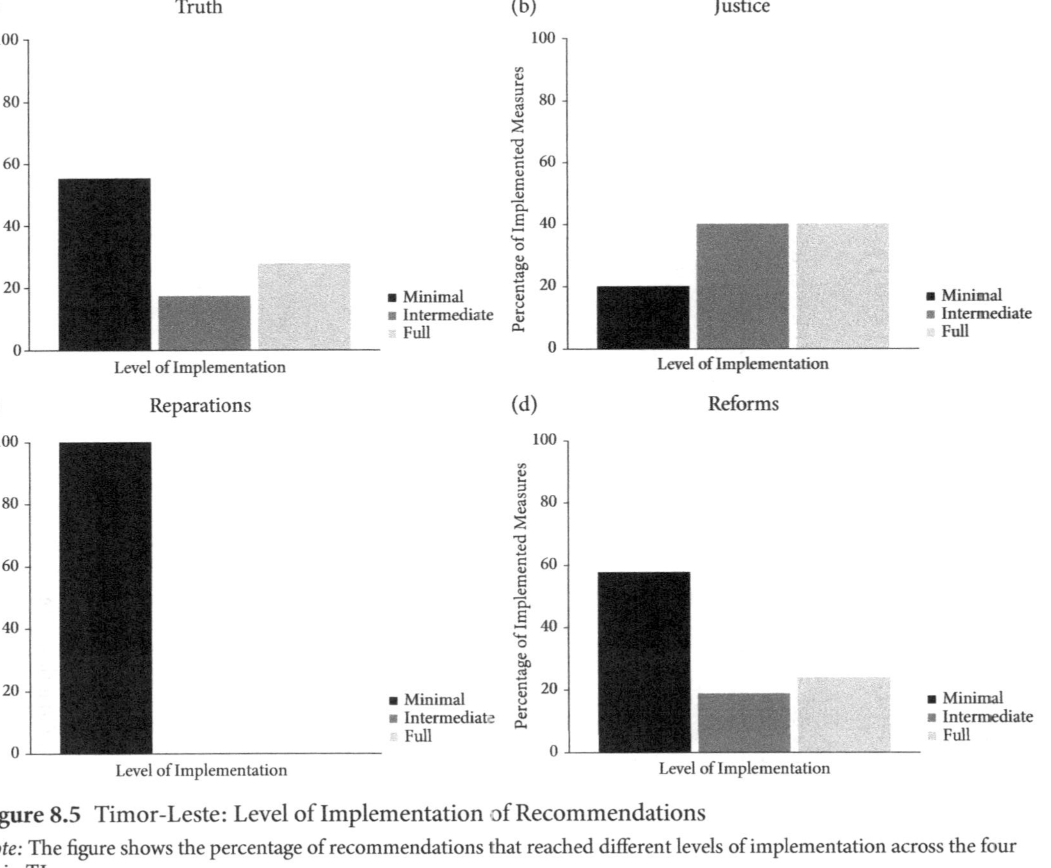

Figure 8.5 Timor-Leste: Level of Implementation of Recommendations

Note: The figure shows the percentage of recommendations that reached different levels of implementation across the four main TJ areas.

Quantitative Analysis: Implementation

I now assess the relationship between NGO advocacy and implementation of CAVR recommendations. Tables 8.2 and 8.3 present the results of logit and ordered logit regressions, with *Implementation Initiated* and *Implementation Level* as the outcome variables. With respect to initiation, *NGO Advocacy* is a positive and statistically significant predictor of the outcome ($p < 0.01$). In this way, Timor-Leste is different from Guatemala, where the relationship was not statistically significant, but similar to South Africa, where the relationship was significant. *NGO Coalition Size*, though small, is also positive and statistically

Table 8.2 Analysis: NGO Advocacy and Implementation of Recommendations in Timor-Leste: Initiation

	Implementation Initiated			
	(1)	(2)	(3)	(4)
NGO Advocacy	1.22**			1.13**
	(0.29)			(0.31)
NGO Coalition Size		0.01**		0.02**
		(0.01)		(0.01)
INGO Coalition Size			−0.03**	−0.06**
			(0.01)	(0.01)
Observations	247	244	247	244

Logit models. Standard errors in parentheses.
$^{+}p < 0.10$, $^{*}p < 0.05$, $^{**}p < 0.01$

Table 8.3 Analysis: NGO Advocacy and Implementation of Recommendations in Timor-Leste: Level

	Implementation Level			
	(1)	(2)	(3)	(4)
NGO Advocacy	−0.12			−0.10
	(0.44)			(0.45)
NGO Coalition Size		−0.00		−0.00
		(0.01)		(0.01)
INGO Coalition Size			−0.01	−0.01
			(0.02)	(0.02)
Observations	120	120	120	120

Ordered logit models. Standard errors in parentheses.
$^{+}p < 0.10$, $^{*}p < 0.05$, $^{**}p < 0.01$

significant ($p < 0.01$) in this case. *INGO Coalition Size* is negative and statistically significant, though also small—similar to the Guatemalan case.

INGOs may coalesce around hard cases—a potential explanation for the negative association with the outcome. There *is* notable variation in INGO coalitions across the four major TJ areas in Timor-Leste. The average INGO coalition comprised seventeen groups, with thirteen in the area of truth, thirty-four in the area of justice, six in the area of reparations, and eleven in the area of reforms. Consistent with a hard-case logic, the area with the most INGO representation, justice, did in fact have the lowest rate of policy initiation (approximately 22 percent). However, the area with the least INGO representation, reparations, did not have the highest rate of initiation (29 percent, compared to 40 percent for truth and 74 percent for reforms). A second explanation, and which seems to ring true in Guatemala, is that the Timorese government has effectively devolved its TJ responsibilities to other actors like INGOs and IOs like the United Nations, which are still active in Timorese TJ more than twenty years since the commission concluded and more than twenty-five years since the occupation and conflict ended. A third explanation is that the Timorese government may resent, and has therefore resisted, long-term external advocacy. My research interviews lend credence to the second explanation.

Different from Guatemala, yet again similar to South Africa, neither *NGO Advocacy* nor *NGO Coalition Size* is a positive and statistically significant predictor of the level of implementation of recommendations in Timor-Leste. Whereas government unresponsiveness to civil society activism in South Africa has mostly been due to a lack of commitment to further TJ, in Timor-Leste this has also been due to successive crises in the country since the CAVR. Just one year after the commission, the nation was beset by a range of security challenges that, from the government's vantage point, likely diminished TJ's relative importance. So while civil society may have moved the government to launch many post-commission TJ policies, advocacy groups were ultimately not decisive for progress on them.

My conversations with Eduardo González and Cristián Correa further contextualize these results. In terms of recommendations related to Indonesia, González said flatly, "Xanana and his people . . . didn't bat an eye abandoning those ideals and those demands." Correa echoed these sentiments, saying very pointedly that he did not see much interest beyond giving the international community just enough to gain support, power, resources, and prestige—a classic case of "playing along to get along," but not much else beyond that.[36] Correa did clarify, "That's not a phenomenon in [just] Timor; that's everywhere."[37]

[36] Commenting on the CTF, La'o Hamutuk (2005*b*), among other civil society groups, reported that the commission brought neither truth nor friendship.

[37] Cronin-Furman 2022.

Qualitative Analysis: Implementation

The Timorese state's decision to implement further TJ measures could potentially be the result of socialization into TJ norms—a process inspired by civil society. I evaluate socialization at three levels: low, moderate, and high. At a low level, implementation is reactive, almost exclusively prompted by civil society. At a high level, implementation is part of the state's new identity, occurring independently of external actors and pressure.

Timor-Leste since the CAVR appears to be at the lowest level of socialization, delivering TJ measures in a piecemeal fashion, after long stretches of time have elapsed, only for some issues, and almost exclusively due to civil society activism. In this way, the country is on par with Guatemala and South Africa, as examined in Chapters 6 and 7. These "poster children" of truth commissions and TJ have made many programmatic changes but are still behind on substantive progress. The Guatemalan internal armed conflict ended, South African apartheid was overthrown, and Timorese independence was established. Nonetheless, a robust, underlying, intrinsic commitment to truth, justice, reparations, and guarantees of nonrepetition has been lacking. I grant, in the context of Timor-Leste, the significant achievement of establishing the CNC in 2017, more than a decade after the CAVR. But even then, the center does not work independently; in fact, it depends on civil society to meet its mandate. Low socialization is also apparent when we view the civil society side. Recall, at the lowest level of socialization, NGOs, to the extent that they can, assume the duty of the state to provide additional TJ.

Building the Legal and Judicial System

In the legal and judicial arena, NGO advocacy has helped move the needle on a whole-of-government reform process to bring Timorese institutions in line with international human rights principles and standards. Organizations' advocacy for compliance with international law, including holding accountable perpetrators of crimes against humanity, has not gone as far as some advocates would like, however, in part because of Timor-Leste's mixed relationship with Indonesia.[38]

Withdrawals of two key sets of international actors have further undermined criminal accountability for conflict-related abuses.[39] UNTAET and UNMISET were always meant to be temporary but their conclusion had important consequences, including, just one year after UNMISET withdrew, the 2006 security crisis. The United Nations, through its peacekeeping forces, strove to restabilize

[38] Author interviews with Eduardo González and Adriana Sri Adhiati and her associate Mark X.
[39] La'o Hamutuk 2012, 2013.

the country and left in 2012 when it had done so. But throughout, they only addressed the symptom, not the cause.

International judges, who had been helping with trials for well over a decade, likewise departed in 2014, effectively halting criminal investigations and prosecutions related to the occupation and armed conflicts. But, at least until that point, NGOs meaningfully influenced court outcomes. US judge Phillip Rapoza, who served on the Special Panels for Serious Crimes, is recorded saying:

> [T]he judges with whom I served, both Timorese and international, paid very close attention to the views expressed by JSMP. I sincerely believe that the work of JSMP made us better judges in the difficult work we had to do and, even if we did not always agree with JSMP or they with us, we always considered what they had to say.[40]

Despite or perhaps because of the departure, JSMP and its partners have had a strong impact on Timorese courts, somewhat moving away from advocacy for conflict-related abuses to broader issues like SGBV. Judge Rapoza affirmed, "JSMP has provided a framework for describing and analyzing the challenges we currently face in the realm of charging, trials and sentencing in cases of sexual violence. . . . Just as importantly, it proposes a way forward for addressing them."[41] Because of this advocacy, Timorese courts have made some progress.

JSMP's work with the Asia Foundation is exemplary of burden sharing in institutional reform. Based in San Francisco, the foundation has featured JSMP's work in its reports, validating JSMP's contributions to Timor-Leste. This support has bolstered JSMP's credibility as a go-to actor in helping the government develop and implement reforms at a local and national level. Relatedly, JSMP and the Asia Foundation have collaborated on research, including to understand the effect of community justice on dispute resolution. The formal justice system is important, but so too is the customary justice system, and JSMP understands this. Rather than advance one system at the other's expense, JSMP has collaborated with the Asia Foundation to determine how the two can be integrated and harmonized—much like how the CAVR and customary practices like *lisan* were integrated during Timor-Leste's transition.[42]

In keeping with burden sharing, the Asia Foundation (the international group) has strengthened the work that JSMP (the domestic group) has initiated. This collaboration exemplifies how *NGOs contribute to and provide oversight over the legal and judicial system.*

[40] Rapoza 2016.
[41] Rapoza 2016.
[42] Asia Foundation 2013, 2019; JSMP 2023.

Securing the Security Sector

Security sector-focused organizations have helped establish formal and informal mechanisms for dispute resolution, as well as for citizen participation and civilian oversight. Mahein spearheaded and organized one of these mechanisms, Security Sector Discussions, which bring together key stakeholders, including members of the public, to help identify persistent and emerging issues in the security sector. Some of these issues include indiscipline and misconduct within security institutions (e.g., police brutality), inadequate responses to organized crime, and low budget allocations.

There has been some progress, though modest, around improving the conduct of military and police personnel. A 2018 Asia Foundation survey indicated improving public perceptions of security institutions in Timor-Leste.[43] The foundation's survey research is helpful to local organizations like JSMP and Mahein: It highlights areas of growth and areas still needing improvement, helping local groups focus their efforts and resources, while putting state actors on notice.[44] The foundation is also a valued funder. These are yet other examples of burden sharing: Domestic NGOs lead with INGO support.

Budgetary allocations to the security sector have also increased, and the government has made strides toward combating organized crime through domestic policy and bilateral action with Indonesia. Moreover, anti-drug and anti-sex trafficking laws have been approved.[45] But corruption threatens to undermine these gains.[46] *NGOs' work as watchdogs for the security sector remains vital.*

Responding to Violence Against Women and Children

Due to their close relationships with survivors, relationships that date back decades in some cases, NGOs dedicated to gender issues have been the first places women survivors of CRSV and domestic violence turn for counseling and to be connected with support groups. NGOs have also lobbied for and helped survivors gain access to the services they need, including "medical, psycho-social and economic assistance, safe spaces, support to develop vocational skills or to resume educational opportunities, legal aid, and access to justice,"[47] through public and private institutions. And because these groups have also been at the forefront of children's issues, they have worked directly with the government on getting stolen children back to their families and communities—crucial work that led then-Prime Minister Rui de Araújo, whose own sister was taken, to

[43] Asia Foundation 2013, 2019.
[44] Asia Foundation 2013, 2019.
[45] Fundasaun Mahein 2014.
[46] Fundasaun Mahein 2022.
[47] ACbit and AJAR 2017, 6.

"realize that there's this huge potential in the recommendations of the CAVR."[48] His stint as prime minister was short, just two years, from 2015 to 2017. But he used this time to develop in 2016 a working group to analyze the extent of implementation of the CAVR's recommendations and inaugurate a follow-up institution, the CNC, in 2017. "So it just shows that picture of the importance of the role of civil society," Wandita underscored, as well as "leaders like Rui who have open eyes and open hearts, and they suddenly see this important piece."

Domestic and international NGOs focused on women's issues have exemplified burden sharing from the start. Recall FOKUPERS' founding as Timor-Leste's first women's NGO in 1997. The organization had to reach out and develop connections and strategies beyond Timor-Leste's borders, including in Indonesia and Southeast Asia. For this reason, some members have moved between organizations, like Wandita between FOKUPERS in Dili and AJAR in Jakarta.

Humanitarian organizations with a wider remit, such as the International Committee of the Red Cross (ICRC), have also lent their support (e.g., by assessing the needs of families of the missing and advocating for Timor-Leste and Indonesia to meet those needs). As the foremost expert organization on international humanitarian law—which defines, prohibits, and sets standards for resolving missing persons cases—the ICRC is an important ally that lends its powerful voice to its domestic NGO partners.[49]

Consistent with burden sharing, international groups have strengthened the work local women's groups have spearheaded. This partnership illustrates how *NGOs are leading in the response to violence against women and children.*

Remembering and Teaching the Past

Reflecting Timorese conflict history in educational curricula has also proved to be slow and difficult work. The same can be said of memorializing a broad cross-section of victims. This is due in part to the major delay in establishing the CNC. Between the CAVR's conclusion and the center's creation, there were no real opportunities for survivors and victims' relatives to share, be listened to, and have their experiences recorded and disseminated beyond their families and communities. As in Guatemala and South Africa, this work largely fell to civil society groups, with ACbit facilitating intergenerational dialogues to build up community history, and its regional NGO partner AJAR, in collaboration with the National University of East Timor and Peace University, developing a curriculum for university students.[50]

48 Author interview with Galuh Wandita.
49 Robins 2010.
50 AJAR 2018.

In 2013, eight years after the CAVR, the Ministry of Education, in cooperation with ACbit, published the book *CHEGA* to teach new generations about the conflict, the movement for self-determination, Independence, and TJ and human rights. "Timor-Leste needs to prevent the conflict, because the country's independence was gained with the people's suffering," ACbit director Manuela Leong said when the book was launched. One way to achieve this goal is for young people "[to] know this History, so that, in the future, they stay away from violence."[51] Since 2017, in close collaboration with civil society, the CNC has built on these initiatives and helped the state make progress on CAVR recommendations. The CNC itself is the fulfillment of the recommendation to build a memory center at the former Comarca-Balide prison, where members of the Resistance were detained and tortured and, in some cases, disappeared or killed.[52]

The CNC typifies the results of burden sharing in education and memorialization. Plans were devised by a working group involving representatives of domestic and international NGOs (FOKUPERS, the Hak Association, and the ICTJ), the Post-CAVR Technical Secretariat, the Timorese national human rights institution, and the UN Integrated Mission in East Timor. These stakeholders were put on equal footing to create what is arguably the most important Timorese TJ institution since the CAVR.[53]

So, *civil society governs key aspects of memorialization and education.*

A Legacy of Progress

So, we see NGOs helping to build and monitor the legal and judicial system; working to make the security sector safer and more effective; answering the unmet needs of women and child survivors of violence; and contributing to memorialization and education of Timorese people on the past. This is significant work and shows civil society actors as TJ governors, even though it sometimes feels like they are "always on the losing [side]," as Wandita poignantly expressed. A key player in TJ in Timor-Leste, Walsh confirmed that civil society advocacy has been critical. He maintains:

> Though restricted mainly to the human rights sector, civil society [has been] inventive, sustained against the odds over many years, principled and, as the establishment of the [CNC] demonstrates, effective. Had their voices and representations on behalf of victims gone silent, I fear the recommendations would have remained dormant if not dead.[54]

[51] Government of Timor-Leste 2013.
[52] Byrne et al. 2024.
[53] Working Group 2009.
[54] Author interview with Pat Walsh.

Implementing Like a State: Civil Society Substitution in Post-CAVR Timor-Leste

"That the UN, and the international community in general, washed their hands and walked away was [Timor-Leste's] main problem," La'o Hamutuk's Charles Scheiner expressed to me with a degree of frustration. Timor-Leste was and is, after all, "a small, new country, which has a lot of other problems to deal with." And TJ was not just the Timorese government's responsibility but also the responsibility of Indonesia, its enablers like the United States, and the broader international community.[55] This is important to remember when making judgments about the implementation of CAVR recommendations. Still, NGOs pointed the Timorese government toward many policy areas where action was needed and feasible. Wandita emphasized, "Timor should have been better." And it could have been better, not leaving so much of the unfinished business of the CAVR—that is, the recommendations—to NGOs to agitate for, to assist with, and, indeed, to deliver on their own.

Domestic and foreign government actors in many ways ceded their duty and failed to uphold victims' rights and international TJ norms. As in Guatemala and South Africa, it is regrettable that the Timorese government's TJ actions were episodic, fragmented, and delayed. However, as I have laid out, NGOs in Timor-Leste, much like their Guatemalan and South African counterparts, did not wait or rely solely on the state to enact further measures; they have worked with and separately from the state to realize important TJ outcomes.

Notable areas of civil society assistance to and substitution for the state, building on the analyses above, include crime prevention via dialogue and dispute resolution at the community level.[56] Mahein believes this minimizes tension and suspicion among neighbors and reduces the security sector's workload. With respect to technical advice on legislation and court proceedings, members of Parliament and judges "always ask" for advice from NGOs like JSMP.[57] In terms of submissions to UN treaty bodies and special rapporteurs, Timorese activist organizations like La'o Hamutuk consistently fill gaps the government leaves. Regarding reducing the stigma around sexual violence and children born from rape, groups like ACbit and FOKUPERS help survivors come together, heal, and access the resources they need and deserve.[58] NGOs like AJAR and PRADET are also the ones that receive CNC funding to, respectively, reunify families and

[55] La'o Hamutuk 2005*a*, 2010*a*, 2010*b*, 2012.
[56] Author interview with Nélson Belo.
[57] Author interview with Casimiro dos Santos.
[58] Author interviews with Patrick Burgess.

provide mental health services.[59] NGOs will also lead the newly developed School of Social Justice in Timor-Leste.

Araújo's two-year tenure as prime minister marked the beginning of the Timorese government more sincerely pursuing implementation of the CAVR's recommendations, specifically via the CNC. It was a breakthrough moment, and implementation of recommendations is progressing (except for those concerning reparations and criminal accountability for conflict-era abuses, which were deliberately cut out of the institution's mandate). The Center is "funded . . . competently led and well respected."[60] Nonetheless, Wandita noted, as did many of her NGO colleagues who I interviewed, "It's really late. . . . There was a gap . . . 2005 to 2017, so twelve years. . . . And the price, the cost, is human lives and survivors feeling that they were found [by the CAVR] and then they were lost again."[61] The CNC also depends on civil society to meet its mandate, the center's executive director, Hugo Fernandes, told me. Collaboration with and delegation to civil society is part of its design and operation. Devolution of state responsibility to the third sector, as I warned in previous chapters, could undermine TJ norms and efforts domestically and internationally. So all stakeholders should remain alert, lest gains become losses.

Discussion

Part Two examined how Timorese NGOs help make proposals policy. I tracked the strategies they use to motivate government action on CAVR recommendations. I found that groups advocate for their policy priorities through lobbying legislators, monitoring judges, and designing and helping to carry out programs in security, services, and memory and education.

In statistical analyses of recommendation implementation in Timor-Leste, I found a significant effect for NGO representation and coalition breadth on policy initiation, but not ultimate policy completion. The Timorese case is thus similar to the South African case but different from the Guatemalan case, where NGO representation did matter for policy completion. Government unresponsiveness has been due in part to a lack of commitment to continuing TJ, as well as the myriad security crises the nation faced after the CAVR. But change seems afoot.

In addition, I found through qualitative analysis that where the government has been unwilling or unable to provide further remedies, NGOs have intervened, assisting the government in policy areas where there was at least a modest

[59] Author interviews with Hugo Fernandes and Galuh Wandita.
[60] Author interview with Pat Walsh.
[61] Author interview with Galuh Wandita.

commitment to a positive outcome and substituting for the government where there was not such a commitment. Very similar to the other cases I have studied, INGOs and IOs have lent Timorese NGOs operational support. However, this has not been a cure-all for low political will, sociopolitical issues, and geopolitical challenges.

In keeping with burden sharing, local advocates played a leading role in the second half of the implementation and follow-up stage. Of course, domestic groups do not have limitless resources, and their institutional power and authority are limited; they cannot force the government to act. Neither can they implement all types of recommendations on their own. So, those with an interest in truth and justice—especially external actors like foreign governments, INGOs, and IOs—should support domestic civil society before, during, and perhaps especially after truth commissions.

9
Conclusion

Over the past half-century, scholars, practitioners, civil society actors, and policymakers have intensely debated TJ norms, practices, and institutions. Nonetheless, our collective understanding of global TJ has trailed behind its implementation. This book has proposed a framework for thinking about TJ's nature, consequences, and limits.

I systematically studied the actors who govern TJ as a set of norms, practices, and institutions: domestic and international civil society actors who compose a transnational network of activists, experts, funders, and service providers, and who represent survivors of political violence, victims' families, and broader affected communities. In addition, I identified civil society's main challengers: governments that are responsible for abuses and/or that do not prioritize TJ among other regime goals. Moreover, I examined how civil society groups have nevertheless induced governments to implement TJ policies: burden sharing in advocacy, expert consultancy, policy agenda setting, and policy implementation.

My work is thus a rejoinder to two major misreadings in much scholarship: first, that TJ is a set of government-led processes, and second, that these processes are domestic in nature. These misreadings together suggest that TJ adoption, design, operation, and impacts are entirely or mainly determined by governments and that processes around the world are unrelated to each other. Yet the local implementation of TJ is inextricably tied to its global development and spread, and governments' responsibility to provide TJ is often disconnected from their interest in doing so. TJ, therefore, cannot simply be a set of domestic, government-led processes. In fact, it is not. Rather, it is a transnational, civil society-led institution.

My research contrasts with existing TJ scholarship in several ways. I focused on civil society instead of privileging governments and IOs.[1] De-centering states as the primary, if not exclusive, governors in TJ and world politics and instead centering civil society is a hallmark of my work. I showed that members of the global TJ network have mediated between governments and citizens, channeling the interests of survivors, victims' families, and affected communities in an organized fashion. As representatives of affected populations, network members

[1] In so doing, I built on efforts by Bakiner (2015), Collins (2010), González-Ocantos (2020), Kim (2014), Lessa (2022), Medie (2020), and Michel (2018), among many others.

Governing Truth. Kelebogile Zvobgo, Oxford University Press. © Oxford University Press (2026).
DOI: 10.1093/oso/9780197815663.003.0009

have been more interested in TJ than governments. What's more, network members have refined, institutionalized, and normalized TJ around the globe.[2] In this way, my study also differs from research that sees TJ as a foreign imposition and that effectively ignores civil society's importance at both a grassroots and global level.

The preceding chapters showed network members' centrality to TJ around the world: They promoted and defended victims' rights to truth, justice, reparations, and guarantees of nonrepetition and were vital to every stage of TJ. They initiated demands for TJ processes, assisted with design and operation, and monitored government responses. In some instances, their efforts even eclipsed those of state actors. TJ network members, NGOs in particular, leveraged their delegated, moral, and expert authority and availed themselves of a range of political strategies like protest mobilization and litigation to motivate governments to produce meaningful outcomes.

Rather than approach the TJ network as a homogenous unit, where members engage in similar activities and can thus substitute for each other, this project presented a novel model of transnational advocacy and advocacy networks: the burden sharing model.[3] Under this model, domestic and international civil society actors exercise their comparative advantages in knowledge and expertise, material and political resources, and access to policymaking bodies and decision makers. By so doing, they economize on resources and improve their prospects of success.

I operationalized success in three ways: institutional adoption, strong design, and implementation and follow-up. In contrast to earlier, more static frameworks, my approach was dynamic: I proposed changes in leading and supporting roles in the multistage political process that is TJ. I showed that domestic groups are critical for TJ adoption, international experts are vital for strong TJ design, and domestic groups are essential for TJ delivery and follow-up. Thus, my project and model went beyond policy advocacy and policy adoption, which have been prior scholarship's focus: I brought important attention to civil society's significant role in policy design and policy execution.

Certainly, the TJ network's success is not inevitable or guaranteed. And domestic and international groups do not always collaborate as described under the model. Rather, their success, I argued, and the empirical findings showed,

[2] TJ is a complex, multidimensional project—a project that is too complex for any one actor to address on its own. That is why civil society groups team up with each other and attempt to do the same with governments. To extend Henry and Sundstrom (2021, 3), TJ is an area where civil society groups can provide "expertise, information, and representation." This is why states and IOs have "created space for [these] nonstate actors . . . to play a role in advocating for global governance, negotiating its provisions, and promoting its rules."

[3] Consistent with Stroup and Wong (2017), NGOs working in the TJ space vary considerably, including in terms of their power, resources, and authority.

depends in large part on them doing so. With different members essentially tagging in when they enjoy a comparative advantage relative to their colleagues, and tagging out when they do not, I demonstrated the TJ network's agility, which helps explain the network's success in producing important TJ outcomes over the past fifty years.

I showed four factors that influence TJ network members' success at three key stages of truth commissions—the mechanism that I took as a point of departure for my investigation. First, domestic NGOs pleaded the cause of survivors, victims' families, and affected communities, and INGOs amplified their messages. Domestic and international groups' leveraging of *information* and *moral authority* over governments contributed to commission adoption. Second, international experts drew on *professional experience* and *technical expertise* to encourage governments to afford commissions strong jurisdictional and operational powers. This helped strengthen legal mandates. Third, domestic NGOs, with their international partners' material and political support, pressed governments to implement commission recommendations through *agenda setting* and *policy advocacy*. And, where governments proved unwilling or unable to produce the recommended policies, NGOs engaged in *substitution*, assuming for themselves the burden of realizing further TJ.

To be sure, the network's effectiveness at each stage was/is circumscribed by members' political, knowledge, and financial resources, as well as governments' sensitivity to advocacy, censure, and sanction. My project has thus offered a new perspective on the potential and limits of civil society and TJ and helps us understand differences and similarities across contexts.

Findings

I evaluated the implications of my argument using a variety of original data and multiple social science research methods. I established the global TJ network's influence on the origins, contours, and consequences of TJ institutions and programs in ways prior scholarly accounts had not fully explored or appreciated. TJ network members did this by burden sharing between and among themselves.

In Chapter 3, a systematic, multi-method study of truth commission adoption, I found clear evidence of domestic and international civil society actors leading governments to adopt commissions. Domestic groups took the crucial first steps during the period of violence, recording and sharing their research findings with their international partners and cultivating the local appetite for truth and justice. Then, from a supporting position, international groups adapted and broadcasted this information, with a view to mobilizing different foreign actors—whether publics, governments, or IOs—to also demand accountability.

The cross-national statistical analysis showed a robust relationship between the strength of domestic civil society groups and commission adoption, as well as between international HRO shaming campaigns and commission adoption. The analysis addressed a shortcoming in existing single-country and small-*N* comparative studies: limited generalizability. Indeed, this chapter put idiosyncrasies of particular cases into perspective: Truth commission adoption has more often than not been influenced by transnational advocacy.

Careful tests indicated that the results are not simple artifacts of regional or global diffusion or byproducts of the construct and measurement of political transitions. Interview and focus group data "thickened" the analysis, contributing to a key conclusion: Domestic actors' ability to shine the light on abuses, transmit information to international partners, and mobilize support for redress during and after political violence matters most for commission adoption. Accordingly, the first policy implication of my research is this: Those with an interest in human rights and TJ should reinforce domestic civil societies during authoritarian regimes, internal armed conflicts, and other periods of repression and violence—by amplifying their voices and experiences, strengthening their demands, and leaning on governments to confront past violence and injustice.

In Chapter 4, a rigorous cross-national examination of truth commission institutional design, I demonstrated international TJ experts' influence over governments' decisions to endow commissions with strong investigative powers. Using innovative quantitative data on commission mandates, I illuminated a strong association between international expert advice and commissions that possess the power to uncover root causes of abuses and that possess the power to preserve evidence. More broadly, international experts have contributed to commissions having a wider material scope of inquiry and effective evidence-gathering powers and having stronger overall designs. The statistical analysis also suggested that a strong domestic civil society can influence commissions' subpoena powers.

Both the quantitative analysis and the qualitative analysis that followed it made clear that domestic political and institutional factors can be equally if not more important for commission design than civil society actors' efforts. Nonetheless, my interviews and a focus group I conducted with leading practitioners underscored the significance of evidence-based, practice-refined, expert advice in the design of commissions around the world. An important policy implication of these findings is that commissions are not created equally and, thus, may not produce similar outcomes. In light of this, foreign donors—whether IOs, governments, or foundations—should, in collaboration with civil society groups, devise ways to guide differently situated governments toward the same goal: strong commission designs that enable high-quality investigations.

This could involve, for example, making funding conditional on implementing particular design features, like the power to subpoena witness testimony.

Chapter 5 introduced original data on truth commission recommendations. While scholars have traditionally treated commissions as backward looking, I argued that they are also forward looking. Through their extensive reports, commissions have validated civil society's claims about abuses and furnished public policy proposals. Essentially, commissions have operated as norm and policy entrepreneurs, and civil society actors have used commissions' outputs to push governments to implement additional measures.

With my unusually comprehensive and granular data, I mapped the expansion of commission recommendations over time and I revealed commissions' increasingly holistic approach to recommendations. Whereas commissions in the 1970s and 1980s focused primarily on institutional reforms, commissions in the 1990s, 2000s, and 2010s better addressed TJ's other three pillars: truth, justice, and reparation. Nonetheless, the ongoing emphasis on institutional reforms indicates that commissions have seen themselves as reformers, with an express interest in addressing structural problems.

To spur scholarly engagement with the data, I also provided a glimpse into the relationships between different policy prescriptions and different political contexts. Indeed, taking commission recommendations seriously can improve our understanding of democratic consolidation, human rights respect, and durable peace (or the absence thereof) in countries that have implemented commissions and other TJ measures.

While paradigmatic transitional commissions like Guatemala's Historical Clarification Commission have been the subject of a number of studies to date, my project's broad cross-national perspective showed that there are many things that are not unique to them (e.g., the types of recommendations they make). Non-paradigmatic commissions like the Moroccan Equity and Reconciliation Commission, which was implemented under an established monarchy, also make recommendations about institutional reforms, among a range of remedial and preventive measures. My interviews with former commission officials shed light on why commissions have made dozens, even hundreds, of recommendations.

Recommendations, I discovered, tend to represent just a fraction of the issues and concerns that commission officials encounter during their investigations and that they believe must be addressed, if not through implementation then at least through acknowledgment. Here, too, I found evidence of civil society's influence. NGO representatives, along with survivors and victims' relatives, have made recommendations of their own for commissions to include in their reports. Critically, NGOs have used commission recommendations to push governments beyond their initial TJ pledges.

In the first part of Chapters 6, 7, and 8, cross-case qualitative studies of NGOs defining the terms of what additional TJ measures should follow a truth commission, I showed that domestic groups have often set the post-commission agenda, with the backing of their international partners. While some scholarly accounts would lead us to expect that NGOs choose to advocate for certain issues and not others because of their organizational histories and existing issue portfolios, I tracked NGOs in Guatemala, South Africa, and Timor-Leste expanding their platforms and activities to encompass new issues. Beyond issue selection, I showed that domestic NGOs frame commission findings and recommendations, contend with prohibitive political conditions, and exploit mobilizing structures like international networks.

Finally, in the second part of Chapters 6, 7, and 8, mixed-method studies of civil society groups advancing post-commission TJ outcomes, I found compelling evidence of TJ network members' importance for the implementation of commission recommendations. Domestic NGOs pressed for their policy objectives through a variety of means, including contentious politics and legal action—all with the support of their international partners. In response, governments implemented recommendations, albeit often in a piecemeal fashion.

More precisely, in the South Africa and Timor-Leste studies, I showed that NGO-supported recommendations were more likely to be initiated by the respective governments, though NGOs did not strongly influence the level of implementation (i.e., minimal, intermediate, or full). I found different results in Guatemala. There, NGO-supported recommendations were not more likely to be launched, though they were more likely to reach intermediate and full implementation if initiated.

With regard to initiation, the cross-country differences may owe to the fact that the world had its eyes on South Africa and Timor-Leste in a manner distinct from Guatemala. South Africa catapulted the idea of commissions globally, and Timor-Leste was one of the first post-South Africa commission laboratories. So the respective countries may have wanted to show the world something—not necessarily a lot, but "just enough" to maintain international support, resources, and prestige, per ICTJ senior expert Cristián Correa in one of my fieldwork interviews.

In terms of the level of implementation, cross-country differences may be due in part to the number of recommendations. Guatemala had roughly one-third the number of recommendations that South Africa and Timor-Leste had, so follow-up on initiated measures may have been easier in Guatemala. Future research should tease out these relationships by expanding the set of cases studied, to discern possible pre- and post-South Africa differences globally, as well as differences in recommendation quantity (and, possibly, quality).

Interestingly, in both Guatemala and Timor-Leste, the data showed negative correlations between INGO coalition breadth and initiation of implementation—a finding that suggests government resistance to INGOs. This is one avenue that future research should explore. With growing global crack-downs on domestic NGOs and their INGO partners, it will be important to study the degree to which this form of government backlash has limited their effectiveness.

Crucially, I found that governments' decisions to deliver further TJ measures have been made tactically—in other words, due to civil society pressure—even in countries that scholars have upheld as human rights and justice exemplars among post-violence societies. Further, civil society actors have in some instances abandoned attempts to persuade and socialize governments into TJ and human rights. Indeed, where governments have been unwilling or unable to deliver, domestic organizations, with their international partners' material and political support, have effectively substituted for governments and themselves implemented many commission recommendations.

Given limited resources, private foundations, foreign governments, and IOs would do well to invest in domestic NGOs, politically and materially, not only before and during commissions and other TJ processes but also afterward. For their part, mainstream scholars should more meaningfully address transnational civil society actors when analyzing TJ, human rights, and world politics, attending to internal dynamics of advocacy networks (like burden sharing) and more carefully tracking the causes of policy adoption, design, and implementation and follow-up.

Contributions and Implications

This book contributes to several key areas of scholarship. To begin, comparative politics and international relations scholars have long understood the importance of transnational civil society actors in domestic and international politics, notably in the area of human rights. However, before this book, theory had not been refined for, nor had systematic evidence been extended to, TJ—a distinct set of norms, practices, and institutions within human rights.

In particular, what I term the "global TJ network" had not been well defined in scholarship, and network members' relationships were not apparent. Indeed, cooperation between and among domestic and international groups was not clearly identified, and groups' relative competencies were not modeled to explain multiple outcomes of interest (i.e., institutional adoption, design, and implementation and follow-up). Scholarship was thus unable to comprehend in a global sense civil society actors' manifold contributions to TJ or explain why governments do or do not adopt TJ mechanisms, design them to succeed, and ultimately act on their results.

This book asked and answered these questions directly. The evidence presented makes clear that the global TJ network has been the force behind key outcomes, with domestic groups necessary for institutional adoption, international groups critical for strong institutional design, and domestic groups essential to policy delivery and follow-up.

Taking Truth Commissions and Civil Society Seriously

Some scholars and legal practitioners have suggested that governments respond to calls for justice with truth commissions in an effort to avoid if not subvert it. Adherents to this school of thought hold that only criminal prosecutions produce "true" or "real" justice and that commissions and other nonretributive TJ mechanisms are simply a means to co-opt civil society's demands. Yet my project makes clear that civil society groups have often been the first to articulate the need for TJ and, more specifically, commissions.

Where we might worry about co-optation is where civil society groups are left out of the process. Yet even here, we would expect to see, and indeed have seen, civil society mobilizing against top-down approaches. Besides, the multiple case studies and analytical vignettes that I presented in previous chapters suggest that the mere installation of a commission or other mechanism would not pacify, let alone satisfy, civil society. The groups I studied have continuously agitated to ensure that TJ efforts are genuine and robust. Building on this, commissions have often preceded and, as this book has shown, enabled subsequent TJ measures via civil society. Commissions, therefore, need not be orthogonal to other measures but can indeed be central to them.

I hope that scholars who study other TJ measures—such as prosecutions, reparations, and reforms—will evaluate how well the burden sharing model applies beyond truth commissions. As evidenced in preceding chapters, domestic NGOs, with INGOs' support, have advocated before, advised, assisted, and substituted for governments in delivering different types of TJ that commissions have recommended. This is because civil society groups are concerned with all four TJ pillars, not just truth. Moreover, commissions often call for such measures as trials, victim compensation, and legal and institutional reforms—calls that civil society carries forward. For these reasons, I see burden sharing as a general model for understanding TJ.

It is possible that NGOs are less influential for the development, design, and delivery of TJ modalities other than truth commissions. It is possible, too, that NGOs are less effective in realizing other modalities without commissions as a basis for advocacy. To determine the full scope of the burden sharing model, further empirical investigation is needed. We especially need detailed data on institutional adoption, strong design, and implementation and follow-up in other TJ areas. Examining NGO advocacy in the absence of commissions would also be beneficial. Civil society groups help and are helped by commissions, but existing studies, including this one, have not shown exactly how much commissions help.

Taking Politics Seriously

Many scholars have grown wary of TJ over the years. This is not without basis: Research has found that TJ mechanisms are not necessarily correlated with positive outcomes like respect for human rights and the rule of law, democratization and democratic consolidation, and peacebuilding. Some research has found a neutral, if not negative, effect on these outcomes. But perhaps these results do not reflect the consequences of TJ *as a set of norms, practices, and institutions* but, rather, of TJ *as a process and as a site of political contestation.*

Null or negative results may be due to backlash from TJ opponents, within and outside of government, or the lack of a veritable commitment by governments to human rights and TJ, as my research has suggested. Additionally—or alternatively—neutral or negative impacts could indicate that a particular TJ process was not done well. I offer three possible ways this might be the case—three ideas future research should examine.

First, adverse impacts may result from a top-down, rather than bottom-up, process. As this project argues, civil society is key in all aspects: institutional adoption, strong design, and implementation and follow-up. The chief prosecutor for human rights in Guatemala, Hilda Pineda, conveyed to me that civil society groups "are organized. They have the data. They are committed." Moreover, they "listened to the victims before the State did."[4] Second, it could be that a given TJ institution was not designed well and, therefore, was not as helpful as it could have been—a point that Priscilla Hayner relayed in our conversations. Third, it could be that the institution or program was not implemented well, as part of a holistic TJ agenda. This last point merits elaboration.

TJ is a set of tools intended by TJ governors to be sequenced or used contemporaneously. Perhaps it is the lack of reparations after a truth commission or the absence of institutional reforms alongside trials and lustrations that explains

[4] Michel (2018, 16) shows that private prosecution, often involving NGOs, both "improve[s] the chances of a case to reach a court when facing an unresponsive state" and "improve[s] victims' perceptions of being 'seen' or 'heard' by the system, even when the public prosecutor is working efficiently."

adverse outcomes and, in cross-national studies, negative, null, or mixed results. I recall a statement from Emir Mejía in the Secretariat for Peace in Guatemala. He conveyed, "If we had implemented the accords holistically, we would have had such a change in Guatemala; it would be a different country." So, while scholars may document programmatic changes in various post-violence societies like Guatemala, scholars should investigate more finely and study more minutely substantive progress in the months, years, and decades following violence and initial efforts toward truth and justice. Doing this type of work, as I have attempted, will require bringing together a range of novel data and a multi-method approach. Indeed, large-*N* quantitative studies combined with single-country or small-*N* comparative case studies that center relevant actors' perspectives can illuminate cross-national patterns and delineate subnational causal pathways and mechanisms.

Quantitative Transitional Justice

Historically, in cross-national TJ datasets, scholars have only captured whether a country adopted a given TJ mechanism.[5] Some of these scholars have then estimated how different TJ tools, which have almost always been dichotomously coded, relate to a range of political processes and outcomes like democratization and democratic consolidation, respect for human rights and the rule of law, and durable peace.[6] The problem with this approach is that it implies unit homogeneity. It supposes, for example, that a truth commission in Peru is equivalent to one in Sri Lanka, when in fact they are starkly different. "One can reasonably question whether it is appropriate to treat all trials (or truth commissions, amnesties, etc.) as being the same for theory testing," write Stewart and Wiebelhaus-Brahm.[7]

Today's emphasis on TJ as a *process*, and growing circumspection about TJ's ability to contribute to these outcomes, has been accompanied by greater recognition of variation within classes of TJ tools (e.g., truth commissions) and across classes of tools (e.g., trials and reparations). The "same" mechanism may look different in different countries and produce different outcomes. In a similar vein, particular TJ mechanisms may be tied to particular outcomes (e.g., certain personnel reforms, democratic representation, and trust in government).[8]

[5] See, for example, Binningsbø et al. (2012), Kim (2012*b*, 2019), Kim and Sikkink (2010), Lie et al. (2007), Olsen, Payne, and Reiter (2010), Olsen, Payne, Reiter, and Wiebelhaus-Brahm (2010), Powers and Proctor (2016), Sikkink and Walling (2007), and Wiebelhaus-Brahm (2010).

[6] For more, see Stewart and Wiebelhaus-Brahm's (2017) helpful review and critique. Dancy et al. (2019) carry forward this critique and use it to motivate their Transitional Justice Research Collaborative database.

[7] Stewart and Wiebelhaus-Brahm 2017, 106.

[8] Horne 2014; Nalepa 2022.

Accordingly, TJ data must be disaggregated. This means that scholars may have to restrict certain projects to studying a single class of tools so that we can deeply understand origins, inputs, outputs, and outcomes. My project contributes to this shift in scholarship and offers a model for finely measuring and studying TJ tools and processes.

There are also several areas future research can explore using the *Varieties of Truth Commissions* datasets. For instance, scholars could "slice" the recommendations data to examine implementation of different types of TJ projects across countries, rather than assess all projects for a limited number of cases. The recommendations data allow scholars to examine both realized and, crucially, unrealized projects. Byrne and coauthors have done this for memorialization projects, which encompass everything from the removal of monuments, to the installation of museums, to the establishment of national days of remembrance.[9] Scholars could conduct similar studies focused on education recommendations, reparations proposals, and suggested reform packages. To best understand TJ politics, we need to study both the "ones" and the "zeros." My data help scholars begin to do just that.

Moving Beyond Political Transitions

While I focused much of my analysis on transitional truth commissions, my theory and data are useful for understanding TJ in non-transitional settings as well. Take, for instance, South Korea, where policymakers answered civil society demands to establish commissions to investigate events that occurred many decades before.[10] Consider also Canada, where the government engaged international experts and enumerated key investigative powers in commission mandates.[11]

In a similar vein, my theory can with some modification be applied beyond democracies, transitional or otherwise—an important point of contrast with much prior work. My datasets also include non-democracies.[12] Previous datasets have often neglected commissions in autocracies and have essentially precluded the possibility of civil society actors being active and influential in non-democratic settings. Yet we have seen civil society mobilization leading to commissions in autocracies like Morocco.[13]

[9] Byrne et al. 2024

[10] Kim 2014.

[11] Nagy 2008. Civil society advocacy notwithstanding, elites and large contingents of the public may simply want to "move on." See the Spanish case, for example (Aguilar et al. 2011).

[12] Gillooly et al. 2024.

[13] Wiebelhaus-Brahm 2021*b*.

Building on this point, should TJ outside of political transitions and outside of democracies "count"? What lessons can we extend from paradigmatic sites for TJ like South Africa in the 1990s? And what can we learn from non-paradigmatic contexts like the United States and Zimbabwe today? While perhaps innocuous to scholars working outside of TJ, these questions are intensely debated in academic TJ circles. While practitioners do not really discriminate between TJ institutions and programs created in different contexts and instead focus on inputs, outputs, and outcomes, as evidenced by the work of the ICTJ and other organizations, many academics *do* discriminate between them, and often to the detriment of our understanding of TJ politics on the ground.

To illustrate, early work on TJ in newly democratic countries in Central and South America led some scholars to conflate TJ and democracy when, in fact, versions of both have existed without the other. For this reason, scholars missed many cases like postwar Uganda, where, in 1986, Yoweri Museveni established a truth commission that conducted a fairly robust investigation into abuses under his predecessors—Idi Amin, Milton Obote, and lesser-known interim leaders—from Uganda's independence from Britain in 1962 up to 1986. Continuing autocratic rule notwithstanding, a type of TJ was possible.[14]

The resilience of non-democratic institutions should not imply that TJ is not possible, just as the resilience of democratic institutions should not suggest that TJ is not required. The exact events that precede TJ in non-transitional and non-democratic contexts may be different, but that is something to be addressed theoretically and empirically, not simply ignored. Certainly, there can be conceptual and theoretical reasons for studying non-paradigmatic cases separately, but there are no conceptual or theoretical reasons for neglecting them altogether.

There have been growing calls in recent years for, and in some instances implementation of, TJ institutions and programs in standing autocracies like Zimbabwe and standing democracies like the United States. Rather than view them as cases that we cannot make sense of, as I mentioned above, scholars should study them seriously, extending and refining our theories and, where necessary, developing new ones that help us comprehend the emergence of TJ institutions and programs where we might least expect them.[15]

The inequalities, discrimination, and violence that racial, ethnic, and religious minority groups face in democracies like the United States are not so different from those that Black people experienced in apartheid South Africa. And there is an abiding need to reckon with the past and remedy historical wrongdoing in the United States just as there was in South Africa. Moreover, we see today in

[14] Excellent work by Quinn (2011), Winston (2021), and others on Uganda and similar cases has unfortunately not entered TJ's mainstream.

[15] Cronin-Furman 2022; Gillooly et al. 2024; Murphy and Zvobgo 2023; Posthumus and Zvobgo 2021.

countries like the United States the types of civil society mobilization and contentious politics that we observed in paradigmatic TJ sites like Argentina and Guatemala. We may very well see what happened then happening now. Domestic civil society mobilization could be helpful now as it was then. Likewise, we see in countries like Zimbabwe, since former President Robert Mugabe's ouster and death, some of the same sensitivities to external pressure that we saw in Indonesia, Timor-Leste, and elsewhere. Continued and perhaps more intense pressure could help produce TJ processes. Crucial in both places would be the arming of civil society with ideas, resources, and methods proven to be useful in historical cases.

Today, we have the benefit of knowing the things that make TJ adoption more likely and, importantly, the things that make a robust process and serious follow-up more likely. Monitoring the degree to which non-paradigmatic cases do and do not follow what has been done in other places will likely be instructive. Some differences, like in the temporal scope of truth commission investigations or in proposed remedies for harms, are to be expected. But there should not be substantial differences in, say, the types of powers that truth commissions need (e.g., the power to subpoena testimony).

Taking seriously and studying rigorously both paradigmatic and non-paradigmatic cases will help us better understand positive and negative TJ outcomes around the world. On the policy-practice side, stakeholders like external funders should, for example, not support commissions in autocracies that carry out selective investigations. Neither should they support reparations programs that limit the number of beneficiaries on the basis of sectarianism, political or otherwise. All of these processes should be closely monitored.

Moving Forward

As this project concludes, I highlight additional work that remains. To begin, as scholarship advances and attempts to identify with greater precision and certainty TJ's effects on politics, it will be increasingly important for researchers to address how earlier stages of TJ processes influence later ones. I showed that TJ institutions and programs, truth commissions in particular, are not created equally. Given this, can scholars reasonably expect similar effects across contexts?

Take, for instance, truth commission design, which I examined in Chapter 4. Can commissions with weak investigative powers construct an equally comprehensive historical account as commissions with strong investigative powers? Consider, also, commission recommendations, which I studied across Chapters 5, 6, 7, and 8. Can commissions that make different recommendations and whose recommendations are variably implemented nevertheless contribute in similar ways to democracy, human rights, and peace? And can there be meaningful TJ in contexts where civil society is marginalized in the process?

It will also be important for scholars to address from a more normative perspective whether democracy, human rights respect, and durable peace, while desirable, are reasonable and appropriate goals for TJ.[16] Are expectations of what TJ mechanisms can do too high? And should scholarship, at least for a time, focus on studying "mediate goals"—for example, the implementation of commission recommendations, the conduct of human rights trials, and the practice of vetting, lustrations, and purges—rather than "final goals" like democracy? Certainly, there exists a tradeoff between breadth and depth in scholarship. Previous research attempted to give us breadth of understanding. And, in many ways, it did. However, this work also left us with many mixed results. Research may do well to now offer *depth* of understanding.

Relatedly, to identify causal effects and pathways with greater certainty, researchers should collect more fine-grained data and/or locate potential sites for natural (or quasi-) experiments. One area where this would be especially useful is in the study of TJ's spread across world regions.[17] My project's cross-national and comparative analyses provided support for the argument that transnational civil society advocacy produces outcomes of interest. Specific actors engaged in specific behaviors to help deliver specific outcomes, like truth commission adoption. But the question of whether transnational advocacy is a driver or a pathway of regional diffusion of commissions and other TJ mechanisms remains to be systematically investigated.[18]

While much research, including mine, typically views diffusion as an alternative explanation, it may be a complementary one, especially over time. The nature of transnational civil society partnerships has been changing in recent years. Before TJ ideas, norms, and practices were in place, international experts like those at the ICTJ used to teach domestic groups about what TJ is and how to adapt it to their local contexts. Now that these ideas are in place, groups like the ICTJ are connecting domestic groups in one country to domestic groups in other countries so that they can learn from each other. Through domestic-to-domestic partnerships, advocates from countries that have delivered commissions can, for example, share with advocates in other

[16] Scholars like Nalepa (2022) have examined the prospective nature of truth commissions and TJ, connecting their by-products, notably transparency, to the quality of democratic representation and, more broadly, to democratic stability. But scholars like Dancy and Thoms (2022) have found "no measurable effect" for outcomes like free and fair elections and checks and balances across branches of government.

[17] Subotić 2012.

[18] Sikkink's (2011) work on human rights prosecutions is exemplary.

countries strategies for setting and implementing a TJ agenda that includes commissions.[19] If domestic-to-domestic partnerships become concentrated within certain geographic regions, we may in effect observe transnational diffusion through transnational advocacy.

Finally, there is the question of what TJ's future looks like if, in even the most promising of contexts like Guatemala, South Africa, and Timor-Leste, governments have not been socialized into TJ, among a broader set of human rights norms. As I raised in the last empirical chapters, is civil society substitution sustainable and, if not, what could help make it so?

I am not suggesting that we resign ourselves to government inaction and instead rely on civil society.[20] TJ is a right of survivors and victims' families and an obligation of governments to provide. Civil society substitution is a last resort and has real downsides. Rather, the question I am posing is this: How can we support civil society actors in challenging post-violence contexts where they are forced into this position?

Moreover, given that governments around the world are restricting civic space and cracking down on civil society, using both physical and bureaucratic repression, how can allies support and sustain advocates' efforts to fight impunity and promote truth and justice? When we consider this and other questions, it is clear that TJ remains ripe for inquiry and merits our continued time and attention.

[19] This is a phenomenon that Rodrigues (2016) observes in the environmental advocacy space.
[20] Like Kochanski (2021) and Quinn (2021), I encourage scholars to interrogate state abdication.

Afterword

The human rights situation in transitional and "post-transitional" countries is ever evolving, and the countries to which I dedicated separate chapters—Guatemala, South Africa, and Timor-Leste—are no exception. In this afterword, I briefly reflect on political developments in Guatemala since my fieldwork, developments that exemplify the challenges and challengers the TJ network and the broader human rights movement face around the world.

On August 20, 2023, reformist Bernardo Arévalo won the Guatemalan presidency, with the support of civil society and Indigenous movements concerned with democracy and human rights in the country. But his ascent to the highest office in the land was anything but straightforward. Between the election and Inauguration Day, the incumbent president Alejandro Giammattei's attorney general, María Consuelo Porras, moved to temporarily suspend Arévalo's Seed Movement party. Porras also moved to strip the president-elect's legal immunity. Moreover, the administration intimidated independent judges, including election magistrates, leading some to flee the country. This flagrant antidemocratic behavior generated domestic protests and international criticism. After some last-ditch efforts in Congress to delay the inauguration, Arévalo was finally sworn in as president on January 15, 2024—nearly five months after winning office.[1]

In his first year in office, Arévalo has faced more than a dozen impeachment requests, his coalition in Congress has fallen apart, and his opponents in Congress have moved to appoint Supreme Court justices who are expected to obstruct his reforms.[2] Arévalo would hardly be the first leader to have his reform agenda derailed. Recall former Chief Prosecutor for Human Rights Hilda Pineda who I interviewed. She was leveraging limited resources to undertake strategic prosecutions of wartime abuses. She knew her team could not prosecute every case and that time was running out for victims' aging relatives all these decades later. So she aimed to litigate emblematic cases that would speak to broader trends and acknowledge different victims' suffering. She expressed hope that these cases would validate victims' truth and help rebuild social trust. But her plans were cut short. In 2021, Porras, the same attorney general who would try to obstruct Arévalo's rise, removed Pineda from her post.[3]

These moves undermine the work of human rights, justice, and peace in Guatemala. Other incidents include arbitrary detentions of journalists and violence against Indigenous people, LGBTQIA+ individuals, and women.[4] Deeply problematic for civil society is insecurity for human rights defenders, as well as for independent prosecutors, judges,

[1] Amnesty International 2023; Freedom House 2024*a*; US Department of State 2024*a*.

[2] Bosworth 2024.

[3] HRW 2022. In South Africa, corruption is likewise rampant, with current and former leaders and members of government indicted on, and sometimes convicted of, multiple charges of corruption and abuse of power (Freedom House 2024*b*, US Department of State 2024*b*).

[4] In South Africa and Timor-Leste, we see multiple instances of police brutality, as well as lengthy pretrial detentions, overcrowded prisons, and custodial deaths. We also see state failures to investigate and prosecute allegations of violence against women (Freedom House 2024*b*, 2024*c*, US Department of State 2024*b*, 2024*c*).

journalists, and others who have been important allies. Congress has also introduced laws to impede the work of NGOs engaged in human rights work. This is far from an exhaustive list.[5]

Why end the book here? For some, the examples presented suggest the opposite of the book's thesis, that civil society actors govern TJ. But I start where I began, with a message of encouragement for both this book's readers and its protagonists. Civil society's persistence—across decades, against unbelievable odds, to produce and maintain change after profound and sustained political violence (and minimize losses where possible)—is nothing short of remarkable.

I mentioned in Chapter 6 that at the time of my fieldwork, President Giammattei was threatening to dissolve a number of institutions created by the 1996 peace accords, including the Secretariat for Peace and the National Reparations Program. He succeeded in dissolving the former but not the latter, only managing to render it inactive. Why? The evidence points to the TJ network and the human rights movement.

Civil society's story, contained in these pages and so many more that I did not write, teaches us to not assume and accept losses, but to instead continue the fight for truth, justice, reparation, and nonrepetition—as NGOs and civil society movements in Guatemala, South Africa, Timor-Leste, and countless other countries have so earnestly and unrelentingly done and will no doubt continue to do.

We must hear, see, and not be silent. Never again.

[5] Amnesty International 2023; Freedom House 2024*a*.

References

ACbit and AJAR. 2017. *Our Path Is Upwards; Becoming Strong Together: Strengthening Women Survivors of Violence in Timor-Leste Through Participatory Action Research (PAR)*. Asosiasaun Chega! ba ita and Asia Justice and Rights. asia-ajar.org/wp-content/uploads/2018/02/Final-English-PAR-Report.compressed.pdf. Accessed June 7, 2022.

Aeby, Katia and María Jesús García Barrachina. 2007. *10 Years Without War... Waiting for Peace: The State of Compliance with the Peace Accord on Strengthening Civilian Power and the Role of the Armed Forces in a Democratic Society*. Peace Brigades International.

Aguilar, Paloma, Laia Balcells, and Héctor Cebolla-Boado. 2011. "Determinants of Attitudes Toward Transitional Justice: An Empirical Analysis of the Spanish Case." *Comparative Political Studies* 44(10): 1397–1430.

AJAR. 2018. *Timor-Leste: International Educators' Workshop on Strengthening the Capacity for Education on History and Violence Prevention*. Asia Justice and Rights. asia-ajar.org/2018/06/29/timor-leste-international-educators-workshop-on-strengthening-the-capacity-for-education-on-history-and-violence-prevention/. Accessed June 7, 2022.

Akhavan, Payam. 2001. "Beyond Impunity: Can International Criminal Justice Prevent Future Atrocities?" *American Journal of International Law* 95(1): 7–31.

Al Jazeera. 2023. "Guatemala Releases Military Officials Convicted of Grave Crimes." *Al Jazeera*. https://www.aljazeera.com/news/2023/6/10/guatemala-releases-military-officials-convicted-of-grave-crimes. Accessed October 17, 2024.

Alldén, Susanne. 2007. "Internalising the Culture of Human Rights: Securing Women's Rights in Post-Conflict East Timor." *Asia-Pacific Journal on Human Rights and the Law* 8(1): 1–23.

Alter, Karen J. 2014. *The New Terrain of International Law: Courts, Politics, Rights*. Princeton University Press.

Amnesty International. 1990. *AMR 34/06/90/s: Temor de Ejecución Extrajudicial, Desaparición y Malos Tratos*. Amnesty International. amnesty.org/download/Documents/200000/amr340061990es.pdf. Accessed May 15, 2020.

Amnesty International. 1993. *ACT 33/36/93: Political Killings and Disappearances: Medicolegal Aspects*. Amnesty International. amnesty.org/download/Documents/188000/act330361993en.pdf. Accessed May 15, 2020.

Amnesty International. 1994. *AMR 34/10/94/s: Temor de Seguridad/Amenazas de Muerte*. Amnesty International. amnesty.org/download/Documents/184000/amr340101994es.pdf. Accessed May 15, 2020.

Amnesty International. 1995*a*. *AMR 34/024/1995: Victims of 1982 Army Massacre at Las Dos Erres Exhumed*. Amnesty International. amnesty.org/download/Documents/172000/amr340241995en.pdf. Accessed May 15, 2020.

Amnesty International. 1995*b*. *AMR 34/48/89/s: Temor de "Desaparición"*. Amnesty International. amnesty.org/download/Documents/200000/amr340481989es.pdf. Accessed May 15, 2020.

Amnesty International. 1995*c*. *POL 10/03/95: Amnesty International Report 1995*. Amnesty International. amnesty.org/download/Documents/176000/pol100031995en.pdf. Accessed May 15, 2020.

Amnesty International. 1996. *ASA 21/08/96: East Timor Prisoners in Becora Prison, Dili*. Amnesty International. amnesty.org/download/Documents/168000/asa210081996en.pdf. Accessed May 15, 2020.

Amnesty International. 1998. *ASA 21/106/98: Fear for Safety / Arbitrary Arrests / Unlawful Killings*. Amnesty International. amnesty.org/download/Documents/152000/asa211061998en.pdf. Accessed July 1, 2020.

Amnesty International. 1999. *ASA 21/37/99: Several Human Rights Organizations, Including Yayasan Hak, Fokupers, Kontras*. Amnesty International. amnesty.org/download/Documents/144000/asa210371999en.pdf. Accessed July 1, 2020.

Amnesty International. 2008. *Battling Impunity in Guatemala*. Amnesty International. amnestyusa.org/blog/battling-impunity-in-guatemala/. Accessed October 17, 2024.

Amnesty International. 2023. *Guatemala 2023*. Amnesty International. amnesty.org/en/location/americas/central-america-and-the-caribbean/guatemala/report-guatemala/. Accessed October 18, 2024.

Ancelovici, Marcos and Jane Jenson. 2013. "Standardization for Transnational Diffusion: The Case of Truth Commissions and Conditional Cash Transfers." *International Political Sociology* 7(3):294–312.

Ang, Milena and Monika Nalepa. 2019. "Can Transitional Justice Improve the Quality of Representation in New Democracies?" *World Politics* 71(4):631–666.

Annan, Kofi. 2007. *Address by H.E. Mr. Kofi Annan to both Houses of Parliament*. United Nations Office on Drugs and Crime. unodc.org/unodc/en/about-unodc/speeches/speech_2007_05_08.html. Accessed September 29, 2020.

Appel, Benjamin J. 2018. "In the Shadow of the International Criminal Court: Does the ICC Deter Human Rights Violations?" *Journal of Conflict Resolution* 62(1):3–28.

Arenhövel, Mark. 2008. "Democratization and Transitional Justice." *Democratization* 15(3):570–587.

Ariav, Roee. 2012. "National Investigations of Human Rights Between National and International Law." *Goettingen Journal of International Law* 4:853–871.

Arieli, Tamar and Nissim Cohen. 2013. "Policy Entrepreneurs and Post-Conflict Cross-Border Cooperation: A Conceptual Framework and the Israeli–Jordanian Case." *Policy Sciences* 46:237–256.

Arthur, Paige and Christalla Yakinthou. 2018. *Transitional Justice, International Assistance, and Civil Society: Missed Connections*. Cambridge University Press.

Asal, Victor, Kathleen Deloughery, and Amanda Murdie. 2016. "Responding to Terrorism? Human Rights Organization Shaming and Terrorist Attacks." *Studies in Conflict & Terrorism* 39(3):240–259.

Asia Foundation. 2013. *Timor-Leste Law & Justice Survey 2013*. Asia Foundation.

Asia Foundation. 2019. *Community Police Perceptions Survey: Summary of Key Findings*. Asia Foundation. asiafoundation.org/wp-content/uploads/2019/09/Timor-Leste-Community-Police-Perceptions-Survey-Summary-of-Key-Findings_EN.pdf. Accessed June 6, 2022.

Asmal, Kader. 1992. "Victims, Survivors and Citizens: Human Rights, Reparations and Reconciliation." *South African Journal on Human Rights* 8(4):491–511.

Avant, Deborah D., Martha Finnemore, and Susan K. Sell. 2010. *Who Governs the Globe?* Cambridge University Press.

Ayoub, Phillip M. and Kristina Stoeckl. 2024. "The Double-Helix Entanglements of Transnational Advocacy: Moral Conservative Resistance to LGBTI Rights." *Review of International Studies* 50(2):289–311.

Backer, David. 2003. "Civil Society and Transitional Justice: Possibilities, Patterns and Prospects." *Journal of Human Rights* 2(3):297–313.

Bakiner, Onur. 2014. "Truth Commission Impact: An Assessment of How Commissions Influence Politics and Society." *International Journal of Transitional Justice* 8(1):6–30.

Bakiner, Onur. 2015. *Truth Commissions: Memory, Power, and Legitimacy*. University of Pennsylvania Press.

Balcells, Laia, Valeria Palanza, and Elsa Voytas. 2022. "Can Transitional Justice Improve the Quality of Representation in New Democracies?" *Journal of Politics* 84(1):496–510.

Baldwin, Maria T. 2009. *Amnesty International and US Foreign Policy: Human Rights Campaigns in Guatemala, the United States, and China*. LFB Scholarly Publishing.

Barnett, Michael and Martha Finnemore. 2004. *Rules for the World: International Organizations in Global Politics*. Cornell University Press.

Bass, Gary Jonathan. 2002. *Stay the Hand of Vengeance: The Politics of War Crimes Tribunals*. Princeton University Press.

Bates, Genevieve, Ipek Cinar, and Monika Nalepa. 2020. "Accountability by the Numbers: Introducing the Global Transitional Justice Events Dataset (1946–2016)." *Perspectives on Politics* 18(1):161–184.

Becker, Megan, Benjamin A. T. Graham, and Kelebogile Zvobgo. 2021. "The Stewardship Model: An Inclusive Approach to Undergraduate Research." *PS: Political Science & Politics* 54(1):158–162.

Bell, Sam R., Tavishi Bhasin, K. Chad Clay, and Amanda Murdie. 2014. "Taking the Fight to Them: Neighborhood Human Rights Organizations and Domestic Protest." *British Journal of Political Science* 44(4):853–875.

Ben-Josef Hirsch, Michal, Megan MacKenzie, and Mohamed Sesay. 2012. "Measuring the Impacts of Truth and Reconciliation Commissions: Placing the Global 'Success' of TRCs in Local Perspective." *Cooperation and Conflict* 47(3):386–403.

Bennett, Andrew. 2010. Process Tracing and Causal Inference. In *Rethinking Social Inquiry: Diverse Tools, Shared Standards, 2nd edition*, ed. Henry E. Brady and David Collier. Rowman and Littlefield pp. 207–219.

Bennett, Andrew and Jeffrey T. Checkel. 2015. *Process Tracing: From Metaphor to Analytic Tool*. Cambridge University Press.

Benneyworth, Garth. 2011. "Armed and Trained: Nelson Mandela's 1962 Military Mission as Commander in Chief of Umkhonto we Sizwe and Provenance for His Buried Makarov Pistol." *South African Historical Journal* 63(1):78–101.

Benomar, Jamal. 1993. "Justice After Transitions." *Journal of Democracy* 4(1):3–14.

Berg, Sonja. 2012. "Child Diversion Programme Minimum Standard Compliance in the Western Cape: An Exploratory Study." (PhD thesis University of South Africa).

Binningsbø, Helga Malmin, Cyanne E. Loyle, Scott Gates, and Jon Elster. 2012. "Armed Conflict and Post-Conflict Justice, 1946–2006: A Dataset." *Journal of Peace Research* 49(5):731–740.

Bob, Clifford. 2002. Globalization and the Social Construction of Human Rights Campaigns. In *Globalization and Human Rights*, ed. Alison Brysk. University of California Press pp. 133–147.

Bob, Clifford. 2005. *The Marketing of Rebellion: Insurgents, Media, and International Activism*. Cambridge University Press.

Boix, Carles, Michael Miller, and Sebastian Rosato. 2013. "A Complete Data Set of Political Regimes, 1800–2007." *Comparative Political Studies* 46(12):1523–1554.

Bosworth, James. 2024. *Guatemala's "Coalition of the Corrupt" Is Derailing Arevalo's Agenda*. World Politics Review. worldpoliticsreview.com/guatemala-arevalo-corruption-reforms/. Accessed October 18, 2024.

Bowsher, Josh. 2020. "The South African TRC as Neoliberal Reconciliation: Victim Subjectivities and the Synchronization of Affects." *Social & Legal Studies* 29(1):41–64.

Brahm, Eric. 2007. "Uncovering the Truth: Examining Truth Commission Success and Impact." *International Studies Perspectives* 8(1):16–35.

Brouwer, Stijn. 2015. *Policy Entrepreneurs in Water Governance: Strategies for Change*. Springer.

Brysk, Alison. 1993. "From Above and Below: Social Movements, the International System, and Human Rights in Argentina." *Comparative Political Studies* 26(3):259–285.
Brysk, Alison. 2013. *Speaking Rights to Power: Constructing Political Will.* Oxford University Press.
Burke, Jason. 2016. "Four Former Apartheid-Era Guards on Trial over 1983 Student Murder." *The Guardian.* theguardian.com/world/2016/feb/26/four-former-apartheid-era-guards-on-trial-over-1983-student. Accessed May 15, 2020.
Burt, Jo-Marie. 2007. *Silencing Civil Society: Political Violence and the Authoritarian State in Peru.* Palgrave Macmillan.
Burt, Jo-Marie. 2016*a*. "Defense Witnesses Testify in Sepur Zarco Trial Ahead of Closing Arguments." *International Justice Monitor.* ijmonitor.org/2016/02/defense-witnesses-testify-in-sepur-zarco-trial-ahead-of-closing-arguments/. Accessed October 17, 2024.
Burt, Jo-Marie. 2016*b*. "Military Officers Convicted in Landmark Sepur Zarco Sexual Violence Case." *International Justice Monitor.* ijmonitor.org/2016/03/military-officers-convicted-in-landmark-sepur-zarco-sexual-violence-case/. Accessed October 17, 2024.
Bush, Sarah Sunn. 2015. *The Taming of Democracy Assistance.* Cambridge University Press.
Byrne, Alexandra, Bilen Zerie, and Kelebogile Zvobgo. 2024. "Producing Truth: Public Memory Projects in Post-Violence Societies." *Human Rights Quarterly* 46(2):207–233.
Byrne, Catherine C. 2004. "Benefit or Burden: Victims' Reflections on TRC Participation." *Peace and Conflict* 10(3):237–256.
Call, Charles T. 2004. "Is Transitional Justice Really Just?" *Brown Journal of World Affairs* 11(1):101–114.
Capella, Ana Cláudia Niedhardt. 2016. "Agenda-Setting Policy: Strategies and Agenda Denial Mechanisms." *Organizações & Sociedade* 23(79):675–691.
Carpenter, R. Charli. 2007*a*. "Setting the Advocacy Agenda: Theorizing Issue Emergence and Nonemergence in Transnational Advocacy Networks." *International Studies Quarterly* 51(1):99–120.
Carpenter, R. Charli. 2007*b*. "Studying Issue (Non)-Adoption in Transnational Advocacy Networks." *International Organization* 61(3):643–667.
CAVR. 2005. *Chega! The Report of the Commission for Reception, Truth and Reconciliation in Timor-Leste (CAVR).*
CEH. 1999. *Guatemala, Memoria del Silencio.* Comisión para el Esclarecimiento Histórico.
Chapman, Audrey R. and Hugo van der Merwe. 2008. *Truth and Reconciliation in South Africa: Did the TRC Deliver?* University of Pennsylvania Press.
Chaudhry, Suparna. 2022. "The Assault on Civil Society: Explaining State Crackdown on NGOs." *International Organization* 76(3):549–590.
Chaudhry, Suparna. Forthcoming. *Civil Societies, Uncivil States: State Repression of NGOs.* Cornell University Press.
Chaudoin, Stephen. 2023. "How International Organizations Change National Media Coverage of Human Rights." *International Organization* 77(1):238–261.
Chenoweth, Erica and Maria J. Stephan. 2011. *Why Civil Resistance Works: The Strategic Logic of Nonviolent Conflict.* Columbia University Press.
Civil Society Prison Reform Initiative. 2020. *CSPRI Newsletter Nr 10 April 2005.* dullahomarinstitute.org.za/acjr/resource-centre/10%20-%20April%202005.pdf. Accessed October 17, 2024.
Civil Society Prison Reform Initiative. 2022. *Submissions on Combating of Torture of Persons Bill [B 21 of 2012].* dullahomarinstitute.org.za/acjr/resource-centre/CSPRI_Torture_Bill_submissions-1082012.pdf. Accessed October 17, 2024.
Clark, Ann Marie. 2010. *Diplomacy of Conscience: Amnesty International and Changing Human Rights Norms.* Princeton University Press.

Collier, David. 2011. "Understanding Process Tracing." *PS: Political Science & Politics* 44(4):823–830.

Collins, Cath. 2010. *Post-Transitional Justice: Human Rights Trials in Chile and El Salvador*. Pennsylvania State University Press.

Congreso de la Nación de Argentina. 1984. Decreto 187. Comisión Nacional Sobre la Desaparición de Personas – Constitución – Integración y funciones. B.O. 19/12/1983. In *Anales de Legislación Argentina*, ed. Carlos M. Oliva Velez. Sociedad Anonima pp. 137–138.

Coppedge, Michael et al. 2018. "V-Dem Country-Year Dataset v8." *Varieties of Democracy (V-Dem) Project*.

Correa, Cristián. 2013. *Reparations in Peru: From Recommendations to Implementation*. International Center for Transitional Justice.

Correa, Cristián, Shuichi Furuya, and Clara Sandoval. 2020. *Reparation for Victims of Armed Conflict, Vol. 3*. Cambridge University Press.

Crenzel, Emilio. 2012. *The Memory of the Argentina Disappearances: The Political History of Nunca Más*. Routledge.

Cronin-Furman, Kate. 2013. "Managing Expectations: International Criminal Trials and the Prospects for Deterrence of Mass Atrocity." *International Journal of Transitional Justice* 7(3):434–454.

Cronin-Furman, Kate. 2022. *Hypocrisy and Human Rights: Resisting Accountability for Mass Atrocities*. Cornell University Press.

CSVR. 2004. *Symbolic Reparations: A Fractured Opportunity*. Institute for Justice and Reconciliation. http://www.csvr.org.za/docs/livingmemory/symbolicreparations.pdf. Accessed November 28, 2024.

CVR. 2001. *Informe final de la Comisión de la Verdad y Reconciliación*. Comisión de la Verdad y Reconciliación.

Dancy, Geoff. 2018. "Deals with the Devil? Conflict Amnesties, Civil War, and Sustainable Peace." *International Organization* 72(2):387–421.

Dancy, Geoff, Bridget E. Marchesi, Tricia D. Olsen, Leigh A. Payne, Andrew G. Reiter, and Kathryn Sikkink. 2019. "Behind Bars and Bargains: New Findings on Transitional Justice in Emerging Democracies." *International Studies Quarterly* 63(1):99–110.

Dancy, Geoff, Hun Joon Kim, and Eric Wiebelhaus-Brahm. 2010. "The Turn to Truth: Trends in Truth Commission Experimentation." *Journal of Human Rights* 9(1):45–64.

Dancy, Geoff and Oskar Timo Thoms. 2022. "Do Truth Commissions Really Improve Democracy?" *Comparative Political Studies* 55(4):555–587.

Danner, Allison and Erik Voeten. 2010. "Who Is Running the International Criminal Justice System?" *Cambridge Studies in International Relations* 114(1):35–71.

De Greiff, Pablo. 2012. Theorizing Transitional Justice. In *Transitional Justice*, ed. Melissa S. Williams, Rosemary Nagy, and Jon Elster. New York University Press pp. 31–77.

de la Rey, Cheryl and Ingrid Owens. 1998. "Perceptions of Psychosocial Healing and the Truth and Reconciliation Commission in South Africa." *Peace and Conflict* 4(3):257–270.

Della Porta, Donatella and Sidney Tarrow. 2005. *Transnational Protest and Global Activism*. Rowman and Littlefield.

DeTommaso, Meghan M., Mario Schulz, and Steve B. Lem. 2017. "Choices of Justice: Effects of Civil War Termination on Postconflict Justice Mechanisms Implemented by the State." *International Journal of Transitional Justice* 11(2):218–238.

Dietrich, Simone. 2013. "Bypass or Engage? Explaining Donor Delivery Tactics in Foreign Aid Allocation." *International Studies Quarterly* 57(4):698–712.

Dietrich, Simone and Amanda Murdie. 2017. "Human Rights Shaming Through INGOs and Foreign Aid Delivery." *Review of International Organizations* 12(1): 95–120.

Duke, Lynne. 1998. "After Apartheid, a Need to Heal." *Washington Post*. washingtonpost.com/archive/politics/1998/11/15/after-apartheid-a-need-to-heal/d377c2ce-4fff-4f00-95ce-36c25ac95ee7/. Accessed May 15, 2020.

Dullah Omar Institute. 2023. *About Us*. Dullah Omar Institute. dullahomarinstitute.org.za/about-us/about-the-institute. Accessed April 20, 2023.

EAAF. 2018. *Guatemala*. Equipo Argentino de Antropología Forense. eaaf.org/wp-content/uploads/2018/08/guatemala1999.pdf. Accessed October 17, 2024.

Eck, Kristine and Lisa Hultman. 2007. "One-Sided Violence Against Civilians in War: Insights from New Fatality Data." *Journal of Peace Research* 44(2): 233–246.

Edward Flores, Thomas and Irfan Nooruddin. 2009. "Democracy Under the Gun: Understanding Postconflict Economic Recovery." *Journal of Conflict Resolution* 53(1):3–29.

Edwards, Michael. 2009. *Civil Society*. Polity.

Elster, Jon. 2004. *Closing the Books: Transitional Justice in Historical Perspective*. Cambridge University Press.

Escribà-Folch, Abel and Joseph Wright. 2015. "Human Rights Prosecutions and Autocratic Survival." *International Organization* 69(2):343–373.

Farbstein, Susan. 2015. *New Revelations of Political Interference in Prosecution of Apartheid-Era Crimes*. International Human Rights Clinic. https://humanrightsclinic.law.harvard.edu/new-revelations-of-political-interference-in-prosecution-of-apartheid-era-crimes/. Accessed November 9, 2024.

Fariss, Christopher J. 2014. "Respect for Human Rights Has Improved over Time: Modeling the Changing Standard of Accountability." *American Political Science Review* 108(2):297–318.

Finnemore, Martha. 1996*a*. *National Interests in International Society*. Cornell University Press.

Finnemore, Martha. 1996*b*. "Norms, Culture, and World Politics: Insights from Sociology's Institutionalism." *International Organization* 50(2):325–347.

Fletcher, Laurel E. and Harvey M. Weinstein with Jamie Rowen. 2009. "Context, Timing and the Dynamics of Transitional Justice: A Historical Perspective." *Human Rights Quarterly* 31(1):163–220.

FOKUPERS. 1999. *The End of the Dry Season: Efforts by East Timorese Women to End Violence: A Beginning*. Forum Komunikasaun Ba Feto Timor Loro Sa'e.

Franklin, James C. 2008. "Shame on You: The Impact of Human Rights Criticism on Political Repression in Latin America." *International Studies Quarterly* 52(1):187–211.

Freedom House. 2024*a*. *Freedom in the World 2024: Guatemala*. Freedom House. freedomhouse.org/country/guatemala/freedom-world/2024. Accessed October 18, 2024.

Freedom House. 2024*b*. *Freedom in the World 2024: South Africa*. Freedom House. freedomhouse.org/country/south-africa/freedom-world/2024. Accessed October 18, 2024.

Freedom House. 2024*c*. *Freedom in the World 2024: Timor-Leste*. Freedom House. freedomhouse.org/country/timor-leste/freedom-world/2024. Accessed October 18, 2024.

Fundasaun Mahein. 2014. *The Thematic Issues of the Security Sector in 2014*. Fundasaun Mahein. fundasaunmahein.org/wp-content/uploads/2015/01/MNL-95-_Thematic-Issue_30012015_Englisg-Version.pdf. Accessed June 6, 2022.

Fundasaun Mahein. 2022. *Reflections on the 20th Anniversary of Timor-Leste's Restored Independence: Fundasaun Mahein's Call to the Historic Leaders of RDTL*. Fundasaun Mahein. fundasaunmahein.org/wp-content/uploads/2022/05/MNL-157-Reflections-on-the-20th-Anniversary-of-Independence-Eng-1.pdf. Accessed June 6, 2022.

Fyall, Rachel and Michael McGuire. 2015. "Advocating for Policy Change in Nonprofit Coalitions." *Nonprofit and Voluntary Sector Quarterly* 44(6):1274–1291.

George, Alexander L. and Andrew Bennett. 2005. *Case Studies and Theory Development in the Social Sciences*. MIT Press.

Georgetown Institute for Women, Peace and Security. 2015. *Women Leading Peace: A Close Examination of Women's Political Participation in Peace Processes in Northern Ireland, Guatemala, Kenya, and the Philippines.* Georgetown Institute for Women, Peace and Security. giwps.georgetown.edu/wp-content/uploads/2017/08/Women-Leading-Peace.pdf. Accessed May 26, 2023.
Gerring, John. 2007. "Is There a (Viable) Crucial-Case Method?" *Comparative Political Studies* 40(3):231–253.
Gibson, James L. 2004. *Overcoming Apartheid.* Russell Sage Foundation.
Gillespie, Ciaran. 2013. "Terror and the Search for Justice in South Africa: An Interview with Shirley Gunn." *Critical Studies on Terrorism* 6(3):473–481.
Gillooly, Shauna, Daniel Solomon, and Kelebogile Zvobgo. 2024. "Co-Opting Truth: Explaining Quasi-Judicial Institutions in Authoritarian Regimes." *Human Rights Quarterly* 46(1):67–97.
Gizelis, Theodora-Ismene. 2011. "A Country of Their Own: Women and Peacebuilding." *Conflict Management and Peace Science* 28(5):522–542.
González, Eduardo. 2013. *Drafting a Truth Commission Mandate: A Practical Tool.* International Center for Transitional Justice.
González, Eduardo, Elena Naughton, and Félix Reátegui. 2014. *Challenging the Conventional Can Truth Commissions Strengthen Peace Processes?* International Center for Transitional Justice.
González, Eduardo and Howard Varney. 2013. *Truth Seeking: Elements of Creating an Effective Truth Commission.* Amnesty Commission of the Ministry of Justice of Brazil and International Center for Transitional Justice.
González-Ocantos, Ezequiel A. 2020. *The Politics of Transitional Justice in Latin America: Power, Norms, and Capacity Building.* Cambridge University Press.
Government of Timor-Leste. 2013. *Ministry of Education Launches the Book "CHEGA" to the New Generations.* Government of Timor-Leste. timor-leste.gov.tl/?p=8588&lang=en. Accessed June 8, 2022.
Grandin, Greg. 2005. "The Instruction of Great Catastrophe: Truth Commissions, National History, and State Formation in Argentina, Chile, and Guatemala." *The American Historical Review* 110(1):46–67.
Gready, Paul. 2010. *The Era of Transitional Justice: The Aftermath of the Truth and Reconciliation Commission in South Africa and Beyond.* Routledge.
Green, Jessica F. 2013. *Rethinking Private Authority: Agents and Entrepreneurs in Global Environmental Governance.* Princeton University Press.
Greenstein, Claire. 2024. "Reparations, but for What? Presenting a New Approach to Coding Reparations." *Law & Social Inquiry* 49(1):90–117.
Grodsky, Brian K. 2010. *The Costs of Justice: How New Leaders Respond to Previous Rights Abuses.* University of Notre Dame Press.
Grunebaum, Heidi. 2017. *Memorializing the Past: Everyday Life in South Africa After the Truth and Reconciliation Commission.* Routledge.
Guest, Iain. 1990. *Behind the Disappearances: Argentina's Dirty War Against Human Rights and the United Nations.* University of Pennsylvania Press.
Haas, Peter M. 1992. "Introduction: Epistemic Communities and International Policy Coordination." *International Organization* 46(1):1–35.
Haddad, Heidi Nichols. 2013. "After the Norm Cascade: NGO Mission Expansion and the Coalition for the International Criminal Court." *Global Governance* 19(2):187–206.
Haddad, Heidi Nichols. 2018. *The Hidden Hands of Justice: NGOs, Human Rights, and International Courts.* Cambridge University Press.
Hafner-Burton, Emilie M. 2008. "Sticks and Stones: Naming and Shaming the Human Rights Enforcement Problem." *International Organization* 62(4):689–716.
Haines, Herbert H. 1984. "Black Radicalization and the Funding of Civil Rights: 1957–1970." *Social Problems* 32(1):31–43.

Hamber, Brandon. 1998. "The Burdens of Truth: An Evaluation of the Psychological Support Services and Initiatives Undertaken by the South African Truth and Reconciliation Commission." *American Imago* 55(1):9–28.

Hamber, Brandon. 2001. Who Pays for Peace? Implications of the Negotiated Settlement in a Post-Apartheid South Africa. In *Ethnopolitical Warfare: Causes, Consequences, and Possible Solutions*, ed. Daniel Chirot and Martin E.P. Seligman. American Psychological Association pp. 235–258.

Handlarski, Denise. 2009. Women's Speech and Silence. In *(Re)Interpretations: The Shapes of Justice in Women's Experience*, ed. Lisa Dresdner and Laurel S. Peterson. Cambridge Scholars Publishing pp. 48–51.

Hayner, Priscilla B. 2001. *Unspeakable Truths: Confronting State Terror and Atrocity.* Routledge, 1st edition.

Hayner, Priscilla B. 2011. *Unspeakable Truths: Transitional Justice and the Challenge of Truth Commissions.* Routledge, 2nd edition.

Healy, Lynne M. 2008. "Exploring the History of Social Work as a Human Rights Profession." *International Social Work* 51(6):735–748.

Hegre, Havard, Tanja Ellingsen, Nils Petter Gleditsch and Scott Gates. 2001. "Towards a Democratic Civil Peace? Opportunity, Grievance, and Civil War, 1816–1992." *American Political Science Review* 95(1):33–48.

Helfer, Laurence R. and Anne E. Showalter. 2017. "Opposing International Justice: Kenya's Integrated Backlash Strategy Against the ICC." *International Criminal Law Review* 17(1):1–46.

Hendrix, Cullen S. and Wendy H. Wong. 2014. "Knowing Your Audience: How the Structure of International Relations and Organizational Choices Affect Amnesty International's Advocacy." *Review of International Organizations* 9(1):29–58.

Henisz, Witold J. 2002. "The Institutional Environment for Infrastructure Investment." *Industrial and Corporate Change* 11(2):355–389.

Henry, Laura A. and Lisa McIntosh Sundstrom. 2021. *Bringing Global Governance Home: NGO Mediation in the BRICS States.* Oxford University Press.

Herrold, Catherine E. 2020. *Delta Democracy: Pathways to Incremental Civic Revolution in Egypt and Beyond.* Oxford University Press.

Hertel, Shareen. 2006. *Unexpected Power: Conflict and Change Among Transnational Activists.* Cornell University Press.

Hillebrecht, Courtney. 2021. *Saving the International Justice Regime: Beyond Backlash Against International Courts.* Cambridge University Press.

Hirst, Megan and Howard Varney. 2005. *Justice Abandoned? An Assessment of the Serious Crimes Process in East Timor.* International Center for Transitional Justice.

Hopgood, Stephen. 2013. *Keepers of the Flame: Understanding Amnesty International.* Cornell University Press.

Horne, Cynthia M. 2012. "Assessing the Impact of Lustration on Trust in Public Institutions and National Government in Central and Eastern Europe." *Comparative Political Studies* 45(4):412–446.

Horne, Cynthia M. 2014. "The Impact of Lustration on Democratization in Postcommunist Countries." *International Journal of Transitional Justice* 8(3):496–521.

HRMC. 2023. *Transitional Justice.* Human Rights Media Centre. hrmc.org.za/transitional-justice-2/. Accessed April 20, 2023.

HRW. 2000*a*. *Human Rights Watch World Report 2000: Asia Overview.* Human Rights Watch. hrw.org/legacy/wr2k/Asia.htm#TopOfPage. Accessed May 15, 2020.

HRW. 2000*b*. *Human Rights Watch World Report 2000: Indonesia and East Timor.* Human Rights Watch. hrw.org/legacy/wr2k/Asia-05.htm#TopOfPage. Accessed May 15, 2020.

HRW. 2022. "Guatemala: Attorney General Arbitrarily Fires Prosecutors." *Human Rights Watch.* hrw.org/news/2022/07/14/guatemala-attorney-general-arbitrarily-fires-prosecutors. Accessed October 10, 2024.

Huber, John D. and Charles R. Shipan. 2002. *Deliberate Discretion? The Institutional Foundations of Bureaucratic Autonomy*. Cambridge University Press.
Hunt, Janet. 2016. FOKUPERS – The East Timorese Women's Communication Forum: The Development of Timor's First Women's NGO. In *Women and the Politics of Gender in Post-Conflict Timor-Leste: Between Heaven and Earth*, ed. Sara Niner. Routledge.
Huyse, Luc. 1995. "Justice After Transition: On the Choices Successor Elites Make in Dealing with the Past." *Law & Social Inquiry* 20(1):51–78.
IACtHR. 2004. *Case of Molina-Theissen v. Guatemala Judgment of May 4, 2004*. Inter-American Court of Human Rights.
IACtHR. 2009. *Case of the "Las Dos Erres" Massacre v. Guatemala Judgment of November 24, 2009*. Inter-American Court of Human Rights.
ICSC. 2022. *Centro Nacional Chega! (Timor-Leste)*. International Coalition of Sites of Conscience. sitesofconscience.org/en/membership/centro-nacional-chega-timor-leste/. Accessed June 8, 2022.
ICTJ. 2002. *2001/2002 Annual Report*. International Center for Transitional Justice.
ICTJ. 2011*a*. "South Africa: Constitutional Court Upholds Right to Express the Truth." *International Center for Transitional Justice*. ictj.org/news/south-africa-constitutional-court-upholds-right-express-truth. Accessed October 17, 2024.
ICTJ. 2011*b*. "South Africa: New Reparations Plan Embitters Many Victims." *International Center for Transitional Justice*. ictj.org/news/south-africa-new-reparations-plan-embitters-many-victims. Accessed October 17, 2024.
ICTJ. 2012. "Zuma's Presidential Pardons Process "Unconstitutional""." *International Center for Transitional Justice*. https://bit.ly/4919kM8. Accessed October 17, 2024.
ICTJ. 2014. "20 Years On, ANC Rules but Legacy of Apartheid Still Lingers." *International Center for Transitional Justice*. ictj.org/news/20-years-anc-rules-legacy-apartheid-still-lingers. Accessed October 17, 2024.
ICTJ. 2015. "Family Seeks Justice in South Africa for Anti-Apartheid Activist 32 Years after her Torture and Disappearance." *International Center for Transitional Justice*. ictj.org/news/justice-south-africa-anti-apartheid-activist-disappearance. Accessed October 17, 2024.
Ignatieff, Michael. 1998. *The Warrior's Honor: Ethnic War and the Modern Conscience*. Metropolitan Books.
IJR. 2021. *SA Reconciliation Barometer Survey 2021 Report*. Institute for Justice and Reconciliation. ijr.org.za/home/wp-content/uploads/2021/12/IJR_SA-Reconciliation-Barometer-2021.pdf. Accessed June 21, 2022.
Impunity Watch. 2008. *Reconociendo el Pasado: Desafíos para Combatir la Impunidad en Guatemala*. Impunity Watch. corteidh.or.cr/tablas/28969.pdf. Accessed May 15, 2020.
Impunity Watch. 2023. "Guatemala: Attorney General Arbitrarily Fires Prosecutors." *Impunity Watch*. impunitywatch.org/wp-content/uploads/2023/12/20-Years-of-the-PNR-Impact-of-the-National-Reparation-Program-for-the-victims-of-the-armed-conflict-in-Guatemala-Impunity-Watch-Dec2023.pdf. Accessed October 11, 2024.
Instituto Interamericano de Derechos Humanos. 2005. *Verdad, Justicia y Reparación: Desafíos para la Democracia y la Convivencia Social*. Instituto Interamericano de Derechos Humanos. idea.int/sites/default/files/publications/verdad-justicia-y-reparacion-desafios-para-la-democracia-y-la-convivencia-social.pdf. Accessed May 26, 2023.
Irgil, Ezgi, Anne-Kathrin Kreft, Myunghee Lee, Charmaine N. Willis, and Kelebogile Zvobgo. 2021. "Field Research: A Graduate Student's Guide." *International Studies Review* 23(4):1495–1517.
Jackson, Michael. 2005. "Storytelling Events, Violence, and the Appearance of the Past." *Anthropological Quarterly* 78(2):355–375.
Joachim, Jutta M. 2007. *Agenda Setting, the UN, and NGOs: Gender Violence and Reproductive Rights*. Georgetown University Press.

Johnston, Emma and Mishel Stephenson. 2016. "DNA Profiling Success Rates from Degraded Skeletal Remains in Guatemala." *Journal of Forensic Sciences* 61(4): 898–902.

JSMP. 2015. *JSMP Presentation at the Timor-Leste Development Partners Meeting: Strengthening the Legislative and Judicial Framework*. Judicial System Monitoring Program. laohamutuk.org/econ/15TLDPM/JSMPen.pdf. Accessed May 25, 2022.

JSMP. 2023. "JSMP Signs an MoU with Leaders from Samalete Village for the Community Security Support Program (PASK)." *Judicial System Monitoring Program*. jsmp.tl/wp-content/uploads/PrAsinaMOUSukuSamaleteERMERA_ENGLISH.pdf. Accessed October 14, 2023.

Kagan, Jennifer A. 2024. "How Do Environmental Advocacy Nonprofits Perceive Their Representational Role? A Three Dimensional Approach." *VOLUNTAS: International Journal of Voluntary and Nonprofit Organizations* 35:202–213.

Keck, Margaret E. and Kathryn Sikkink. 1998. *Activists Beyond Borders: Advocacy Networks in International Politics*. Cornell University Press.

Kellow, Aynsley and Hannah Murphy-Gregory. 2018. NGOs and Global Politics. In *Handbook of Research on NGOs*, ed. Aynsley Kellow and Hannah Murphy-Gregory. Edward Elgar Publishing pp. 1–14.

Keohane, Robert O. 1984. *After Hegemony*. Princeton University Press.

Kim, Hun Joon. 2012*a*. "Local, National, and International Determinants of Truth Commissions: The South Korean Experience." *Human Rights Quarterly* 34(3): 726–750.

Kim, Hun Joon. 2012*b*. "Structural Determinants of Human Rights Prosecutions After Democratic Transition." *Journal of Peace Research* 49(2):305–320.

Kim, Hun Joon. 2014. *The Massacres at Mt. Halla: Sixty Years of Truth Seeking in South Korea*. Cornell University Press.

Kim, Hun Joon. 2019. "Why Do States Adopt Truth Commissions After Transition?" *Social Science Quarterly* 100(5):1485–1502.

Kim, Hun Joon and Kathryn Sikkink. 2010. "Explaining the Deterrence Effect of Human Rights Prosecutions for Transitional Countries." *International Studies Quarterly* 54(4):939–963.

Kingdon, John W. 1984. *Agendas, Alternatives, and Public Policies*. Little, Brown and Company.

Kiss, Elizabeth. 2000. Moral Ambition Within and Beyond Political Constraints. In *Truth v. Justice: The Morality of Truth Commissions*, ed. R.I. Rotberg and Dennis Thompson. Princeton University Press pp. 68–98.

Klotz, Audie. 1995. "Norms Reconstituting Interests: Global Racial Equality and US Sanctions Against South Africa." *International Organization* 49(3):451–478.

Klotz, Audie. 2002. "Transnational Activism and Global Transformations: The Anti-Apartheid and Abolitionist Experiences." *European Journal of International Relations* 8(1):49–76.

Koc-Menard, Nathalie. 2014. "Notes from the Field: Exhuming the Past After the Peruvian Internal Conflict." *International Journal of Transitional Justice* 8(2):277–288.

Kochanski, Adam. 2020. "Mandating Truth: Patterns and Trends in Truth Commission Design." *Human Rights Review* 21:113–137.

Kochanski, Adam. 2021. "State (Ir)Responsibility and the (Un)Making of Transformative Reparations at the Extraordinary Chambers in the Courts of Cambodia." *Peacebuilding* 9(2):129–144.

Koremenos, Barbara. 2016. *The Continent of International Law: Explaining Agreement Design*. Cambridge University Press.

Kostelka, Filip. 2017. "Does Democratic Consolidation Lead to a Decline in Voter Turnout? Global Evidence Since 1939." *American Political Science Review* 111(4):653–667.

Kreutz, Joakim. 2010. "How and When Armed Conflicts End: Introducing the UCDP Conflict Termination Dataset." *Journal of Peace Research* 47(2):243–250.

Kurtz, Lester. 2010. *The Anti-Apartheid Struggle in South Africa (1912–1992).* International Center on Nonviolent Conflict.

La'o Hamutuk. 2005*a*. *Commission of Experts: Lack of Political Will Blocks Justice for Timor-Leste.* La'o Hamutuk. laohamutuk.org/Bulletin/2005/Aug/bulletinv6n3.html. Accessed December 1, 2024.

La'o Hamutuk. 2005*b*. *Editorial: Commission of Truth and Friendship Brings Neither.* La'o Hamutuk. laohamutuk.org/Bulletin/2005/Aug/bulletinv6n3.html. Accessed December 1, 2024.

La'o Hamutuk. 2010*a*. *Justice for Timor-Leste: An International Obligation Not Yet Met.* La'o Hamutuk. laohamutuk.org/Bulletin/2010/Feb/bulletinv11n1-2.html#justice. Accessed December 1, 2024.

La'o Hamutuk. 2010*b*. *Submission to Committee A, National Parliament Democratic Republic of Timor-Leste.* La'o Hamutuk. laohamutuk.org/Justice/Reparations/LHSubCommAReparationsEn.pdf. Accessed December 1, 2024.

La'o Hamutuk. 2012. *Letter to UN Security Council.* La'o Hamutuk. laohamutuk.org/Justice/LHUNSC4Nov2012en.pdf. Accessed December 1, 2024.

La'o Hamutuk. 2013. *Editorial: Together We Can End Impunity.* La'o Hamutuk. laohamutuk.org/Bulletin/2013/Jul/bulletinv13n1en.html#editorial. Accessed December 1, 2024.

Lebovic, James H. and Erik Voeten. 2006. "The Politics of Shame: The Condemnation of Country Human Rights Practices in the UNCHR." *International Studies Quarterly* 50(4):861–888.

LeRoux, Kelly. 2009. "The Effects of Descriptive Representation on Nonprofits' Civic Intermediary Roles: A Test of the 'Racial Mismatch Hypothesis in the Social Services Sector." *Nonprofit and Voluntary Sector Quarterly* 38(5):741–760.

Lessa, Francesca. 2022. *The Condor Trials: Transnational Repression and Human Rights in South America.* Yale University Press.

Lie, Tove Grete, Helga Malmin Binningsbø, and Scott Gates. 2007. *Post-Conflict Justice and Sustainable Peace.* World Bank.

Light, Paul Charles. 1982. *The President's Agenda.* Johns Hopkins University Press.

Linzer, Drew A. and Jeffrey K. Staton. 2015. "A Global Measure of Judicial Independence, 1948–2012." *Journal of Law and Courts* 3(2):223–256.

Lira, Elizabeth. 2017. "The Chilean Human Rights Archives and Moral Resistance to Dictatorship." *International Journal of Transitional Justice* 11(2):189–196.

Lodge, Tom. 1995. "The South African General Election, April 1994: Results, Analysis and Implications." *African Affairs* 94(377):471–500.

Loken, Meredith, Milli Lake, and Kate Cronin-Furman. 2018. "Deploying Justice: Strategic Accountability for Wartime Sexual Violence." *International Studies Quarterly* 62(4):751–764.

Loveman, Mara. 1998. "High-Risk Collective Action: Defending Human Rights in Chile, Uruguay, and Argentina." *American Journal of Sociology* 104(2):477–525.

Loyle, Cyanne E. and Helga Malmin Binningsbø. 2018. "Justice During Armed Conflict: A New Dataset on Government and Rebel Strategies." *Journal of Conflict Resolution* 62(2):442–466.

Lutz, Ellen and Kathryn Sikkink. 2001. "The Justice Cascade: The Evolution and Impact of Foreign Human Rights Trials in Latin America." *Chicago Journal of International Law* 2(1):1–33.

Madlingozi, Tshepo. 2010. "On Transitional Justice Entrepreneurs and the Production of Victims." *Journal of Human Rights Practice* 2(2):208–228.

Mahoney, James. 2010. "After KKV: The New Methodology of Qualitative Research." *World Politics* 62(1):120–147.

Mamdani, Mahmood. 2002. "Amnesty or Impunity? A Preliminary Critique of the Report of the Truth and Reconciliation Commission of South Africa (TRC)." *Diacritics* 32(3):33–59.

Martín, Héctor Centeno, Eric Wiebelhaus-Brahm, Ana Belén Nieto-Librero, and Dylan Wright. 2022. "Explaining the Timeliness of Implementation of Truth Commission Recommendations." *Journal of Peace Research* 59(5):710–726.

Martínez, Marta. 2017. *Impunity's Eclipse: The Long Journey to the Historic Genocide Trial in Guatemala.* International Center for Transitional Justice.

McConnachie, Kirsten. 2004. *Truth Commissions and NGOs: The Essential Relationship (The "Frati Guidelines" for NGOs Engaging with Truth Commissions).* International Center for Transitional Justice.

Medie, Peace A. 2020. *Global Norms and Local Action: The Campaigns to End Violence Against Women in Africa.* Oxford University Press.

Meernik, James. 2005. "Justice and Peace? How the International Criminal Tribunal Affects Societal Peace in Bosnia." *Journal of Peace Research* 42(3):271–289.

Meernik, James, Rosa Aloisi, Marsha Sowell, and Angela Nichols. 2012. "The Impact of Human Rights Organizations on Naming and Shaming Campaigns." *Journal of Conflict Resolution* 56(2):233–256.

Mendeloff, David. 2004. "Truth-Seeking, Truth-Telling, and Postconflict Peacebuilding: Curb the Enthusiasm." *International Studies Review* 6(3):355–380.

Merry, Sally Engle. 2006. "Transnational Human Rights and Local Activism: Mapping the Middle." *American Anthropologist* 108(1):38–51.

Michel, Verónica. 2018. *Prosecutorial Accountability and Victims' Rights in Latin America.* Cambridge University Press.

Mihr, Anja and Hans Peter Schmitz. 2007. "Human Rights Education (HRE) and Transnational Activism." *Human Rights Quarterly* 29(4):973–993.

Minow, Martha. 1998. *Between Vengeance and Forgiveness: Facing History After Genocide and Mass Violence.* Beacon Press.

Mitchell, George E. and Hans Peter Schmitz. 2014. "Principled Instrumentalism: A Theory of Transnational NGO Behaviour." *Review of International Studies* 40(3): 487–504.

Mitchell, Lincoln A. 2009. *Uncertain Democracy: US Foreign Policy and Georgia's Rose Revolution.* University of Pennsylvania Press.

Mulesky, Suzie, Wayne Sandholtz, and Kelebogile Zvobgo. 2024. "Do Human Rights Treaty Obligations Matter for Ratification?" *Journal of Human Rights* 23(1):1–18.

Murdie, Amanda. 2014. *Help or Harm: The Human Security Effects of International NGOs.* Stanford University Press.

Murdie, Amanda and David R. Davis. 2012. "Looking in the Mirror: Comparing INGO Networks Across Issue Areas." *Review of International Organizations* 7(2):177–202.

Murdie, Amanda and Dursun Peksen. 2013*a*. "The Impact of Human Rights INGO Activities on Economic Sanctions." *Review of International Organizations* 8(1):33–53.

Murdie, Amanda and Dursun Peksen. 2013*b*. "The Impact of Human Rights INGO Shaming on Humanitarian Interventions." *Journal of Politics* 76(1):215–228.

Murdie, Amanda and Johannes Urpelainen. 2015. "Why Pick on Us? Environmental INGOs and State Shaming As a Strategic Substitute." *Political Studies* 63(2): 353–372.

Murphy, Colleen and Kelebogile Zvobgo. 2023. Transitional Justice for Historical Injustice. In *Research Handbook on Transitional Justice*, ed. Cheryl Lawther and Luke Moffett. Edward Elgar Publishing pp. 421–435.

Nagy, Rosemary. 2008. "Transitional Justice as Global Project: Critical Reflections." *Third World Quarterly* 29(2):275–289.

Nagy, Rosemary. 2014. "The Truth and Reconciliation Commission of Canada: Genesis and Design." *Law and Society Review* 29(2):199–217.

Nalepa, Monika. 2022. *After Authoritarianism: Transitional Justice and Democratic Stability*. Cambridge University Press.

Nalepa, Monika and Emilia Justyna Powell. 2016. "The Role of Domestic Opposition and International Justice Regimes in Peaceful Transitions of Power." *Journal of Conflict Resolution* 60(7):1191–1218.

National Security Archive. 2001. *Ford and Kissinger Gave Green Light to Indonesia's Invasion of East Timor, 1975: New Documents Detail Conversations with Suharto*. National Security Archive. nsarchive2.gwu.edu/NSAEBB/NSAEBB62/index2.html. Accessed May 26, 2023.

Nevins, Joseph. 2018. Mass Killing at a Distance: US Complicity in the East Timor Genocide and International Structural Violence (1975–1999). In *Dirty Hands and Vicious Deeds: The US Government's Complicity in Crimes Against Humanity and Genocide*, ed. Samuel Totten. University of Toronto Press.

New Tactics in Human Rights. n.d. "Accountability After Abuses: Organizing survivors to expand reparations to heal individuals and communities.". newtactics.org/tactic/accountability-after-abuses-organizing-survivors-expand-reparations-heal-individuals-and. Accessed May 15, 2020.

Niner, Sara. 2016. *Women and the Politics of Gender in Post-Conflict Timor-Leste: Between Heaven and Earth*. Routledge.

Ntsebeza, Dumisa. 2000. The Uses of Truth Commissions: Lessons for the World. In *Truth v. Justice*, ed. R.I. Rotberg and Dennis Thompson. Princeton University Press.

ODHAG. 1998. *Nunca Más: Informe del Proyecto lnterdiocesano de Recuperación de la Memoria Histórica Guatemala*. Oficina de Derechos Humanos del Arzobispado de Guatemala.

O'Donnell, Guillermo and Philippe C. Schmitter. 2013. *Transitions from Authoritarian Rule: Tentative Conclusions About Uncertain Democracies*. Johns Hopkins University Press.

Oduro, Franklin and Rosemary Nagy. 2014. "What's in an Idea? Truth Commission Policy Transfer in Ghana and Canada." *Journal of Human Rights* 13(1):85–102.

Oettler, Anika. 2006. "Encounters with History: Dealing with the 'Present Past' in Guatemala." *European Review of Latin American and Caribbean Studies* 81 (October):3–19.

OHCHR. 2009. *NGOs Alternative Report: Implementation of the Convention on the Elimination of All Forms of Discrimination Against Women (CEDAW) in Timor-Leste*. United Nations. tbinternet.ohchr.org/Treaties/CEDAW/Shared%20Documents/TLS/INT_CEDAW_NGO_TLS_44_10156_E.pdf. Accessed May 15, 2020.

Olsen, Tricia D. and Andrew G. Reiter. 2010. *Transitional Justice in Balance: Comparing Processes, Weighing Efficacy*. United States Institute of Peace.

Olsen, Tricia D., Leigh A. Payne, and Andrew G. Reiter. 2010. "Transitional Justice in the World, 1970–2007: Insights from a New Dataset." *Journal of Peace Research* 47(6):803–809.

Olsen, Tricia D., Leigh A. Payne, Andrew G. Reiter, and Eric Wiebelhaus-Brahm. 2010. "When Truth Commissions Improve Human Rights." *International Journal of Transitional Justice* 4(3):457–476.

Osiel, Mark J. 2000. "Why Prosecute? Critics of Punishment for Mass Atrocity." *Human Rights Quarterly* 22(1):118–147.

Pallas, Christopher L. and Elizabeth A. Bloodgood. 2022. *Beyond the Boomerang: From Transnational Advocacy Networks to Transcalar Advocacy in International Politics*. University of Alabama Press.

Parliament of the Republic of South Africa. 1995. *Promotion of National Unity and Reconciliation Act No. 34 of 1995*. Parliament of the Republic of South Africa.

Pettersson, Therése and Kristine Eck. 2018. "Organized Violence, 1989–2017." *Journal of Peace Research* 55(4):535–47.

Pigou, Piers. 2003. *Crying Without Tears: In Pursuit of Justice and Reconciliation in Timor-Leste – Community Perspectives and Expectations.* International Center for Transitional Justice.

Posthumus, Daniel and Kelebogile Zvobgo. 2021. "Democratizing Truth: An Analysis of Truth Commissions in the United States." *International Journal of Transitional Justice* 15(3):510–532.

Powers, Kathy L. and Kim Proctor. 2016. "Victim's Justice in the Aftermath of Political Violence: Why Do Countries Award Reparations?" *Foreign Policy Analysis* 13(4):787–810.

Prentice, Christopher R. and Jeffrey L. Brudney. 2017. "Nonprofit Lobbying Strategy: Challenging or Championing the Conventional Wisdom?" *VOLUNTAS: International Journal of Voluntary and Nonprofit Organizations* 28:935–957.

Presbey, Gail M. 2006. "Evaluating the Legacy of Nonviolence in South Africa." *Peace & Change* 31(2):141–174.

Price, Richard. 2003. "Transnational Civil Society and Advocacy in World Politics." *World Politics* 55(4):579–606.

Prorok, Alyssa K. 2017. "The (In)compatibility of Peace and Justice? The International Criminal Court and Civil Conflict Termination." *International Organization* 71(2):213–243.

Puwana, Zukiswa and Rita Kesselring. 2018. Persistent Injuries, the Law and Politics: The South African Victims' Support Group Khulumani and Its Struggle for Redress. In *Advocating Transitional Justice in Africa: The Role of Civil Society*, ed. Jasmina Brankovic and Hugo van der Merwe. Springer pp. 91–110.

Quinn, Joanna R. 2011. *The Politics of Acknowledgement: Truth Commissions in Uganda and Haiti.* University of British Columbia Press.

Quinn, Joanna R. 2021. "The Impact of State Abdication on Transitional Justice: When Non-State Actors and Other States Fill the Post-Transition Gap." *Peacebuilding* 9(2):114–128.

Ramírez-Barat, Clara. 2011. *Making an Impact: Guidelines on Designing and Implementing Outreach Programs for Transitional Justice.* International Center for Transitional Justice.

Rana, Sameer S.J.B and Kelebogile Zvobgo. 2021. "Safeguarding Truth: Supporting Children's Participation at Truth Commissions." *Journal of Human Rights* 20(3):282–303.

Rapoza, Phillip. 2016. *Charging, Trials and Sentencing in Cases of Sexual Violence in Timor-Leste 2012–2015.* East Timor Law and Justice Bulletin. easttimorlawandjusticebulletin.com/2016/12/charging-trials-and-sentencing-in-cases.html. Accessed June 3, 2022.

Raustiala, Kal. 1997. "States, NGOs, and International Environmental Institutions." *International Studies Quarterly* 41(4):719–740.

Rede Feto Timor Leste. 2015. *NGO Shadow Report: Implementation of the Convention on the Elimination of All Forms of Discrimination Against Women (CEDAW) in Timor-Leste.* United Nations. tbinternet.ohchr.org/Treaties/CEDAW/Shared%20Documents/TLS/INT_CEDAW_NGO_TLS_21963_E.pdf. Accessed June 30, 2020.

Reimann, Kim D. 2006. "A View from the Top: International Politics, Norms and the Worldwide Growth of NGOs." *International Studies Quarterly* 50(1):45–67.

Reiners, Nina. 2022. *Transnational Lawmaking Coalitions for Human Rights.* Cambridge University Press.

Reiners, Nina. 2024. "The Power of Interpersonal Relationships: A Socio-Legal Approach to International Institutions and Human Rights Advocacy." *Review of International Studies* 50(2):252–270.

Risse, Thomas, Stephen C. Ropp, and Kathryn Sikkink. 1999. *The Power of Human Rights: International Norms and Domestic Change.* Cambridge University Press.

Risse, Thomas, Stephen C. Ropp, and Kathryn Sikkink. 2013. *The Persistent Power of Human Rights: From Commitment to Compliance.* Cambridge University Press.
Robins, Simon. 2010. *An Assessment of the Needs of Families of the Missing in Timor-Leste.* Post-War Reconstruction & Development Unit.
Rodrigues, Maria Guadalupe Moog. 2016. "The Prospects for Transnational Advocacy Across the IBSA Bloc – A View from Brazil." *Third World Quarterly* 37(4):703–720.
Roht-Arriaza, Naomi. 2001. The Role of International Actors in National Accountability Processes. In *The Politics of Memory: Transitional Justice in Democratizing Societies*, ed. Alexandra Barahona De Brito, Carmen Gonzalez Enriquez, and Paloma Aguilar. Oxford University Press pp. 40–64.
Roht-Arriaza, Naomi. 2002. "Civil Society in Processes of Accountability." *Post-Conflict Justice* 97:97–98.
Ross, Amy. 2004. "Truth and Consequences in Guatemala." *GeoJournal* 60(1):73–79.
Ross, Amy. 2006. "The Creation and Conduct of the Guatemalan Commission for Historical Clarification." *Geoforum* 37(1):69–81.
Rothfield, Philipa, Cleo Fleming, and Paul A. Komesaroff. 2008. *Pathways to Reconciliation: Between Theory and Practice.* Ashgate Publishing.
Rowen, Jamie. 2017. *Searching for Truth in the Transitional Justice Movement.* Cambridge University Press.
Royaume du Maroc. 2005. *Rapport Final.* Instance Equité et Réconciliation.
Rudling, Adriana. 2019. "What's Inside the Box? Mapping Agency and Conflict within Victims' Organizations." *International Journal of Transitional Justice* 13(3):458–477.
SáCouto, Susana, Alysson Ford Ouoba, and Claudia Martin. 2022. *Documenting Good Practice on Accountability for Conflict-Related Sexual Violence: The Sepur Zarco Case.* UN Women. unwomen.org/sites/default/files/2022-07/Research-paper-Documenting-good-practice-on-accountability-for-conflict-related-sexual-violence-Sepur-Zarco-en.pdf. Accessed October 17, 2024.
SACTJ. 2022. *About.* South African Coalition for Transitional Justice. unfinishedtrc.co.za/the-south-african-coalition-for-transitional-justice/. Accessed June 17, 2022.
Salamon, Lester M. and Stefan Toepler. 2015. "Government-Nonprofit Cooperation: Anomaly or Necessity?" *VOLUNTAS: International Journal of Voluntary and Nonprofit Organizations* 26:2155–2177.
Salvesen, Hilde. 2002. *Guatemala: Five Years After the Peace Accords — The Challenges of Implementing Peace.* International Peace Research Institute, Oslo.
Sandholtz, Wayne. 2000. Globalization and the Evolution of Rules. In *Globalization and Governance*, ed. Aseem Prakash and Jeffrey Hart. Routledge pp. 77–102.
Sandholtz, Wayne. 2017. "Domestic Law and Human Rights Treaty Commitments: The Convention against Torture." *Journal of Human Rights* 16(1):25–43.
Sarkin-Hughes, Jeremy. 2004. *Carrots and Sticks: The TRC and the South African Amnesty Process.* Intersentia.
Scharf, Michael P. 1996. "The Case for a Permanent International Truth Commission." *Duke Journal of Comparative & International Law* 7(2):375–410.
Schnattschneider, Elmer Eric. 1960. *The Semisovereign People: A Realist's View of Democracy in America.* Holt, Rinehart, and Winston.
Schoner, Rachel J. 2023. "Empowering Your Victims: Why Repressive Regimes Allow Individual petitions in international Organizations." *Review of International Organizations* pp. 1–37, Online First. doi.org/10.1007/s11558-023-09512-5. *Review of International Organizations.*
Schoner, Rachel J. 2024. "Naming and Shaming in UN Treaty Bodies: Individual Petitions' Effect on Human Rights." *Review of International Organizations* pp. 1–40, Online First. doi.org/10.1007/s11558-024-09564-1. Accessed November 25, 2024.
Shelton, Dinah. 1994. "The Participation of Nongovernmental Organizations in International Judicial Proceedings." *American Journal of International Law* 88(4):611–642.

Sikkink, Kathryn. 2011. *The Justice Cascade: How Human Rights Prosecutions Are Changing World Politics.* W.W. Norton & Company.

Sikkink, Kathryn and Carrie Booth Walling. 2007. "The Impact of Human Rights Trials in Latin America." *Journal of Peace Research* 44(4):427–445.

Simmons, Beth A. 2009. *Mobilizing for Human Rights: International Law in Domestic Politics.* Cambridge University Press.

Simpson, James G.R. 2012. "Boipatong: The Politics of a Massacre and the South African Transition." *Journal of Southern African Studies* 38(3):623–647.

Skaar, Elin, Adriana Rudling, Lisa-Marie Måseidvåg Selvik, Eric Wiebelhaus-Brahm, and Jemima García-Godos. 2025. "The Implementation of Truth Commission Recommendations: Exploring the 'Beyond Words' Database for Latin America." *Conflict Management and Peace Science* 42(1):82–103.

Skaar, Elin and Eric Wiebelhaus-Brahm. 2013. "The Drivers of Transitional Justice." *Nordic Journal of Human Rights* 31(2):127–148.

Skaar, Elin, Eric Wiebelhaus-Brahm, and Jemima García-Godos. 2022*a*. *Exploring Truth Commission Recommendations in a Comparative Perspective: Beyond Words, Vol. I.* Intersentia.

Skaar, Elin, Eric Wiebelhaus-Brahm, and Jemima García-Godos. 2022*b*. *Latin American Experiences with Truth Commission Recommendations: Beyond Words, Vol. II.* Intersentia.

Smith, Charles Anthony. 2012. *The Rise and Fall of War Crimes Trials: From Charles I to Bush II.* Cambridge University Press.

Smith, Jackie and Dawn Wiest. 2005. "The Uneven Geography of Global Civil Society: National and Global Influences on Transnational Association." *Social Forces* 84(2):621–652.

Snow, David A., E. Burke Rochford Jr., Steven K. Worden, and Robert D. Benford. 1986. "Frame Alignment Processes, Micromobilization, and Movement Participation." *American Sociological Review* 51(4):464–481.

Snyder, Jack and Leslie Vinjamuri. 2003/2004. "Trials and Errors: Principles and Pragmatism in Strategies of International Justice." *International Security* 28(3):5–44.

South African History Online. 2020. *Shirley Gunn.* South African History Online. sahistory.org.za/people/shirley-gunn. Accessed April 20, 2023.

South African Press Association. 1996. *Bomber-Accused Gunn Pursues Vlok.* South African Press Association. justice.gov.za/trc/media/1996/9606/s960625f.htm. Accessed April 20, 2023.

Sriram, Chandra Lekha. 2003. "Revolutions in Accountability: New Approaches to Past Abuses." *American University International Law Review* 19(2):301–429.

Stahn, Carsten. 2005. "The Geometry of Transitional Justice: Choices of Institutional Design." *Leiden Journal of International Law* 18(3):425–466.

Stewart, Brandon and Eric Wiebelhaus-Brahm. 2017. "The Quantitative Turn in Transitional Justice Research: What Have We Learned About Impact?" *Transitional Justice Review* 1(5):97–133.

Stromseth, Jane, David Wippman, and Rosa Brooks. 2006. *Can Might Make Rights? Building the Rule of Law After Military Interventions.* Cambridge University Press.

Stroup, Sarah S. and Amanda Murdie. 2012. "There's No Place Like Home: Explaining International NGO Advocacy." *Review of International Organizations* 7:425–448.

Stroup, Sarah S. and Wendy H. Wong. 2017. *The Authority Trap: Strategic Choices of International NGOs.* Cornell University Press.

Struett, Michael. 2008. *The Politics of Constructing the International Criminal Court: NGOs, Discourse, and Agency.* Springer.

Subotić, Jelena. 2009. *Hijacked Justice: Dealing with the Past in the Balkans.* Cornell University Press.

Subotić, Jelena. 2011. "Expanding the Scope of Post-Conflict Justice: Individual, State and Societal Responsibility." *Journal of Peace Research* 48(2):157–169.
Subotić, Jelena. 2012. "The Transformation of International Transitional Justice Advocacy." *International Journal of Transitional Justice* 6(1):106–125.
Subotić, Jelena. 2015. "Truth, Justice, and Reconciliation on the Ground: Normative Divergence in the Western Balkans." *Journal of International Relations and Development* 18:361–382.
Subotić, Jelena. 2022. "Holocaust and the Meaning of the Srebrenica Genocide: A Reflection on a Controversy." *Journal of Genocide Research* 24(1):71–82.
Sutter, Daniel. 1995. "Settling Old Scores: Potholes Along the Transition from Authoritarian Rule." *Journal of Conflict Resolution* 39(1):110–128.
Svolik, Milan. 2008. "Authoritarian Reversals and Democratic Consolidation." *American Political Science Review* 102(2):153–168.
Svolik, Milan W. 2015. "Which Democracies Will Last? Coups, Incumbent Takeovers, and the Dynamic of Democratic Consolidation." *British Journal of Political Science* 45(4):715–738.
Teitel, Ruti G. 2003. "Transitional Justice Genealogy." *Harvard Human Rights Journal* 16(2003):69–94.
Tepperman, Jonathan. 2002. "Truth and Consequences." *Foreign Affairs* 81(2): 128–145.
Totten, Christopher D. 2009. "The International Criminal Court and Truth Commissions: A Framework for Cross-Interaction in the Sudan and Beyond." *Northwestern University Journal of International Human Rights* 7(1):1–33.
TRC. 2002. *Truth and Reconciliation Commission of South Africa Report*. Government of South Africa.
Trejo, Guillermo, Juan Albarracín, and Lucía Tiscornia. 2018. "Breaking State Impunity in Post-Authoritarian Regimes: Why Transitional Justice Processes Deter Criminal Violence in New Democracies." *Journal of Peace Research* 55(6): 787–809.
UNCHR. 1997. *Question of the Impunity of Perpetrators of Human Rights Violations (Civil and Political). E/CN.4/Sub.2/1997/20/Rev.1*. United Nations.
UNCHR. 1999. *Report of the Special Rapporteur on Violence Against Women, Its Causes and Consequences, Ms. Radhika Coomaraswamy. E/CN.4/1999/68/Add.3*. United Nations.
UNCHR. 2001. *Report of the Special Rapporteur on Violence Against Women, Its Causes and Consequences, Radhika Coomaraswamy, in Accordance with Commission on Human Rights Resolution 2000/45*. United Nations.
UNSG. 1999. *Situation of Human Rights in East Timor: Note by the Secretary-General A/54/660*. United Nations.
UNTAET. 2000*a*. *Daily Briefing 06 Oct 2000*. United Nations Transitional Administration for East Timor. peacekeeping.un.org/en/mission/past/etimor/DB/DB061000.htm. Accessed May 15, 2020.
UNTAET. 2000*b*. *Daily Briefing 12 Dec 2000*. United Nations Transitional Administration for East Timor. peacekeeping.un.org/en/mission/past/etimor/DB/db121200.htm. Accessed May 15, 2020.
UNTAET. 2000*c*. *Daily Briefing 13 Oct 2000*. United Nations Transitional Administration for East Timor. peacekeeping.un.org/en/mission/past/etimor/DB/DB131000.HTM. Accessed May 15, 2020.
UNTAET. 2000*d*. *Daily Briefing 22 Sep 2000*. United Nations Transitional Administration for East Timor. peacekeeping.un.org/en/mission/past/etimor/DB/db220900.htm. Accessed May 15, 2020.
UNTAET. 2001. *On the Establishment of a Commission for Reception, Truth and Reconciliation in East Timor. UNTAET/REG/2001/10*. United Nations.

US Department of State. 2024*a*. *2023 Country Reports on Human Rights Practices: Guatemala*. US Department of State. https://www.state.gov/reports/2023-country-reports-on-human-rights-practices/guatemala/. Accessed October 21, 2024.

US Department of State. 2024*b*. *2023 Country Reports on Human Rights Practices: South Africa*. US Department of State. https://www.state.gov/reports/2023-country-reports-on-human-rights-practices/south-africa/. Accessed October 21, 2024.

US Department of State. 2024*c*. *2023 Country Reports on Human Rights Practices: Timor-Leste*. US Department of State. https://www.state.gov/reports/2023-country-reports-on-human-rights-practices/timor-leste/. Accessed October 21, 2024.

van Zyl, Paul. 1999. "Dilemmas of Transitional Justice: The Case of South Africa's Truth and Reconciliation Commission." *Journal of International Affairs* 52(2):647–667.

VanAntwerpen, Jonathan. 2008. Reconciliation Reconceived: Religion, Secularism, and the Language of Transition. In *The Politics of Reconciliation in Multicultural Societies*, ed. Will Kymlicka and Bashir Bashir. Oxford University Press pp. 25–47.

VanAntwerpen, Jonathan. 2009. Moral Globalization and Discursive Struggle: Reconciliation, Transitional Justice, and Cosmopolitan Discourse. In *Globalization, Philanthropy, and Civil Society: Projecting Institutional Logics Abroad*, ed. David C. Hammack and Steven Heydemann. Indiana University Press pp. 95–136.

Vilán, Andrea. Forthcoming. *Universal Rights, Uneven Impacts: The Domestic Politics of Treaty Incorporation*. Cambridge University Press.

Villamil, Francisco and Laia Balcells. 2021. "Do TJ Policies Cause Backlash? Evidence from Street Name Changes in Spain." *Research & Politics* 8(4):1–7.

Vinjamuri, Leslie and Jack Snyder. 2015. "Law and Politics in Transitional Justice." *Annual Review of Political Science* 18(1):303–327.

Walter, Barbara F. 2002. *Committing to Peace: The Successful Settlement of Civil Wars*. Princeton University Press.

Wandita, Galuh, Karen Campbell-Nelson, and Manuela Leong Pereira. 2006. Learning to Engender Reparations in Timor-leste: Reaching Out to Female Victims. In *What Happened to the Women? Gender and Reparations for Human Rights Violations*, ed. Ruth Rubio-Marín. Social Science Research Council pp. 284–334.

Wells, Rachel and Theresa Anasti. 2020. "Hybrid Models for Social Change: Legitimacy Among Community-Based Nonprofit Organizations." *VOLUNTAS: International Journal of Voluntary and Nonprofit Organizations* 31(6):1134–1147.

Wiebelhaus-Brahm, Eric. 2010. *Truth Commissions and Transitional Societies: The Impact on Human Rights and Democracy*. Routledge.

Wiebelhaus-Brahm, Eric. 2021*a*. "Competition for Control of the State and the Transitional Justice Agenda Among Tunisian Civil Society Organisations." *Peacebuilding* 9(2):160–174.

Wiebelhaus-Brahm, Eric. 2021*b*. "Global Transitional Justice Norms and the Framing of Truth Commissions in the Absence of Transition." *Negotiation and Conflict Management Research* 14(3):170–186.

Wiebelhaus-Brahm, Eric, Dylan Wright, Centeno Héctor Martín, and Ana Belén Nieto Librero. 2023. "Examining Compliance with Domestic Human Rights Bodies: The Case of Truth Commission Recommendations." *Journal of Human Rights* 22(3):406–424.

Wigglesworth, Ann. 2013. "The Growth of Civil Society in Timor-Leste: Three Moments of Activism." *Journal of Contemporary Asia* 43(1):51–74.

Winston, Carla. 2021. "Truth Commissions as Tactical Concessions: The Curious Case of Idi Amin." *The International Journal of Human Rights* 25(2):251–273.

WOLA. 2019. *The Government of Guatemala Should Guarantee the Protection and Access to the Historic Archive of the National Police*. Washington Office on Latin America. wola.org/wp-content/uploads/2019/05/Comunicado-AHPN-GUA-English.pdf. Accessed October 17, 2024.

Wong, Wendy H. 2014. *Internal Affairs: How the Structure of NGOs Transforms Human Rights.* Cornell University Press.

Woo, Byungwon and Amanda Murdie. 2017. "International Organizations and Naming and Shaming: Does the International Monetary Fund Care about the Human Rights Reputation of Its Client?" *Political Studies* 65(4):767–785.

Working Group. 2009. *Concept Paper on CAVR and CTF Follow-up Institution.* Fokupers, Hak Association, ICTJ, PDHJ, STP-CAVR, UNMIT. laohamutuk.org/Justice/Reparations/ConceptOct09En.pdf. Accessed November 27, 2024.

Working Group on Reparations. 2008. *Concept Paper on a National Reparations Program for Timor-Leste.* Working Group on Reparations. ictj.org/sites/default/files/ICTJ-TimorLeste-Reparations-Concept-2008-English.pdf. Accessed May 15, 2020.

World Bank. 2018. *Overcoming Poverty and Inequality in South Africa: An Assessment of Drivers, Constraints and Opportunities.* World Bank.

Yoshioka, Takayuki. 2014. "Representational Roles of Nonprofit Advocacy Organizations in the United States." *VOLUNTAS: International Journal of Voluntary and Nonprofit Organizations* 25:1062–1090.

Zvobgo, Kelebogile. 2019*a*. "Designing Truth: Facilitating Perpetrator Testimony at Truth Commissions." *Journal of Human Rights* 18(1):92–110.

Zvobgo, Kelebogile. 2019*b*. "Human Rights versus National Interests: Shifting US Public Attitudes on the International Criminal Court." *International Studies Quarterly* 63(4):1065–1078.

Zvobgo, Kelebogile. 2020. "Demanding Truth: The Global Transitional Justice Network and the Creation of Truth Commissions." *International Studies Quarterly* 64(3):609–625.

Zvobgo, Kelebogile. 2022. Research Labs: Concept, Utility, and Application. In *Handbook of Research Methods in International Relations*, ed. R. Joseph Huddleston, Thomas Jamieson, and Patrick James. Edward Elgar Publishing pp. 729–747.

Zvobgo, Kelebogile and Benjamin A.T. Graham. 2020. "The World Bank as an Enforcer of Human Rights." *Journal of Human Rights* 19(4):425–448.

Zvobgo, Kelebogile, Charmaine N. Willis, Myunghee Lee, Anne-Kathrin Kreft, and Ezgi Irgil. 2022. Fieldwork. In *Strategies for Navigating Graduate School and Beyond*, ed. Kevin G. Lorentz, Daniel J. Mallinson, Julia Marin Hellwege, Davin Phoenix, and J. Cherie Strachan. American Political Science Association pp. 129–134.

Zvobgo, Kelebogile and Claire B. Crawford. 2023. "Performing Truth? Examining Transitional Justice Practice in West Africa." *Unpublished manuscript.*

Zvobgo, Kelebogile, Paula M. Pickering, Jaime E. Settle, and Michael J. Tierney. 2023. "Creating New Knowledge with Undergraduate Students: Institutional Incentives and Faculty Agency." *PS: Political Science & Politics* 56(4):512–518.

Zvobgo, Kelebogile and Stephen Chaudoin. 2025. "Complementarity and Public Views on Overlapping Domestic and International Courts." *Journal of Politics* 87(3): 1028–1044.

Zvobgo, Kelebogile, Wayne Sandholtz, and Suzie Mulesky. 2020. "Reserving Rights: Explaining Human Rights Treaty Reservations." *International Studies Quarterly* 64(4):785–797.

Index

Page numbers in **bold** denote illustrations.

D

I

J